AF778387

Youth and the Labour Market in Romania

ADAPT LABOUR STUDIES BOOK-SERIES

International School of Higher Education in Labour and Industrial Relations

Series Editors
Tayo Fashoyin, University of Lagos (*Nigeria*)
Michele Tiraboschi, University of Modena and Reggio Emilia (*Italy*)

Guest Editors
Cristina Lincaru, Researcher at INCSMPS (*Romania*)
Vasilica Ciucă, General Manager of the National Institute for Scientific Research on Labour and Social Protection, Bucharest (*Romania*)

English Language Editor
Pietro Manzella, ADAPT Senior Research Fellow (*Italy*)

ADAPT (www.adapt.it) is a non-profit organisation founded in 2000 by Professor Marco Biagi with the aim of promoting study and research in the field of labour law and industrial relations from an international and comparative perspective. Our purpose is to encourage and implement a new approach to academic research, by establishing ongoing relationships with other universities and advanced studies institutes, and through promoting academic and scientific exchange programmes with enterprises, institutions, foundations and associations. In collaboration with the Centre for International and Comparative Studies on Law, Economics, Environment and Work (DEAL) at the Marco Biagi Department of Economics of the University of Modena and Reggio Emilia, ADAPT set up the International School of Higher Education in Labour and Industrial Relations, an internationally accredited centre of excellence for research, study and postgraduate programmes in the area of industrial and labour relations.

ADAPT International Scientific Committee
Bertagna Giuseppe *(University of Bergamo, Italy)*, Bulgarelli Aviana *(ISFOL, Italy)*, Fashoyin Tayo *(University of Lagos, Nigeria)*, Frommberger Dietmar *(Universität Magdeburg, Germany)*, Grisolia Julio Armando *(Universidad Nacional de Tres de Febrero, Argentina)*, Hajdù Jòzsef *(University of Szeged, Hungary)*, Kai Chang *(Renmin University, China)*, Ouchi Shynia *(University of Kobe, Japan)*, Quinlan Michael *(University of New South Wales, Australia)*, Raso Delgue Juan *(Universidad de la Republica, Uruguay)*, Ryan Paul *(King's College, University of Cambridge, United Kingdom)*, Sanchez Castaneda Alfredo *(Universidad Nacional Autonoma de Mexico, Mexico)*, Sargeant Malcolm *(Middlesex University, United Kingdom)*, Tiraboschi Michele *(University of Modena and Reggio Emilia, Italy)*, Tucker Erick *(York University, Canada).*

Youth and the Labour Market in Romania

Edited by

Cristina Lincaru and Vasilica Ciucă

CAMBRIDGE SCHOLARS PUBLISHING

Youth and the Labour Market in Romania,
Edited by Cristina Lincaru and Vasilica Ciucă

This book first published 2014

Cambridge Scholars Publishing

12 Back Chapman Street, Newcastle upon Tyne, NE6 2XX, UK

British Library Cataloguing in Publication Data
A catalogue record for this book is available from the British Library

Copyright © 2014 by Cristina Lincaru, Vasilica Ciucă and contributors

All rights for this book reserved. No part of this book may be reproduced, stored in a retrieval system, or transmitted, in any form or by any means, electronic, mechanical, photocopying, recording or otherwise, without the prior permission of the copyright owner.

ISBN (10): 1-4438-5974-5, ISBN (13): 978-1-4438-5974-5

TABLE OF CONTENTS

LIST OF ILLUSTRATIONS

List of Tables

FOREWORD

VASILICA CIUCĂ

The cases of the Romanian labour market and of youth employment performance were analyzed in an attempt to improve the quality and efficiency of youth employment. Recent developments in labour market participation of young people indicate an accentuation of labour market segmentation and a decrease in job security for young people with the risk of exclusion and marginalization, fuelled by longer transition processes towards decent employment.

This transition may seem clear when one looks at two aspects: education and employment. However, the diversity that characterizes young people as a group makes this transition a difficult and blurred process to categorize. The challenge the transition towards employment presents is faced by all, regardless of one's level of education, as employment security is uncertain. The map and the schedule of this journey are anticipated and projected by society and communities through policies and initiatives to stimulate the entry of young people into the labour market through for instance Public Employment Services (PES).

The situation young people find themselves in when they finish school and have no job opportunities is a rather delicate one as society offers no "safety nets". Families are also powerless while the function of PES itself becomes useless.

Under the "intangibles are the major drivers of growth" paradigm, the greatest challenge faced by labour market management is assuring a new security model while creating value through innovation, research and development, brand construction and networking according to specific community needs. Demand and supply must be approached holistically by all labour market actors. PES should act as an institutional integrator that continuously monitors, evaluates and analyzes the state of the Business System's effectiveness.

The pathway to employment for those under the age of 25 should facilitate the gaining of skills needed for integration into a social system (organization, community, etc.). Only in a community which is open to them will young people learn how to grow and transform their host community in a sustainable way.

This book, as well as others in the ADAPT Labour Studies Book-Series, intends to explain the challenges young people deal with while playing a vital role within the community they live in. As Kafka has been quoted as saying, "Youth is happy because it has the ability to see beauty. Anyone who keeps the ability to see beauty never grows old". Therefore, young people, and those young at heart perform an integral role in society, and they must be well integrated to enable their successful engagement within our communities.

INTRODUCTION

IMPROVING THE QUALITY OF EMPLOYMENT FOR YOUTH: GLOBAL CHALLENGES AND INITIATIVES

VASILICA CIUCĂ

1. Introductory Remarks

Romania assumed the ambitious targets set by the Europe 2020 Strategy to achieve a smart, sustainable and inclusive growth, goals which were reiterated in the Conclusions of the European Council (June 28 to 29, 2012). These complex objectives require a national response that would provide an adequate framework based on sound public finances, structural reforms and investments to boost competitiveness. The success of this complex process is conditioned by the capacity at national level to formulate concrete innovative measures and initiatives on employment, education and skills, according to the specific country's need, and to focus on obtaining results.

In achieving this goal, an important objective is to stimulate employment among young people, by providing opportunities for acquiring work experience and through job-creation initiatives for young people. These interventions were to be financed through structural funds.

Therefore, the Ministry of Labour, Family and Social Protection (MMFPS) in partnership with the Ministry of European Affairs, the Ministry of Education, Youth and Sports and other central administration bodies in 2012 promoted a "National Plan for Jobs", which was integrated into the National Reform Plan (2007-2013). This action was a response to the rising trend of unemployment, particularly that of young people, due to the prevailing negative impacts and amplification of the economic crises in Romania and across the globe. To the same end, the European Council approved a "Pact for Growth and Jobs"[1] in June 2012.

[1] European Council. 2012. *European Council Conclusions.* European Council Brussels, 29 June 2012 (COD), EUCO 76/12, CO EUR 4 CONCL 2 European Council:Bruxelles 29 June 2012 (COD).

In the context of high unemployment and the global financial and economic crisis, the following are supported as viable solutions regarding the employment of young people. These reforms aimed at:

> (d) Tackling unemployment and addressing the social consequences of the crisis effectively; pursuing reforms to improve employment levels; stepping up efforts to increase youth employment, notably to improve young people's first work experience and their participation in the labour market, with the objective that within a few months of leaving school, young people receive a good quality offer of employment, continued education, an apprenticeship, or a traineeship, which can be supported by the ESF; and developing and implementing effective policies to combat poverty and support vulnerable groups. Member States will swiftly implement their National Job Plans and develop more ambitious and precise National Job Plans for the next European Semester ones. Member States should use the possibilities of financing temporary recruitment subsidies from the European Social Fund.[2]

The June 2012 Council established that "Boosting employment, for both women and men, in particular for young people and the long-term unemployed, is a clear priority", with special recommendation that youth unemployment policies and actions pursue initiatives presented in the Commission's 'Employment package', putting emphasis on quality job creation, structural reform of labour markets and investment in human capital.[3] As a result, the Commission launched the reform bearing in mind that "one of the priorities for action is to ensure a smooth school-to-work transition for young people."[4]

This integrated approach to the transition from school to work as a process offers a fresh perspective on an innovative and positive youth trajectory, either to education or to employment or to a mixed one, eliminating as far as possible the risk of social exclusion, and the risk of poverty that comes along with inactivity.[5] The 2012-2013 National Plan

---

[2] European Council. 2012. *European Council Conclusions*. European Council Brussels, 29 June, 2012 (COD), EUCO 76/12, CO EUR 4 CONCL 2 The European Council Brussels, 29 Junie 2012 (COD) 8. Brussels: European Union.

[3] European Council. 2012. *European Council Conclusions*. European Council Brussels, 29 June, 2012 (COD), EUCO 76/12, CO EUR 4 CONCL 2 The European Council Brussels, 29 June 2012 (COD) 13. Brussels: European Union.

[4] European Commission. 2012. *European Commission Press Release, July 2012 Youth Unemployment: Shows that Apprenticeships and Traineeships are Useful but Need to be Improved*, IP/12/731. Brussels: European Commission.

[5] Definition of "inactive": a person who is neither in education nor in school, or who drops out of school, has low education and no practical skills.

developed under the coordination of the MMFPS reflects recommendations from the Council to

> Ensure that young people are either in employment, education or training within four months of leaving school, and the definition of a Quality Framework for Traineeships.[6]

Within this context, the role and responsibility of the PES is to identify and formulate solutions, to design Active Labour Market Policies (ALMPs) and other suitable active measures, and to present an integrated approach for young people so as to obtain a positive transition towards quality and sustainable employment.

2. International Labour Standards Concerning Youth Employment Promoted by the ILO

In July 2012, the ILO at its 101st International Labour Conference (ILC) adopted a Resolution concerning the youth employment crisis: a call for action continuing the Resolution concerning youth employment adopted at the 93rd ILC of 2005. This new call for action was made in order to tackle the new and severe youth employment crisis.[7] The framework of the employment policy provided by the ILO is sound and comprehensive.

The ILO encouraged the development of employment strategies in its 1964 Convention 122, the Employment Policy Convention, ratified and enforced in Romania since 6 June 1973 (C122/1973),[8] providing that:

> 1. With a view to stimulating economic growth and development, raising levels of living, meeting manpower requirements and overcoming unemployment and underemployment, each Member shall declare and pursue, as a major goal, an active policy designed to promote full, productive and freely chosen employment.

---

6 European Commission. 2012. *European Commission Press Release, July 2012 Youth Unemployment shows that Apprenticeships and Traineeships are Useful but Need to be Improved*, IP/12/731. Brussels: European Commission.

7 *Resolution Concerning the Youth Employment Crisis: A Call for Action*, Resolutions adopted by the ILC at its 101st Session, Geneva, 14 June 2012, 3.

8 http://www.ilo.org/dyn/normlex/en/f?p=1000:11200:0::NO:11200:P11200_COUNTRY_ID:102824 (accessed 14 March 2013).

2. The said policy shall aim at ensuring that:
(a) There is work for all who are available for and are seeking work;
(b) Such work is as productive as possible;
(c) There is freedom of choice of employment and the fullest possible opportunity for each worker to qualify for, and to use his skills and endowments in a job for which he is well suited, irrespective of race, colour, sex, religion, political opinion, national extraction or social origin.

3. The said policy shall take due account of the stage and level of economic development and the mutual relationships between employment objectives and other economic and social objectives, and shall be pursued by methods that are appropriate to national conditions and practices.[9]

The C122/1973 was fulfilled through the Job Creation in Small and Medium-Sized Enterprises Recommendation, 1998 (No. 189), and the Promotion of Cooperatives Recommendation, 2002 (No. 193). These recommendations promote the valorisation of all the employment opportunities in a diversified form, benefitting existing jobs and job-creation strategies, including cooperatives.

The second major fulfilment of the C122/1973 was made by the ILO in 1975 through the Human Resources Development Convention, 1975 (C No. 142), the Convention concerning Vocational Guidance and Vocational Training in the Development of Human Resources (enforcement: 19 July 1977) adopted in Geneva, at the 60th ILC Session (23 June 1975)—Status: Up-to-date instrument (Technical Convention). Convention 142/1975 has not been ratified by Romania, and assumes that:

Each Member shall adopt and develop comprehensive and coordinated policies and programmes of vocational guidance and vocational training, closely linked with employment, in particular through public employment services. (Article 1, Co 142 /1975).

2.1. Recent Resolutions Concerning Youth Employment

Since 1978, the ILO has adopted five resolutions regarding employment during the International Labour Conferences, three of which are directed to youth.[10] The most recent documents concerning youth employment are:

---

[9] C 122: *Employment Policy (Supplementary Provisions)* Recommendation, 1984 (No. 169). Guidance on the Implementation of Convention No. 122.

[10] The 2005 Resolution contained an appendix listing international labour standards relevant to work and young persons, actualised by the Resolution

a) Resolution Concerning Youth Employment ILC, 64th Session, 1978;

b) Resolution Concerning follow-up to the World Employment Conference ILC, 65th Session, 1979;

c) Resolution Concerning Young People and the ILO's Contribution to the International Youth Year ILC, 69th Session, 1983;

d) Resolution Concerning Young People, with a Detailed Set of Conclusions ILC, 72nd Session, 1986;

e) Resolution Concerning Youth Employment ILC, 86th Session, 1998, called for the Prioritization of Youth Employment (62);

f) Resolution on Promoting Youth Employment (A/RES/57/165), 2002;

g) Resolution Concerning Policies and Programmes involving Youth A/RES/58/133, 2004;

h) Resolution Concerning Youth Employment, Resolutions adopted by the ILC at its 93rd Session, Geneva, June 2005;[11]

i) Resolution Concerning the Youth Employment Crisis: A Call for Action, Resolutions adopted by the ILC at its 101st Session, Geneva, 14 June 2012.

2.2. ILO Conventions Concerning Youth Employment

Youth employment policy promoted by the ILO through conventions and related recommendations covers three areas: employment policy governance, public and private employment services and other areas influencing youth employment policy. Within the context of an economic crisis, it is very important to keep in mind those actions that prioritise fundamental rights (see point d.). Below are the documents grouped by area of governance, and their status in Romania:

---

concerning the Youth Employment Crisis: *A Call for Action*, Resolutions Adopted by the ILC at its 101st Session, Geneva, 14 June 2012.

11 http://www.ilo.org/public/english/standards/relm/ilc/ilc93/pdf/resolutions.pdf (Accessed May 2013, 13).

a) Governance Convention on employment policy (and related Recommendations)

- C111—Discrimination (Employment and Occupation) Convention, 1958 (No. 111) Convention Concerning Discrimination in Respect of Employment and Occupation (Entry into force: 15 June 1960) Adoption: Geneva, 42nd ILC session (25 June 1958) - Status: Up-to-Date Instrument (Fundamental Convention). Ratified by Romania on 6 June 1973.[12]
- C122—Employment Policy Convention, 1964 (No. 122), Developing a Youth Employment Strategy Ratified by Romania on 6 June 1973.[13]
- R083—Employment Service Recommendation, 1948 (No. 83).
- R111—Recommendations: R111- Discrimination (Employment and Occupation) Recommendation, 1958 (No. 111).
- R122—Employment Policy Recommendation, 1964 (No. 122).
- R169—Employment Policy (Supplementary Provisions) Recommendation, 1984 (No. 169). Guidance on the implementation of Convention No. 122.
- R189—The Job Creation in Small and Medium-Sized Enterprises Recommendation, 1998 (No. 189).
- R193—The Promotion of Cooperatives Recommendation, 2002 (No. 193).
- C142—The Human Resources Development Convention, 1975 (No. 142) —Convention Concerning Vocational Guidance and Vocational Training in the Development of Human Resources (Entry into force: 19 July 1977) Adoption: Geneva, 60th ILC session (23 June 1975)—Status: Up-to-Date Instrument (Technical Convention), (not ratified by Romania).
- R195—Human Resources Development Recommendation, 2004 (No. 195).

---

12 http://www.ilo.org/dyn/normlex/en/f?p=1000:11200:0::NO:11200:P11200_COUNTRY_ID:102824 (Accessed June 24, 2013).

13 http://www.ilo.org/dyn/normlex/en/f?p=1000:11200:0::NO:11200:P11200_COUNTRY_ID:102824 (Accessed May 30, 2013).

a) Conventions Concerning Public and Private Employment Services:

- C2—The Unemployment Convention, 1919 (No. 2), ratified by Romania on 13 June 1921, in force, technical.
- C88—Employment Service Convention, 1948 (No. 88), ratified by Romania on 6 June 1973, in force, technical.
- C181—Private Employment Agencies Convention, 1997(No. 181), not ratified by Romania.
- R188—Private Employment Agencies Recommendation, 1997.
- R198—Employment Relationship Recommendation, 2006 (No. 198).
- C150—The Labour Administration Convention, 1978 (No. 150), ratified by Romania on 4 November 2008.

b) Other influential documents:

- C168—The Employment Promotion and Protection against Unemployment Convention, 1988 (No. 168), ratified by Romania on 15 December 1992, in force, technical.
- C044—Unemployment Provision Convention, 1934 (No. 44), not ratified by Romania.
- C102—Social Security (Minimum Standards) Convention, 1952 (No. 102), Romania has accepted Parts II, III, V, VII and VIII, ratified on 15 October 2009.
- R202—Social Protection Floors Recommendation, 2012 (No. 202) Recommendation concerning National Floors of Social Protection Adoption: Geneva, 101st ILC session (14 June 2012) — Status: Up-to-date instrument (Convention).
- R067—Income Security Recommendation, 1944.
- R069—Medical Care Recommendation, 1944.

c) In addressing the youth employment crisis,[14] actions should take account of

- The ILO Declaration of Philadelphia (1944).
- The ILO Declaration on Fundamental Principles and Rights at Work and its Follow-up (1998).
- The Decent Work Agenda (1999).
- The Global Employment Agenda (2003).
- The Conclusions Concerning the Promotion of Sustainable Enterprises (2007).
- The ILO Declaration on Social Justice for a Fair Globalization (2008).
- The Global Jobs Pact (2009).
- The ILC Conclusions Concerning the Recurrent Discussion on Employment (2010), and the Body of International Labour Standards Relevant to Work and Young Persons.

3. ILO Youth Employment Policy Areas

Regardless of location, whether living in a developed, developing or transition economy, young people are likely to be affected by the economic crisis. The situation of youth employment thus deserves urgent attention. Not only does it threaten to violate the principle of equality and solidarity between generations, which is an important aspect of social justice, but any further prolonging or deepening of the crisis will also increase the likelihood of political and social unrest as more and more young people lose faith in the current economic paradigm. In 2005, motivated by this realisation, a resolution was adopted at the International Labour Conference (ILC) calling for an integrated approach to solving the youth employment crisis. This approach was aimed at combining micro and macroeconomic interventions that would address both the demand and supply sides of the labour market and the quantity and quality of employment.

> The youth employment crisis has reached intolerable dimensions. It poses a threat to political stability and social cohesion. This is evidenced by higher unemployment, lower quality jobs, rising marginalization of youth

[14] ILO. 2012. *Resolution Concerning the Youth Employment Crisis: A Call for Action*, Resolutions adopted by the ILC at its 101st Session, Geneva, 14 June 2012, 3.

and among them, slow transition from school to work, detachment from the labour market, and other symptoms. Young people are particularly vulnerable to volatile and unstable economic conditions and a whole generation of young people, as a result, faces much bleaker life prospects than any previous one.

Therefore, there is a pressing need to adopt a new policy paradigm to promote "pro-employment" growth, and make employment and social protection key objectives of economic policies and development strategies. Youth have to be firmly embedded in the policy-making process, and supported by a sufficient political commitment and consistent resources.

Among the main lessons learnt in this report, mention should be made of the following:

- Young people are not a homogeneous group; therefore, targeting specific groups and specific disadvantages in the labour market is more effective. This requires adequate resourcing and administrative capacities to deliver such complex targeted programmes.
- The quality of, and access to, universal education needs to be improved to reduce school drop-out rates and prevent youth from falling into the unemployment and poverty trap.
- Focusing principally on supply-side interventions will not solve the problem. Demand management and the use of labour market policies, such as wage subsidies and apprenticeships, need to be adopted to promote job creation for youth.
- Entrepreneurship, public investment programmes and employment services should also be encouraged to increase employment opportunities, particularly in disadvantaged economies.
- TVET systems have to be made more responsive to the rapidly changing demand for skills across the world through the use of new information and communication technologies, to improve curricula and extend their outreach. More emphasis on lifelong learning and soft skills is decisive to improving youth employability.
- Social media and networks can be used for youth mobilization, voice and outreach, and potentially for youth employment policies.
- Policies facilitating access to jobs should not undermine young workers' rights at work. They deserve a fair chance to acquire employment security, and to receive decent remuneration.
- Lots of young people are not adequately covered by current systems of unemployment benefits. Therefore, policies and measures should be adopted to provide them with greater social protection.
- Income support and employment assistance should go hand in hand to prevent perverse effects.
- International labour standards can help safeguard workers' rights and should be promoted and adhered to.
- Effective policies require a high degree of policy coordination and coherence nationally and internationally.

- While these and other lessons provide important benchmarks for the design of youth employment policies, there remain gaps in knowledge. Monitoring and evaluation of policies and programmes are required for knowledge building and to assess the impact for future intervention.

Finally, a youth employment crisis of this magnitude can only be tackled with a great deal of mobilization, coordination and partnerships at the global level. The ILO has the lead responsibility for garnering this support, including the promotion of social dialogue and the inclusion of social partners. (Summary Conclusion of 2012 the ILC Report)

The Resolutions adopted by the ILC at its 93rd Session, Geneva, June 2005, recommended four policy areas to enhance youth employment: increase employment creation (through initiating a growth strategy, sustaining entrepreneurship and self employment, promoting cooperatives, and public employment policies), facilitate transitions to work (through education, training and labour market policies), providing social protection (assuring labour standards and social protection) and enhancing youth participation.

Fig I-1. 2005 ILC Resolution Policy Areas.[15]

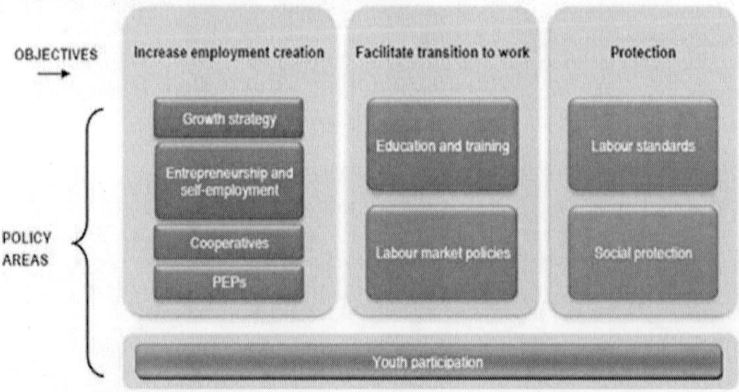

Source: ILO, 2012.

[15] ILO. 2012. *The Youth Employment Crisis: Time for Action* report prepared by Youth for the Youth Employment Forum (Geneva, 23–25 May 2012) is a Summary of the 2012 ILC Report Titled "The Youth Employment Crisis: Time For Action," Committee on Youth Employment of the 101st Session of the International Labour Conference in June 2012. Available at http://www.ilo.org/ilc/ILCSessions/101stSession/reports/reports-submitted/WCMS_175421/lang--fr/index.htm. (Accessed 14 April 2013).

4. Why Do We Need a New Design for ALMPs?

Disadvantaged groups tend to be the targets of ALMPs, but in the context of the crises they are difficult to filter under the current criteria of appropriateness:

> 353. Active labour market policies are an important tool for all youth. They are particularly important for disadvantaged youth and for countering the increase in the number of youth who are detached from both the education and training system and the labour market. Integrated programmes that offer a package of services and tailor them to the heterogeneous needs of their clients tend to be more successful. ALMPs are also important for moderating the rise in youth unemployment during a crisis. Their effectiveness for job creation is more limited where the main problem is a global slump in demand, as in the present context.[16]

1) New categories of potential beneficiaries: NEETs, school drop-outs, young people with high levels of education, and young people with high school education but without having completed the baccalaureate exam. These circumstances indicate the need for diversification of ALMPs.

2) Large scale of demand for ALMPs: increasing numbers, large areas of implementation but under high heterogeneity of local/regional economic-social backgrounds.

3) Action on the short term but effects on the long term: there is a need to develop a knowledge base and to share good practices.

4) High demand for immediate action: ALMPs to be applied to stop or reduce the large accumulation of young people outside the labour market.

5) New employment patterns designed for young people in order to ensure security, decent remuneration, career development, informal productive employment, instead of being part of a fragmented labour market.

6) New trajectories designed for the transitions of young people from rural and informal areas to formal employment.

7) The scope for exploring the self-employment potentials of some professionals in an innovative manner, while establishing cooperatives for young people (see C 122, R 193).

8) The new structure of the ALMPs should be supplemented with integrated programmes with a view of:

---

[16] ILO. 2012. *Report V, the Youth Employment Crisis: Time for Action, Fifth Item on the Agenda*, International Labour Office Geneva, ILC.101/V, First Edition, 107.

> Providing employment and social protection to youth in poverty while generating high economic returns in creating small-scale infrastructure to increase productivity in disadvantaged economies.[17]

9) The setting-up of ALMPs, notwithstanding budgetary and financial constraints amplified by the crises.

10) The extension of social protection to young people who are inadequately covered by unemployment benefits. In this sense:

> 354. Many young people are not adequately covered by current systems of unemployment benefits and social protection. First time job seekers are rarely entitled to unemployment benefits, while youth on temporary contracts are only eligible for limited benefits because of their short contributory period. Ways can be found to give greater social protection to these groups of young people. An important lesson is the need for close synergy between welfare and income support and activation measures to prevent perverse effects.[18]

5. Conclusion

Our main objective has been to focus on LMP developed by PES in the context of European youth employment with the objective to ensure a smooth school-to-work transition in the conditions and recommendations provided by ILO standards for this domain. In order to identify new coordinates for designing new ALMPs in Romania, under these new constraints and opportunities, we explored the experience of the best performers from EU27, identified good practices from ALMPs for young people, and focused on their employment in the short term, also bearing in mind their relative cost-benefit effort.

According to ILO Resolution 195/2004, Human Resources Development Recommendation, with regard to the identified and formulated problem falling under the wording *"how to do?" but do not know "what to do?"*, we have attempted to formulate a solution of ALMPs that could respond to such a challenge. For this last question, we propose the final result of our analysis for the place and role of ALMPs in the knowledge economy, focusing on youth needs.

---

[17] ILO. 2012. *Report V, the Youth Employment Crisis: Time for Action, Fifth Item on the Agenda*, International Labour Office Geneva, ILC.101/V, First Edition, 107.

[18] ILO. 2012. *Report V, the Youth Employment Crisis: Time for Action, Fifth Item on the Agenda*, International Labour Office Geneva, ILC.101/V, First Edition, 107.

References

Bekker S. 2010. "EEO Review: Youth Employment Measures 2010: The Netherlands," European Employment Observatory.

Birchall J., and L. H. Ketilson. 2009. "Resilience of the Cooperative Business Model in Times of Crisis," International Labour Office, Sustainable Enterprise Programme. Geneva: ILO, 3.

Cazes, S., and M. Tonin. 2010. "Employment Protection Legislation and Job stability: A European Cross-Country Analysis," in *International Labour Review*, 149.

Corbanese, V. and G. Rosas. 2009. "Guide to the Design, Monitoring and Evaluation of Innovative Active Labour Market Programmes Targeting Individuals at Risk of Labour Market Exclusion," ILO, Budapest.

Daguerre, A., and D. Etherington. 2009. "Active Labour Market Policies in International Context: What Works Best? Lessons for the UK, Department for Work and Pensions," Working Paper No. 59 (Norwich, HMSO, 2009).

Freedman, D. 2005. *Youth Employment Promotion. A Review of ILO Work and the Lessons Learned.* Employment Strategy Department, http://www.ilo.org/youthmakingithappen/PDF/yenwp1.pdf (accessed 13 March 2013).

Fashoyin T, M. Tiraboschi, Series Editors; Sanchez Castaneda, A., L. Serrani, and F. Sperotti, Guest Editors. 2012. "Youth Unemployment and Joblessness: Causes, Consequences, Responses," *Adapt Labour Studies Book Series*. Cambridge Scholars Publishing.

Fashoyin T, Tiraboschi M, Series Editors; Manzella, P. and L. Rustico. 2011. "Productivity, Investment in Human Capital and the Challenge of Youth Employment," *Adapt Labour Studies Book Series*. Newcastle upon Tyne: Cambridge Scholars Publishing.

Rosas, G., and G. Rossignotti. "Starting the New Millennium Right: Decent Employment for Young People," in *International Labour Review*144, No. 2.

Auer, P., U. Efendioglu, and J. Leschke. 2004. *Active Labour Market Policies around the World: Coping with the Consequences of Globalization.* Geneva: ILO.

World Bank. 2005. *Young People in South Eastern Europe: From Risk to Empowerment.* Washington, DC: The World Bank.

Cunningham, W., M. L. Sanchez-Puerta, an A. Wuermli. 2010. "Active Labour Market Programs for Youth: A Framework to Guide Youth Employment Interventions," Employment Policy Primer Note No. 16. Washington, DC: World Bank.

Hofer, A. R., and A. Delaney. 2010. "Shooting for the Moon: Good Practices in Local Youth Entrepreneurship Support," OECD LEED Working Paper 2010/11. Trento, Italy: OECD Publishing.

European Council. 2012. *European Council Conclusions. June 2012.* European Council, Brussels, 29 June 2012 (COD), EUCO 76/12, CO EUR 4 CONCL 2 The European Council Brussels, 29 June 2012 (COD). Brussels: European Union.

ILO. 1944. "Declaration Concerning the Aims and Purposes of the International Labour Organisation," Adopted at the 26th Session of the ILO, Philadelphia, 10 May 1944 Was Drafted by the then Acting ILO Director, Edward J. Phelan, and C. Wilfred Jenk. Geneva: ILO.

—. 1984. *C 122 ILO- Employment Policy (Supplementary Provisions) Recommendation*, 1984 (No. 169), Guidance on the Implementation of Convention No. 122. Geneva: ILO.

—. 2002. *R193 ILO 2002—Promotion of Cooperatives Recommendation, 2002 (No. 193) Recommendation concerning Promotion of Cooperatives Adoption*, Geneva, 90th ILC session (20 Jun 2002) - Status: Up-to-date instrument (Technical Convention). Geneva: ILO.

—. 2004. *Conclusions of the Tripartite Meeting on Youth Employment, Op. Cit. Tripartite Meeting on Youth Employment: the Way Forward*, 13-15 October 2004, International Labour Organization, TMYEWF/ 2004/7. Geneva: ILO.

—. 2004. "Promoting Employment: Policies, Skills, Enterprises," Report III (Part IB), ILC, 92nd Session, Geneva, 2004, 130. Geneva: ILO.

—. 2005. "Youth: Pathways to Decent Work," Report VI Promoting Youth Employment—Tackling the challenge Sixth item on the agenda International Labour, International Labour Conference, 93rd Session, 2005, International Labour Office Geneva, pg.62. Geneva: ILO.

—. 2009. "ILO Support for the Role of Public Employment Services in the Labour Market," Governing Body, 306th Session, Geneva, Nov. 2009, GB.306/ESP/3/2. Geneva: ILO.

—. 2010. "Global Employment Trends for Youth," August 2010, Special Issue on the Impact of the Global Economic Crisis on Youth, International Labour Office. Geneva: ILO.

—. 2010. "Recovery and Growth with Decent Work," Report of the Director-General, Report I(C), International Labour Conference, 99th Session. Geneva: ILO;

—. 2011. A New Era of Social Justice, Report of the Director-General, Report I(A), International Labour Conference, 100th Session, Geneva.

—. 2010. "Resolution and Conclusions Concerning the Recurrent Discussion on Employment," in Report of the Committee for the

Recurrent Discussion on Employment, International Labour Conference, 99th Session, Geneva: ILO, 56–70.

—. 2010. "Accelerating a Job Rich Recovery in G20 Countries: Building on Experience," An ILO Report, with Substantive Contributions from OECD, to the Meeting of G20 Labour and Employment Ministers, Washington, DC.

—. 2010. Employment and Social Protection Policies from Crisis to Recovery and Beyond: A Review of Experience, an ILO Report to the G20 Labour and Employment Ministers Meeting, Washington, DC, 20–21 April 2010. Geneva: ILO.

—. 2012. *The Youth Employment Crisis: Time for Action*. Report Prepared by Youth for the Youth Employment Forum (Geneva, 23–25 May 2012). Geneva: ILO.

—. 2012. *R 2012 /101 ILC ILO, Resolution Concerning the Youth Employment Crisis: A Call for Action*, Resolutions Adopted by the ILC at its 101st Session, Geneva, 14 June 2012, pg.3. Geneva: ILO.

—. 2012. *Report V ILO 2012, The Youth Employment Crisis: Time for Action*, Fifth Item on the Agenda, International Labour Office Geneva, ILC.101/V, First edition 2012, pg.107. Geneva: ILO.

European Commission. 2012. "Youth Unemployment," European Commission, Press Release, 2 July 2012, IP/12/731. Brussels: European Commission.

United Nations. 2011. *The Universal Declaration of Human Rights*, Retrieved October 25, 2011.

The Increasing Need for Active Labour Market Policies (ALMPs) for Young People

Cristina Lincaru

1. Introduction

The Resolution concerning the youth employment crisis, *A Call for Action*, adopted at the 101st session of the International Labour Conference (ILC) calls for an integrated approach to solve the issue at hand. This approach aims at combining micro and macroeconomic interventions that would address both the demand and supply sides of the labour market and the quantity and quality of employment.[1]

> The youth employment crisis has reached intolerable dimensions. It poses a threat to political stability and social cohesion. This is evidenced by higher unemployment, lower quality jobs, rising marginalization of youth and among them, slow transition from school to work, detachment from the labour market, and other symptoms. Young people are particularly vulnerable to volatile and unstable economic conditions and a whole generation of young people, as a result, faces much bleaker life prospects than any previous one. Therefore, there is a pressing need to adopt a new policy paradigm to promote "pro-employment" growth, and make employment and social protection key objectives of economic policies and development strategies.[2]

---

[1] The Youth Employment Crisis: Time for Action, 2012 ILO, is a report prepared within the youth employment forum (Geneva, 23–25 may 2012) which summarises the 2012 ILC report titled "The Youth Employment Crisis: Time for Action," drafted by the committee on Youth Employment of the 101st Session of the International Labour Conference in June 2012. Available at http://www.ilo.org/ilc/ILCSessions/101stSession/reports/reports-submitted/WCMS_175421/lang--fr/index.htm, 2 (Accessed May 3, 2013).

[2] ILO. 2010. "Recovery and Growth with Decent Work," Report of the Director-General, Report I(C), International Labour Conference, 99th Session, Geneva, 2010; ILO. 2011. "A new Era of Social Justice," Report of the Director-General,

It is generally accepted that the best actions in response to the new developments regarding youth unemployment solutions are provided by the ALMPs:

> 195. Recent ILO research has shown that cost-effective ALMPs are of strategic importance for promoting youth employment in the current economic conjuncture of weak economic recovery and severe fiscal constraints. Simulations show that increasing spending on ALMPs by only 0.5 per cent of GDP increases employment by between 0.2 and 1.2 per cent over the medium term, depending on the country.[3] These results show that countries with the lowest ALMP spending to GDP ratio can harvest the largest benefit by instituting such policies.[4]

The multidimensional nature of ALMPs and their strong correlations with the variations of the socio-economic ecosystem set a limit of transferability of any good practice confirmed and validated by the specific characteristics of the implementation location. Therefore, I shall present the latest evolutions of Romania's background that could influence ALMPs, considering the following factors: the demographic context (pertinent changes within the population, fertility, mean age of women at childbirth, life expectancy at birth, mobility of workers, and the demographic crises), the macroeconomic context (economic growth models for the 2000-2008, 2008-2009 and 2010-2011 periods), the recent labour market and social welfare systems reforms (Labour Code, the Code of Social Dialogue, the "Social Assistance" Law and the "Pension" Law), Romania's performance in global competitiveness, poverty and in-work poverty (labour market participation, employment at regional level, the relative poverty rate, the in-work at-risk-of-poverty rate, productivity in

---

Report I(A), International Labour Conference, 100th Session, Geneva: ILO; ILO. 2010. "Resolution and Conclusions concerning the Recurrent Discussion on Employment," in Report of the Committee for the Recurrent Discussion on Employment, International Labour Conference, 99th Session, Geneva, 2010, 56–70; ILO. 2010. "Accelerating a Job Rich Recovery in G20 Countries: Building on Experience," an ILO Report, with substantive contributions from OECD, to the Meeting of G20 Labour and Employment Ministers, Washington, DC, 20-21 April 2010; ILO. 2010. Employment and Social Protection Policies from Crisis to Recovery and Beyond: A Review of Experience, ILO Report to the G20 Labour and Employment Ministers Meeting, Washington, DC, 20-21 April 2010.

[3] IILS. 2011. *World of Work Report: Making Markets Work for Jobs*. Geneva: ILO, 121.

[4] IILS. 2011. *World of Work Report: Making Markets Work for Jobs*. Geneva: ILO, 126.

rural areas, the labour market vulnerability of Roma people, labour taxation, the shadow economy and undeclared work, as well as perceptions of corruption).

2. The Demographic Context

In 2012, the total population of Romania amounted to 21.36 million people. In the last decade, the overall population decreased by more than 1 million, with a 4.9% rate of natural change of population in comparison to the rate reported in 2000. This tendency was contrary to the EU27 positive trend of increasing the total population to 503.7 million people, with a difference of some 21 million people (4.3% of the total population in 2001). The changes in the population aged 15-24 years old in Romania were similar to the EU27 in both absolute and relative terms. The decreasing number of young people[5] (15 to 24-year-olds) in 2011 was distributed as follows:

a. 1.7 million people in Romania, that is a decrease of 0.28 million people in absolute terms and 1.2% in relative terms with respect to the 2000 levels;

b. 59.8 million people in EU27, that is a decrease of 4.1 million people in absolute terms, and a 0.8% drop in relative terms compared to the 2000 levels.

The demographic structural change expressed through the decrease of the young population share in the total population took place at a speed of more than double that of Romania. In 2011, the percentage of population aged 15-24 years old out of the total population was:

a. 13.4% in Romania, decreasing by 2.8pp with respect to the 2000 levels;

b. 11.9% in EU27, decreasing by 1.3pp if one considers the same cohort in 2000.

The share of total population of Romania in the total EU27 population was 4.3% in 2011 (-0.4pp compared to the 2000 levels). The same tendency was visible for the 15-24 age groups, yet more accelerated. The

---

[5] Data Source: EUROSTAT, Population on 1 January by Five Years Age Groups and Sex [demo_pjangroup].

15-24 year-old age group population in Romania in the same age group in EU27 was 4.8% in 2011 (-0.9pp), more than twice the 2000 levels.

2.2. The Decreasing Tendency of the Rate of Natural Change of Population

The recorded rate of natural change in the population was negative throughout the period 2000-2011, shifting from -0.9% in 2000 to -2.6% in 2011. In the EU27, this indicator constantly increased and recorded a positive trend, from 0.6% in 2000 to 0.8% in 2011.[6] The gap between Romania and the EU27 in this figure has increased, too, from a difference of 1.5 percentage points in 2000, to a difference of 3.4 percentage points in 2011. Between 2008 and 2011, the effect of the crisis was felt stronger in Romania than in the EU27, with the annual rate of population growth declining by 1.1 percentage points in Romania, and by 0.4 percentage points if the EU27 average is taken.

a) Low Levels of Total Fertility Rates

The number of children per woman in Romania was 1.22 in 2011, down from 1.31 in 2000, and well below the 2.1 that ensures the replacement of the population. During the crisis (from 2008 to 2011), this figure dropped by 0.1.[7] As of 2009, the European average fertility rate was 1.59.

b) The Increase of the Mean Age of Women at Childbirth

The mean age of women at childbirth[8] for Romania was found to be 25.7 years in 2000 and 27.1 years in 2011, with the EU27 average which was equal to 29.2 years in 2002 and 29.8 years in 2009 (latest data available). The Romanian gap in relation to the EU27 average for the average age of women at first childbirth has decreased from 3.1 years in 2000 to 2.8 years in 2008, slightly increasing to 2.9 years in 2009, that is, during the crisis.

---

[6] EUROSTAT, *Demographic Balance and Crude Rates* [demo_gind], Crude Rate of Natural Change of Population.

[7] EUROSTAT, [tsdde220] - *Total Fertility Rate* - Number of Children per Woman.

[8] EUROSTAT, *Fertility Indicators* [demo_find], Mean Age of Women at Childbirth.

c) The Increase of the Median Age of Population

The median age of the population in Romania has continuously increased, from 34.4 years in 2000 to 39 years in 2012.[9] Romania's gap in relation to the EU27 average has decreased by one year; from 3.6 years in 2000 to 2.6 years in 2012 (it remained stable from 2008 to 2012).

d) The Increase in Life Expectancy at Birth[10]

For the period 2000-2011, there has been a general increase of life expectancy at birth—by 3.3 years for men and by 3.4 years for women –in line with the general trend of the EU27. In Romania, life expectancy at birth in 2011 was 78.2 years for women, and 71 years for men. Romania closed in on the 1-year gap with the EU27 average for women, from 6.2 years in 2002 to the 5.2 years in 2009, whereas for men the country reduced the gap by 0.2 years, from 7.1 years in 2002 to 6.9 years in 2009.

e) The Explosive Growth in the Number of Young People Migrating for Work following Romania's entry into the European Union

"Free movement of workers" is one of the fundamental values of the European community, as is laid down in its Constitution:

> Article 45 (ex-Article 39 EC) of the Treaty on the Functioning of the European Union (hereinafter "TFEU") and has been developed through secondary law (Regulation (EEC) No 1612/68[11] and Directive 2004/38/EC,[12] as well as Directive2005/36/EC)[13] and by the case-law of the Court of Justice of the European Union (hereinafter "CJ").[14]

---

[9] EUROSTAT. *Population on 1 January: Structure Indicators* [demo_pjanind], *Median Age of Population.* Brussels: EUROSTAT.

[10] EUROSTAT. *Life Expectancy at Birth, by Sex* (tps00025). Brussels: EUROSTAT.

[11] OJ L 257, 19.10.1968, 2, hereinafter "the Regulation".

[12] OJ L 158, 30.4.2004, 77, hereinafter "the Directive".

[13] OJ L 255, 30.9.2005, 22.

[14] Quoted from European Commission. 2010. *Reaffirming the Free Movement of Workers: Rights and Major Developments.* Communication From the Commission to the Council, The European Parliament, The European Economic and Social Committee and The Committee of the Regions, Brussels, 13.7.2010, COM(2010)373 final. Brussels: European Union.

The multi-faceted and large area covered by the mobility process in the context of the Single European Market consolidation has become a complex issue, with major implications reported in many areas (welfare systems, education, health, pensions, recognition of qualifications, etc.) as a consequence of "the most important individual rights that the EU guarantees to its citizens".[15] Following the enlargement wave of 1 January 2007, Romania and Bulgaria joined the EU25, gradually going through three phases of the transitional arrangements:[16]

- 1st phase, from 1 January 2007 to 31 December 2008;
- 2nd phase, from 1 January 2009 to 31 December 2011;
- 3rd phase, from 1 January 2012 to 31 December 2013.

In 2012, the European Commission reported that:

a) As nationals from EU-2 Member States are concerned, their total number in the EU-15 Member States increased from around 700,000 at the end of 2003 to a little over 2.7 million in 2010;[17]

b) As far as EU-2 intra-EU movers are concerned, it should be noted that 80% of them are Romanians and 20% Bulgarians (Idem 12, 253);

c) 85% of the EU-10 as well as of the EU-2 nationals living in other Member States are of working-age (Idem 12, 265);

Moreover, among the working age population (aged 15-64 years old) it appears that recent intra-EU movers are younger than the overall labour force in both the sending and receiving countries (see Chart 16) and that this is particularly true of recent movers from EU-2 and EU-10 countries. Persons under 35 years represent 62 % of EU-2 working-age movers and 70 % of EU-10 working-age movers, compared to only 34 % in the EU-15

---

[15] European Commission. 2010. *Reaffirming the Free Movement of Workers: Rights and Major Developments.* Communication From the Commission to the Council, The European Parliament, The European Economic and Social Committee and The Committee of the Regions, Brussels, 13.7.2010, COM(2010)373 final. Brussels: European Union, 2.

[16] CZ: still under national law; ES: restrictions for workers from Romania (from July 2011); DE and AT: Restrictions also on the Posting of Workers in Certain Sectors.

[17] Directorate-General for Employment, Social Affairs and Inclusion. 2011. *Employment and Social Developments in Europe 2011*, http://ec.europa.eu/employment_social/esde/2011, European Union. 2012, Chapter 6: *Intra-EU Labour Mobility and the Impact of Enlargement*, 265.

labour force. Conversely, some half of EU-15 movers is aged 35 or older. (Idem 12, 265).

f) The Dramatic and Long-Term Negative Effects of the Demographic Crisis

"By 2060, however, the average European level of dependants (population dependency ratio over 65/ population aged 15-64) will double, putting unbearable pressure on public pension systems:"[18] "No pension system can survive such a doubling of retirees/employees report".[19] Base projections made in 2009 for 2060 indicated a possible scenario for Romania. In 2007, this country had a population of 16.9 million people, a share of working age population of 53.6% of total population, and an elderly dependency rate (65 + / 15-64) of 65.3% which almost tripled, drawing a dramatic picture of the major demographic crisis affecting Romania and having major negative effects of change on the age structure of employment and the long-term sustainability of public finances.[20]

3. The Macroeconomic Context

From 2000 so far, the Romanian economy has experienced three major periods of development: an initial period of growth (2000-2008) culminating in a "boom that led to unsustainable balances during 2003-2008", followed by a second period of severe recession during the 2008-2009 global financial crisis,[21] and ending with a third period (2010-2012)

---

[18] UE: Viitoarea Criza Demografica şi a pensiilor va fi de 10 ori mai grava decât actuala criza globala, Asociatia pentru Pensiile Administrate Privat din Romania, www.apapr.ro.

[19] Börsch-Supan, A. 2010. *Note: Economic and Scientific Policies European Parliament's Special Committee on the Financial, Economic and Social Crisis Social Impact of the Crisis - Demographic Challenges and the Pension System.* , Directorate General for Internal Policies Policy Department, Ip/A/Cris/Nt/2009-06 2010, Pe. 429.995 En.

[20] Directorate-General for Economic and Financial Affairs. 2009. "Sustainability Report," *European Economy* 9:135.

[21] International Monetary Fund. 2012. *Staff Report for the 2012 Article IV Consultation, Sixth Review Under the Stand-By Arrangement, and Requests for Waiver of Nonobservance of Performance Criterion and Modification of Performance Criteria* Prepared by the European Department in Consultation with Other Departments, approved by Poul M. Thomsen and Vivek Arora, International Monetary Fund, Romania. Washington DC: IMF, 5.

of "restoration of macroeconomic sustainability"[22] and "modest growth, with modest economic recovery prospects for the future"[23].

3.1. The 2000-2008 Period and the Unsustainable Economic Boom

The economic growth Romania experienced during this period was mostly based on foreign direct investment.

> Foreign direct investment and capital inflows (in part through subsidiaries of foreign banks in Romania) helped finance high consumption and investment growth. Robust export growth to EU countries reflected a process of increasing economic integration with Western European economies.[24]

Domestic demand grew faster, causing current account deficits, which reached 14% of GDP in 2007, that is an increase of over 10 percentage points from 2000. Thus:

> The overheating economy and rapid capital inflows complicated monetary policy, resulting in the real effective exchange rate (REER) (NBR's) inability to achieve its inflation target notwithstanding increases in interest rates and reserve requirements. A real effective exchange rate (REER) was about 50 percent between mid-2004 and mid-2007, driven by the strong capital inflows and expectations of economic convergence under EU membership. Fiscal policy played a strongly pro-cyclical role, with the

---

[22] International Monetary Fund. 2012. *Staff Report for the 2012 Article IV Consultation, Sixth Review Under the Stand-By Arrangement, and Requests for Waiver of Nonobservance of Performance Criterion and Modification of Performance Criteria* Prepared by the European Department in Consultation with Other Departments, approved by Poul M. Thomsen and Vivek Arora, International Monetary Fund, Romania. Washington DC: IMF, 5.

[23] European Union. 2012. *European Economic Forecast, Autumn 2012, Statistical Annex*, pg. 154, Table 13: "Potential GDP," Volume (percentage change on preceding year, 1993-2014), 19.10.2012, http://ec.europa.eu/economy_finance/eu/forecasts/2012_autumn/ro.html. Brussels: European Union.

[24] International Monetary Fund. 2009. *Request for Stand-By Arrangement Prepared by the European Department* (In Consultation with Other Departments) approved by Poul Thomsen and Philip Gerson. Washington DC: International Monetary Fund, 4.

government deficit rising from under 1 percent of GDP in 2005 to near 5 percent of GDP by 2008.[25]

Growth was driven by domestic demand supported by increased lending and rising wages. The average growth of domestic demand was 7.5% for the years 2000 to 2004, and 10.6% for the period 2005-2008. In 2008, the annual growth rate of real GDP was 7.3%. After 2008, due to the financial and banking crisis, there was a sharp fall in domestic demand (12.9%).[26] The annual growth rate of real GDP in Romania was 2.4% in 2000, 1.5 percentage points lower than the EU27 average. From 2001 and until 2008, the annual growth rate of real GDP for Romania was higher than the EU27 average (6.3% for Romania and 2% for the EU27), with a maximum of 8.5% in 2004 and 3.9% in 2000 achieved in Romania and the EU27, respectively. At the end of this period, the real GDP growth rate was 7.3% in Romania and 0.3% in the EU27. Estimates of the output gap—i.e. the difference between the growth rates of real GDP and potential GDP[27]—calculated by the IMF in October 2012 for Romania pointed towards a positive trend; GDP was higher than the sustainable level of existing resources (capital and labour), which led to increasing the inflationary pressures, a fact which was confirmed by potential GDP.[28]

Thus, the *IMF Romania Output Gap* (5th revision) indicates ongoing trends of an increasing distance from an equilibrium state, originally amounting to 0.6 percentage points in 2000, up to 10 percentage points in 2008. As a result of applying new and multivariate models, the output gap estimated by the IMF was at 2.4 percentage points in 2000, rising by 0.9

---

[25] International Monetary Fund. 2009. *Romania: Request For Stand-By Arrangement—Staff Report; Staff Supplements; and Press Release on the Executive Board Discussion*, IMF Country Report No. 09/183. Washington DC: IMF.

[26] Document De Lucru Al Serviciilor Comisiei, Evaluarea Programului Naţional De Reforma Şi A Programului De Convergenţa Din 2011, Pentru România *Care Însoţeşte Documentul* Recomandare De Recomandare A Consiliului Privind Programul Naţional De Reforma Din 2011 Al României Ii De Emitere A Unui Aviz Al Consiliului Privind Programul De Convergenţa Actualizat Al României Pentru Perioada 2011-2014,{Sec(2011) 825 Final}, Comisia Europeana, Bruxelles, 7.6.2011, Sec(2011) 731 Final, 2.

[27] Pibul Potenţial Este Pibul Care Ar Putea Fi Realizat La Capacitatea Totală A Economiei În Condiţii De Maximă Eficienţă, Http://Www.Businessdictionary.Com/Definition/Output-Gap.Html.

[28] PIBul potenţial nu este observat direct, valorile obţinute sunt diferite în funcţie de metoda de calcul.

percentage points in 2006, and maintaining the growth trend up to the maximum of 6.2 percentage points in 2008.

3.2. Severe Recession during 2008-2009

The economic and financial crisis of 2008-2009 led to a dramatic decline of the Romanian economy, and the real GDP growth rate recorded an absolute decline of 14.1 percentage points (expressed as a sudden transition from an annual increase of 7.3% in 2008 to a decrease of -7.1% in 2009), four times that of the EU27 average (3.8%). Government deficit (considering the ESA 95 B.9 methodology) fell from -5.7% to -9% of GDP in 2009. The decline was driven by lower domestic demand, moving from 7.8% in 2007 to -12%[29] in 2009.

In this context, an anti-crisis programme was launched, supported by the International Monetary Fund (IMF), the European Union (EU) and the World Bank (WB), initiated by the First Stand-by Arrangement (SBA) and finally approved on 4 May 2009, which expired on 30 May 2011 and lasted 24 months.[30] The first package of external financing 2009-2011[31] had the main objective of stabilising the Romanian economy, and eliminating economic imbalances to restore confidence in financial markets and create conditions for sustainable economic growth.

> Significant progress has been made under the SBA in achieving fiscal consolidation and safeguarding the financial sector [...]. A structural fiscal deficit of almost 9 percent of GDP in 2008 was halved by 2010, and the government finances are broadly on track toward respecting the 3 percent of GDP Maastricht deficit limit in 2012[...]. Structural reforms in tax administration, pensions, public wages and employment, and social benefits will ease fiscal pressures in the medium-term, while improving

[29] International Monetary Fund. 2012. *Article IV Consultation and Sixth Review Under the Stand-by Arrangement, and Requests for Waiver of Nonobservance of Performance Criterion and Modification of Performance Criteria—Staff Report*; Staff Supplement; Public Information Notice and Press Release on the Executive Board Discussion; and Statement by the Executive Director for Romania. IMF Country Report No. 12/290, 37. Washington DC: IMF.

[30] International Monetary Fund. 2012. *Romania: Financial Position in the Fund* as of November 30, 2012, Summary of IMF Members' Quota, Reserve Position, SDR Holdings, Outstanding Credit, Recent Lending Arrangements, Projected Payments due to the IMF, and Monthly Historical Transactions with the Fund.

[31] Ratificat Printr-o serie de documente legislative cum ar fi: OUG nr.99/2009, OUG nr. 10/2010, Legea nr.257/2010, Legea nr.84/2011, Legea nr.286/ 2011 http://www.mfinante.ro/pachete.html?pagina=pachete.

public sector efficiency and setting the stage for more widespread improvements in the business climate.[32]

The current account deficit fell from 11.5% of GDP in 2008, to 4.2% of GDP in 2009, while consolidated public debt rose from 13.4% of GDP in 2008 to 23.6% of GDP in 2009. Growth was inflationary, and potential aggregate demand was below the productive potential of the economy.

The real GDP growth rate fell from 7.3% in 2008 to -6.6% in 2009. The EU27 Commission estimated the potential GDP growth rates[33] as 2.3% in 2008, and 1.7% in 2009. The output gap transition from the positive inflation in 2008 to the negative output gap (the economy operates below capacity) was supported by several calculation methodologies in 2009. More specifically:

a) The new method for calculating the output gap used by the IMF shows a shift from 10% in 2008 to -0.3% in 2009;[34]

b) The multivariate approach resorted to by the IMF points to a shift from 6.2% in 2008 to -1.1% in 2009;[35]

c) The output gap calculated by the European Commission shows a shift from 2.3% in 2008 to -8.9% in 2009.[36]

3.3. Restoring Macroeconomic Sustainability: Vulnerable Recovery (2010-2011)

In September 2012, the IMF issued the following conclusions regarding the latest progression of the Romanian economy:

---

[32] România: Scrisoare De Intenţie, Bucureşti, 10 martie 2011, 6, http://www.imf.org/external/pubs/ft/scr/2011/cr1180.pdf (accessed 13 March 2013).

[33] PIB potenţial—nivelul PIB real care poate fi produs de economie fără a genera presiuni inflaziomiste.

[34] FMI. 2012. *Romania: Selected Issues Paper*, IMF Country Report No. 12/291, Publication Services. Washington DC: IMF, 6.

[35] FMI. 2012. *Romania: Selected Issues Paper*, IMF Country Report No. 12/291, Publication Services. Washington DC: IMF, 6.

[36] European Commission. 2012. "Commission Staff Working Document, European Economic Forecast," *European Economy* 8, Directorate-General for Economic and Financial Affairs, 154.

> Following the severe downturn during the 2008–09 crises, Romania has made significant progress in restoring macroeconomic stability. Large external and fiscal imbalances were reduced to more sustainable levels under two consecutive IMF SBAs, supported by the European Union and the World Bank. The current account deficit declined sharply from 11½ percent of GDP in 2008 to 4½ percent in 2011, and the structural fiscal deficit narrowed from 7½ percent of GDP to 3 percent over the same period. Annual inflation dropped from a high of 8 percent at end-2010 to 2 percent in June 2012, partly reflecting the temporary impact of the good 2011 harvest. Core inflation fell from above 5 percent in 2008 to about 2 percent recently [...]. Growth resumed at 2½ percent in 2011, boosted by a bumper harvest, but nevertheless lagged behind most other European emerging economies. The unemployment rate increased from 5.8 percent in 2008 to 7.3 percent in 2010 and has remained elevated since then. With the euro area entering recession and domestic political tensions on the rise, recent developments point to a stronger growth slowdown in 2012 than previously expected. After two quarters of decline, real GDP rebounded by 0.5 percent (q/q) in 2012:Q2 on the back of solid domestic demand but high-frequency data indicate that the economy may have slowed again since May.[37]

In 2012, Romania's economy continued to be driven by domestic demand.[38] In 2010, GDP growth was -1.6%, domestic demand contributed -1.6% and net exports 0%. In 2011, growth was 2.5% and the contribution of domestic demand was 3.2%, reduced by the negative contribution of net exports of -0.8%. In 2012, GDP growth decreased to 0.7%, the contribution of domestic demand was 1% and the net exports contribution decreased by approximately 0.4%.[39] The annual growth of domestic

---

[37] International Monetary Fund. 2012. *Staff Report for the 2012 Article IV Consultation, Sixth Review Under the Stand-By Arrangement, and Requests for Waiver of Nonobservance of Performance Criterion and Modification of Performance Criteria* Prepared by the European Department in Consultation with Other Departments, approved by Poul M. Thomsen and Vivek Arora. Washington DC: IMF, 5.

[38] European Commission. 2012. "Commission Staff Working Document, European Economic Forecast," *European Economy* 8, Directorate-General for Economic and Financial Affairs.

[39] *CNP: Comisia Naţională de Prognoză, Proiecţia Principalilor Indicatori Macroeconomici* pentru Perioada 2012-2016, Prognoza de toamnă 2012, 23 noiembrie 2012, NOTĂ: Prognoza de toamnă este elaborată în concordanţă cu prevederile Regulamentului nr. 1175/2011 al Parlamentului European şi al Consiliului de modificare a Regulamentului nr. 1466/97 al Consiliului privind consolidarea supravegherii poziţiilor bugetare şi supravegherea şi coordonarea politicilor economice.

demand was negative (-1.5% in 2010 compared to 2009), with a return to 3.1% in 2011, and estimated at 1% in 2012. The European Forecast, in autumn 2012, estimated for 2012 a slight increase in real GDP (0.8%), found in approximately one third of the annual growth rate of 2.1% of GDP potential, which indicates that the economy is still functioning well below potential. The main country-specific downside risks in 2012 relate to:

a) Ongoing domestic political uncertainties that could increase financing costs and hold back investment; and

b) A higher-than expected impact of the drought on agriculture.[40]

Here are the recent findings of the IMF:

> Staff projects real GDP growth to slow to about 1 percent in 2012, and to gradually pick up to 2½ percent in 2013, due to diminished confidence, continued low capital inflows and EU funds absorption, and the slowdown in external demand related to the euro area recession. Moreover, the recent drought will weaken agricultural output in the second half of 2012. Unemployment would only slightly decline.[41]

As a result of maintaining the context of uncertainty and enhancement of turbulence in 2012, the Romanian authorities have argued for further fiscal consolidation by reducing spending, including measures to keep the wage bill under control. In addition, significant pension reforms have improved the financial soundness of the public pension system. They are pursued simultaneously for improving the design capital budgets in order to achieve long-term investment.

A new programme called Precautionary Assistance was launched which was supported by the International Monetary Fund (IMF), the European Union (EU) and the World Bank (WB), by means of the Second Stand-By Agreement, and was intended to continue to adjust and to

---

[40] European Commission. 2012. "Commission Staff Working Document, European Economic Forecast," *European Economy* 8, Directorate-General for Economic and Financial Affairs, 99.

[41] International Monetary Fund. 2012. *Staff Report for the 2012 Article IV Consultation, Sixth Review Under the Stand-By Arrangement, and Requests for Waiver of Nonobservance of Performance Criterion and Modification of Performance Criteria* Prepared by the European Department in Consultation with Other Departments, approved by Poul M. Thomsen and Vivek Arora. Washington DC: IMF, 37.

mitigate the effects of possible future shocks. This second package[42] of external financing, which was launched on 31 May 2011 and completed on 30 March 2013,[43] announced that:

> The proposed follow-up programme aims to provide precautionary support against possible future economic shocks, while assisting Romania in continuing its economic adjustment. Building on the achievements of the current SBA, the key objectives of the new programme are to: (i) continue the fiscal adjustment process while attacking problems of revenue and expenditure efficiency, and arrears; (ii) boost growth potential through structural reforms and improved flexibility of the economy, which will allow for continued competitiveness as Romania prepares for eventual euro area entry; and (iii) continue fostering confidence, facilitating improved private capital flows, by improving policy stability and the business climate.[44]

A number of priority actions were agreed to have direct effects on the labour market and promote state-owned enterprises through:

- Structural benchmarking;

- The appointment of legal advisors for privatisation of CFR Marfa, TAROM, Transelectrica, Transgaz, and Romgaz;

- The setting-up of action plans for the remaining SOEs of the central government;

- Mechanisms to facilitate restructuring and securitising SOE arrears,[45] as well as a follow-up reform of the labour market.

---

[42] Reglementat în legislaţie prin: Lege 285/2011 Lege 205/2012, http://www.mfinante.ro/pachete.html?pagina=pachete.

[43] International Monetary Fund. 2012. *Romania: Financial Position in the Fund* as of November 30, 2012, Summary of IMF Members' Quota, Reserve Position, SDR Holdings, Outstanding Credit, Recent Lending Arrangements, Projected Payments Due to the IMF, and Monthly Historical Transactions with the Fund. Washington DC: IMF.

[44] România: Scrisoare De Intenţie, Bucureşti, 10 martie 2011, 3, http://www.imf.org/external/pubs/ft/scr/2011/cr1180.pdf, 9.

[45] International Monetary Fund. 2012. "Romania: Fourth Review under the Stand-By Arrangement and Request for Modification of Performance Criteria," Staff Report, Staff Supplement, Press Release on the Executive Board Discussion; and Statement by the Executive Director for Romania. IMF Country Report No. 12/73. Washington DC: IMF.

4. Recent Substantial Reforms of the Labour Market and Social Welfare Systems

A coordinated reform of the labour market and social welfare systems took place in 2011. The Labour Code, the Code of Social Dialogue, the "Social Assistance" Law and the "Pension" Law were amended in order "to increase the flexibility of labour markets, improve collective bargaining efficiency—while protecting the rights of workers and employers –and increase labour force participation." Among the tools to increase Romanian labour market flexibility, mention should be made of the objective of more flexible working hours.

4.1. The New Labour Code

The New Labour Code (Law No. 53 of January 24, 2003, published on 18 May 2011 and enforced on 21 May 2011) "aims to improve labour market flexibility by promoting employment and temporary extension of probationary periods, and increasing flexibility of working time."[46]

Amendments to the Labour Code were intended to increase labour market flexibility, by promoting the diversification of individual employment contracts, through the adoption of fixed-term employment contracts, extending probationary periods, and increasing working flexibility.

4.2. The Code of Social Dialogue

The Code of Social Dialogue[47] (Law No. 62 of 10 May 2011, enforced on May 13, 2011) establishes a new regulatory framework for social dialogue in Romania. It aims to "strengthen legislation on trade unions to resolve labour disputes, define the notion of employers and collective

---

[46] International Monetary Fund. 2011. *Romania. Letter of Intent and Technical Memorandum of Understanding.* Washington DC: IMF.

[47] Lincaru, C., V. Ciucă. 2012. broşura Echilibrul între muncă– familie şi timpul de muncă la nivel European, naţional şi local: Sisteme de conciliere si bune practici pentru negocieri colective în România, publicaţie în cadrul proiectului LIBRA „Să îmbunătăţim Negocierea, Relaţiile şi acordurile privind echilibrul dintre viaţa profesională şi cea personală", LIBRA este un proiect cofinanţat de Comisia Europeană, DG Ocuparea Forţei de Muncă, Afaceri Sociale şi Incluziune, Budget Heading 04.03.03.01/ Relaţii Sociale şi Dialog Social, care beneficiază de susţinerea Ministerului Muncii, Familiei şi Protecţiei Sociale din România. Proiect realizat cu susţinerea Uniunii Europene, 10.

agreement, and review the Economic and Social Council, amending the mechanisms of collective bargaining and labour relations. "Raising the quota of representation in trade unions and employers' associations, eliminating collective bargaining at national level, repealing the *erga omnes* effect of collective agreements at a sectoral level are among the main initiatives".[48] Following the abolition of the collective agreement at a national level, Romania is now integrated into the mainstream of European industry-level agreements.

The implementation of the Social Dialogue Code was postponed due to a prolonged consultation process with the social partners on defining the sectors for collective bargaining".[49] The new Social Dialogue Code came into force by means of an agreement between the social partners laying down the definition of a "sector" in the new collective agreements. On 29 December 2011, Decision No. 1260 of 21 December 2011 regarding business sectors determined in accordance with Law No. 62/2011 entered into force. In accordance with the new criteria of representation concerning the organization and functioning of trade unions and employers, a review processes has commenced on the new structures for unions at the industry level. The Social Dialogue Code proposes:

- Conditions and new criteria on the minimum procedures to establish and dissolute trade unions; Law No. 62/2011, Article 3 (2), Article 40.

- New conditions for acquiring legal personality on the part of the union; Law No. 62/2011, Article 14, (1, 2, 3); Article 17 (1); Article 18; Article 46.

- New criteria to allow different trade union bodies to associate legally; Law No. 62/2011, Art. 41.

- New conditions to gain representativeness; Law No. 62/2011, Art-29; Article 51.

- New conditions allowing delegates or representatives to assist labour organizations and pursue their legal interests; Law No. 62/2011 Article 31.

- A new procedure for evaluating the levels of representation at different stages; Law No. 62/2011; Article 52.

---

48 IMF. 2011. *Romania. Letter of Intent and Technical Memorandum of Understanding.* Washington DC: IMF.

49 IMF. 2011. *Romania. Letter of Intent and Technical Memorandum of Understanding.* Washington DC: IMF.

- New conditions of initiating and proposing legislation of interest to the union; Law No. 62/2011Art. 29;

- Local collective bargaining; Law No. 62/201141, Article 43; Article 46; Article 52;

The Romanian authorities assume to continue the major reform process of the labour law system, by way of consultations and compliance with EU directives and ILO core conventions. In response to the amended version of the Code of Social Dialogue, which lays down a new structure of the Economic and Social Council, and in the absence of government and civil society representatives, members of trade union confederations and employers' associations jointly concluded a national agreement that led the government to create a National Tripartite Council.

Both parties criticized the proposals for labour market reform. Unions have unanimously expressed their opinions on these changes, considering that it is the proposal process and tripartite social dialogue that will be at risk, making collective agreements null and void while preventing social partners from gaining representativeness. The solution supported by the social partners, which ensures the successful implementation of the new framework for consolidating democracy, could promote and encourage effective social dialogue based on consultation.

4.3. Social Assistance

The new provision on social assistance, Act No. 292/2011[50] is an important step in streamlining social benefits and improving the possibility to direct them to the most disadvantaged groups. "The authorities will ensure that the newly designed social assistance law is fully effective by January 2013, prior to households facing energy price liberalisation."[51]

The implementation of new legislation on labour market and social welfare progresses, and has yielded some positive results so far.[52]

---

[50] Lege nr. 292 din 20/12/2011, Publicat in Monitorul Oficial, Partea I nr. 905 din 20/12/2011, Intrare in vigoare: 23/12/2011, Lege a asistenţei sociale.

[51] International Monetary Fund. 2012. *Staff Report for the 2012 Article IV Consultation, Sixth Review Under the Stand-By Arrangement, and Requests for Waiver of Non-observance of Performance Criterion and Modification of Performance Criteria* Prepared by the European Department in Consultation with Other Departments, approved by Poul M. Thomsen and Vivek Arora. Washington DC: IMF.

[52] International Monetary Fund. 2012. *Staff Report for the 2012 Article IV Consultation, Sixth Review Under the Stand-By Arrangement, and Requests for*

4.4. Main Amendments to Extant Legislation

4.4.1. The Labour Code

- The extension of the scope and duration of fixed-term employment contracts;

- The extension of probationary periods;

- The extension of the period to be entitled to compensation for overtime work;

- The introduction of a performance evaluation system among the criteria considered at the time of initiating collective dismissals.

4.4.2. The Social Dialogue Code

- A cap on the maximum duration of collective agreements;

- The repeal of collective agreements at a national level;

- The tightening-up of the requirements to establish trade unions at firm level, also in terms of representation;

- The removal of the automatic *erga omnes* extension of collective agreements concluded at a sectoral level;

- Public sector wage-setting carried out by the government after consultation with social partners;

- The introduction of dialogue through collective bargaining.

4.4.3. The "Social Assistance" Law

- The widening of the scope of the beneficiaries (54 new types of social benefits to be assigned to nine groups);

Waiver of Nonobservance of Performance Criterion and Modification of Performance Criteria Prepared by the European Department in Consultation with Other Departments, approved by Poul M. Thomsen and Vivek Arora. Washington DC: IMF, 29.

- Guaranteed minimum wage, disability and child allowances, and disaster relief programmes;

- Improved surveillance and anti-fraud control;

- Integration into the social service delivery system.

4.4.4. Reforming the Retirement System to ensure Sustainability

The legal framework for welfare reform required continual implementation of the state pension "units". In this sense:

> Law No.263/2010 regarding the unitary public pension system provided a series of measures aimed at improving the financial sustainability of the pension system, based on the principles of contribution and social solidarity through employment pension expenditure and other social insurance rights. The main aspects of this provision concern:
>
> - A gradual shift towards indexing the pension point-based value;
>
> - Equality of treatment for recipients of public pensions, through the elimination of imbalances that still exist in the system;
>
> - A legal framework for occupational pension schemes;
>
> - An increase in the standard retirement age for men and women;
>
> - A discouraging effect to apply for early retirement if failing to pay necessary contributions.
>
> Objectives and implementation measures:
>
> - Ensuring the sustainability of the unit-based public pension system in the medium and long term;
>
> - Maintaining adequate living standards for pensioners;
>
> - Harmonising the national public pension system with European practices and recommendations in this field.[53]

[53] *Strategia Fiscal Bugetară* Pentru Perioada 2013-2015, Guvernul României, Ministerul de Finanţe, 49.

5. Labour Market Challenges to Increase the Competitiveness of the Romanian Economy

While generating, building and developing in a sustainable and intelligent manner, demand is raised by:

> The income that is generated in the process [...]. When these programmes succeed in integrating disadvantaged youth into the labour market, they also yield large economic and social benefits in terms of greater equity and, in some cases, a reduction in anti-social behaviour.[54]

5.1. Romania: Fragile Growth Potential in the Medium Term

The recent developments are illustrative of the great divide existing between the economic and the legal dimension.

> Output contracted sharply during the global crisis and is expected to recover only gradually. In the run up to the crisis, Romania's growth was driven by structural reforms, productivity increases, and above all by foreign-financed investments. With the onset of the crisis, the boom came to a halt and unemployment increased. Medium-term growth projections have been revised down from 4 percent to 3.5 percent due to delays in structural reforms and a lower-than-expected capacity to absorb EU funds. Measuring potential output involves a high degree of uncertainty in transitional economies that experienced boom-bust cycles. The Romanian economy underwent substantial structural changes that spurred an uptake in growth while the declining manufacturing sector pushed large numbers of workers out of the labour force.[55]

Act No. 285/2011 on labour markets made reference to the progress made during 2011, pointing out that the targets for 2010-2012 will contribute in the following manner:

---

[54] Corbanese V., and G. Rosas. 2009. "Guide to the Design, Monitoring and Evaluation of Innovative Active Labour Market Programmes Targeting Individuals at Risk of Labour Market Exclusion," Budapest: ILO.

[55] Fondul Monetar Internaţional România, Raportul Echipei pentru Consultarea din anul 2012 pe Articolul IV, a şasea evaluare în cadrul Acordului Stand-By, şi Solicitare de Derogare pentru Neîndeplinirea unui Criteriu de Performanţă şi Solicitare de Modificare a Criteriilor de Performanţă Întocmit de Departamentul European în consultare cu Alte Departamente, Aprobat de Poul M. Thomsen şiVivek Arora, 13 septembrie 2012, 13.

> Introduce important legislative changes to increase the flexibility of the labour market, improve the efficiency of collective bargaining (while protecting the rights of both parties), and increasing labour force participation. [...] [The Romanian Government] will request [...] that the International Labour Organization conduct labour inspections to improve enforcement and address the large informal labour market. Improving the efficiency of social protection will remain a priority, especially in the area of social inspection.[56]

At the end of 2012, some recommendations for structural reforms were enforced, as well as a roadmap for the liberalization of the energy price. In this sense, it was concluded that "labour market reforms have introduced more flexibility in employment relationships, which has contributed to some recovery in employment rates".[57]

5.3. Romania's Performances in Global Competitiveness and as an Efficiency-driven Economy

Romania's overall competitiveness performances are good, to the extent that it has been included in the "efficiency-driven" group of countries, yet it has deteriorated in the last three years following the crisis.

According to the Global Competitiveness Index produced by the World Economic Forum, Romania ranked at position 77 out of 142 countries in 2012/2011, losing ground with respect to 2011/2010 (67/139), and to 2010/2009 (64/133).[58] Romania's competitiveness erosion was considerably higher than the EU27 average; Europe has lost eight positions in the global competitiveness index between 2010 and 2012. In this paper, competitiveness is defined as:

---

[56] LEGE nr. 285 din 14 decembrie 2011, privind ratificarea Scrisorii de intenţie semnate de autorităţile române la Bucureşti la 10 martie 2011 şi aprobate prin Decizia Consiliului director al Fondului Monetar Internaţional din 25 martie 2011 Emitent: Parlamentul Publicat În: Monitorul Oficial nr. 906 din 21 decembrie 2011.

[57] International Monetary Fund. 2012. *Staff Report for the 2012 Article IV Consultation, Sixth Review Under the Stand-By Arrangement, and Requests for Waiver of Nonobservance of Performance Criterion and Modification of Performance Criteria* Prepared by the European Department in Consultation with Other Departments, approved by Poul M. Thomsen and Vivek Arora. Washington DC: IMF, 6.

[58] Sala-i-Martin, X. 2011. "The Global Competitiveness Report 2011–2012," World Economic Forum, Executive Opinion Survey the Global Competitiveness Report 2011-2012. New York: World Economic Forum.

> the set of institutions, policies, and factors that determine the level of productivity of a country. The level of productivity, in turn, sets the level of prosperity that can be earned by an economy. The productivity level also determines the rates of return obtained by investments in an economy, which in turn are the fundamental drivers of its growth rates. In other words, a more competitive economy is one that is likely to grow faster over time."[59] (Table I-1)

Labour market efficiency (P7) is negative as exhibiting shortcomings in terms of cooperation in labour relations, employment rigidity and the ability to stop the brain drain phenomenon or to attract talented people. A competitive advantage lies in the low cost of redundancy followed by a close correlation between payment and productivity. (Table I-2)

A successful implementation of the reform is strongly dependent on the capacity to develop coordinated innovative active measures under new and dynamic austerity conditions. Important steps in this connection are the consolidation of the progress obtained, the extension of the efforts towards the assumed engagements, and the structural reform of an economy strongly oriented towards tackling the erosion of Romania's global competitiveness performance.

---

[59] World Economic Forum. 2011. *Summary of the Global Competitiveness Report 2011-2012*. New York: World Economic Forum, 4, http://www.mtic.gov.md/img/d2011/download/2012/04-11/Sinteza_Raportului_Competitivitatii_Globale_2011_1.pdf.

Table I-1. Rank and Score for Global Competitiveness Indices for Romania in 2010/2011.

	Rank /142	Score (1 to 7, max is desirable)
Basic requirements (essential for economy driven by factors) 40%	89	4.1
P 1. Institutions	99	3.5
P 2. Infrastructure	95	3.4
P 3. Macroeconomic environment	87	4.5
P 4. Health and primary education	66	5.7
II. Efficiency enhancers (essential for efficiency driven economies) 50%	62	4.1
P 5. Higher education and training	55	4.4
P 6. Good market efficiency	96	4
P 7. Labour market efficiency	92	4.1
P 8. Financial market development	84	3.9
P 9. Technological readiness	60	3.8
P10. Market size	44	4.4
III. Innovation and sophistication factors (essential for innovation driven economy) 10%	99	3.2
P11. Business sophistication	102	3.5
P12. Innovation	95	2.9

Source: Summary of the Global Competitiveness Report 2011-2012 released by the World Economic Forum
http://www.mtic.gov.md/img/d2011/download/2012/0411/Sinteza_Raportului_Competitivitatii_Globale_2011_1.pdf
* Classified in three sub-indices and 12 pillars components.[60]

[60] World Economic Forum. 2011. *Summary of the Global Competitiveness Report 2011-2012.* New York: World Economic Forum. http://www.mtic.gov.md/img/d2011/download/2012/0411/Sinteza_Raportului_Competitivitatii_Globale_2011_1.pdf.

Table I-2. Rank and Score of the Global Competitiveness Index (ICG) for Romania.[61]

Global Competitiveness Index (ICG) 2011-2012	Rank: 77 Total 142	Score: 4.08 / Maximum 7	
Global Competitiveness Index (ICG) 2010-2011	Rank: 67 Total 139	Score: 4.2 / Maximum 7	Lost 10 places in the hierarchy in the last year
Global Competitiveness Index (ICG) 2010-2011	Rank: 64 Total 133	Score: 4.1 / maxim 7	
Pillar 7. Labour market efficiency	Rank: 92 Total 142	Score: 4.1 / Maximum 7 / mean 4,4	
Flexibility			
7.1. Cooperation in labour-employer relations:	Rank: 137 Total 142	Score: 3.3 / Maximum 7 / mean 4.4	1 confrontation relationship type, 7 Cooperation relations generally
7.2. Flexibility of wage determination	Rank: 90 Total 142	Score: 4.8 / Maximum 7 / mean 4.9	1 centralized bargaining process 7 decentralized bargaining processes
7.3. Rigidity of employment index, 0–100 (worst)	Rank: 118 Total 140	Score: 4.6	100% very bad

[61] Table 2 considers Pillar 7-ICG P7: "labour market efficiency" that is a component of "market conditions" in the context of the Romanian performance evaluation in global competitiveness background, including subcomponents that characterize labour market flexibility and the ability to effectively harness the most talented young people. Sinteza Raportului Competitivităţii Globale 2011-2012 publicat de Forumul Economic Mondial (WEF).
http://www.mtic.gov.md/img/d2011/download/2012/0411/Sinteza_Raportului_Competitivitatii_Globale_2011_1.pdf (accessed 20 January 2014).

7.4. Hiring and firing practices	Rank: 91 Total 142	Score: 3,6 / Maximum 7 / mean 3.9	1 hampered by regulations 7 flexibility due to employers
7.5. Redundancy costs, weeks of salary	Rank: 15 Total 139	Score: 8	Cost in number of weeks redundancy pay
Efficient Recourse to Talent			
7.6. Pay and productivity	Rank: 55 Total 142	Score: 4.1 / Maximum 7 / mean 3.9	1 payment is not correlated with productivity 7 strongly linked to worker productivity
7.7. Reliance on professional management	Rank:84 Total 142	Score: 3.9 / Maximum 7 / mean 4.3	1 unrelated family friends and management competencies held 7 in most managers choose based on skills and performance
7.8. Brain drain / attracting talented people	Rank:131 Total 142	Score: 22 / Maximum 7 / mean 3.5	1 usually creative people, talented people does go after opportunities in other countries 7 yes, there are many opportunities for talented people
7.9. Women in labour force, ratio to men	Rank:65 Total 142	0.79	Rate ratio of activities of women / activity rate for men in 2009

Source: Summary of the Global Competitiveness Report 2011-2012, the World Economic Forum.
http://www.mtic.gov.md/img/d2011/download/2012/0411/Sinteza_Raportului_Competitivitatii_Globale_2011_1.pdf. (accessed 20 March 2013).

5.5. The Growing Difficulty of Doing Business

The ease in doing business in Romania measured by the World Bank Ease indicates a loss of 17 positions, i.e. from position 55 in 2010 to position 72 in 2012. The EU27 average position remains constant over this period (39th).[62]

6. High Levels of Poverty and the Working Poor

6.1. Low Levels of Participation in the Labour Market

The implementation of all these major reforms is hampered by low activity rates, which amount to 63%—compared to the 63.3% activity rate for the 15-64 year-old age group in 2011 in Romania, that is 7.9pp lower than the EU27 mean—especially for the elderly (a 41.5% activity rate for 55 to 64 aged persons in 2011 in Romania, that is 9.4pp lower than the EU27 mean) and also high unemployment rates for young people (a 23.7% unemployment rate for those aged 15 to 24 years old in 2011 in Romania, 2.3pp higher than the EU27 mean). The new active measures need to respond to a two-fold function, to wit supporting and accelerating the transitions towards formal employment, taking into account one's income and taxes, and public employment services.

6.2. An Increase in the Heterogeneous Nature of Employment at a Regional Level

Since 2010, the heterogeneous nature of employment at a regional level has become increasingly apparent. In 2011 the best performing areas (North East and Bucharest-Ilfov) recorded high levels of employment, 68.5% and 68.2% respectively, that is, 0.4pp higher than the EU27 average. On the contrary, Centru exhibited an employment rate of 56.5%, 12.1pp lower than the EU27 average.

Among the visible effects of the crisis was the ongoing dispersion of regional employment rates[64] for the 15-64 year-old age group considering the Nomenclature of Territorial Units for Statistics (NUTS2). Such

---

[62] http://www.doingbusiness.org/rankings (Accessed 15 June 2013).

[63] EUROSTAT. *Activity Rates by Sex, Age and Nationality* (%) [lfsa_argan]. Brussels: EUROSTAT.

[64] Source: EUROSTAT, *Dispersion of Regional Employment Rates of Age Group 15-64* by NUTS 3 regions (%).

dispersion was more accentuated in 2011 (7.3%), 3% more than the 4.3% reported in 2008 in Romania, and not far from the 12.5% of the EU in 2011 (+1.2pp from 11.3% in 2008). The same indicator is exhibited if NUTS 3 is taken, with a 1.9pp increase in Romania, from 16.1% in 2008 to 18% in 2010. Estimates for 2020 point to a 1.3pp increase, that is 14.4% from 13.1% in 2008. In 2010 the ratio between the dispersion of regional rates of the 15-64 year-old age group considering the NUTS3 level and the NUTS2 level was 2.5 for EU27 and 12.6 for Romania, indicating dispersion within NUTS3 in Romania which is five times higher than in the EU27.

6.3. Romania is still one of the Poorest Countries in Europe

Romania's relative poverty rate[65] is one of the highest in the EU. Until 2007 –indicating a breakdown in data series –percentages oscillated between 17% and 18%. Romania reported a better position, with one to two percentage points above the European average, close to Greece, Spain, and Portugal. Over the last three years, Romania lost ground in terms of relative poverty, dangerously drifting towards the poorest of the 32 countries included in the EUROSTAT Report. From 2007 to 2009, Romania recorded a poverty rate ranging between 22% and 25%, with only Latvia faring worse. The risk of poverty generally increased between 2010 and 2011; 1.1pp in Romania and 0.5pp in the EU27.

6.4. High Poverty Rates among People in Employment[66]

The in-work at-risk-of-poverty rate is an indicator[67] which refers to people that are simultaneously employed and in poverty, also taking account of income levels and the poverty line. In the EU27, 8.9% of people are in-work poor and at risk of poverty. Yet in Romania this situation is more alarming, with 17 to 19 employees out of 100 facing this

---

[65] The relative poverty rate is an indicator of poverty incidence, which is calculated considering the share of the total population of persons in households with disposable income per adult equivalent (including or excluding the value of consumption from personal resources) below the poverty line. Currently, the indicator is reckoned for 60% of median disposable income per equivalent adult.

[66] According to EUROSTAT, this indicator refers to the share of people who have a job and income equivalent available under the poverty line, which is set at 60% of the national median equalised disposable income.

[67] EUROSTAT, SILC. 2007. *In-Work at-Risk-of-Poverty Rate* (Source: SILC) Pentru anul 2007, ruptură în serie. Brussels: EUROSTAT.

risk. This means that their income levels are below the poverty line, with high rates of income polarization and wage dispersion. This is coupled with an eroding real value, a consequence of the poor functioning of the Romanian economy. Therefore, salaried employment attractiveness is still low due to the in-work poverty rate (17% in 2011).

6.5. Low Productivity Levels in Agriculture: Looming Poverty in Rural Areas

As of 1 January 2011, the Romanian population was distributed as follows: 2.27 million people in predominantly urban regions (UR), 9.39 million people in intermediate regions (IN), 9.76 million in rural regions (PR). Per capita GDP at current market prices by urban-rural area is: €7,800 PR, €10,800 IN, €26,100 PU and €11,000 as national mean.[68] In 2005, in Romania, the risk of relative poverty in rural areas was more than twice that in urban areas (42% and 18%, respectively). In late 2010, the INS estimated that the unemployment rate in urban areas was 9.1%, while in rural areas the unemployment rate was 5%. In 2005, and taking account of NUTS 2, the figures were as follows:

- Employment rates for the 15-64 year-old age group: 58.9% PR, 54.9% IR, 59.3% PU, national average of 57.6%;
- Employment rate for the 55-64 year-old age group: 46.2% PR, IR 32.3%, 26.6% PU, national average of 39.5%;

- Youth unemployment for the 15-24 year-old age group: 6.4% for PR, IR 6%, 6.2% PU national average of 6.3%.

Accordingly:

> With regard to Eastern countries, over dependence of rural areas on agriculture and lack of alternative employment are reported. Moreover, in countries such as Poland, Bulgaria, Lithuania and Romania agricultural productivity is often low, because it is influenced by an unfavourable investment environment, limited agricultural land market, poor technical and environmental status of water management systems (canals, drainage

[68] EUROSTAT. 2012. *Statistics in Focus 30/2012,* (online data code: urt_e3gdp). Brussels: EUROSTAT.

systems, hydraulic structures).[...] Small farmers appear to be a specific group at risk of poverty and social exclusion in rural areas.[69]

6.6. Poverty and Vulnerability amongst the Roma People

According to the World Bank[70]:

- The overall employment rate of Roma people in 2010 was 50%, 13 percentage points lower than the national total employment;

- The employment rate of Roma women in 2010 was 31%, 24 percentage points lower than the employment rate of women at the national level;

- The share of labour income obtained by Roma people is equal to 39% of national average labour incomes.

7. Labour Taxation, the Shadow Economy and Undeclared Work

7.1. Reducing Labour Taxation for Vulnerable, Disadvantaged, and low-skilled People

The share of labour taxation in total taxation charge in Romania compared with the EU mean[71] indicates a decreasing trend in Romania of 2.3 percentage points from 43.8% in 2000 to 41.5% in 2011. The EU average trend is reversed, as labour taxation is increasing by 1.1 percentage points, from a share of 50.1% in 2000 to 51.2% in 2011. The share of taxation in GDP by economic function in Romania[72] indicates a decreasing trend in the share of labour taxation in GDP by 1.9 percentage points, from 13.2% in 2000 to 11.3% in 2011. The EU average presents the same trend but at a slower rate, and the labour share of taxation in GDP falls by 0.6 percentage

[69] European Commission. 2008. "Poverty and Social Exclusion in Rural Areas," Final Study Report, European Commission Directorate-General for Employment, Social Affairs and Equal Opportunities Unit E2. Manuscript completed in August 2008, 21.

[70] The World Bank. 2010. *Roma Inclusion: An Economic Opportunity for Bulgaria, Czech Republic, Romania, and Serbia.* Washington DC: The World Bank.

[71] EUROSTAT. *Structure of Taxes by Economic Function* [gov_a_tax_str]. Brussels: EUROSTAT.

[72] EUROSTAT. *Structure of Taxes by Economic Function* [gov_a_tax_str]. Brussels: EUROSTAT.

points, from 20.2% in 2000 to 19.6% in 2011. For Romanian lawmakers, reducing labour taxation for vulnerable, disadvantaged, and especially low-skilled people remains a challenge.[73]

7.2. High Levels of Shadow Economy and Undeclared Work

Schneider (2012) has estimated that the shadow economy in Romania contributed to 29.1% of GDP in 2012, almost doubling the EU levels (14.9%). This trend was the same between 2005 and 2012, and the shadow economy in Romania faced a 2.1pp decrease, and a 2.5pp in EU27.

Schneider has also pointed out that for the period 1995-2006 undeclared work would account for 16%-21% of GDP in Romania, between two to three times more than the EU27 level of GDP (7.2%, Table I-3).

Table I-3. Estimates of the Shadow Economy and Undeclared Work in Romania and EU27.

Country	Shadow economy dimension (in % GDP)			Undeclared work (% GDP, 1995-2006)
	2005	2010	2012	
EU27	17.4	15.4	14.9	7.2
Ro	32.2	29.8	29.1	16/21

Source: European Commission. "Tax reforms in EU Member States, Tax Policy Challenges for Economic Growth and Fiscal Sustainability 2012 Report," *European Economy* 6.

In 2011, some 2.9 million people (31.4% of those in employment) were involved in informal employment in Romania. The distribution of informal employment was 75.3% in the household sector, 24.0% in the informal sector and 0.7% in the formal sector. Informal employment is more common in rural areas (88.4%) than in urban ones (11.6%). Informal employment in rural areas involved some 2.6 million people, equivalent to 27.8% of overall employment in the Romanian economy. In urban areas, informal workers accounted for only about 3.6% of total employment.[74]

---

[73] European Union. 2012. "Tax Reforms, in EU Member States," *European Economy* 6. (Provisional Version) Economic and Financial Affairs, Tax Policy Challenges for Economic, Growth and Fiscal Sustainability. Brussels: European Commission.

[74] Voinea, L., and L. Liviu Albu. 2011. *Economia informală şi impactual ei asupra pieţei muncii* [Informal economy and its impact on the labour market], BNS,

8. The Risk of Corruption

The perception of corruption measured by the Transparency International's Corruption Perception Index ranked Romania 75th[75] in 2012, that is four positions higher than 2010. The EU27 average was 36 in 2012, up six positions from 2010. In 2012, Romania approved the National Anti-corruption Strategy 2012-2015 which includes preventive measures against corruption and evaluation indicators, and the National Action Plan for the implementation of the National Anti-corruption Strategy 2012-2015.[76]

9. Conclusion

Labour market reform needs to continue in order to ensure the productivity, flexibility and competitiveness of the Romanian labour market, while protecting employees and safeguarding collective bargaining rights under austerity conditions. It follows that decision-makers face the challenge of developing new active measures and strategies which should have an impact on employment growth.

References

Börsch-Supan, A. 2010. *Social Impact of the Crisis—Demographic Challenges and the Pension System*, Directorate General for Internal Policies Policy Department: Economic and Scientific Policies European Parliament's Special Committee on the Financial, Economic and Social Crisis. Brussels:

Bucharest. Constantin Ciutacu, Institute of National Economy, Romanian Academy, http://www.eurofound.europa.eu/ewco/2012/02/RO1202019I.htm (accessed 20 December 2013).

[75] International Monetary Fund. 2012. *Staff Report for the 2012 Article IV Consultation, Sixth Review Under the Stand-By Arrangement, and Requests for Waiver of Nonobservance of Performance Criterion and Modification of Performance Criteria* Prepared by the European Department in Consultation with Other Departments, approved by Poul M. Thomsen and Vivek Arora. Washington DC: IMF, 25.

[76] Hotărâre nr. 215 din 20/03/2012, Publicat in Monitorul Oficial, Partea I nr. 202 din 27/03/2012, Intrare in vigoare: 27/03/2012, privind aprobarea Strategiei naţionale anticorupţie pe perioada 2012-2015, a Inventarului măsurilor preventive anticorupţie şi a indicatorilor de evaluare, precum şi a Planului naţional de acţiune pentru implementarea Strategiei naţionale anticorupţie 2012-2015.

CNP, Comisia Naţională de Prognoză. 23 noiembrie 2012. *Proiecţia Principalilor Indicatori Macroeconomici Pentru Perioada 2012-2016*, Prognoza de toamnă.

Corbanese V., and G. Rosas. 2009. "Guide to the Design, Monitoring and Evaluation of Innovative Active Labour Market Programmes Targeting Individuals at Risk of Labour Market Exclusion," Budapest: ILO.

Directorate-General for Economic and Financial Affairs. 2009. "Sustainability Report 2009," *European Economy* 9. Brussels: Directorate-General for Economic and Financial Affairs. 135.

Directorate-General for Employment, Social Affairs and Inclusion. 2011. *Employment and Social Developments in Europe.* Brussels: European Union http://ec.europa.eu/employment_social/esde/2011 (accessed 13 June 2013)

European Commission. 2008. "Poverty and Social Exclusion in Rural Areas," Final Study Report, European Commission Directorate-General for Employment, Social Affairs and Equal Opportunities Unit E2. Brussels: European Union, 21.

—. 2010. "Tax policy Challenges for Economic, Growth and Fiscal Sustainability," in *Reaffirming the Free Movement of Workers: Rights and Major Developments*, Communication from the Commission to the Council, The European Parliament, The European Economic and Social Committee and The Committee of the Regions, Brussels, 13.7.2010, COM(2010) 373 Final. Brussels: European Commission.

—. 2011. "Assessment of the National Reform Programme and the Convergence Programme 2011," Commission Staff Working Document, accompanying document for Romania Recommendation for a Council Recommendation on the National Reform Programme 2011 of Romania and an opinion on the updated convergence program of Romania for the period 2011-2014 {SEC (2011) 825 final}, 7.6.2011 SEC (2011) 731 final. Brussels: European Commission, 2.

—. 2012. "European Economic Forecast Autumn 2012," *European Economy* 8, Commission Staff Working Document, Directorate-General for Economic and Financial Affairs, 154.

—. 2012. *European Economic Forecast*. Statistical Annex, 154, Table 13: Potential GDP, volume (percentage change on preceding year, 1993-2014). Brussels: European Commission.
http://ec.europa.eu/economy_finance/eu/forecasts/2012_autumn/ro.html.

European Union. 1968. *Regulation (EEC) No 1612/68 of the Council of 15 October 1968 on Freedom of Movement for Workers within the Community.* Brussels: European Union.

—. 2004. *Directive 2004/38/EC of the European Parliament and of the Council of 29 April 2004 on the Right of Citizens of the Union and their Family Members to Move and Reside Freely within the Territory of the Member States amending Regulation (EEC) No 1612/68 and Repealing Directives 64/221/EEC, 68/360/EEC, 72/194/EEC, 73/148/EEC, 75/34/EEC, 75/35/EEC, 90/364/EEC, 90/365/EEC and 93/96/EECOJ L 158, 30.4.2004.* Brussels: European Union.

—. 2005. Directive 2005/36/EC *of the European Parliament and of the Council of 7 September 2005 on the Recognition of Professional Qualifications.* Brussels: European Union.

—. 2012. "Tax Reforms in EU Member States," *European Economy* 6, (Provisional Version) Economic and Financial Affairs. Brussels: European Commission.

—. 2012. *Chapter 6: Intra-EU Labour Mobility and the Impact of Enlargement*. Brussels: European Union, 265.

EUROSTAT. 2012. *Statistics in Focus*, *30/2012*, (online data code: urt_e3gdp). Brussels: European Union.

Guvernul României, Ministerul de Finanţe. 2012. *Strategia Fiscal Bugetară Pentru Perioada 2013-2015,* Guvernul României, Ministerul de Finanţe, 49.

Hotărâre nr. 215 din 20/03/2012. Publicat in Monitorul Oficial, Partea I nr. 202 din 27/03/2012, Intrare in vigoare: 27/03/2012, privind aprobarea Strategiei naţionale anticorupţie pe perioada 2012-2015, a Inventarului măsurilor preventive anticorupţie şi a indicatorilor de evaluare, precum şi a Planului naţional de acţiune pentru implementarea Strategiei naţionale anticorupţie 2012-2015. http://www.eurofound.europa.eu/ewco/2012/02/RO1202019I.htm.

ILO. 2012. "The Youth Employment Crisis: Time for Action," Report prepared by youth for the Youth Employment Forum (Geneva, 23–25 May 2012). Geneva: ILO. http://www.ilo.org/ilc/ILCSessions/101stSession/reports/reports-submitted/WCMS_175421/lang--fr/index.htm, (accessed 13 June 2013), 2.

International Monetary Fund. 2009. *Request for Stand-by Arrangement—Staff Report*; *Staff Supplements; and Press Release on the Executive Board Discussion*. IMF Country Report No. 09/183. Washington DC: IMF.

—. 2011. *Letter of Intent and Technical Memorandum of Understanding.* Washington DC: IMF.

—. 2011. *Romania: Letter of Intent, Bucharest.* Washington DC: IMF, *6.* http://www.imf.org/external/pubs/ft/scr/2011/cr1180.pdf.

—. 2012. *Article IV Consultation and Sixth Review Under the Stand-by Arrangement and Requests for Waiver of Non-observance of Performance Criterion and Modification of Performance Criteria.* Staff Report, October 2012, Staff Supplement, Public Information Notice and Press Release on the Executive Board Discussion; and Statement by the Executive Director for Romania, IMF Country Report No. 12/290. Washington DC: IMF.

—. 2012. *Financial Position in the Fund as of November 30, 2012.* Summary of IMF members' Quota, Reserve Position, SDR Holdings, Outstanding Credit, Recent Lending Arrangements, Projected Payments due to the IMF, and Monthly Historical Transactions with the Fund. Washington DC: IMF.

—. 2012. *Fourth Review Under the Stand-by Arrangement and Request for Modification of Performance Criteria—Staff Report*; April 2012, Staff Supplement; Press Release on the Executive Board Discussion; and Statement by the Executive Director for Romania. IMF Country Report No. 12/73. Washington DC: IMF.

—. 2012. *Selected Issues Paper, October 2012*. IMF Country Report No. 12/291, Washington DC: IMF, 6,

—. 2012. *Staff Report for the 2012 Article IV Consultation, Sixth Review Under the Stand-By Arrangement, and Requests for Waiver of Non-observance of Performance Criterion and Modification of Performance Criteria* Prepared by the European Department in Consultation with Other Departments, approved by Poul M. Thomsen and Vivek Arora. Washington DC: IMF.

Lege nr. 285 din 14 decembrie 2011, privind ratificarea Scrisorii de intenţie semnate de autorităţile române la Bucureşti la 10 martie 2011 şi aprobate prin Decizia Consiliului director al Fondului Monetar Internaţional din 25 martie 2011 EMITENT: PARLAMENTUL

Lege nr. 292 din 20/12/2011, Publicat in Monitorul Oficial, Partea I nr. 905 din 20/12/2011, Intrare in vigoare: 23/12/2011, Lege a asistenţei sociale.

Lincaru, C, and V. Ciucă. 2012. "Work-Life Balance at European, National and Local Levels: Systems Conciliation and Best Practices for Collective Bargaining in Romania," Publication on LIBRA Project.

Sala-i-Martin, X. 2011. "The Global Competitiveness Report 2011-2012," World Economic Forum, Executive Opinion Survey the Global Competitiveness Report 2011-2012. New York: World Economic Forum.

The World Bank. 2010. *Roma Inclusion: An Economic Opportunity for Bulgaria, The Czech Republic, Romania, and Serbia.* Washington DC: The World Bank.

Voinea, L. and L. Liviu Albu. 2011. *Economia informală şi impactual ei asupra pieţei muncii* [Informal Economy and its Impact on the Labour Market], BNS, Bucharest. Constantin Ciutacu, Institute of National Economy, Romanian Academy.

WEF. 2012. *Summary of the Global Competitiveness Report 2011-2012.* New York: World Economic Forum. *pg.4*http://www.mtic.gov.md/img/d2011/download/2012/04-11/Sinteza_Raportului_Competitivitatii_Globale_2011_1.pdf (accessed 13 June 2013).

CHAPTER ONE:

ANALYSIS OF YOUTH LABOUR MARKET ENTRY DURING THE ECONOMIC AND FINANCIAL CRISIS

THE FUZZY CONCEPT OF "YOUTH": DEFINING CHARACTERISTICS

BEATRICE CHIRIAC AND CRISTINA LINCARU

1. Introductory Remarks

In the contemporary socioeconomic scenario, there are a wide range of definitions for "young people," who are frequently seen as a distinct category with a high degree of heterogeneity. Youth are "between childhood and adulthood but still not yet mature."[1] It is the time when critical decisions are made concerning: building social relations, actively and effectively participating in economic life, and taking on new roles, either in one's personal or professional sphere.

In economic terms,[2] maturity manifests as the capability to be economically independent, to manage one's financial resources, and to clarify and crystallize one's professional role in line with future career developments. UNESCO defines youth as:

> "Youth" is best understood as a period of transition from the dependence of childhood to adulthood's independence and awareness of our interdependence as members of a community. Youth is a more fluid category than a fixed age-group.[3]

---

[1] DEX, http://dexonline.ro/definitie/t%C3%A2n%C4%83r.

[2] Mitteraurer, M. 1983. *Ledige Mutter: Zur Geschichte illegitimer Geburten in Europa.* Munchen: Beck, cited by Bologan, M. 2010. *Metode statistice de evaluare a impactului tranziţiei asupra condiţiei tineretului Republicii Moldova*, Specialitatea 08.00.11—Statistică Economică, Teză de doctor în economie, Conducător Elena CARA, Conf. univ., dr., Aspecte privind noţiunea de tânăr şi de adult, Chişinău, 2010.

[3] UNESCO. *What Do We Mean by "Youth?"* UNESCO Social and Human sciences, Youth, http://www.unesco.org/new/en/social-and-human-sciences/themes/youth/youth-definition/ (accessed 13 June 2013).

2. Young VS Mature People: Main Characteristics

In general terms, "youth" are treated as a distinct category.

Accordingly, a young person is not yet an adult or, in a broader sense, a person is not yet mature. Maturity concerns the physical, emotional, and intellectual component, as well as networking, autonomy, determination, and self-knowledge, and differs from individual to individual.

It is frequently the case that one's maturity emerges at the time of taking on new roles, chiefly in terms of interpersonal and professional relations. The social dimension is mainly found in the formation of social skills, geared towards meeting the needs for affiliation, the expression of individuality and family formation at an early age. The economic dimension is reflected through developing the capacity to carry out economic activities, generating income by starting a career and succeeding in a chosen professional field. Further, the concept of youth is a multidimensional one. As such, both universal elements and distinguishing features can be singled out. "Youth" could be seen as a homogeneous group characterized by common elements or, vice versa, as a non-homogeneous group consisting of particular elements (see Table 1-1).

Studying youth is a fascinating research topic *per se*, and so is its analysis as a stage of the human life cycle—that is, the period subsequent to adolescence and prior to adulthood—and the transition from school to work. This transition fixes the age boundaries between youth and adulthood. The struggle to access the labour market confirms the completion of this transition process, which involves transformation, growth, search, and experimentation and is intended to provide emotional, physical and intellectual stability. Thus, "the interests of young people are not focused on self-expression and self-assertion, but more on the fact that a more appropriate and faster ascent to the status of an adult or a person who is economically independent."[4]

[4] Bologan, M. 2010. *Metode statistice de evaluare a impactului tranziţiei asupra condiţiei tineretului Republicii Moldova*: 211 Specialitatea 08.00.11, Statistică Economică, Teză de doctor în economie, Conducător Elena CARA, Conf. univ., dr., Aspecte privind noţiunea de tânăr şi de adult, Chişinău.

Table 1-1. Universal and Particular Elements of the Concept of "Youth".[5]

Universal	Particular
Age	Social status, e.g. class, gender, ethnicity, race, location
Global youth culture	Cultural formation, e.g. subculture
Compulsory Education	Possibilities, opportunities and unequal outcomes
Legal requirements based on age, status offences	State regulation according to social status
Adolescent development	Different life experiences and cultural norms for development
Youth with disabilities	'Young' having several meanings

Source: Wagner P. 2004. "Bazele statisticii": 189, Bucureşti: Editura Universităţii "Titu Maiorescu", cited by Bologan M., Metode statistice de evaluare a impactului tranziţiei asupra condiţiei tineretului Republicii Moldova, Specialitatea 08.00.11—Statistică Economică, Teză de doctor în economie, Conducător Elena CARA, Conf. univ., dr., Aspecte privind noţiunea de tânăr şi de adult, Chişinău, 2010.

If the European perspective is taken, the key milestones to adulthood are the age limit to child benefits, the end of full-time compulsory education, voting rights and the minimum age for standing for elections. In this sense:

> The age limit of child benefits usually ranges from 15 (in the Czech Republic and Latvia) to 18, but it is often prolonged when children are still in education. The end of compulsory education may also be seen as the time when individuals are free to make their own choices. It ranges from 14 to 17 years. Considering civic rights, the voting age for national elections in the European Union is 18 in all countries except Austria (16). In Italy the legal voting age is 18 but the Senate is elected only by people aged 25 and over. The age to stand for election as a candidate varies from 18 to 40 across Member States, and may depend of the type of election."[6]

[5] Wagner, P. 2004. "Bazele Statisticii," Bucureşti: Editura Universităţii Titu Maiorescu, 189, cited by Bologan M., Metode statistice de evaluare a impactului tranziţiei asupra condiţiei tineretului Republicii Moldova, Specialitatea 08.00.11 Statistică Economică, Teză de doctor în economie, Conducător Elena CARA, Conf. univ., dr., *Aspecte privind noţiunea de tânăr şi de adult*, Chişinău, 2010.

[6] European Commission. 2009. *Youth: Investing and Empowering*. Commission Staff Working Document to the Communication from the Commission to the Council, the European Parliament, the European Economic and Social Committee

3. Ages of Youth: Some Statistics

According to the definition of the International Labour Organization (ILO), young people are those aged 15 to 24 years old. Moreover:

> The UN, for statistical consistency across regions, defines 'youth', as those persons between the ages of 15 and 24 years, without prejudice to other definitions by Member States.[7]

European employment policy is built primarily on data and analyses provided by EUROSTAT based on the European Union Labour Force Survey (EU LFS), which in turn, draws on the concepts and definitions of the ILO. In a 2012 accompanying document, subsequent to the launch of the Strategy Europe 2020, the 20 to 64 age group was set as a strategic cycle, in lieu of the 15 to 64 age group previously established. In this context, the period of education is extended and the stages of maturation are diversified, with these changes resulting in prolonged economic dependence and postponed access to the labour market. Romania sets at 16 years old the age at which a person can legally enter the labour market, pursuant to par 1-5, Article 13 of the Labour Code, yet with some exceptions:

(1) An individual becomes able to work at the age of 16.

(2) An individual may enter into an employment contract as an employee at the age of 15, upon the consent of parents or legal guardians for activities suited to the physical, skills and knowledge, if this does not jeopardize the health development and training.

(3) The employment of persons under the age of 15 is prohibited.

(4) The employment of persons under judicial interdiction is prohibited.

(5) Employment in hard, harmful or dangerous jobs is allowed at the age of 18 and following the issuance of a legal authorisation.

---

and the Committee of the Regions, EU Youth Report, {COM(2009) 200}, {SEC(2009) 545}, {SEC(2009) 546}, {SEC(2009) 548}.

[7] UNESCO. *What Do We Mean by "Youth?"* UNESCO Social and Human sciences, Youth, http://www.unesco.org/new/en/social-and-human-sciences/themes/youth/youth-definition/ (accessed 13 June 2013).

At the age of 16, youth may choose to stay in education or look for a job. Normally, all young people graduate from high school no later than 19 years old. The age limit for completion of compulsory education in Romania is 16 years, whereas 18 years is the age at which people enjoy voting rights. The minimum age to hold public office is 23 years and is correlated with the level of representation and type of election.

4. Final Remarks: Youth and Coexisting Development Periods

The complexity of human development calls for a holistic understanding of one's life, in order to ensure the social, economic and creative development of knowledge and its potential to benefit the individual, the family and the community. The manifestation of the knowledge economy through empowering creative autonomy and knowledge capability requires a profound reassessment of the concept of youth. In what follows, some useful information is presented concerning the review of policies which make use of this notion.[8]

The period from 20 to 24 years of age of extended adolescence is known as a period of transition towards adulthood having characteristics and features typical of youth and young adult status.

Activities defining a young person include: social engagement, the manufacturing of goods, the provision of different types of services (paid work), adapting to a certain type of activity, which might be the expression of the social division of labour. Social relations established in the early stages are rare. Relationships with one's family of origin are established freely, given the cultural background of the new family components.

The time period between 20 and 25 years of age is narrowing down the passage to adulthood, yet adolescence remains a period of transition to adult life, also in biological terms.

If females are considered, some authors—including Douvan and Adelson—believe that women do not go through an identity crisis during adolescence, and especially during the transition period (prolonged adolescence).

According to some scholars, the expansion of youth to the upper limit might lead to some consequences in its determination. In this respect, Levinson believes that young adulthood refers to a range of mental

[8] Albu, E. 2007. "Psihologia vârstelor," Universitatea Petru Maior Târgu-Mures, Departamentul I.F.R.D, 81-83.

developments between 17 and 45 years of age, with some differences between the two sexes. Erikson characterized youth (middle age within life cycles) as being dominated by enhancing social identity, employment, and involvement in the making of plans through social tasks. During this time, this group experiences intense love and early family life, leading to the development of privacy. As such, the growing influence of the oscillation period of intimacy, isolation and state of the ego calls for the need to relate new individuals, groups, organizations, causes and so forth.

Many psychologists emphasize that the youth stage plays a central role in that it stresses the institutional demarcation of special events such as: completing schooling, or entering adulthood, marriage and parenthood.

In the classification of Bayley, focusing especially on intellectual development, adulthood is placed as the development occurring between 22 and 44 years. Instead, the World Health Organisation (WHO) considers youth as being between 18/20 years and 35 years, with the young adulthood upper limit coinciding with the age at which all organs and body systems operate under and upper parameters.

Schiopu and Green believe that youth extends beyond 24 and 25 years.

Youth can be divided into three sub-stages: that of adapting to work and family life (between 24 and 28 years), the period of implantation during which experience intensifies until parenthood (between 28 and 32 years), and the third sub-stage (between 32 and 35 years) that is a period of relative stability in terms of values, behaviour and aspirations made in time.

References

Albu, E. 2007. "Psihologia vârstelor," Universitatea Petru Maior, Târgu-Mureş, DEPARTAMENTUL I.F.R.D., 81-83.

Bayley, N. 2006. "Bayley Scales of Infant and Toddler Development–Third Edition. San Antonio, TX: Harcourt Assessment," *Journal of Psycho-educational Assessment* June 2007 25: 180-190;

Bologan, M. 2010. *Metode statistice de evaluare a impactului tranziţiei asupra condiţiei tineretului Republicii Moldova*. Specialitatea 08.00.11, Statistică Economică, Teză de doctor în economie, Conducător Elena CARA, Conf. univ., dr., Aspecte privind noţiunea de tânăr şi de adult, Chişinău.

Collins, W. A., and M. R. Gunnar. 1990. "Social and Personality Development," *American Review of Psychology* 41:387-416.

Douvan, E., and J. Adelson. 1966. *The Adolescent Experience*. New York: John Wiley & Sons, Inc.

Erikson, E. H. 1968. *Identity: Youth and Crisis*. New York: W. W. Norton & Company.

Erikson, E. H., and J. M. Erikson. 1987. *The Life Cycle Completed*. New York: W. W. Norton & Company.

European Commission. 2009. *Youth: Investing and Empowering*. Commission Staff Working Document to the Communication from the Commission to the Council, the European Parliament, the European Economic and Social Committee and the Committee of the Regions, EU Youth Report, {COM(2009) 200}, {SEC(2009) 545}, {SEC(2009) 546}, {SEC(2009) 548}.

Levinson, D. and J. Rousselet. 2012. *Neuropsychiatry of Childhood and Adolescence* Vol. 60 nr. 5S, Juillet 2012 P. S1—S 330 Elseivier Masson SAS, IACAPAP 2012—20 the World Congress, Paris. Brain, Mind and Development.

Mitteraurer M. 1983. *Ledige Mutter: Zur Geschichte illegitimer Geburten in Europa*: 452. , Munchen: Beck, cited.

Official Journal of Romania. 2011. *Labour Code .24/01/2003*. Republished in the Official Journal Part I No. 345 of 05.18.2011 Entered into Force on 21.05.2011.

Rousselet, J. 1969. *Adolescentul acest necunoscut*, 1969 Ed. Politică, Bucureşti.

Şchiopu, U., and E. Verza, E. 1977. *Psihologia vârstelor*. Ciclurile vieții, Ed. Didactică şi Pedagogică R.A., Bucureşti.

Wagner P. 2004. *Bazele statisticii.* Bucureşti: Editura Universităţii Titu Maiorescu.

RECENT DEVELOPMENTS IN THE LABOUR MARKET PARTICIPATION OF YOUNG PEOPLE

VASILICA CIUCĂ AND CRISTINA LINCARU

1. Introduction

In order to investigate youth participation in the labour market, the first quarter of the year will be taken as a reference period, on the grounds that:

- March is the most favourable[1] month for students to access information about their academic studies. Another reason is that in March some of the most desirable European educational destinations, The Netherlands, Denmark, Sweden and France, commence their selection procedures;

- Education and the effects of the legal regulation of the labour market can be harmonised in the first quarter of the year. The academic year starts in September and ends in June/July of each year. However, the procedures to register as unemployed and to be entitled to the relative benefits can start at anytime, yet they are enforced only after a certain period of time for school-leavers;

- Graduates in Romania can register as unemployed with the National Agency for Employment (*ANOFM*) 60 days after their graduation date, usually in September. They can also register at the end of the first quarter, with the unemployment spell lasting no less than 4 months, which is the same amount of time calculated by the Youth Guarantee Report in which one becomes unemployed or leaves formal education:

> (5) The term "Youth Guarantee" refers here to the fact that young people receive a good quality offer of employment, continued education, an

---

[1] http://www.webpr.ro/stiri-webreleases_educatie-14308127-webrelease-tot-mai-multi-romani-apeleaza-servicii-consultanta-educationala-pentru-aplica-studii-strainatate.htm?cfnl= .

apprenticeship or a traineeship within a period of four months of becoming unemployed or leaving formal education.[2]

In Romania, in the first quarter of 2012, the population in the 15-24 year-old age group amounted to 2.74 million, of whom 0.79 million were active and 1.95 million were inactive. Among the active population, 0.6 million people were employed, while 0.19 million people were unemployed. Comparing these figures with the EU27 average, one might note that apart from the share of the unemployed population, a significant difference emerges when taking into account the inactive population.

2. Employment Rates for People Aged 15 to 24 Years Old in the First Quarter of 2012

The employment rate for people aged 15-24 in the EU27 was 32.1%, compared to 21.9% in Romania. Similarly, the inactivity rate was 71.3% in Romania, that is 12.9pp higher than the European average.

Job loss is accompanied by increased transitions from employment to inactivity, raising the chances of being trapped in unemployment. Low employment levels resulting from flexible forms of employment indicated different labour market patterns than those implemented in Europe.

> 10% of the employed population has not kept their jobs in 2011, an increasing tendency as compared to the past. Out of them, about one quarter (2.4% of total) have changed jobs, while three-quarters transited to the status of unemployed or inactive. In 2011, the odds that an employed person became unemployed or inactive were 7.7%, as against 3.3% in 2010. More than 50% of the pupils and students who complete their studies are unemployed or inactive. Thus, 37% of them fall in unemployment, 18% face inactivity, and 45% of them find a job. The continuing unemployment rate was 58% in 2011, 8pp more than in 2010, meaning that 6 out of 10 of the unemployed still have no jobs. Only 2 out of 10 of them are transited from unemployment to employment. In fact, 80% of the unemployed find work. Young people without higher education are the most affected category.[3]

---

[2] European Commission. 2012. *Proposal for a Council Recommendation on Establishing a Youth Guarantee* {SWD (2012) 409 final} COM (2012) 729 final, 2012/0351 (NLE). Brussels: European Commission, 6.

[3] Voinea, L., L. Simionescu, N. Mardari, V. Voineagu, V. Duma, P. Jifcu, L. Sinigaglia, N. Hrehorciuc-Caragea, S. Pisică. 2010. *Mobilitatea forței de muncă și aspecte privind incluziunea socială,* Biroul pentru Observarea pieței muncii și a calității locurilor de muncă, Blocul Național Sindical, Proiect cofinanțat din fondul

2.1. Salaried Employment for Young People in the 15-24 Age Group in Q1 2012

The number of workers in salaried employment in the first quarter (Q1) of 2012 was 17.1 million in the EU27, and 0.35 million in Romania.[4]

A higher diversification of employment by professional status is visible in Romania comparing with the EU27 mean. The share of employed persons in total employment was 93.1% for EU27 and 58.4% for Romania, whereas the share of self-employment in total employment was 4.3% in EU27 and 10.5% in Romania, with the rate of contributing family workers out of total employment corresponding to 2.5% in EU27 and 31.1% in Romania. If professional status is taken into account, one might note that in Romania:

- There is a propensity for employees to work as unpaid family workers. In this case, solutions are needed to increase productivity and to better integrate the related benefits with the labour market protection systems; and

- There are high levels of self-employment, pointing to a tendency towards entrepreneurship and autonomous work.

2.2. Low Levels of Temporary Employment for Young People Aged 15-24 Years in Q1 2012

Temporary employment is a necessary tool for improving youth labour market inclusion and directly contributing to the implementation and the enforcement of flexicurity. Temporary working schemes also serve as a ladder towards quality employment, which is coupled with career and personnel developments, benefits in terms of social security and so forth.

In the first quarter of 2012, 17.5 thousand people aged 15-24 years old in Romania were employed on a temporary basis, that is 0.6% of the total population in the same age group. The EU27 average for the same indicator was about 13% in the first quarter of 2011.

This structural difference indicates a potentially important, albeit untapped, aspect of the labour market in Romania, which would increase youth employment. The relevance of temporary employment in the labour

---

Social european prin Programul Operaţional Sectorial Dezvoltarea Resurselor Umane 2007-2013, 51.

[4] Source: *Employment by Sex, Age and Professional Status* (1,000) [lfsq_egaps].

market in Q1 2012 is reflected by the percentage of temporary employment contracts in total employment. The average share of temporary employment for young people aged 15-24 years old in the EU27 in Q1 2012 was 40.6%, while in Romania it was 5% for the same period. Importantly, in 2011 this tool was given fresh momentum by new legislation amending the Labour Code, although not being fully implemented. Another aspect that should be pointed out is that in the first quarter of 2012, temporary employment among the population aged 15-64 years was 13.1% of total employment for the EU27 average and 1.5 % for Romania. The same tendency is visible in the 20-64 age group, with temporary employment accounting for 12.3% for the EU27 and 1.4% for Romania.

2.3. Full-time and Part-time Employment for the 15-24 Age Group

In the first quarter of 2012, part-time employment for young people aged 15 to 24 years was 31.3% of total employment for EU27, and 16.1% for Romania. Similarly to self-employment, part-time work has been poorly implemented. This aspect is evidenced by the fact that during the first quarter of 2012, part-time work for the 15-64 age group made up 19.3% of total employment for the EU27 average, and 9% for Romania.

The same trend is apparent in the 20 to 64 age group, as part-time employment accounted for 18.7% in the EU27 and 8.8% in Romania.

In the first quarter of 2012, there were 96.2 thousand people aged 15-24 years old in part-time employment,[5] of whom 53.3 thousand having low levels of education (ISCED97 0:2), 41.5 thousand possessing medium levels of education (ISCED97 3-4) and about 1.4 thousand who were regarded as highly educated (ISCED97 5-6). In Q1 2012, part-time employment was structured as follows:

- Romania: part-time employment contracts were entered into by 55.4% of young people with low educational levels, 43.1% of the population with medium levels of education, and by 1.5% of those with higher levels of education.

---

[5] Source: EUROSTAT: *Full-time and Part-time Employment by Sex, Age and the Highest Level of Education Attained.*

- On average in the EU27, part-time employment contracts were entered into by 30% of young people with low educational levels, 58.2% of the population with medium levels of education, and by 11.5% of highly-educated people.

3. Independent Employment

3.1. Self-employment by Sex, Age and Educational Attainments

Self-employment among high calibre graduates in the first quarter of 2012 in Romania included 2.3% of the population aged 15-24, totalling 63 thousand people. Of them, 60.6 thousand people were employed as self-employed without employees—2.2% of the total population—either possessing secondary upper education (53.3%, ISCED97 3-4), or secondary lower education (45%, ISCED97 1-2).

As for the EU27, 1.4% of the total population aged 15-24 years worked as self-employed—784.4 thousand people—either with (0.1%) or without employees (1.2%). In educational terms, 2% of the total population aged 15-24 years old was an employer, while 1.7% of the total population in the same age cohort were self-employed. Within the self-employed population in the 15-24 age group, 62.3% of people had middle-level education (ISCED97 3-4), 23.9% of them obtained low levels of education (ISCED97 1-2), and 13.1% of them were highly educated (ISCED97 5+).

If one were to apply the EU27 structure for self-employment in Romania taking account of the educational levels, the number of people in this sector would rise by 5.6 thousand people among those with secondary education (ISCED97 3-4), and by 6.3 thousand among those with higher education.

3.2. Youth and Entrepreneurship in Romania

The report on entrepreneurship carried out by the Global Entrepreneurship Monitor (GEM) in Romania in 2011 pointed out a number of factors with respect to the development trends of young people:

- Potential entrepreneurial activity in Romania for the population aged 18-24 years old was 28.9% in 2011, increasing from 24.2% in 2007, a rise which was second only to that reported for the 25-34 age group (32.1% in

2011).[6] Potential entrepreneurs are those individuals aged between 18 and 64 years old who intend to start a business within three years.[7]

> The Romanian potential entrepreneurs' profile indicates that they are usually young, males with a secondary degree and earn above the 33% household income. The distribution of potential entrepreneurs by age categories did not show significant changes in the period surveyed. In 2011, some 58.8% of the potential entrepreneurs were males. The highest share of potential entrepreneurs by household income can be found among those above the 33%-limit, even though their share decreased from 57.1% in 2007 to 49.9% in 2011. According to our findings, potential entrepreneurs with secondary degree represent 48.9% in 2011, although their share in 2007 was only 4.2%. On the other hand, the share of those who obtained a university degree decreased from 41.1% in 2007 to 5.4% in 2011.[8]

- The early stage entrepreneurial activity rate for the population aged 18-24 years old was 7.87% in 2011, increasing from 1.09% in 2007, and slightly lower than that reported for the 55-64 age group (4.55% in 2011). The highest level of involvement in entrepreneurial activities has been reported by the 25-34 year-old age group in 2011 (14.64 %), almost twice the level reached in 2007 (7.54%). The second highest level included the 45-54 year-old age group with a rate of involvement of 10.20% in 2011, increasing by almost 3 times the percentage reported in 2007 (3.69%).[9] "Early-stage entrepreneurs" (TEA) females aged between 18 and 64 are those identified as nascent or young entrepreneurs. When considering themselves as both nascent and young business entrepreneurs, they are usually counted as "nascent" entrepreneurs only.[10]

---

[6] GEM. *Adult Population Survey, Romania, 2007-2011*. Cited in Petru, T.-P., A. Benyovszki, L.-Z. Györfy, Á. Nagy, D. Matiş, Ş. Pete. 2011. "Entrepreneurship in Romania 2011," Country Report, Sponsoring institutions OTP Bank Romania S.A., Babeş-Bolyai University of Cluj-Napoca, Pro Oeconomica Association, 16.

[7] Petru, T.-P., A. Benyovszki, L.-Z. Györfy, Á. Nagy, D. Matiş, Ş. Pete. 2011. "Entrepreneurship in Romania 2011," Country Report, Sponsoring institutions OTP Bank Romania S.A., Babeş-Bolyai University of Cluj-Napoca, Pro economica Association, 8.

[8] *Ibid.*, 16.

[9] GEM. *Adult Population Survey, Romania, 2007-2011*. Cited in Petru, T.-P., A. Benyovszki, L.-Z. Györfy, Á. Nagy, D. Matiş, Ş. Pete. 2011. "Entrepreneurship in Romania 2011," Country Report, Sponsoring institutions OTP Bank Romania S.A., Babeş-Bolyai University of Cluj-Napoca, Pro Oeconomica Association, 17.

[10] GEM. *Adult Population Survey, Romania, 2007-2011*. Cited in Petru, T.-P., A. Benyovszki, L.-Z. Györfy, Á. Nagy, D. Matiş, Ş. Pete. 2011. "Entrepreneurship in

Nascent entrepreneurs are those individuals aged between 18 and 64 years who are actively planning a new venture. These entrepreneurs have committed during the previous 12 months to starting a new business that they will own at least partly. Activities such as organizing the start-up team, looking for equipment, saving money for the start-up or drafting a business plan would all be considered as active commitments to starting a business. This business does not provide remuneration, wages or any other payments to the owners for more than three months.[11] Young business entrepreneurs or new business owners are those entrepreneurs who own and manage a new business at least partly for 4 to 42 months and are not remunerated for longer than this period. These new ventures are launched in the first 42 months following their establishment.

- The share of established business owners in Romania in 2007-2011 for the population aged 18 to 24 was 1.36% in 2011, increasing from 0.0% in 2007.

The established business owners' rate reached its highest levels in the last five years in all age groups in 2011. The highest share of established entrepreneurs can be found in the 55-64 age category. The rate indicates a significant increase among men, from 2.16% in 2010 to 6.28% in 2011. From 2010 to 2011, the rate has also increased for the three household incomes, but the most important increase is in the upper 33% category, from 1.69% in 2010 to 5.55% in 2011. The highest established business owner rate by educational levels can be identified among those who have a university degree.[12] Established business owners (EB) are those entrepreneurs who have set up businesses that they have continued to own and manage and which have provided remuneration for more than 42 months.[13]

4. The Worsening of Long-term Unemployment for People Aged 15 to 24 in Q1 2012

In the first quarter of 2012, there were 187.6 thousand unemployed aged between 15 and 24 —calculated considering the ILO methodology—

Romania 2011," Country Report, Sponsoring institutions OTP Bank Romania S.A., Babeş-Bolyai University of Cluj-Napoca, Pro Oeconomica Association, 16.

[11] *Ibid.,* 8.

[12] *Ibid.,* 18.

[13] Petru, T.-P., A. Benyovszki, L.-Z. Györfy, Á. Nagy, D. Matiş, Ş. Pete. 2011. "Entrepreneurship in Romania 2011," Country Report, Sponsoring institutions OTP Bank Romania S.A., Babeş-Bolyai University of Cluj-Napoca, Pro Oeconomica Association, 9.

114.1 thousand were males and 73.6 thousand were females, amounting to 43.8% of the total number of long-term unemployed. Over the same period, in the EU27 there were 5.47 million people without a job, 3.09 million of whom were males and 2.38 million were females (28.9% of the long-term unemployed). In the EU27, in the first quarter of 2012 (Q1 2012) and 2011 (Q1 2011), the total number of unemployed aged 15 to 24 increased by 266.6 thousand people, 177.1 thousand were males and 89.6 thousand females. The reverse took place in Romania during the same time frame: a decrease was reported among the total number of unemployed aged 15 to 24 (-17.4 thousand people), where 6.4 thousand were males and 10.9 thousand were women.

The persistence of long-term unemployment for young people –more than 1 year[14]—is a major challenge in Romania. In Q1 2012, the percentage of Romanian youth facing unemployment for 12 to 17 months was 15.7% of total unemployment, whereas the share of those without a job for 24 to 47 months was 21.1%, that is 3.1pp and 10.6pp higher than the EU27 mean, respectively.

Evidently, long-term unemployment was accentuated by the economic slowdown. Between Q1 2012 and Q1 2011, the long-term unemployment rate increased by 6.5pp in Romania and 2.5pp in the EU27, with a gap in Q1 2012 amounting to 12.2pp.

In Romania, the long-term unemployment rate for young people aged 15 to 24 was 43.8% in Q1 2012, exceeding the rates reported for both the 15-64 age group (42.9%), and the 20-64 age group (43.5%). We also noticed that in Q1 2012, the rate of long-term unemployment for 15 to 64-year-olds and 20 to 64-year-olds increased by 3.1pp and by 2.6pp, respectively. Simply put, the long-term unemployment rate for young people in Q1 2012/Q1 2011 was twice that reported for the working age population. In Romania, this was more evident for men (7.2%) than for women (4.1%). The trend was reversed in Europe, since long-term unemployment for men and women rose by 2.1pp and 2.9pp, respectively.

4.1. Unemployment for the 15-24 year-old Age Group in the Q1 2012: Some Worrying Trends

Unemployment rates in Romania follow trends which are different from those in Europe, especially if one considers that in Romania in Q1 2012, the youth unemployment rate was 23.9%, three times as high as that

[14] EUROSTAT. *Long-term Unemployment* (12 months or more) as a Percentage of Total Unemployment, by Sex and Age (%) [lfsq_upgal]. Brussels: EUROSTAT.

reported for the working age population, and twice as high the EU27 average (22.9%). In Romania, the relationship between the unemployment rate and the unemployment rate of the working age population by sex is 2.9 for males and 3.3 for females, whereas in the EU27 it is 2.2 and 2.1 for males and females, respectively. Thus in Romania the unemployment rate reported small quarterly variations by the end of 2011 (-0.2pp/+0.3pp). In Q1 2012, the unemployment rate for people in the 15-64 age group was 7.9%, and 7.6% for those in the new working age (20 to 64-year-olds), that is lower than the European mean for the same age cohort (2.8pp and 2.7 pp, respectively). The convergence towards the European mean is generally due to rising unemployment levels in Europe and not to lower unemployment rates in Romania. In Q1 2011, the unemployment rate in Romania was 23.6%, 2.2pp higher than the EU27 level. Finally, in Q1 2012 the unemployment rate was 23.9%, that is 1pp higher than the EU27 average.

4.2. Youth and Working Age People in Q1 2012: the Degree of Urbanization and the Effects on the Labour Market

Below are some statistics concerning urbanization and employment in both Romania and the EU27 (EUROSTAT data):

1) In Romania, the areas regarded as Predominantly Urban (PU) –that is consisting of at least 500 inhabitants/km²—are home to 917.4 thousand people (37.5%) in the 15-24 age group (36% in the EU27).

2) The areas deemed as Intermediate (IR) in Romania –that is consisting of between 100 and 499 inhabitants/km²—are home to 626.2 thousand (23.3%) people in the 15-24 age group (38.7% in the EU27);

3) In Romania, the areas regarded as Predominantly Rural (PR)—that is consisting of less than 100 inhabitants / km ²)—are home to 1.192,500 people (39.2%), in the 15-24 year-old age group (25.3% in the EU27).

Major differences exist between Romania and the EU27 concerning the territorial distribution of the population aged 15 to 24 by employment status, expressed in relative terms. If one considers the Q1 2012:

- An unemployment rate of 6.8% is reported in densely populated areas (PU) among the 15-24 age group, 2.1pp lower than the EU27 rate for the same age group (9%).

- An unemployment rate of 10% is recorded in intermediate urbanized areas (IR) among the 15 to 24-year-olds, which is almost the same as the EU27 rate for the same age group (10.2%).

- An unemployment rate of 5.2% is reported in sparsely populated areas (PR) among the 15 to 24-year-olds, 4.2 lower than the EU27 rate for the same age group (9.4%).

As for the employment rate:

- An employment rate of 16.7% is reported in densely populated areas (PU) among the 15 to 24-year-olds (29.3% for the EU27).

- An employment rate of 18.7% is reported in intermediate urbanized areas (IR) among the 15 to 24-year-olds (36.1% for the EU27).

- An employment rate of 27.6% is reported in sparsely urbanized areas (PR) among the 15 to 24-year-olds (28.9% for the EU27).

As for the inactivity rate:

- An inactivity rate of 76.5% is reported in densely populated areas (PU) among the 15 to 24-year-olds (61.7% for the EU27).

- An inactivity rate of 71.3% is reported in intermediate urbanized areas (IR) among the 15 to 24-year-olds (53.8% for the EU27).

- An inactivity rate of 67.2% is reported in sparsely urbanized areas (PR) among the 15 to 24-year-olds (60.7% for the EU27).

As for labour market participation, those living in intermediate urbanized areas are closely followed by densely populated areas, with this trend that is different from that reported in Europe. The spatial heterogeneity is increasing and justifies the need for extensive research to identify the most important contributing factors to this state of affairs from a spatial integrated perspective. Regarding sparsely populated areas, the trend is consistent with the European one, indicating the scope for transferring of best practices in this connection.

5. Young People not in Education, Employment, and Training (NEETs) by Educational Attainments, Age and Sex in 2011

In 2011, the number of Romanian young people classified as NEETs was 495 thousand, that is 17.4% of the total population aged 15 to 24 (+ 1 pp from 2010). As for Europe, NEETs were 12.9% of the 15 to 24-year-olds, (+0.1pp from the previous year).

As for labour market participation, in 2011 6.8% of total population aged 15-24 years old were unemployed NEETs (+0.5pp from 2010), and 10.5% in the same age group were inactive (+0.4pp from 2010). In 2011 in EU27, 6.6% of total population aged 15-24 years old were unemployed NEETs (+ 0.1pp from 2010), while inactive NEETs were roughly the same as the previous year (6.3%). Therefore, one might conclude that Romanian unemployment rates for those NEETs followed almost the same trends as that in Europe, while for inactivity rates it is almost double the EU mean (accentuating the divergent tendency by 0.4pp/year).

In addition, if one considers NEETs' willingness to work in 2011, 11.9% (338.7 thousand) of those in the 15-24 year-old age group show intention to work (whether seeking employment or not), with only 5.5% (156.6 thousand) of those in the same age group expressing no intention to work. As for the EU27, 9.3% of those aged 15 to 24 were NEETs who were willing to work, while 3.6% of individuals aged 15-24 were NEETs without any intention to work. In 2011, the potential number of people estimated to move from inactivity to activity amounted to 142.3 thousand in the 15 to 24 age group. This estimation was calculated by subtracting 156 thousand NEETs in the 15 to 24 age group from the total number of inactive people in the same age cohort (298 thousand).

6. Young Graduates Who Passed the Baccalaureate Entry Exam upon Completion of the High School: A Specific Target Group in Romania

The reform of the education system following the passing of Education Law No. 1/2011 brought about a significant decrease in the rate of high school graduates. In 2012, only 43.79% of students graduated—the lowest trend reported in Romania ever—thus exhibiting a significant decrease compared to 2009 (80%). The number of potential candidates estimated by the Ministry of Education that entered a baccalaureate degree course in

2012 was 330 thousand.[15] The National Agency for Employment[16] reported a rise in the number of high school and college graduates registered as unemployed without entering a baccalaureate programme.[17]

Pursuant to Law No. 76/2002, the 2011 and 2012 graduates that failed the Baccalaureate exam are to be regarded as unemployed:

Article 17[18]

(2) People are assimilated to unemployed persons in the cases provided in Article 16, letter b) if the following conditions are met:

a) They are graduates aged 16 years old who failed to be employed in positions in line with their educational paths within 60 days from graduation;

b) They graduated in special schools for people with disabilities, are 16 years old and failed to be employed in positions in line with their educational paths;

Article 34

(3) Unemployed people referred to in Article17/(2) are entitled to unemployment benefits if the following conditions are met:

a) They are registered with local employment agencies;

b) Their income resulting from legal activities is less than the gross minimum wage;

c) Under the conditions laid down by the law, they do not qualify for retirement.

---

[15] Declarație Ministrul interimar al Educației, Liviu Pop, iulie 2012 http://www.romanialibera.ro/actualitate/educatie/bacalaureat-2012-peste-330-000-de-absolventi-de-liceu-ar-putea-participa-la-bacalaureat-in-acest-an-265773.html (accessed 13 June 2013).

[16] http://www.realitatea.net/cat-de-mare-este-valul-de-tineri-someri-dupa-dezastrul-de-la-bac_981088.html (accessed 13 June 2013).

[17] http://www.realitatea.net/cat-de-mare-este-valul-de-tineri-someri-dupa-dezastrul-de-la-bac_981088.html (accessed 13 June 2013).

[18] LEGE Nr. 76 din 16 ianuarie 2002 privind sistemul asigurărilor pentru somaj si stimularea ocupării forței de muncă (accessed 13 June 2013).

Article 40

(1) Unemployed people can claim unemployment benefits referred to in Article 17/ (2) during a period of 6 months. The amount of such benefits is a fixed one and amounts to 50% of the reference social indicator in force at the time of its determination;

(2) The unemployment benefits referred to in paragraph (1) are collected pursuant to Article 17. (2) let. a) and b).

The reference social indicator (ISR) is calculated considering par. 3, Article 14, and Article 33 of Law No.76/2002. For 2012, the ISR was 500 lei (Romanian currency); thus the amount of the unemployment benefits to be assigned was 250 lei. Regarding the number of young people who have access to the baccalaureate exam:

- 199,272 young people entered the 2012 exam session, corresponding to 60.3% (154,367) of the total high school graduates in 2012, and 39.7% (44,905) of the total high school graduates in 2011.

- There were 87,261 baccalaureate graduates in 2012 (26.4% of the total number of enrolled students);

- 112,011 students failed the baccalaureate entrance exam (33.9% of those who registered to the exam in 2011 and 2012);

- 130,728 young people did not register for the baccalaureate entrance exam even if they were eligible (39.6% of total 2011 high school graduates);

- 242,739 high school graduates in 2011 and 2012 did not pass the baccalaureate entry exam in the 2012 summer session, that is 70% of all high school graduates in 2011 and 2012 who attempted the exam. They can complete secondary education, stay on in higher education, or acquire further skills acquisition to enter the labour market;

- As of July 2012, 34.2 thousand unemployed youth in the 15 to 24 age group were high school graduates who did not pass the baccalaureate entry exam, that is 46.7% of the total number of unemployed young people aged 15 to 24 (+40% from 2011).

- In 2012, there were 208,539 youth facing the risk of inactivity, mostly high school graduates from the 2011 and 2012 classes who did not pass the baccalaureate entry exam in the 2012 summer session and did not register as unemployed. In other words, only 14% of high school graduates in 2011 and 2012 who did not pass the entry examination in 2012 summer session applied for unemployment benefits.

- Those 23,288 high school graduates who did not pass the baccalaureate entry examination in 2011 and 2012 and are registered as unemployed had studied in specialized secondary schools.

In economic terms, that 14% (34.2 thousand) of high school graduates who registered as unemployed after failing the baccalaureate exam cost the country 250 lei per graduate, that is 8.5 million lei per month in benefits resulting from passive measures. It has been estimated that 80.9 million lei have been allocated to unemployment high school graduates, that is 6.2% of the financial resources assigned to passive measures.

In a context of rampant unemployment, young people face increasing difficulty to find a job, thus many of them might decide to stay on in education. This could be an investment for the future only if they acquire the right skills. In the EU27, 7.5 million people in the 15-24 age group were NEETs, reporting a rise from 10.8% in 2008 to 12.8% in 2010.

Tellingly, in Bulgaria, Estonia, Greece, Ireland, Italy, Latvia, Romania, Slovakia and Spain, over 14% of young people do not study or work.

7. Conclusion

Job loss is accompanied by increased transitions from employment to inactivity, with the risk of being trapped in unemployment which is far from remote. In the first quarter of 2012, there were 187.6 thousand people aged 15 to 24 who were unemployed in Romania—114.1 thousand were males and 73.6 thousand were females–signalling that the long-term unemployment rate was 43.8%.

Flexible working arrangements like temporary and part-time employment are not yet fully implemented. Progress has been made in self-employment, but there is still room for improvement, particularly in unpaid family work and strategies to promote entrepreneurship. This is true if one considers certain ILO recommendations, among others R189 – The Job Creation in Small and Medium-Sized Enterprises Recommendation, 1998 (No. 189), and R 193—The Promotion of Cooperatives Recommendation, 2002 (No. 193).

Evidently, the efforts made so far are insufficient to help youth fare well in employment. Young people should be supported through innovative action in view of achieving satisfying job outcomes, enrolling in further education, or taking part in apprenticeships and traineeships:

> (2) Young people have been hit particularly hard during the crisis. They are vulnerable because of the transition periods of life they are going through, their lack of professional experience, their sometimes inadequate education or training, their often limited social protection coverage, restricted access to financial resources, and precarious work conditions. Young women are more likely to be affected by low pay and precarious employment, while young parents, primarily young mothers, lack adequate work-life balance measures. Furthermore, some young people are at a particular disadvantage or at risk of discrimination. Appropriate supportive measures are therefore required.[19]

Romania is urged to find solutions regarding the high levels of youth inactivity and unemployment, and especially high rates of NEETs. The pathways to employment for young people are increasingly diverse and might contribute to reduce the costs to deal with these issues also in the years to come.

References

European Commission. 2012. *Proposal for a Council Recommendation on Establishing a Youth Guarantee* {SWD (2012) 409 Final}, COM (2012) 729 Final, 2012/0351 (NLE). Brussels: European Commission, 6.

EUROSTAT. *Long-term Unemployment (12 months or more) as a Percentage of the Total Unemployment, by Sex and Age* (%) [lfsq_upgal]. Brussels: EUROSTAT.

—. *Population by sex, age, degree of urbanisation of residence and labour status* (1 000) [lfsq_pgauws]. Brussels: EUROSTAT.

—. *Population by Sex, Age, Nationality and Labour Status* (1 000) [lfsq_pganws]. Brussels: EUROSTAT.

—. *Population, Aged 15 to 74 Years by Sex, Age and Highest Level of Education Attained* (1 000) [lfsq_pgaed], 2012Q1. Brussels: EUROSTAT.

[19] European Commission. 2012. *Proposal for a Council Recommendation on Establishing a Youth Guarantee* {SWD (2012) 409 final} COM (2012) 729 final, 2012/0351 (NLE). Brussels: European Commission, 6.

—. *Self-employment by Sex, Age and Highest Level of Education Attained* (1 000) [lfsq_esgaed]. Brussels: EUROSTAT.

—. *Unemployment by Sex, Age and Duration of Unemployment* (1 000) [lfsq_ugad]. Brussels: EUROSTAT.

—. *Young People Not in Employment and Not in Any Education and Training, by Educational Attainment Level, Age Group and Sex* (in % points of NEET rates) [edat_lfse_21]. Brussels: EUROSTAT.

GEM. *Adult Population Survey, Romania, 2007-2011*. Cited in Petru, T.-P., A. Benyovszki, L.-Z. Györfy, Á. Nagy, D. Matiş, Ş. Pete. 2011. "Entrepreneurship in Romania 2011," Country Report, Sponsoring institutions OTP Bank Romania S.A., Babeş-Bolyai University of Cluj-Napoca, Pro Oeconomica Association, 16.

Lege Nr. 76 din 16 ianuarie 2002 *privind sistemul asigurărilor pentru somaj si stimularea ocupării forţei de muncă.*

Petru, T.-P., A. Benyovszki, L.-Z. Györfy, Á. Nagy, D. Matiş, Ş. Pete. 2011. "Entrepreneurship in Romania 2011," Country Report, Sponsoring institutions OTP Bank Romania S.A., Babeş-Bolyai University of Cluj-Napoca, Pro Oeconomica Association, 8.

Voinea, L., L. Simionescu, N. Mardari, V. Voineagu, V., Duma, P. Jifcu, L. Sinigaglia, N. Hrehorciuc-Caragea, S. Pisică. 2010. *Mobilitatea forţei de muncă şi aspecte privind incluziunea socială.* Biroul pentru Observarea pieţei muncii şi a calităţii locurilor de muncă, Blocul Naţional Sindical, Proiect cofinanţat din fondul Social european prin Programul Operaţional Sectorial Dezvoltarea Resurselor Umane 2007-2013, 51.

YOUTH EMPLOYMENT: THE ACCENTUATION OF LABOUR MARKET SEGMENTATION AND OTHER CHALLENGES

CRISTINA LINCARU, VASILICA CIUCĂ AND CODRUTA DRAGOIU

1. Introduction

A possible response to the crisis is that of increasing flexibility, since "more flexible labour markets allow for adjustments to [such] shocks with little to no employment loss".[1] The other side of the coin is rigidity and an accentuation of labour market segmentation.

> Labour market segmentation theory initially distinguishes two labour market segments, the one characterised by better, permanent, well-paid jobs with career prospects (the "primary segment"), and the other having temporary, badly paid jobs without any career prospects (the "secondary segment"). [...] Those who work in the latter segment of the labour market have a weak link with the labour market.[2]

The impact of the economic crisis on the Romanian labour market slowed down its dynamism and increased the risks of segmentation. Like many other countries, in 2011 Romania took exceptional measures to break the vicious cycle resulting from this state of play. These measures were mainly directed towards reviewing the Labour Code in the area of employment protection legislation, in view of increasing labour market

---

[1] Friedrich, K., and M. Axel. *Labour Market Flexibility* http://www.oecd.org/eco/growth/35558438.pdf (accessed 13 June 2013).

[2] De Grip, A., I. Sieben, D. van Jaarsveld. 2006. "Labour Market Segmentation Revisited: A Study of the Dutch Call Centre," Sector ROA-W-2006/8E, Research Centre for Education and the Labour Market http://www.roa.unimaas.nl/pdf_publications/2006/ROA-W-2006_8E.pdf (accessed 13 June 2013).

flexibility—either external or internal—and reducing labour market segmentation. More specifically, these measures included:

Job Protection:[3]

External flexibility: The reform in the area of employment protection legislation has been sustained, chiefly in countries with a strong need of facilitating labour market adjustment and with rigid employment protection legislation;

- A number of countries have introduced changes to legislation regulating individual and collective dismissals, under the pressure of mass unemployment and a highly segmented labour market;

- Many initiatives include longer probationary periods.

With regard to the regulation of temporary contracts, the purpose of several reforms has been either to inject more flexibility in the labour market or to limit the abuse of these working schemes, thus preventing problems related to labour market segmentation;

- The access to fixed-term contracts has been facilitated, by extending their scope;

- The duration of temporary contracts has been extended;

Working Time Regulation:[4]

Internal flexibility has been largely used as a tool to complement external flexibility and to stimulate employment within specific groups;

- More flexible working time arrangements have been introduced by adapting overtime regulations;

- Employers have been given more leeway to amend working time arrangements;

---

[3] European Commission. 2012. "Labour Market Developments in Europe," *European Economy* 5, Directorate-General for Economic and Financial Affairs, 51.
[4] *Ibid.*, 52.

After causing a fall in demand and sector contraction, the decline of Romanian labour market dynamism narrowed down the access to quality employment, diminished labour income, and contributed to poverty and social exclusion, generating irrecoverable losses and hampering the reallocation of workers and sustainable growth in the expanding sectors:

> As some sectors expand and other contract, the ability of workers to move into expanding sectors can be critical to the employment situation.[5]

From the perspective of the dual labour market, significant flows of jobs and workers have been reported between the primary and the secondary segment, as well as independent trajectories for the component groups:

> The primary sector generally contains the higher-grade, higher-status, and better-paid jobs, with employers offering the best terms and conditions. It is a male dominated sector. The secondary sector is characterised by jobs which are mostly low-skilled and require relatively little training. There are few barriers to job mobility within the secondary sector. Because the jobs are unattractive, there is little incentive to stay, and there are high levels of labour turnover, with workers moving on to other jobs or employers. Wages are low, and terms and conditions of the job are poor. It is a female dominated sector.[6]

As for job market flows:

> The analysis of labour market flows provides an indication of the sources of unemployment fluctuations, notably whether changes in unemployment rates are mostly related to fluctuations in separation, job finding rates or both [...]. At the end of 2011, the probability of finding a job fell considerably in Cyprus, Denmark, Greece, Spain, Ireland and Romania.[7]

---

[5] Fallon P. R., and R. E. B. Lucas. 2012. "The Impact of Financial Crises on Labour Markets, Household Incomes and Poverty, A Review of Evidence," *The World Bank Research Observer* 17, No. 1:21-45, http://siteresources.worldbank.org/INTLM/Resources/390041-11411418 01867/2275364-1287763239841/lucas_crisis.pdf (accessed 13 June 2013).

[6] http://understandingsocialscience.wordpress.com/2010/01/08/key-term-definition-segmented-labour-markets/ (accessed 20 June 2013).

[7] European Commission. 2012. *Labour Market Developments in Europe*, 23. Brussels: European Commission.

2. Young People in the Romanian Labour Market

2.1. Gross Worker Flows in the 15-24 Year-Old Age Group: Main Characteristics of Youth Mobility in Romania

In this section, the aggregate employment dynamics of Romanian youth aged 15 to 24 are presented for 2010, by implementing an alternative method to evaluate gross worker flows[8] and using aggregate data provided by EUROSTAT.

Based on the OECD Employment Outlook 2009[9] and 2010,[10] and drawing on the methodology illustrated by Davis and Haltiwanger (1999), the "employment by time since job started" indicator provided quarterly data as a proxy for job tenure[11] that was used to calculate the annual hiring flows (number of hires per year). This new indicator (lfsq_egdn2) has been provided by EUROSTAT since 2008 and is calculated considering the National Labour Force Survey, thus opening up new opportunities to explore the labour market characteristics, including perspectives that are more dynamic. Total employment is broken down into job tenure intervals making up the proxy indicator for hiring. Under this methodology, we consider "hiring" as the act of entering employment and "separation" as that of exiting employment, irrespective of one's status. Transition is referred to by taking account of the employment status, not the position *per se*. We have calculated the annual values for workers' hiring flows, workers' separation flows, workers' total reallocation flows and workers' excess reallocation flows in both relative and absolute terms:

Where workers' mobility is described in absolute indicators:

Ht-1; t– Hiring represents the number of hired workers during an interval of 1 year.

---

[8] Cristina, L., C. Vasilica, and P. Speranța. 2011. *Alternative Method of Gross Worker Flows Measurement. Study Case Romania*, Poster Session IV, EALE Conference 22-24 September 2011, Paphos, Cyprus,
http://www.eale.nl/Conference2011/Programme.htm (accessed 13 June 2013).

[9] OECD. 2009. *Employment Outlook Tackling the Jobs Crisis. How Do Industry, Firm and Worker Characteristics Shape Job and Worker Flows*? Chapter 2, 121.

[10] OECD. 2010. *Employment Outlook Moving Beyond the Job Crisis, Institutional and Policy Determinants of Labour Market Flows*. Chapter 3, 167.

[11] Definition: Total Employment is Broken Down by Job Tenure Intervals
http://www.oecd.org/document/34/0,3746,en_2649_37457_40917154_1_1_1_37457,00.html#jobduration (accessed 13 June 2013).

St-1; t– Separation, or workers' separation, represents the number of separated workers during an interval of 1 year (regardless of the reasons and irrespective of whether it was individual or collective redundancies).

TRNt-1; t—Workers' total reallocation represents the total number of workers undergoing hiring and separations during an interval of 1 year.

ERNt-1; t—"Workers' excess reallocation is that between firms of the same industry" (OECD). The absolute modification of net employment includes the reallocation measures between different groups of firms/ different industries, during an interval of 1 year.

This indicator (calculated for 2008 and 2009, see Table 1-3) for Romania points to certain effects stemming from the global economic crisis, such as increased labour market flexibility and reduced rigidity.

This is the result of a slowdown in the allocation of workers and reduced levels of worker flows.

- Employment rates for youth: the share of employed population aged 15 to 24 hired in Romania was 24.2% in 2009—almost 1/4 of the young population that accessed employment in the reference year—decreasing by 3.4pp from 2008. As for the EU27, the employment rate was 52.3% in 2009 (-6.7% from 2008). The employment rate for 15 to 24-year-olds in Romania was almost half of that in theEU27;

- In 2008, employment growth for the 15-24 age group reported a trend which was as positive as that of the 15-64 age group. In Romania, the employment rate for 15 to 64-year-olds was 9.4% that is 0.7pp higher than the separation rate (8.7%). The 15-24 year-old age group had an employment rate of 27.6%, which was higher than the separation rate by 0.8pp (26.8%). In the EU27, the employment rate for the 15-64 age group was 18.2%, 0.4pp higher than the separation rate (17.8%). Further, those aged 15 to 24 reported an unemployment rate of 59%, 2.5pp lower than the separation rate (61.5%). Finally, the annual employment growth rate was 0.7% in Romania and 0.4% in the EU27 for those aged 15 to 24, and 0.8% and 0.4% for those aged 15 to 64.

A perturbing trend concerning young people losing their job was visible in 2009, mainly owing to the dramatic decrease of the hiring rates, with the separation rates remaining almost constant or even decreasing.

This tendency indicates a diminution of employment access for young people. In Romania, the employment rate for 15 to 64-year-olds was 7.6%, -1.8pp from 2008 and lower than the separation rate of 9.3% (1.7pp). For those aged 15 to 24, the employment rate was 24.2%, -3.4pp from 2008, and lower than the separation rate by 1.9pp (26.1%). In the EU27, the employment rate for the 15-64 age group was 15.6%, with a 2.6pp decrease compared to 2008, and 2.1pp lower than the separation rate (17.7%). For those aged 15 to 24, the employment rate was 52.3%, which is 9.6pp lower than the separation rate (60.7%). The employment growth rate for 2009/2008 for the 15-64 year-old age group was -1.7% in Romania and -2.1% in the EU27. As for those aged 15 to 24, the employment growth rates correspond to -2.1% for Romania and -9.6% for EU27.

- The volume of the reallocation of young workers in Romania and the EU27 is respectively 3 times and 3.4 higher than the reallocation of the working age population. In 2009, the share of employed population aged 15 to 64 which experienced hiring or separation in Romania was 16.9%—that is 1.2pp lower than in 2008—and 33.3% in the EU27, decreasing by 2.7pp from 2008. In 2009, the share of employed population aged 15-24 years old that experienced hiring or separation was 50.3% in Romania—with a 4pp decrease from 2008—and 113% in EU27, decreasing by 6.5pp from 2008. In Romania, young workers' reallocation experienced a 4pp decrease between 2008 and 2009, that is almost 3.3 times higher than the reallocation of total population of working age (-1.2pp). In the EU27, young workers' reallocation decreased by 6.5pp between 2008 and 2009, 2.4 times higher than the whole working age population (-2.7pp in the EU27).

- In Romania, the excess of young workers' reallocations also within the same industry between 2009 and 2008 decreased by 5.1pp, more than twice that of the population of working age (2.1pp). In the EU27 and over the same period, the excess of young workers' reallocations, also within the same industry, decreased by 3.4pp, lower than that reported by the population in employment (4.4pp).

- A decrease in the flows of foreign workers was also reported.

In terms of labour market dynamics by flows of workers, a few aspects arise with reference to the 15-24 year-old age group:

- There are many workers entering the labour market for the first time, the performances of whom are investigated in terms of school-to-work transition. In the normal run of things, high rates of excess reallocation are reported (over 100%) alongside employment growth, as a reflection of new entrants to the labour market;

Table 1-3. Workers' Flows Estimation for Romania and EU27 in 2010.

***rH** annual rate of workers hirings:*

	Romania						UE27					
age gr	rHintT2008	rHintT2009	rHintM2008	rHintM2009	rHintF2008	rHintF2009	rHintT2008	rHintT2009	rHintM2008	rHintM2009	rHintF2008	rHintF2009
15-64	9,4	7,6	12,6	8,9	8,4	6,8	18,2	15,6	21,2	14,8	19,3	14,4
15-24	**27,6**	**24,2**	**42,5**	**25,9**	**26,7**	**21,8**	**59,0**	**52,3**	**67,8**	**49,5**	**62,4**	**55,6**
50-64	4,8	3,6	7,3	4,3	2,5	1,7	15,8	13,6	18,1	13,0	16,7	11,0
25-49	8,6	6,9	11,0	8,2	8,2	6,8	7,2	6,4	9,2	6,3	7,3	6,5

***rS** annual rate of workers separations*

age gr	rSintT2008	rSintT2009	rSintM2008	rSintM2009	rSintF2008	rSintF2009	rSintT2008	rSintT2009	rSintM2008	rSintM2009	rSintF2008	rSintF2009
15-64	8,7	9,3	9,0	10,3	8,4	8,7	17,8	17,7	17,4	17,8	18,2	15,4
15-24	**26,8**	**26,1**	**26,7**	**31,3**	**27,0**	**18,6**	**61,5**	**60,7**	**58,8**	**59,7**	**64,7**	**62,0**
50-64	0,6	5,7	-0,9	7,5	1,2	2,2	15,8	16,0	15,7	16,1	16,0	12,5
25-49	9,2	8,4	10,0	8,5	8,6	9,8	4,3	5,3	4,7	6,2	3,7	4,1

***rTR** annual rate of workers total reallocation*

age gr	rRTintT2008	rRTintT2009	rRTintM2008	rRTintM2009	rRTintF2008	rRTintF2009	rRTintT2008	rRTintT2009	rRTintM2008	rRTintM2009	rRTintF2008	rRTintF2009
15-64	18,1	16,9	19,1	19,2	16,8	15,5	36,0	33,3	34,7	32,6	37,5	29,8
15-24	**54,3**	**50,3**	**54,8**	**57,2**	**53,7**	**40,4**	**120,5**	**113,0**	**115,0**	**109,1**	**127,1**	**117,5**
50-64	5,4	9,3	4,8	11,8	3,8	3,8	31,6	29,6	30,7	29,1	32,7	23,6
25-49	17,7	15,4	19,1	16,7	16,9	16,6	11,5	11,7	11,8	12,5	11,0	10,7

***rER** annual rate of workers excess reallocation*

age gr	rERintT2008	rERintT2009	rERintM2008	rERintM2009	rERintF2008	rERintF2009	rERintT2008	rERintT2009	rERintM2008	rERintM2009	rERintF2008	rERintF2009
15-64	17,4	15,3	18,0	17,7	16,8	13,6	35,6	31,2	34,6	29,6	36,4	28,7
15-24	**53,5**	**48,4**	**53,3**	**51,7**	**53,4**	**37,1**	**118,0**	**104,6**	**112,4**	**99,0**	**124,7**	**111,2**
50-64	1,2	7,2	-1,8	8,6	2,5	3,3	31,6	27,3	30,0	26,0	31,9	22,1
25-49	17,1	13,9	18,3	16,4	16,5	13,6	8,5	10,6	9,3	12,5	7,5	8,3

Source: Authors' Own Elaboration.

- In 2009, the separation rates were higher than the hiring rates across the EU27, as a result of the economic slowdown (Fig. 1-2).

- The higher the performance of the labour market in terms of provision of employment, the higher the hiring and separation rates. In Sweden and Finland, all youth aged 15 to 24 experience both hiring and separation at least once a year. Regardless of the age group, the variations in hiring and separation rates are below 30%, save for the 15 to 24 age group (20% to 120%, Fig. 1-2).

Fig. 1-2. Hiring and Separation Rates for the Age Groups 15-24, 25-49, and 50-64 Years in 2009.

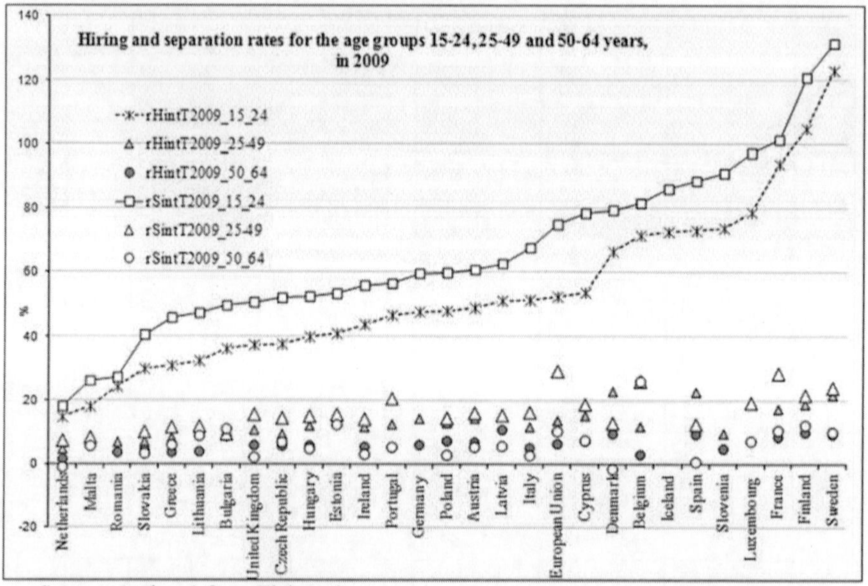

Source: Authors' Own Elaboration.

- Providing more flexibility and containing problems related to labour market segmentation translate into a response to demand through the diversification of the employment arrangements: fixed-term contracts, probationary periods, internships and traineeships;

- There is a widely recognized difficulty to intervene on young people entering the labour market, which however is offset by various active labour market policies, including encouraging employers to stimulate and accelerate the school-to-work transition.

In addition to these specific aspects, the dynamism of young workers in the labour market is decisive in Romania:

> Youth exclusion from the labour market represents a major issue in Romania. The decrease of youth employment in terms of stock is a manifested trend against the overt strategic objectives to support youth employment. Along with the obvious decline in employment, separations are more frequent than employment (S >> H), and are accompanied by decreased levels of workers' reallocation in the same industry.
>
> The low variation levels of workers' flows aged 15 to 24 indicate that the entry of young people into the labour market was lagging behind the economic crisis, being the cause a deep-rooted one. What lacks in particular is the implementation of specific working schemes that can stimulate the inclusion of youth in the labour market.
>
> From 2008 through 2009, the number of permanent and fixed-term contracts for young people decreased, as evidenced by decreasing worker gross flows, without major differences between dynamic regimes for men and women.
>
> The lower allocation of young workers in the same industry indicates an extremely limited propensity towards specialization among them. Low levels of flow allocation within the same industry for young people in Romania reveal serious risks arising from inadequate allocation according to the specialization of individuals. This state of affairs limits the emergence of new industries that are in need of those new skills that can be easily learnt by youth.
>
> Not surprisingly, a recent study[12] shows that those in the 15-24 age group were more willing to transit between jobs. In this sense, only 80.2% of the employed persons in this age group preserved their job in 2010-2011, with a significant difference from those in the 25-49 year-old age group (91.4%), and those in the 50-64 age group (88.9%). However, what is emphasized is that young people who have kept their job enter unemployment and inactivity (14.4%), rather than remain in the labour market (5.4%).[13]

---

[12] Voinea, L., L. Simionescu, N. Mardari, V. Voineagu,V. Duma, P. Jifcu, L. Sinigaglia, N. Hrehorciuc-Caragea, S. Pisică. 2010. *Mobilitatea forţei de muncă şi aspecte privind incluziunea socială.* Biroul pentru Observarea pieţei muncii şi a calităţii locurilor de muncă, Blocul Naţional Sindical, Proiect cofinanţat din fondul Social european prin Programul Operaţional Sectorial Dezvoltarea Resurselor Umane 2007-2013, 26.

[13] Lincaru C., V. Ciucă, et.al. 2013. Studiu: Flexibilitatea pieţei muncii din România, descrisă din perspectiva fluxurilor de lucrători la nivel naţional şi în context european: dinamica pieţei muncii şi mobilitatea lucrătorilor, 110, Investeşte în oameni! Fondul Social European Programul Operaţional Sectorial pentru Dezvoltarea Resurselor Umane 2007—2013 Axa prioritară: 3 Domeniul

2.2. Occupational Mobility of Young People aged 15 to 24

As for occupational mobility of young people aged 15 to 24 in 2010:

> The highest levels of occupational mobility by age group were reported for those aged 15 to 24, as 15.9% of people in employment in this age group have changed their occupation. One might thus assume that this age group is the most mobile one. Yet differences in 25-49 age groups are negligible, for here the percentage of employed persons engaged in job swapping was 14.6%.[14]

3. Labour Market Segmentation and Exceeding Demand: Risks and Consequences

The concept of "labour market segmentation" involves the analysis of the market considering the available contractual relationships between employees and employers—which might offer different degrees of security—while concurrently taking account of possible positive transitions to permanent employment. Many factors may contribute to labour market segmentation, such as temporary working arrangements, misused forms of flexible employment, and insufficient social protection, particularly in the absence of positive transitions between jobs.

3.1. A Reported Increase of Youth aged 15 to 24 who are forced to Engage in Temporary Employment during the Economic Crisis

The proportion of fixed-term employment points to a rise in labour market segmentation. This is a general trend in Europe and another consequence of the economic and social crisis. In the EU27, the percentage of youth aged 15 to 24 in fixed-term employment contracts out

---

major de intervenţie: 3.2 Proiect cofinanţat dinFondul Social European prin Programul Operaţional Sectorial Dezvoltarea Resurselor Umane 2007—2013Titlul proiectului: "Răspunsul pieţei muncii româneşti la criză: creşterea flexibilităţii şi adaptabilităţii întreprinderilor şi consolidarea securităţii lucrătorilor" Cod contract: POSDRU/63/3.2/S/41637.

[14] Voinea, L., L. Simionescu, N. Mardari, V. Voineagu,V. Duma, P. Jifcu, L. Sinigaglia, N. Hrehorciuc-Caragea, S. Pisică. 2010. Mobilitatea forţei de muncă şi aspecte privind incluziunea socială, Biroul pentru Observarea pieţei muncii şi a calităţii locurilor de muncă, Blocul Naţional Sindical, Proiect cofinanţat din fondul Social european prin Programul Operaţional Sectorial Dezvoltarea Resurselor Umane 2007-2013, 20.

of total employed persons was on the increase, from 40.2% in 2008 to 42.5% in 2011 (+2.3pp).[15] The same occurred in Romania, where a 1.5pp increase was reported, from 4.3% in 2008 to 5.8% in 2011. In 2011, the share of those aged 15 to 24 who entered into fixed-term employed contracts because they could not find stable employment in Romania was 68.8% (-5.8pp from 2008) and 36.7% in the EU27 (+0.4pp from 2008).

This difference between Romania and the EU average is similar to that concerning those who engaged in temporary employment[16] because they are still in education or training (40.1%) in the same year.

3.2. A Reported Increase of Youth aged 15 to 24 who are forced to Engage in Involuntary Part-time Employment during the Economic Crisis

The share of involuntary temporary employment indicates a rise in labour market segmentation. This is a general European trend and another consequence of the economic and social crisis. In the EU27, the percentage of youth aged 15 to 24 in involuntary temporary employment out of the total employed persons was on the increase, from 26.3% in 2008 to 29.8% in 2011 (+3.5pp).[17]

The same occurs in Romania, where a 3.5pp increase was reported—5.9pp for males and 1.8pp for females—from 14.7% in 2008 to 18.2% in 2011.[18] In 2011, the share of involuntary part-time employment as a percentage of total part-time employment in Romania for 15 to 24-year-olds was 62.7%, that is -7.9pp from 2008, which was mainly due to the young males' willingness to enter this employment pattern. In this sense, the share of involuntary male part-timers decreased from 81.1% in 2008 to 72.1% in 2011 (9pp), while a small variation was reported among females, from 61.3% in 2008 to 63% in 2011. The convergence process towards the European model is emphasised by the 10.2pp decrease of the gap between involuntary part-time employment in Romania and the EU27, from 44.9 pp in 2008 to 34.7pp in 2011. Yet high levels of segmentation of the labour market have been exhibited, while this rate was as twice in

---

[15] EUROSTAT. *Temporary Employees as Percentage of the Total Number of Employees, By Sex And Age* (%) [lfsa_etpga]. Brussels: EUROSTAT.

[16] EUROSTAT. *Main Reason for the Temporary Employment—Distributions by Sex and Age* (%) [lfsa_etgar]. Brussels: EUROSTAT. Brussels: EUROSTAT.

[17] EUROSTAT. *Temporary Employees As Percentage of the Total Number of Employees For A Given Sex And Age Group* (%).Brussels: EUROSTAT.

[18] EUROSTAT. *Part-time Employment as Percentage of the Total Employment, by Sex and Age* (%) [lfsa_eppga]. Brussels: EUROSTAT.

Romania as in the EU27. In 2011, involuntary part-time employment in Romania as a percentage of total part-time employment for 15 to 24-year-olds was 11.4 pp higher than the same indicator for those aged 25 to 64 (9.1pp for men and 11.9pp for women), whereas only a 2.2pp difference was reported in the EU27 (12.4 for men and 6.2 for women, an aspect pointing to a labour deficit).

3.3. High Prospects for Self-employed Youth, but Inadequate Income is still Reported

The Labour Force Survey (AMIGO, INS) measures the statistic unit per person taking account of the employment status, thus involving self-employed persons (either with or without employees).

Additional information regarding the income of those in non-salaried employment—save for employers—could be gathered from the HBS Household Budget Survey (ABG, INS) that calculates the statistic unit per household. Notwithstanding the limits in terms of methodology, the aim here is to draw a picture of the income vulnerability of self-employment in Romania. In 2011, the self-employed aged 15 to 24[19] were 70.6 thousand, thus reporting a decrease from 2008 (16.2 thousand). One third of them lived in urban areas and the rest were based in rural areas.

> More than 30% of the employed population work in agriculture, and these are considered to be self-employed persons or unpaid family workers; the incidence of low-paid jobs is significant.[20]

3.3.1. Self-employed Persons in Rural Areas and Monthly Average Total Income for Farmers in Rural Households

In 2011, out of 1.4 million self-employed in rural areas (AMIGO/LFS), 46.8 thousand were in the 15-24 age group, that is 6.9% of those employed in this age group and 3.3% of the total self-employed population in rural areas. The general tendency in 2008 through 2011 for average total income

---

[19] INS, TEMPO, AMIGO. *Employment by Age Group, By Status in Employment and By Urban/Rural Area.*

[20] Luminita, C. 2009. *Romania: Self-employed Workers.* Institute of National Economy, Romanian Academy,
http://www.eurofound.europa.eu/comparative/tn0801018s/ro0801019q.htm
(accessed 13 June 2013).

(ABF/HBS)[21] for self-employed (farm or non-agricultural activities) in households in rural areas is on the increase, especially for farmers (the difference between farm households and non-agricultural activities increased from 2.4pp in 2008 to 7.2 in 2011):

- In 2011, the monthly average total income (ABF/HBS) for farm households in rural areas was equal to 67.8% of the total income calculated for salaried workers (ABF) (3146.5 lei—€744—with €1 = 4.23 lei), increasing by 12.1pp from 2008.

- The monthly average total income (ABF/HBS) for the self-employed in non-agricultural activities in rural households in 2011 was 60.6% of the total income calculated for salaried workers (ABF) (3146.5 lei—€744—with €1 = 4.23 lei), increasing by 7.3pp from 2008.

3.3.2. Self-employed Persons in Urban Areas and Monthly Average Total Income of the Self-employed in Non-agricultural Activities in Urban Households

In 2011, out of 0.3 million self-employed in urban area (AMIGO/LFS) 23.8 thousand were in the 15-24 age group, amounting to 3.5% of those employed in this age group and 7.7% of the total self-employed population in the urban areas.

b1. The monthly average total income (ABF/HBS) for farm households in urban areas in 2011 was 49.2% of the monthly average total income calculated for those in salaried employment (ABF), (3146.5 lei—€744—with €1 = 4.23 lei), decreasing by 11.1pp from 2008.
b2. The monthly average total income (ABF/HBS) for the self-employed in non-agricultural activities in urban households in 2011 was 64.6% of the monthly average total income calculated for those in salaried employment (ABF) (3146.5 lei—€744—with €1 = 4.23 lei), increasing by 0.3pp from 2008. In addition, with reference to:

Lower income tax rate for micro-enterprises:

A favourable (i.e. lower) income tax rate has been applied to micro-enterprises since 2007. Set at 2% in 2007, the rate gradually increased to

[21] ABF: *Monthly Averages of Total Income per Household, by Income Categories and Main Social Categories by Areas*.

2.5% and then to 3% in 2009, but it was eliminated in 2010 by the government, within its crisis budgetary consolidation plan.[22]

3.3.3. Contributing Family Workers: The Highest and Most Recent Employment Growth for Youth, but Inadequate Income is still Reported

During the period 2008-2011, contributing family workers[23] in the 15-24 age group experienced the highest growth rates among all other employment categories, which amounted to 12% (24.9% in urban areas and 11.5 in rural areas). In 2011, the number of contributing family workers in the 15-24 age group was 226.8 thousand, +24.3 thousand persons from 2008, meaning that 1 out of 3 employed persons aged 15 to 24 was a contributing family worker. They are concentrated in rural areas (95.6%) rather than in urban ones (4.4%). At present, no official data are available regarding the household monthly average total income for contributing family workers.

4. Wage Adjustment and Labour Costs Recent Trends

4.1. The Close Connection between Productivity and Wage

In 2010, labour productivity[24] in Romania was 5.3 Euros/hour worked, decreasing by 0.3 Euros/hour worked in 2008. Significantly, labour productivity in 2010 was 5.9 times lower than the EU27 average, with such difference that has increased by 0.3pp since 2008. In the previous period, the percentage change of real labour productivity per person employed was 2.9% for Romania in 2011, slightly recovering from the 2009 dramatic fall (12pp, from 7.3% in 2008 to -4.7% in 2009). The same tendency was reported in EU27, yet with less significant variations, for real labour productivity growth, decreasing from -0.6% in 2008 to the late minimum of -2.6% in 2009, and standing at 2.5% in 2010. Projections for

[22] European Commission. 2010. *European Employment Observatory Review, Self-Employment in Europe 2010*. European Commission Directorate-General for Employment, Social Affairs and Equal Opportunities Unit D.2 Brussels: European Commission.

[23] INS, TEMPO, AMIGO. *Employment by Age Group, By Status in Employment and by Urban/Rural Area.*

[24] EUROSTAT. *Labour Productivity, Annual Data* [nama_aux_lp]. Brussels: EUROSTAT.

2012 indicate another fall of real labour productivity growth at -0.2% for Romania and at -0.1% for the EU27.

In Romania, the percentage change in the previous period of real labour productivity per hour worked decreased by 12.4pp, from 7.3% in 2008 to -5.1% in 2009, and slightly recovered at 0.5% in 2010. As for the EU27, this trend was similar but real labour productivity per hour worked decreased only by 1pp, from -0.5% in 2008 to -1.4% in 2009, recovering at 2.2% in 2010.

The rise in labour productivity brought about real wage growth in Romania, as well as in Denmark, France, Finland, the United Kingdom and the Czech Republic, where "there was a close connection between wages and productivity growth"[25]:

> The nominal unit labour cost (NULC) is defined as the ratio of total compensation of employees (D1), in millions of national currency per total number of employees in persons divided by the ratio of GDP in market prices in millions of chain-linked volumes for the reference year 2005 (CLV05), at 2005 exchange rates in national currency per total number of persons employed in persons. The change in nominal unit labour cost is the change in total compensation of employees per number of employees not covered by the change in labour productivity plus the change in share of employees in total employment. Input data is obtained through official transmissions of national accounts' country data in the ESA95 transmission programme. NULC is calculated by the formula: (total D1 in national currency/ total employees in persons) / (GDP in market prices in CLV05 in national currency/ total employment in persons). Data are expressed as percentage change of indexes comparing year Y with year Y-1, Y-5 and Y-10.

4.2. High Risks of Losing Cost Competitiveness: Annual Unit Labour Costs Experience Growth

The annual percentage change of Unit Labour Costs (ULC),[26] defined as the total labour costs required to produce a unit of output, is used to compare international cost competitiveness. In 2008, the ULC annual percentage change in Romania was 6.6 %, indicating a significant loss in cost competitiveness also in 2011, with annual positive growth for ULC at 7.8%. During 2009 and 2010, an increase of cost competiveness for

[25] ILO. 2013. *Global Wage Report 2012/13, Wages and Equitable Growth.* Geneva: ILO, 12.

[26] EUROSTAT. *Unit Labour Cost, Annual Data* [nama_aux_ulc]. Brussels: EUROSTAT.

Romania was reported, which resulted from a negative annual growth rate for ULC of -1.2% and -7.7%, respectively. The ULC annual growth rate of 0.3% for 2012 and 2013 points to an irrelevant decrease in cost competitiveness for Romania, with good prospects to break even after 2014. As for the EU27, the loss in cost competiveness is generated by a positive annual growth rate of ULC, from 1.1% in 2008 to 3.2% in 2009.

The annual growth rate of ULC decreased by -1.6% in 2010 and -0.5% in 2011 and indicated an increase in cost competitiveness. Following a period of economic recovery in 2012, recession is expected also in Romania, being characterised by a positive ULC annual growth rate of 1.5%. In this sense:

> ULC will rise (that is, cost competitiveness will decline) when the labour cost increase is higher than the corresponding increase in productivity.[27]

4.3. Labour Costs are Seven Time Slower than the Highest EU27 Average

In Romania, the hourly labour cost in the business economy in 2010 was 3.85 Euros/hour (monthly labour cost: €594 in 2010),[28] slightly decreasing from 3.88 Euros/hour in 2008. In 2010, social contributions and other labour costs paid by the employer in the business economy was 23.2%, while the share of total wages and salaries was 76.8%, almost similar to the share in 2008[29] (23.6%, if we consider social contributions only).

> Average hourly labour costs are defined as total labour costs divided by the corresponding number of hours worked and the average monthly labour costs are defined as total labour costs per 12 and divided by the yearly average number of employees, expressed as full-time units.[30]

---

[27] Havlik, P. 2005. "Unit Labour Costs in the New EU Member States," Statistika 3, Vienna: Institute for International Economic Studies, 288.

[28] EUROSTAT. *Hourly labour Cost Labour Costs Annual Data*, NACE Rev. 2 [lc_an_cost_r2], Business Economy. Brussels: EUROSTAT. Note that these figures cover not only the compensation of employees (earnings) but also vocational training costs, other expenditure, as well as taxes and subsidies that are incurred or received by the enterprise.

[29] EUROSTAT. *Structure of Labour Costs (%), NACE Rev. 2* [lc_an_struc_r2] Business Economy. Brussels: EUROSTAT.

[30] EUROSTAT. *Labour Costs Annual Data, NACE Rev. 2* http://epp.EUROSTAT.ec.europa.eu/tgm/web/table/description.jsp (accessed 13 June 2013). Brussels: EUROSTAT.

The costs borne by the employer concerning labour and social security as a share of the total labour costs[31] amounted to 23.2% in 2010, lower than 23.6% in 2008 and 24.4% in 2009.

4.4. Average Gross Earnings by Working Type Programme and Share of the Minimum Wage

In Romania, average annual gross earnings in the business economy by working type programme in 2010 were:

- €5,408[32] for full-time units (€450.7 if calculated on a monthly basis). The minimum average wage (€139.47 in 2010) was paid to 30.9% of full-time units in the business economy;

- €2,190[33] for part-time units (€182.5, if calculated on a monthly basis). The average minimum wage (€139.47 in 2010) was paid to 76.4% of full-time units in the business economy;

Further, one out of four Romanian employees is a low-wage earner.[34] In 2010, the Romanian population with less than 60% of median gross earnings was 26.85% of all those in full-time employment,[35] decreasing by 1.25pp from 2006, yet higher than the EU27 average (+8.64pp).

Higher shares of low-wage earners among employees under 30 years old are also reported. In Romania, if apprentices are excluded, 32.37% of low-wage earners were less than 30 years old in 2010, reporting a decrease of 11.57pp from 2006, yet higher than the EU27 average (30.43%). In Romania, the gap between the young and the total population of low-wage earners in 2010 was equal to 7.13pp.

---

[31] EUROSTAT. *Social Security and Other Labour Costs Paid by Employer - % of Total Labour Costs* [tps00114]. Brussels: EUROSTAT.

[32] EUROSTAT. *Average Annual Gross Earnings by Economic Activity*, NACE Rev. 2 [earn_gr_nace2]. Brussels: EUROSTAT.

[33] EUROSTAT. *Average Annual Gross Earnings by Economic Activity*, NACE Rev. 2 [earn_gr_nace2]. Brussels: EUROSTAT.

[34] EUROSTAT. *Low-wage Earners as a Proportion of All Employees (Excluding Apprentices) by Age* [earn_ses_pub1a]. Brussels: EUROSTAT.

[35] EUROSTAT. *Enterprises with 10 Employed Persons or More, NACE Rev. 1.1, C-O excluding L,* http://appsso.EUROSTAT.ec.europa.eu/nui/setupModifyTableLayout.do (accessed 13 June 2013).

As far as the relationship between low-wage earners and working arrangements is concerned, the highest shares of low-wage earners were found among workers in fixed-term contracts[36] (35.41% in 2010), reporting a 3.22pp decrease from 2006, yet 4.14pp higher than the 2010 EU27 average (31.27%). In Romania, the gap between the young and the total population of low-wage earners in 2010 was equal to 10.06pp. In addition:

> Earnings are the wage or salary paid to an employee. There are two main types:
>
> Gross earnings are paid in cash directly to an employee before any deductions for income tax and social security contributions paid by the employee. All bonuses, whether or not regularly paid, are included (the 13th or 14th month, holiday bonuses, profit-sharing, untaken paid leave, occasional commissions, etc.).
>
> Net earnings represent the part of remuneration that employees can actually spend and are calculated by deducting social security contributions and income taxes payable by employees from gross earnings and by adding family allowances if there are children in the family.[37]

4.5. Gender Pay Gap

In 2010, the unadjusted gender pay gap (GPG) in Romania was 6.9% in the business economy and 8.4%[38] in the whole economy, yet:

> In spite of some progress, there remains an important gender pay gap in the difference between average earnings of men and women in the EU-27. For the EU-27 as a whole, women were paid, on average, 16.4 % less than men in 2010.[39]

---

[36] EUROSTAT. *Low-Wage Earners as a Proportion of All Employees* (Excluding Apprentices) by Employment Contract [earn_ses_pub1t]. Brussels: EUROSTAT.

[37] http://epp.EUROSTAT.ec.europa.eu/statistics_explained/index.php/Glossary:Net_earnings (accessed 13 June 2013).

[38] EUROSTAT. *Gender Pay Gap in an Unadjusted Form by Age in %, NACE Rev. 2, B-S Excluding O* (structure of earnings survey methodology) [earn_gr_gpgr2ag]. Brussels: EUROSTAT.

[39] http://epp.EUROSTAT.ec.europa.eu/statistics_explained/index.php/Wages_and_labour_costs.

The lowest levels of GPG involve young employees less than 25 years old, with 1.7% of women who were paid less than men in 2011, reporting a 0.2pp decrease from 2007.[40]

4.6. Incentives for Labour Demand and Supply Provided by Tax-Benefit Related Indicators

Performance and policy indicators "describing the circumstances under which individuals take their behavioural decisions, rather than representing the final outcome of policies for households or individuals" provided by EUROSTAT[41] to measure the incentives for labour demand and supply and to monitor work attractiveness[42] are:

a) Tax wedge on labour costs, focusing on incentives for labour demand;

b) The unemployment trap, focusing on labour supply incentives when moving from unemployment to employment;

c) A low-wage trap, focusing on labour supply incentives when increasing work efforts.

Information on the tax wedge on labour costs - whereas the tax wedge measures the burden of tax and social security contributions relative to labour costs - is provided in relation to low wage earners (that is considering the average worker without children that earns less than 67% of average gross earnings) and also taking into account that:

> The tax wedge is the difference between the employer's labour costs and the employee's net take-home pay, including any cash benefits from government welfare programmes.[43]

The Methodological note is also of relevance:

---

[40] EUROSTAT. *Gender Pay Gap in Unadjusted Form by Age in %, NACE Rev. 2, B-S excluding O (Structure of Earnings Survey Methodology)* [earn_gr_gpgr2ag]. Brussels: EUROSTAT.

[41] EUROSTAT Quality Profile. *Tax Rate on Low Wage Earners by Marginal Effective Tax Rates on Employment Incomes*. Brussels: EUROSTAT.

[42] http://epp.EUROSTAT.ec.europa.eu/statistics_explained/index.php/Wages_and_labour_costs (accessed 13 June 2013).

[43] http://epp.EUROSTAT.ec.europa.eu/statistics_explained/index.php/Glossary:Tax_wedge (accessed 13 June 2013).

> While the values of these indicators vary from an individual situation to another, the above-mentioned limited family types have been selected on the basis of in-depth discussions by a Commission Experts Group and considering an extensive study on the variation of the indicators across family types and earnings levels (ECFIN Economic Paper No. 197, Indicators of unemployment and low-wage traps) to be presented as structural indicators in order to provide simple and easily interpretable indicators. Tax wedge on labour costs, defined as income tax on gross wage earnings plus employee's and the employer's social security contributions, expressed as a percentage of the total labour costs of the earner. The total labour costs of the earner are defined as his/her gross earnings plus the employer's social security contributions plus payroll taxes (where applicable). The tax wedge on labour costs structural indicator is available only for single persons without children earning 67% of the AW (average worker). The data refer to an average worker at national level for different illustrative cases, defined on the basis of marital status (single vs. married), number of workers (only in the case of couples), number of child dependants, and level of gross earnings, expressed as a percentage of the average earnings of an average worker (AW). Notice that all these indicators were based in 2006 on a new wage benchmark which extends the range of industries: AW (average worker) in industry and services (NACE C-K) rather than old APW ("average production worker") definition (NACE D).

As a result, in 2010, the tax wedge was 43.1% in Romania, (+2.2pp from 2008) among the highest in Europe, being 3.8pp higher than the EU27 average:

> The tax wedge for the EU-27 was 39.3 % in 2010 that is slightly lower than five years earlier. The highest tax burdens on low wage earners in 2010 were recorded in Belgium, France, Germany, Hungary, Italy, Latvia, Austria, Romania and Sweden (all above 40%). On the other hand, the lowest tax burdens for low wage earners were recorded in Cyprus (11.9%, in 2007) and Malta (18.1%); the United Kingdom, Luxembourg and Ireland were the only Member States to report a tax burden for low wage earners between 20 % and 30 %.[44]

[44] EUROSTAT. *Net Earnings and Tax Rates Reference.* Metadata in Euro SDMX Metadata Structure (ESMS) Compiling Agency: EUROSTAT, the Statistical Office of the European Union. Brussels: EUROSTAT.

4.7. The Tax Rate on Low-wage Earners: The Unemployment Trap[45]

In 2010, the tax rate on low wages earners was 59% in Romania, increasing by 2pp from 2008. The relative easiness to transit from unemployment to employment was more visible in Romania. The tax rate on low-wage earners was 16.4pp lower than the EU27 average in 2010, with a tendency to be eroded by this decrease (-5pp between 2008 and 2009).

> The unemployment trap measures the percentage of gross earnings which is "taxed away" through higher tax and social security contributions and the withdrawal of unemployment and other benefits when an unemployed person returns to employment. This indicator is available only for single persons without children earning 67% of a full-time production worker (APW).[46]

c) Tax Rate on Low Wage Earners: The Low-wage Trap

In 2010, the tax rate on low-wages earners[47] at 33% of AW (average wage) in Romania was equal to:

- 31% for *single persons without children,* increasing by 2pp from 2008, and 16.42pp lower than the EU27 average. This means that one must produce an additional effort to transit from low incomes (unemployment) to higher incomes (employment), which translates into 31% of earnings that will be taxed away.

- 32% for *one-earner married couple with two children*, decreasing by 3 pp from 2008, and 11.89pp lower than the EU27 average.

> The low-wage trap provides information on the financial consequences for an employed person when increasing his/her work effort and thus his/her wages while taking into account the combined effects of tax and benefit systems. If a relatively large part of the increase in earned income is 'taxed

---

[45] EUROSTAT. *Tax Rate on Low Wage Earners: the Unemployment Trap* [earn_nt_unemtrp]. Brussels: EUROSTAT.

[46] EUROSTAT. *Net Earnings and Tax Rates Reference* Metadata in Euro SDMX Metadata Structure (ESMS) Compiling Agency: EUROSTAT, the Statistical Office of the European Union. Brussels: EUROSTAT.

[47] EUROSTAT. *Tax Rate on Low Wage Earners - Low Wage Trap* [earn_nt_lowwtrp]. Brussels: EUROSTAT.

> away' through higher taxes and reduced benefits, a low-wage trap (formerly known as "poverty trap") prevails in a situation where increased work effort does not pay [...] The overall figures for the EU-27 show that there was a slight decrease between 2005 and 2010 in the incentive for low wage earners to seek higher incomes, as a higher proportion of their earnings would be "taxed away"; there was no change between 2005 and 2010 in the proportion of earnings that would be "taxed away" when an unemployed person moved into employment.[48]

5. Reducing the Costs for Low-Skilled Youth

Although showing prospects for high productivity, Romania is a low-wage country characterised by low minimum wages (the lowest in EU as of July 2012) and extremely low labour costs. Hourly labour costs in Romania were 7.4 times lower than The Netherlands—the EU27 country with the highest labour cost levels in EU27—and this gap rose to 8.2 times in 2010.[49] Apart from boosting Romanian competitiveness, by increasing productivity and trimming the labour costs, another aspect to be considered is the introduction of the minimum wage for young people.

This move will help reduce labour costs for youth to favour their access to the labour market, in line with what has been promoted in a number of EU countries.

5.1. Minimum Wage in Romania

In Romania, the monthly minimum wage in the first semester of 2013 was €157,26, increasing by €18,67 from the first semester in 2008 (138,59).[50] Starting from 1st February 2013, Provision GD23/22 of January 2013[51] guaranteed a minimum of 750 lei per month for 168,667 monthly hours (4.44 lei/ hour). As of July 1, 2013, the statutory gross minimum wage was set at 800 lei per month for a full-time programme of 168,667 hours per month in 2013 (4.74 lei/ hour).[52]

---

[48] EUROSTAT. *Net Earnings and Tax Rates Reference* Metadata in Euro SDMX Metadata Structure (ESMS) Compiling Agency: EUROSTAT, the Statistical Office of the European Union. Brussels: EUROSTAT.
[49] EUROSTAT. *Tps00173*. Brussels: EUROSTAT.
[50] EUROSTAT. *Monthly Minimum Wages*. Bi-Annual Data [earn_mw_cur]. Brussels: EUROSTAT.
[51] http://www.mmuncii.ro/nou/images/Documente/Legislatie/HG23-2013.pdf (access 13 June 2013).
[52] *Hotărâre pentru stabilirea salariului de bază minim brut pe ţară garantat în plată*,

> As of 1 July 2012, 20 of the EU's Member States (all except Denmark, Germany, Italy, Cyprus, Austria, Finland and Sweden) had national legislation setting a minimum wage by statute or by national inter-sectoral agreement, as had Croatia and Turkey. Monthly minimum wages varied considerably in July 2012, ranging from EUR 1.801 per month in Luxembourg to EUR 148 in Bulgaria. When adjusted for differences in purchasing power, the disparities between EU Member States are reduced from a ratio of 12:1 (the highest compared with the lowest) in Euro terms to a ratio of 5:1 in purchasing power standard (PPS) terms with the highest level of minimum wages in Luxembourg (PPS 1 478) and the lowest in Romania (PPS 272).[53]

In order to promote social cohesion, and taking into account the principles laid down in the European Social Charter and the European Social Model, the economic and social policy objective was specified to set at 50% the difference between the gross minimum and average wage.

In this connection, on 24 July 2008 a tripartite agreement[54] was concluded between the government, employers' and workers' representative bodies, to ensure a minimum wage increase during the 2008 to 2014 period. In January 2009, a 11.1% increase in the nominal change of minimum wage rates was reported in Romania, while the annual consumer price increased by 7.8%, 5.6% and 6.1% in 2008, 2009, and 2010, respectively:

> A larger number of countries, including France, Mexico, Nepal, the Netherlands, Peru, Romania, Serbia, Thailand, Turkey and the United Kingdom, increased the minimum wage over the period 2009–2010 in accordance with consumer price increases "thereby maintaining the purchasing power of minimum wage workers without increasing the burden on enterprises during this difficult period".[55]

---

http://www.mmuncii.ro/nou/images/Documente/Proiecte_in_dezbatere/2013-01-21-Proiect%20HG%20sal%20min%202013.pdf (accessed 13 June 2013).

[53] http://epp.EUROSTAT.ec.europa.eu/statistics_explained/index.php/Wages_and_labour_costs (accessed 13 June 2013).

[54] http://www.fml.ro/fmlpage/fmlpage_main/news/acord_tripartit_salariu_minim.htm (access 13 June 2013).

[55] ILO. 2011. *Global Wage Report 2010/2011*. Geneva: ILO, 65. Bonnet F., S. Catherine, and A. Weber. 2012. "Social Protection and Minimum Wages Responses to the 2008 Financial and Economic Crisis: Findings from the ILO/World Bank Inventory," Economic and Labour Market Analysis Department Social Security Department Conditions of Work and Employment Branch, International Labour Organization 2012, 48.

In 2011, the annual mean of the monthly minimum wage was €157.55 (€157.2 and €157.89 in S1 2011 and S2 2011, respectively), which corresponded to 34.5% of the mean value of average monthly earnings in the business economy.[56] In 2008 the annual mean of the monthly minimum wage was €137.95 (€138.59 in S1 and €137.31 in S2 2008), which amounted to 31.3% of the mean value of average monthly earnings in the business economy (+ 4.1pp).

The latest data reveal signs of stagnation in the implementation of the tripartite agreement, thus hampering wage growth.

5.2. Expected Earnings of Young Romanians

Minimum wage is an important indicator especially for career starters without any previous work experience. The most generous salaries for entry-level workers are offered in the IT sector, where young people can earn between €500 and €900. In the telecommunications industry, experienced employees may be paid between €400 and €700. In addition, remuneration for entry-level workers in 2011 was between €350 and €600 in Engineering and Consulting; between €250 and €600 in Finance, and between €250 and €500 in Customer service and call centres:

> Young people of up to 18 years of age enjoy the same monthly minimum wage even though, according to the Romanian Labour Code, their work schedule may not exceed six hours/day, i.e. 30 hours/week.[57]

Considering that in the last five years higher education graduates in Romania reported gross annual average earnings amounting to 1,087 lei (€258,8),[58] estimates for 2010 concerning remuneration of youth exhibit a decrease in the interval of shares [30.9%, 57.4%] from total to full-time unit average gross annual earnings in the business economy. A number of countries enforced minimum wage regulations for youth in order to reduce

---

[56] Monthly Minimum Wage as a Proportion of Average Monthly Earnings (%) - NACE Rev. 2 (from 2008 onwards).

[57] Ciutacu, C. 2012. *National Report on Traineeships—Romania*, Institute of National Economy Romanian Academy, 724, Study on a Comprehensive Overview on Traineeship Arrangements in Member States, Final Synthesis Report, European Commission Directorate-General for Employment, Social Affairs and Inclusion, Unit C3. Brussels: European Commission.

[58] *Piaţa Muncii Pentru Absolvenţii De Studii Superioare*, http://legislatiamuncii.manager.ro/a/4734/analistul-liviu-voinea:-noul-cod-al-muncii-va-reduce-numarul-de-contracte-permanente-si-veniturile-la-buget.html, 17 Octombrie 2011.

the relevant labour costs (Belgium, France, Greece, Ireland, Luxembourg, Latvia, Malta, The Netherlands, Poland and the UK). The European Industrial Relation Observatory (EIRO) reports that:

> A number of countries have set lower minimum wages for young people. Table (2) presents a summary of these rates. The exception is Latvia, where the adult minimum wage also applies to young people, although they have a shorter working week by regulation. Hence, young people in Latvia have in fact a minimum wage that stands at 114% per hour of the full adult rate. For Belgium, it has been reported that a significant number of sectoral agreements have in recent years abandoned the lower, specific "youth rates", in order to conform with European Union anti-discrimination laws. Youth minimum wages have also been abandoned in Slovakia in 2008. Two new developments regarding youth rates concern Greece and the UK. In Greece, Law No. 3863/2010 introduced apprenticeship contracts for a one-year term for young people aged 15–18 years, who receive 70% of the general minimum wage. Employers and persons aged 15–18 years may conclude special apprenticeship agreements for a maximum term of one year, aiming at the acquisition of skills. A similar regulation, according to the same criteria, is enacted also for entrants to the labour market. Entrants to the labour market who are under 25 years of age receive 84% of the minimum salary or wage, as specified each time by the EGSSE, while the Greek Manpower Employment Organization (OAED), without further formality, undertakes to cover part of the social security contributions, in an effort to support the enterprises in question (compare also GR1007019I). In the UK, changes to the labour law (Equality Act) came into force on 1 October 2010: the full adult rate now applies to employees aged 21 (instead of 22). Furthermore, an apprentice rate (for apprentices under the age of 19 or those aged 19 and over in the first 12 months of their apprenticeship) was introduced in October 2010 and stands at GBP 2.50 (€2.91) per hour. In all other countries with specific rates for young workers no specific changes to the youth minimum wage have been reported.[59]

---

[59] http://www.realitatea.net/vezi-salarii-minime-pentru-tineri-in-mai-multe-tari-din-europa_871947.html preluat din http://www.eurofound.europa.eu/eiro/studies/tn1109060s/tn1109060s.htm#hd42

Table 1-4. Minimum Wage for Young People, 2010.[60]

Recipients	Rate or percentage of full rate	Rate or percentage of full rate
Belgium (minimum wage 1,415/m Euros)	Workers aged 16 years old	70%
	Workers aged 17 years old	76%
	Workers aged 18 years old	82%
	Workers aged 20 years old	94%
	Workers aged 21 years old and over	100%
The Czech Republic (minimum wage, 316 /m Euros)	Workers aged below 18 years old	80%
	Workers aged 18–21 years old	90%
France (minimum wage 1,343/m Euros)	Workers aged below 17 years old	80%
	Workers aged 17–18 years old	90%
Greece (minimum wage 739/m Euros)	Workers aged 15–18 years old	70%
Ireland (minimum wage 8,65 Euros/h)	Workers aged below 18 years old	€6,06 per hour
	Workers aged over 18 years, in their first year of their first job	€6,92 per hour
	Workers aged over 18 years, in their second year of their first job	€7,79 per hour
	Workers aged over 18, training or study undertaken in normal working hours (1st / 2nd / 3rd period)	€6,49/€6,92/€ 7,79 per hour
Luxembourg (minimum wage 1724 Euros/m)	Workers aged 15 and 16 years	75%
	Workers aged 17–18 years	80%

60 Aumayr, C., J. Cabrita and D. Stavroula. 2011. *Pay Developments 2010.* Dublin: Eurofound, Eiro, http://www.eurofound.europa.eu/eiro/studies/tn1109060s/tn1109060s.htm#hd42 (accessed 13 June 2013).

Latvia (minimum wage 254 Euros/m)	Workers aged 15–18 years	114% (LVL 1,23 (€1,75) per hour)
Malta (minimum wage 152 Euros/m)	Workers aged under 17 years	94%
	Workers aged over 17 years	96%
Netherlands (minimum wage 1,416 Euros/m)	Workers aged 15 years	30%
	Workers aged 16 years	34.5%
	Workers aged 17 years	39.5%
	Workers aged 18 years	45.5%
	Workers aged 19 years	52.5%
	Workers aged 20 years	61.5%
	Workers aged 21 years	72.5%
	Workers aged 22 years	85%
Poland (minimum wage 329Euros)	First year in employment	80%
UK (minimum wage 6.5 Euros/h)	Workers aged 16–17 years	GBP 3,63 (€4,23) per hour
	'Development rate': 18–21 years (until 2009); 18–20 (from 2010)	GBP 4,83 (€5,63) per hour
	Apprentices (introduced in Oct 2010)	GBP 2,50 (€2,91) per h

Source: Aumayr, C., J. Cabrita and D. Stavroula. 2011. *Pay Developments 2010*. Dublin: Eurofound, Eiro, http://www.eurofound.europa.eu/eiro/studies/tn1109060s/tn1109060s.htm#hd42 (accessed 13 June 2013).

5.3. Median Gross Hourly Earnings by Age and Contract Type

In 2010, median hourly earnings for units with 10 employees or more in Romania were 1,7 Euros/hour for those with less than 30 years, the lowest rate by age group if one considers median hourly earnings for employees in the 30-49 age group (-0,26 Euros/hour) and for 50-year-olds and older (-0,56).[61] Median hourly earnings for under 30-year-olds rose to 1,7 Euros/hour worked, incrementing by 1 Euro/hour in 2006 and an

[61] EUROSTAT. *Median Hourly Earnings*, All Employees (Excluding Apprentices) by Age [earn_ses_pub2a]. Brussels: EUROSTAT.

additional 0,7 Euros/hour in 2010, that is more than the total increase reported among the employed persons (0,58 Euros/hour workers) and for any other age group presented before. In 2010, median hourly earnings in EU27 were 5.6 times higher than those reported in Romania (0.3 pp lower than the EU27/Romania ratio for labour productivity). If the employment contracts[62] are taken, median hourly earnings for open-ended employment contracts in 2010 were 1.97 Euros/hour worked, that is a 0.58 Euros/hour worked increase from 2006. As for fixed-term employment contracts (excluding apprenticeships), this value decreased to 1.62 Euros/hour worked, that is €0,35 less than median hourly earnings for open-ended ones. Low-wage threshold is 2/3 of median gross hourly earnings calculated in Euros.

5.3.1. Median Gross Hourly Earnings of Employees by Educational Level[63]

Education was rewarding in Romania in 2010: workers with tertiary education reported median gross hourly earnings amounting to €3.3 per hour, considering firms with 10 employees or more listed in NACE Rev. 2, sections B to S. Their earnings were 2.5 times higher than those of workers with low levels of education - who earned 1.3 Euros/h - but less than 5 times those of workers with higher education in the EU27. Still with reference to median gross hourly earnings, the EU27-Romania ratio was 7:1. Perhaps this could explain the high propensity to mobility among poorly educated individuals. It might be also relevant to note that:

> Employees with a high level of education are defined as those who have at least completed the first level of tertiary education whereas those who have completed secondary education but not tertiary level are considered as being in the medium level. Employees whose level of education is not beyond the second stage of basic education are considered of low levels of education.[64]

---

[62] EUROSTAT. *Median Hourly Earnings*, All Employees (Excluding Apprentices) by Employment Contract [earn_ses_pub2t]. Brussels: EUROSTAT.

[63] http://epp.EUROSTAT.ec.europa.eu/statistics_explained/index.php/Earnings_statistics#Low-wage_earners (accessed 13 June 2013).

[64] http://epp.EUROSTAT.ec.europa.eu/statistics_explained/index.php/Earnings_statistics#Low-wage_earners (accessed 13 June 2013).

6. Conclusions

6.1. A Decrease in Employment Protection and in the Share of Working Poor

Some serious social consequences arise from excessive market segmentation. At a macroeconomic level, such excess translates into an increase in labour market volatility. During the latest crisis, a reduction in fixed-term work was reported which affected particularly young and poorly trained people, who underwent separation processes. Out of the total number of fixed-term employment contracts in the EU, some 42.2% are youth, an aspect which further highlights their vulnerability. In addition, research carried out on retirement patterns has shown that workers in fixed-terms employment contracts will be entitled to lower pensions than those in open-ended ones. Naturally, providing low remuneration in the absence of productivity growth —or with such growth being higher than that of labour costs—leads to in-work poverty, that involves more than 60% of low-income employees, if the median income is considered.

As far as the EU27 is concerned, in-work poverty affects 8.5% of the employed persons after granting social transfers, and 18.4% of them following the provision of social transfers. For Romania, in-work poverty concerns 17.3% of the employed population after social transfers were allocated and 29.9% before their assignment. This means that almost 1/3 of the employed population earns less than 60% of the average income.

The large number of working poor is indicative of a high degree of polarization of the labour income, placing Romania at the high end among the EU27 and calling into question the quality of one third of existing jobs.

Significantly, the relationship between work poverty and the employment contracts in force in Romania is somehow puzzling. The EU27 average in 2010 indicated that 12.9% of the employed population on temporary working schemes report earnings 60% below the average income. In Romania, this percentage drops to 8.9% that is 4pp lower than the European mean. In 2010, the number of those regarded as working poor hired with open-ended contracts was 5.1% in the EU27, and 4.8% in Romania, thus reporting a 0.3pp difference.

In 2010, the share of the population at risk of poverty or social exclusion in Romania was 41.4%—mainly children and the elderly—almost twice the EU27 average (23.4%). If the same year is considered, the severe material deprivation rate[65] in Romania was equal to 36.7% for children aged less than 18 years old, that is six times higher than the EU27 average (9.5%). For people aged over 65 years old, this rate was 32.4% in Romania, five times higher than in the EU27 (6.4%).

6.2. Work Experience as an Essential Component to Employment

A national study carried out by the National Trade Union Bloc-BNS concerning the recruitment processes reveals that employers regard as pivotal work experience, which is more relevant than the prestige of the university where school-leavers graduated or obtained a specialization.

Moreover, holding a master's or a bachelor's degree is not considered as important by 76% of employers. To the contrary, 17% of them pointed out that preference would be given to candidates holding a master's degree, and only 7% of employers argued that possessing a bachelor's degree would be a preferred condition during the recruitment process. In addition, previous work experience is an important component of the selection procedures, irrespective of the position held before.[66]

6.3. Rapid Demographic Changes Bring About Risks, an Increase in Labour Costs and a Decrease in Productivity

Ageing population is a defining feature of the Romanian labour market that can lead to serious consequences for youth. Pinpointing the main employment issues for this group is a necessary step towards meeting the objectives set down in the Create Jobs National Plan. Ageing takes place when the "population pyramid" is reversed:

> A reduction of the share of youth aged 0 to 14 has been reported, from 22.7% (in 1992) to 15.1% (in 2010), with a concurrent increase of the

---

[65] Rata de privaţiune materială severă (severe material deprivation rate in English): ponderea persoanelor care au o experienţă de cel puţin 4 din 9 privaţiuni: oamenii nu-şi pot permite să i) îşi plătească chiria sau de utilitate facturile, ii) să-şi asigure căldura în locuinţă, III), se facă faţă la cheltuieli neprevăzute, IV) să mănânce carne, peşte, sau un echivalent de proteine in fiecare a doua zi, v), se bucură de o săptămână de vacanţă departe de casă o dată pe an, vi) să aibă o maşina, vii) să aibă o maşină de spălat, viii) să aibă un televizor color, sau ix) să aibă un telefon.

[66] http://legislatiamuncii.manager.ro/a/4734/analistul-liviu-voinea:-noul-cod-al-muncii-va-reduce-numarul-de-contracte-permanente-si-veniturile-la-buget.html, 17 Octombrie 2011.

elderly population—65 years and older—from 11% (in 1992) to 14.9% (in 2010), and the adult population aged 15 to 64, from 66% (in 1992) to 70 % (in 2010). In 2020 the share of young people will drop significantly—between 9.2% and 14.2%—while elderly people consist of 28.41% of the population. With fertility remaining stable, in 2050 youth will account for only 10.0% of the population, with the share of the elderly corresponding to 31.5%.[67]

Similarly to the rest of Europe, an ageing and declining workforce will bring about a range of economic and social problems. By way of example:

- With the share of over 80-year-olds on the increase, major issues will arise concerning the provision of healthcare.

- The larger share of people in the 50 to 64 age group might question the issue of active ageing.

- Finally, problems in terms of human resources development might loom large with the decline of those in the 15 to 24 age group.[68]

The decline of the population aged 15 to 24 is more pronounced in Mediterranean countries, but there are important differences in terms of future developments among EU countries at a regional level. This asymmetry adds to local differences. As a consequence, many socioeconomic and demographic dynamics can be seen, which call for a more holistic approach and integrated adaptation of policies to specific realities. Despite such differences, it is expected that even during the first decade of this millennium, the majority of EU Member States will be involved in a rapid demographic transition that may call into question the European social model. So-called "senescence" of the population is arrived at by the replacement rate being lower than the fertility rate.

Dealing with ageing requires the harmonization of policies and more consideration for the different domains involved, also through forward planning. Along with monitoring education policies, human resources development and the youth labour market, it is pivotal to promote geographical mobility and flexible skills to be integrated also with work-

---

[67] Voineagu, V. *Îmbătrânirea demografică a populației României o problema*! http://www.amosnews.ro/2011/Vergil_Voineagu_Imbatranirea_demografica_a_populatiei_Romaniei_o_problema_-29-66198.html (accessed 13 June 2013).
[68] Bălaşa, A. *Population Aging: Challenges and Responses in Europe, Quality of Life*, XVI, nr. 3–4, 2005, 273–288, http://www.revistacalitateavietii.ro/2005/CV-3-4-05/5.pdf (accessed 13 June 2013).

life balance, health, demography and other factors. Europe is dealing with a rapidly ageing population and the implications on employment might affect labour market performances in aspects that may be anticipated. Yet a number of questions are in need of further research (the societal changes induced by globalization, the impact of knowledge-based economy, technology progress, and so forth):

> In the context of an ageing population and international migration, it is expected that employers in Romania will face a significant shortage of labour. Labour shortages act on employers either indirectly—affecting their ability to meet labour market demand—or indirectly, by increasing staff turnover, bringing about a rise in the labour costs. Concurrently, the lack of qualified workers contributes to an increase in the level of technology designed to boost productivity and the product quality, making companies more competitive both on the internal and the external. Consequences in terms of labour market participation involve more retirees, along with a decrease of active population.[69]

References

Aumayr, C., J. Cabrita and D. Stavroula. 2011. *Pay Developments 2010.* Dublin: Eurofound, Eiro, http://www.eurofound.europa.eu/eiro/studies/tn1109060s/tn1109060s.htm#hd42 (accessed 13 June 2013).

Bălaşa, A. 2005. "Population Aging: Challenges and Responses in Europe," *Quality of Life* 26, No. 3–4:273–288, http://www.revistacalitateavietii.ro/2005/CV-3-4-05/5.pdf (accessed 13 June 2013).

Bonnet, F., S. Catherine, and A. Weber. 2011. "Social Protection and Minimum Wages Responses to the 2008 Financial and Economic Crisis: Findings from the ILO/World Bank Inventory," Economic and Labour Market Analysis Department Social Security Department Conditions of Work and Employment Branch. Geneva: ILO, 48.

Ciutacu, C. 2012. "National Report on Traineeships—Romania," Institute of National Economy Romanian Academy, 724, Study on a Comprehensive Overview on Traineeship Arrangements in Member States, Final Synthesis Report, European Commission Directorate-General for Employment, Social Affairs and Inclusion, Unit C3. Brussels: European Commission.

---

[69] M. Şerban, A. Toth, Piaţa forţei de muncă şi imigraţia, fundaţia Soros, România, 2007, 17.

De Grip, A., I. Sieben, D. van Jaarsveld. 2006. "Labour Market Segmentation Revisited: A Study of the Dutch Call Centre," Sector ROA-W-2006/8E, Research Centre for Education and the Labour Market http://www.roa.unimaas.nl/pdf_publications/2006/ROA-W-2006_8E.pdf (accessed 13 June 2013).

European Commission. 2010. "Self-employment in Europe 2010," European Employment Observatory Review, European Commission Directorate-General for Employment, Social Affairs and Equal Opportunities Unit D.2. Brussels: European Commission.

—. 2012. "Labour Market Developments in Europe, 2012," European Economy 5, European Commission Directorate-General for Economic and Financial Affairs, 51.

EUROSTAT. *Average Annual Gross Earnings by Economic Activity* - NACE Rev. 2 [earn_gr_nace2]. Brussels: EUROSTAT.

—. *Gender Pay Gap in Unadjusted Form by Age in* % - NACE Rev. 2, B-S excluding O (structure of earnings survey methodology) [earn_gr_gpgr2ag]. Brussels: EUROSTAT. http://epp.EUROSTAT.ec.europa.eu/statistics_explained/index.php/Wages_and_labour_costs (accessed 13 June 2013).

—. *Hourly Labour Cost Labour Costs Annual Data, NACE Rev. 2* [lc_an_cost_r2] - Business Economy. Brussels: EUROSTAT.

—. *Labour Productivity*—Annual Data [nama_aux_lp]. Brussels: EUROSTAT.

—. *Low-Wage Earners as a Proportion of all Employees* (Excluding Apprentices) *by Age* [earn_ses_pub1a](Enterprises With 10 Employed Persons or More)—NACE Rev. 1.1, C-O excluding L. Brussels: EUROSTAT. http://appsso.EUROSTAT.ec.europa.eu/nui/setupModifyTableLayout.do (accessed 13 June 2013).

—. *Low-Wage Earners as a Proportion of All Employees* (Excluding Apprentices*) by Employment Contract* [earn_ses_pub1t]. Brussels: EUROSTAT. http://epp.EUROSTAT.ec.europa.eu/statistics_explained/index.php/Glossary:Net_earnings (accessed 13 June 2013).

—. *Main Reason for the Temporary Employment. Distributions by Sex and Age* (%) [lfsa_etgar]. Brussels: EUROSTAT.

—. *Median Hourly Earnings, all Employees (Excluding Apprentices*) *by Age* [earn_ses_pub2a]. Brussels: EUROSTAT.

—. *Median Hourly Earnings, All Employees (Excluding Apprentices) By Employment Contract* [earn_ses_pub2t]. Brussels: EUROSTAT.

—. *Metadata, EUROSTAT Quality Profile, Tax Rate on Low Wage Earners by Marginal Effective Tax Rates on Employment Incomes.* Brussels: EUROSTAT. http://Epp.EUROSTAT.Ec.Europa.Eu/Statistics_Explained/Index.Php/Wages_And_Labour_Costshttp://epp.EUROSTAT.ec.europa.eu/statistics_explained/index.php/Glossary:Tax_wedge (accessed 13 June 2013).

—. *Metadata: Net Earnings and Tax Rates,* Reference Metadata in Euro SDMX Metadata Structure (ESMS). Brussels: EUROSTAT.

—. *Metadata: Net Earnings and Tax Rates,* Reference Metadata in Euro SDMX Metadata Structure (ESMS). Brussels: EUROSTAT.

—. *Monthly Minimum Wage as a Proportion of Average Monthly Earnings* (%)—NACE Rev. 2 (from 2008 onwards). Brussels: EUROSTAT.

—. *Monthly Minimum Wages—Bi-Annual Data* [earn_mw_cur]. Brussels: EUROSTAT. http://www.mmuncii.ro/nou/images/Documente/Legislatie/HG23-2013.pdf (accessed 13 June 2013).

—. *Part-time Employment as Percentage of the Total Employment, by Sex and Age* (%) [lfsa_eppga]. Brussels: EUROSTAT.

—. *Social Security and Other Labour Costs Paid by Employer - % of Total Labour Costs* [tps00114]. Brussels: EUROSTAT.

—. *Structure of Labour Costs* (%)—NACE Rev. 2 [lc_an_struc_r2] Business Economy. Brussels: EUROSTAT.

—. *Tax Rate on Low Wage Earners—Low Wage Trap* [earn_nt_lowwtrp]. Brussels: EUROSTAT.

—. *Tax Rate on Low Wage Earners—Unemployment Trap* [earn_nt_unemtrp]. Brussels: EUROSTAT.

—. *Temporary Employees As Percentage Of The Total Number Of Employees*, by Sex And Age (%) [lfsa_etpga]. Brussels: EUROSTAT.

—. *Temporary Employees as Percentage of the Total Number of Employees for a Given Sex and Age Group* (%). Brussels: EUROSTAT.

—. *Unit Labour Cost* - Annual Data [nama_aux_ulc]. Brussels: EUROSTAT.

Fallon, P. R., and R. E. B. Lucas. 2002. "The Impact of Financial Crises on Labour Markets, Household Incomes and Poverty: A Review of Evidence," *The World Bank Research Observer* 17, No. 1:21-45.

Havlik, P. 2005. "Unit Labour Costs in the new EU Member States," Statistika 3: 288.

ILO. 2011. *ILO Global Wage Report 2010/2011*. Geneva: ILO, 65.

—. 2013. *Global Wage Report 2012/13, Wages and Equitable Growth*. Geneva: ILO, 12.

INS, TEMPO, AMIGO. *Employment by Age Group, by Status in Employment and by Urban/Rural Area.*

Klau, F. and A. Mittelstadt. *Labour Market Flexibility* http://www.oecd.org/eco/growth/35558438.pdf (Brussels: European Commission).

Lincaru C., V. Ciucă, et.al. 2011. *Studiu: Flexibilitatea pieţei muncii din România, descrisă din perspectiva fluxurilor de lucrători la nivel naţional şi în context european: dinamica pieţei muncii şi mobilitatea lucrătorilor*—pg.110, Investeşte în oameni! FONDUL Social European Programul Operaţional Sectorial pentru Dezvoltarea Resurselor Umane 2007—2013 Axa prioritară: 3 Domeniul major de intervenţie: 3.2 Proiect cofinanţat din Fondul Social European prin Programul Operaţional Sectorial Dezvoltarea Resurselor Umane 2007—2013Titlul proiectului: "Răspunsul pieţei muncii româneşti la criză: creşterea flexibilităţii şi adaptabilităţii întreprinderilor şi consolidarea securităţii lucrătorilor" Cod contract: POSDRU/63/3.2/S/41637.

Lincaru, C., V. Ciucă, and S. Pîrciog. 2011. *Alternative method of Gross worker flows measurement- Study case Romania*, Poster Session IV, EALE Conference 22-24 September 2011, Paphos, Cypru, http://www.eale.nl/Conference2011/Programme.htm.

Luminita, C. 2009. *Romania*: *Self-employed Workers*. Institute of National Economy, Romanian Academy, http://www.eurofound.europa.eu/comparative/tn0801018s/ro0801019q.htm.

Şerban, M., and A. Toth. 2007. *Piaţa forţei de muncă şi imigraţia*. Fundaţia Soros, România, 17.

OECD. 2009. "How Do Industry, Firm and Worker Characteristics Shape Job and Worker Flows?" in *Employment Outlook: Tackling the Jobs Crisis*, *Chapter 2*, 121.

—. 2010. "Institutional and Policy Determinants of labour Market Flows," in *Employment Outlook: Moving Beyond the Job Crisis*, *Chapter 3*, 167.

Voinea, L., L. Simionescu, N. Mardari, V. Voineagu,V. Duma, P. Jifcu, L. Sinigaglia, N. Hrehorciuc-Caragea, S. Pisică. 2010. *Mobilitatea forţei de muncă şi aspecte privind incluziunea socială*, Biroul pentru Observarea pieţei muncii şi a calităţii locurilor de muncă, Blocul Naţional Sindical, Proiect cofinanțat din fondul Social european prin

Programul Operaţional Sectorial Dezvoltarea Resurselor Umane 2007-2013, 26.

Voineagu, V. *Îmbătrânirea demografică a populaţiei României - o problema!* http://www.amosnews.ro/2011/Vergil_Voineagu_Imbatranirea_demografica_a_populatiei_Romaniei_o_problema_-29-66198.html (accessed 13 June 2013).

PROJECTIONS OF LABOUR DEMAND FOR UNIVERSITY GRADUATES IN ROMANIA

SPERANTA PIRCIOG, EVA MILITARU
AND MONICA MAER-MATEI

1. Introduction

The projected demand for labour is an important component when it comes to policies concerning the educational and training system; anticipating labour demand by occupation serves as a tool for the planning of the academic courses. Consequently, establishing input-output models to predict labour force demand becomes pivotal.

Among the foregoing models, factors such as the enrolment rates are determinants of economic growth. Since the existing lag between the two processes must be considered, the influence of variables shall be provided by the previous enrolment figures and not the current ones. The models employed along the way for estimating the future labour force demand and implicitly for labour force planning make use of employment figures on the levels of economic sectors, occupations and training. These models require following the stages[1] outlined below:

1. Estimating the future level as well as the growth rate for the total economic output of the analysed country. The reasoning behind this stage is that in an economy with accentuated economic growth rates, there will be a more prominent need for qualified labour force, rather than in slow developing economies.

2. Establishing the structure of the previously estimated output considering the economic sector. This structure will constitute a key element for estimating the requirements of the labour market which allow obtaining such outputs.

---

[1] Spalletti, S. 2008. "The History of Manpower Forecasting in Modelling Labour Market," Working paper No. 18, University of Macerata.

3. The demand for labour estimated in the second stage shall be transposed in terms of educational requirements, on the assumption that each occupation or profession corresponds to a certain level of training.

4. The projected demand for individuals with a certain level of training is compared to the actual roster of those who meet the same educational requirements and—based on this difference—one might decide whether an increase or a reduction in the education system outputs is necessary.

The difficulty of this approach mainly consists in obtaining long-term projections of the initial variables, in consideration that compiling a human resources development plan requires a prediction horizon of at least 10 years. This claim is primarily supported by the fact that it takes a considerable period to train qualified graduates. Depending on the method used for the projections,[2] the following approaches were used for planning labour force and education:

1. Collecting information from employers regarding the labour force requirements for the following time periods. Combining the answers conveys projections of the number of jobs available according to professions/occupations and training levels.

2. Projecting the structure of qualified labour force in the total occupation, based on the demographic information and certain hypotheses related to the structure of the national economic activity singled out by economic sector. In order to implement such a method, it is necessary to analyse the prior evolution of labour force use.

3. Considering that an approach which also allows comparisons between countries originates from the hypothesis that different countries can follow the same trajectory when referring to structure according to the professions and training levels of the labour force. It is thus considered that the labour force prognosis for one particular country can be obtained by analysing time series which characterize countries with superior development level.

4. Starting from the objectives related to economic growth, projections are compiled for the output related to the national economic activities. In the following stage of this approach, certain hypotheses are imposed, referring

[2] Spalletti, S. 2008. "The History of Manpower Forecasting in Modelling Labour Market," Working paper No. 18, University of Macerata.

to productivity, which shall lead to the estimation of total employment and also of employment according to economic activities. The following steps are taken as part of such an approach, with the end purpose of projecting the demand for the labour force:

a) Obtaining certain projections for the Gross Domestic Product (GDP);

b) Estimating the future structure of the economy, in the form of GDP structure by economic sector;

c) Estimating labour productivity according by economic sector;

d) Estimating the labour force structure according to occupations/ professions within each economic sector;

e) Estimating the structure of employed population according to training levels, and of each occupation/profession within a certain activity sector.

5. By means of an econometric approach, identifying the dependency between the requirements of the labour market and the other economic processes. Thus, the impact of certain factors which are significant for the employment levels is investigated. The final output of these models consists in obtaining estimates for the employment levels according to the economic sectors. Such a model was compiled by Tinbergen and Correa, whose linear equations evidenced the dependencies between the number of higher education graduates or high school graduates and economic growth rates. The final objective was to determine the structure of the education system which would contribute to a certain economic growth rate.

The ideas set forth by these approaches can also be found in the model developed for Finland's economy (2009). This model is based on the analysis of the changes occurred in the structure of the labour force according to occupations/professions as a result of modifying the employment structure by occupation, as well as resulting from certain variations in the value of total employment. Anticipating the occupational structure entailed taking three steps:

Step 1. Predicting the employment trend according to national economic activities;

Step 2. Evaluating the expected modification in an occupational group from each activity;

Step 3. Cumulating the numbers related to a certain occupation group from each activity.

This paper is structured as follows: in the next section, we describe the methodological framework, while the third section details the main results. Some concluding remarks will be placed at the end of the work.

2. Methodology

This paper attempts to make projections regarding the labour force demand in the occupational structure in Romania, considering that, according to the analysis carried out in previous research during the past 10 years, significant changes have taken place in the evolution of the employed population with higher education in occupational terms, an aspect which leads to assume that the forthcoming years shall also be characterized by changes in the evolution of the demand for those professions which require higher education.

The focus of this research has been on professionals belonging to the occupational group *2—Professionals,* for whom, according to the 2012 Classification of Professions in Romania (ISCO 08), higher education is explicitly required, and who constitute approximately 70% of the total employed persons with higher education in Romania (between 2000—2010). The remaining 30% of the employed population with higher education are occupied in such professions as: *1- legislators, senior officials and managers*, which do not necessarily require higher education, or professions which do not require higher education at all. The occupational group *2—Professionals* includes the following sub-major groups: *21—Science and engineering professionals, 22—Health professionals, 23—Teaching professionals, 24—Business and administration professionals, 25—Information and communication technology professionals* and *26—Legal, social and cultural professionals*, also divided into minor groups (three digits).

The projection of the labour demand with higher education by minor groups of profession and occupation has been reckoned considering three stages:

a) The initial projection of the employed population with higher education according to minor groups;

b) The projection of the employed population with higher education according to minor groups and economic activities (intersection) based on a); and

c) The projection of the potential demand for labour force with higher education according to minor groups based on the evolution of the structure related to the employed population by minor group and economic activities (b) and adjustments with the prognoses related to the demand for labour force with higher education according to economic activities.

Further on, we will detail the forecasting methodology, justifying our selection of methods and econometric techniques. The three modules unreel logically in the presented order of succession, under the control of an adjustment mechanism which cross-references the employed population with higher education and the demand for labour force with higher education by means of the predictions regarding the evolution of economic activities in the prospects for 2020. In this context, it is necessary to make a distinction between the *projection of employed population* and the *projection of potential demand for labour force*, the latter estimating a requirement of employed population according to the scenarios related to economic development. The projection of employed population takes into account the nominal and structural evolution trends of the employed population according to professions and economic activities.

Therefore, Module 1 covers the projection of employed population according to minor groups (3 digits). As part of this module, an initial iteration is performed in view of estimating the employed population in 2020, considering the history of the evolution of the employed population with higher education in occupational group 2.

The econometric method of *exponential smoothing* was used, a highly useful method when analysing small series of data in a large prognosis horizon (in this case, 11 historical dates and 10 years of prognosis). It is not only a simple estimation of the trend, but an adaptive projection method, because past observations gain a more reduced weight as time elapses, thus making the more recent observations those with the most important weight within the projection process.

This method was selected because it was considered difficult to relate the variable of employed population in a certain profession to other explicative variables. Unlike regression equations with fixed coefficients, the *exponential smoothing* method allows for coefficients to be continuously adjusted based on the past projection error. Out of the various smoothing methods, the *Holt-Winters* and *Double smoothing* ones were utilized because it was ascertained that the analysed series displayed a linear trend, the difference between the two methods being provided by the number of parameters used in the estimation (i.e. two parameters). The general form of the recursive equation for *Double smoothing* is:

$$S_t = \alpha y_t + (1-\alpha)S_{t-1} \quad (1)$$

$$D_t = \alpha S_t + (1-\alpha)D_{t-1} \quad (2)$$

where S is the series smoothed by means of the *Single smoothing* method, and D is the series smoothed by means of *Double smoothing*, if the parameter assumes values ranging between 0 and 1.

The resulting projections are calculated as follows:

$$\hat{y}_{T+k} = \left(2 + \frac{\alpha k}{1-\alpha}\right) S_T - \left(1 + \frac{\alpha k}{1-\alpha}\right) D_T = \left(2S_T - D_T + \frac{\alpha}{1-\alpha}(S_T - D_T)k\right) \quad (3)$$

In the case of the *Holt-Winters method*, the smoothed series is provided by:

$$\hat{y}_{t+k} = a + bk \quad (4)$$

where a and b are the permanent component, respectively the trend component, defined by the following recursive formulas:

$$a(t) = \alpha y_t + (1-\alpha)\big(a(t-1) + b(t-1)\big) \quad (5)$$

$$b(t) = \beta\big(a(t) - a(t-1)\big) + 1 - \beta b(t-1) \quad (6)$$

and α and β are parameters.

The resulting projections are calculated as follows:

$$\hat{y}_{T+k} = a(T) + b(T)k \quad (7)$$

Subsequently, as part of Module 2, an estimate of the employed population is performed, at the intersection between profession (Classification of Professions in Romania, minor groups, 3 digits) and economic activity (Classification of National Economic Activities Rev.2, 2 digits). For every “cell” (job) thus defined by profession and economic activity, we built an equation to estimate the evolution of the employed population in the respective profession and economic activity. We started from the same general form of the regression equation for each cell, and then eliminated certain variables or changed the form of the equation depending on the significance of the parameters. Therefore, the initial equation is the following:

$$(\log(oc_{ij}))_t = \alpha + \beta d\left(\log(oc_{ij})_{t-1}\right) + \delta d\left(\log(oc_{total,j})_t\right) + \theta d\left(\log(oc_{total,j})_{t-1}\right) + \sigma\left(\log(oc_{ij})_{t-1} - \log(oc_{total,j})_{t-1}\right) + \varepsilon_t \qquad (8)$$

Where oc_{ij} is the population employed in economic activity i and profession j *and* $oc_{total,j}$ is the population employed in profession j, in all economic activities.

Because, while analysing the data series, we ascertained that, for the most part, these were not stationary, the logarithm model was used in the majority of cases, with differences of order 1 producing other logarithm models.

As previously mentioned, valid equations were established from a statistical standpoint for every economic activity/relevant profession cell (360 equations). For 217 of the 360 equations it was necessary to perform interpolations of data series, because there were some cells with 0 values, which affected the quality of the estimates. For 203 intersections, the data series did not allow the estimation of a significant equation, mainly because of the values equal to 0 from the data series. This affects the projection values, in the sense that approximately 5% of the volume of historical data could not be taken into consideration while compiling the projections, hence the gap between the values of 2010 (last data of the series) and 2011 (first projection value).

Module 3 constitutes, in fact, the stage of adjusting the projections to the evolutions of economic activities, by relating the structures obtained in Module 2 to the predictions regarding the demand for labour force with higher education according to economic activities. Due to the fact that for the projection of the labour force demand according to professions with higher education, only the professions included in occupational group 2 were analysed (*2- Professionals*), the projections of the demand for labour force with higher education according to economic activities shall be weighted with a vector representing the structure of employed population with higher education in group 2 in the total employed population with higher education. This vector shall relate to the data of 2010, based on the premise that there will be no major modifications in this structure, also confirmed by analysing the data from the time period ranging between 2000 and 2010.

3. Results

The forecasts of the demand for labour force with higher education for occupational group *2- Professionals* suggests that, between 2011 and 2020, there will be an increase in the volume of the demand for labour force for these professions, as exhibited in the chart below. The light bars indicate the projections adjusted for professions in which the estimate of the demand around year 2020 could not be performed due to inconsistencies in the time series. It is estimated that, between 2011 and 2020, an increase shall take place in the demand for labour force with higher education for the professions in group 2 by approximately 14.8%, which represents approximately 145,000 people. The distribution of the increases according to professional subgroups is fairly heterogeneous, as shall be shown later on.

Fig. 1-3. Labour Force Demand Projection for Occupational Group 2-Professionals, 2011-2020 (Persons).

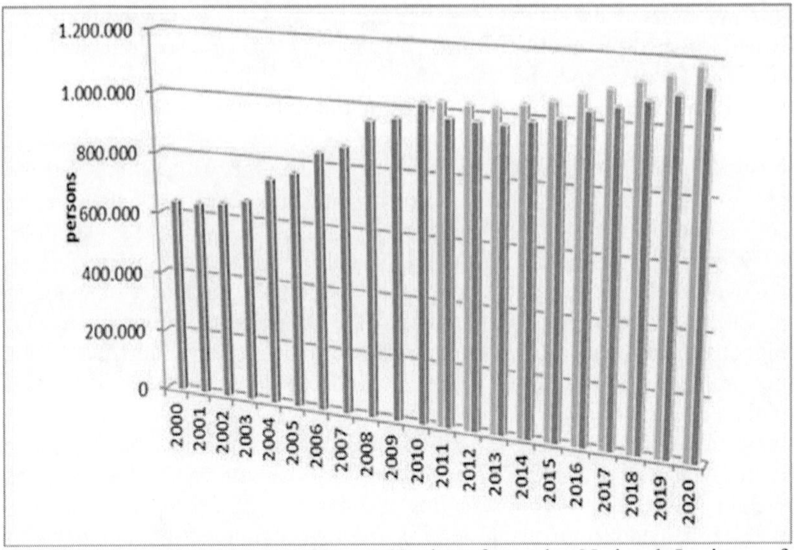

Source: Own calculation based on LFS data from the National Institute of Statistics, Romania.

As previously stated, the distribution of the modifications in the demand for labour force with a university degree displays notable differences among sub-major groups. Therefore, as exhibited in the table below, the most important relative growth in demand is registered for sub-major group *25—Information and communication technology professionals* (39.7%), this being the category for which the demand shows the most significant increases during the past 10 years. Growth in the labour demand are also reported for *24—Business and administration professionals* and *26—Legal, social and cultural professionals*, albeit at slower paces (27% and 20.2%, respectively). We must note that in the latter two professional groups, the increase in demand between 2000 and 2010 was significant, approximately 3 times as high. We also observe a rise in demand for the *21—Science and engineering professionals*, by approximately 12.8%, which in nominal terms represents approximately 34 thousand people. The demand for specialists in the field of healthcare continues to grow, as increases by 17% are estimated throughout the projection horizon. The only professional sub-major category for which decreases are projected in the demand for labour force is that of *23—Teaching professionals*. The demand in this case drops by 0.3% between 2011 and 2020, also due to a decrease in the numbers of pre-school and school children.

Table 1-5. Labour Force Demand for Professionals, changes (persons, %).

	Changes (persons)		Changes (%)
	2000-2010	2011-2020	%
21 - Science and engineering professionals	44829	34357	12,8
22 - Health professionals	37197	17060	17,0
23 - Teaching professionals	38626	-626	-0,3
24 - Business and administration professionals	61358	20891	27,0
25 - Information and communication technology professionals	28941	14933	39,7
26 - Legal, social and cultural professionals	168099	58447	20,2
All Professionals	379050	145062	14,8

Source: Own calculation based on LFS data from the National Institute of Statistics, Romania.

The structural changes of the labour force demand throughout the projection horizon are not particularly significant. *Legal, social and cultural professionals* are likely to continue to hold the largest ratio, with a slight increase from 29.6% in 2010 to 30.8% in 2020. The share of teaching professionals decreases from 20.2% in 2010 to 18.5% in 2020 while the share of *Information and communication technology professionals* reaches the highest values in structural terms, from 3.6 in 2010 to 4.7% in 2020.

Fig. 1-4. Changes in the Structure of the Labour Force Demand for Higher Education (%).

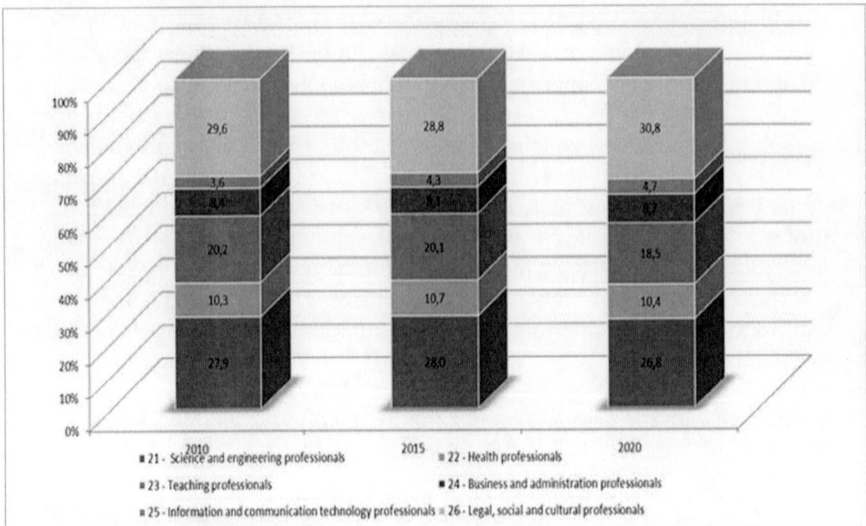

Source: Own calculation based on LFS data from the National Institute of Statistics, Romania.

In the following, we shall detail the main predicted changes in the labour force demand for university graduates by occupations in minor groups.

3.1. Science and Engineering Professionals

As mentioned above, the demand for *science and engineering professionals* will increase between 2011 and 2020 by approximately 13%, which amounts to approximately 34 thousand people. The most relevant rise in demand is observed for *engineers*, whereas a slight decrease in the demand for labour force is observed in the case of *life science professionals.* Stable evolutions, slightly ascending, are observed in the case of the labour force demand for *mathematicians, actuaries and statisticians*.

Fig. 1-5. Science and Engineering Professionals, Past and Projected Changes in Employment (Persons).

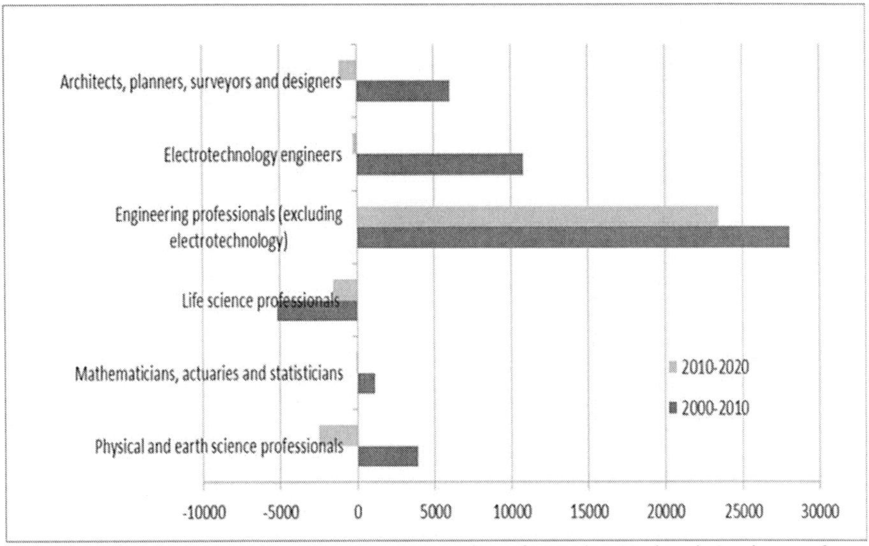

Source: Own calculation based on LFS data from the National Institute of Statistics, Romania.

The past evolution of the number of *life science professionals* was oscillating between 2000 and 2010, with a significant decrease in the first two years analysed. The performed projections indicate a continual decrease in the number of people holding this profession. The number of *engineers* (with the exception of those involved in electro-technology) displayed an ascending trend between 2000 and 2010, which is maintained in the following years, according to projections.

With regard to the economic activities in which *engineers* conduct their tasks, the same rising trend is observed. The main activity framework in which engineers (with the exception of those involved in electro-technology) operate is the construction of buildings, and for this activity, the projection is highly optimistic, given the fact that it reports an increase until 2020 by approximately 35% (as opposed to the value registered in 2010).

3.2. Health Professionals

Labour demand for *health professionals* is experiencing an upward trend; in the case of Romania, we can still talk of a labour shortage regarding health professionals in recent years. As a consequence of low wages and often inadequate working conditions or lack of resources for the provision of adequate health services, well trained Romanian medical staff was forced to migrate. For instance in 2004, medical brain drain from Romania accounted for 3,913 professionals, that is 8.7% of the physicians trained in the country.[3] Instead, during recent years and especially after Romania's accession to the European Union, brain drain has intensified.

Fig. 1-6. Health professionals, Past and Projected Changes in Employment (Persons).

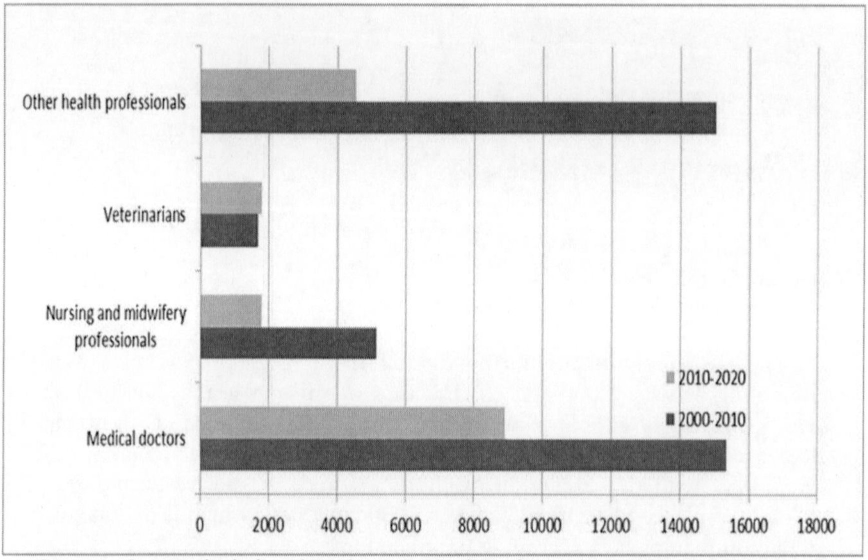

Source: Own calculation based on LFS data from the National Institute of Statistics, Romania.

Thus, the Romanian Physicians Organization (*Colegiul Medicilor din Romania*) reports that in 2010 and 2011 a total of 5,620 physicians

[3] Bhargava, A., F. Docquier , and Y. Moullan. 2010. *Modeling the Effect of Physician Emigration on Human Development.* http://perso.uclouvain.be/frederic.docquier/oxlight.htm (accessed 20 June 2013).

requested professional certificates in order to apply for a job overseas, and since 2007, 10,000 Romanian medical practitioners migrated for work, while the number of employed physicians in Romania reaches approximately 52,000 people. Bearing in mind these evolutions and the fact that the number of physicians to 1,000 inhabitants is still low in Romania, we expect labour demand for health professionals to increase for the next decade. The most significant growth seems to be in the case of *medical doctors*, while for *nursing, midwifery professionals* and *veterinarians* such increase is slighter. On the whole, the growth forecast for labour demand for health professionals reaches 17%, approximately 17 thousand persons between 2011 and 2020.

3.3. Teaching Professionals

The forecasts for labour demand for *teaching professionals* display a very slight decreasing tendency, especially in the case of *university and higher education teachers* and *primary school and early childhood teachers*. We note slow demand increases for *secondary and vocational education teachers*.

Fig. 1-7. Teaching Professionals, Past and Projected Changes in Employment (Persons).

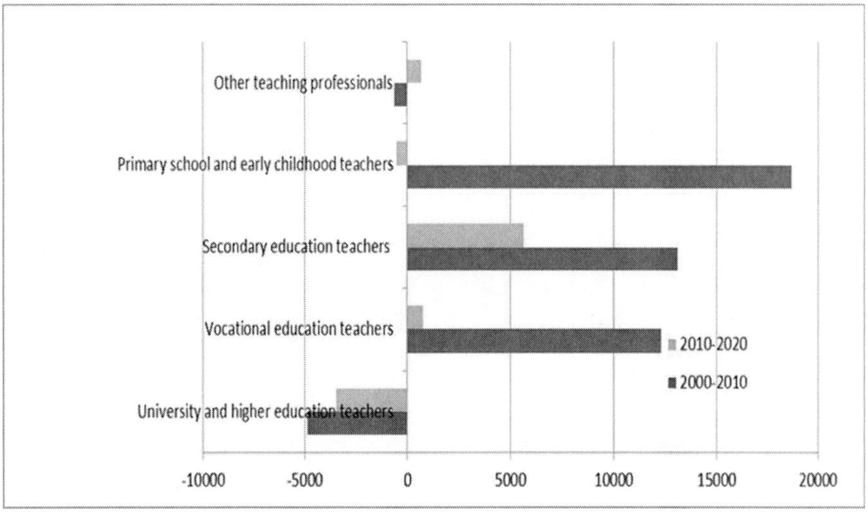

Source: Own calculation based on LFS data from the National Institute of Statistics, Romania.

Employment for *university and higher education teachers* has been slightly decreasing during the last decade, and is likely to be following this trend up to 2020. The harsh austerity measures adopted by the Romanian government through the economic crisis resulted in a significant decrease of university and higher education teachers during 2008 to 2010.

The employment evolutions for this category of teaching professionals are mainly explained by the employment variation of university and higher education professors in the educational sector, as the research sector barely employs university and higher education professionals.

For *secondary school teachers*, the employment evolutions were characterized by ups and downs during 2003-2009, while forecasts show a moderate recovery for 2020.

Following the contraction of preschool aged children cohorts during recent years in Romania, the demand for *primary and early childhood teachers* seems to be reducing for the next decade.

3.4. Business and Administration Professionals

The economic developments in Romania during the last two decades with pre-crisis significant economic growth rate have driven the upward evolution of *business and administrative professionals* in 2000 and 2010.

This growth pattern seems to have been slowed down by the economic crisis, but still, the tendency for 2020 is an increase of labour demand for business and administration professionals, mainly for *finance professionals*. Demand is growing for *administration professionals* as well, but at a slower pace as approaching 2020.

Forecast results show that labour demand for *business and administration professionals* is growing by 27% between 2011 and 2020, accounting for approximately 20 thousand people.

Fig. 1-8. Business and Administration Professionals, Past and Projected Changes in Employment (persons).

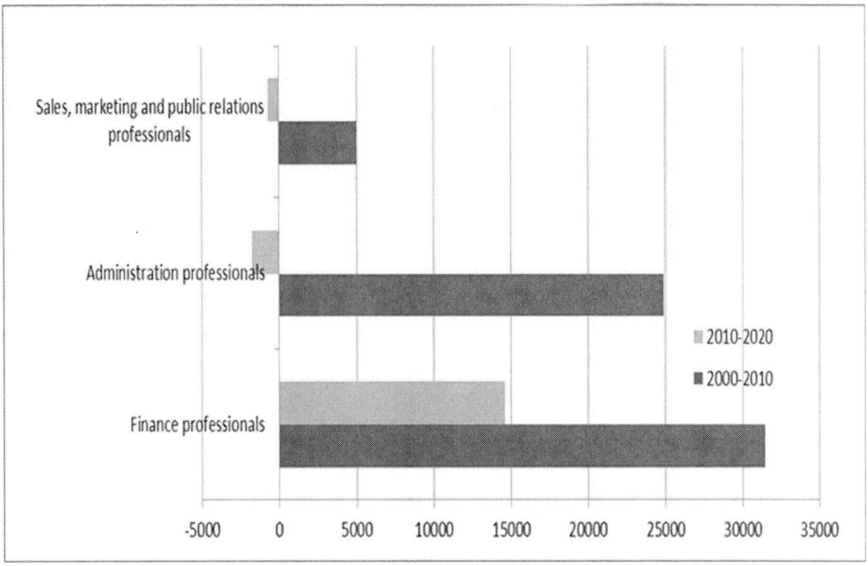

Source: Own calculation based on LFS data from the National Institute of Statistics, Romania.

3.5. Information and Communication Technology (ICT) Professionals

The occupations that display the highest growth rates among higher education employees are those in the group of ICT technology professionals. Here, a relative increase by almost 40% of the number of persons employed has been estimated.

Fig. 1-9. ICT Professionals, Past and Projected Changes in Employment (Persons).

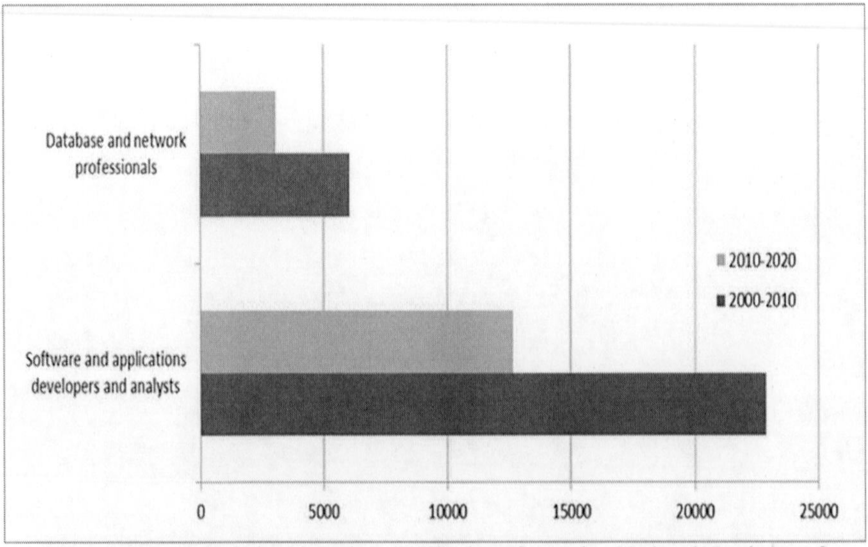

Source: Own calculation based on LFS data from the National Institute of Statistics, Romania.

The expansion of labour demand for *Information and Communication Technology professionals* can be seen in the structural changes of employment trends for professionals as well. Yet the share of *Information and Communication Technology professionals* among the entire group of professionals is below 5%, that is the most positive evolution in the past and the most likely one for the next decade as well. Thus, if those employed as *Information and Communication Technology professionals* made up 3.6% of total professionals in 2010, we estimate an increased share of 4.7% in 2020. However, we note that the demand increase for *Information and Communication Technology professionals* is growing at a slower pace after 2011 as compared to the previous decade (2000-2010).

Both the two minor groups included in the sub-major group *Information and Communication Technology professionals,* namely *Software and applications developers and analysts* and *database and network professionals,* experience growth in labour demand, but this is mostly relevant for the former. As a result of the rapid development of the local IT sector, and with Romania being one of the fastest-growing IT markets in Central and Eastern Europe, the Romanian labour market is now absorbing approximately 4.7 times more IT specialists than it did in 2000.

This is mainly due to IT outsourcing activities, as most important IT global corporations are developing their R&D and software production activities in Romania. They have been greatly encouraged by national legislation, especially Tax Law.

Therefore, the demand for *software and applications developers and analysts* has been growing constantly during the last decade, and our estimates indicate that this upward trend will be maintained in the future.

It also seems that the demand for this profession has not been affected by the latest economic downturn. As for the *database and network professionals,* though the labour demand evolutions have not been linear, the trend still reports an upward slope.

It is also worth noting that between 2009 and 2011 employment has slightly decreased for this profession; however, forecasts exhibit a slowly increasing trend until 2020.

3.6. Legal, Social and Cultural Professionals

Mainly following the pronounced growth rate of labour demand for *legal, social and cultural professionals* during the last decade, 2020 forecasts report the same evolutions, though at a slower pace. Therefore, we expect a relative growth by 20% of the demand for legal, social and cultural practitioners in the next decade, meaning somewhere in the region of 58 thousand people. The most important shares concern *social and religious professionals* and *legal professionals*, because estimates show continual demand growth for both categories.

Fig. 1-10. Legal, Social and Cultural Professionals, Past and Projected Changes in Employment (Persons).

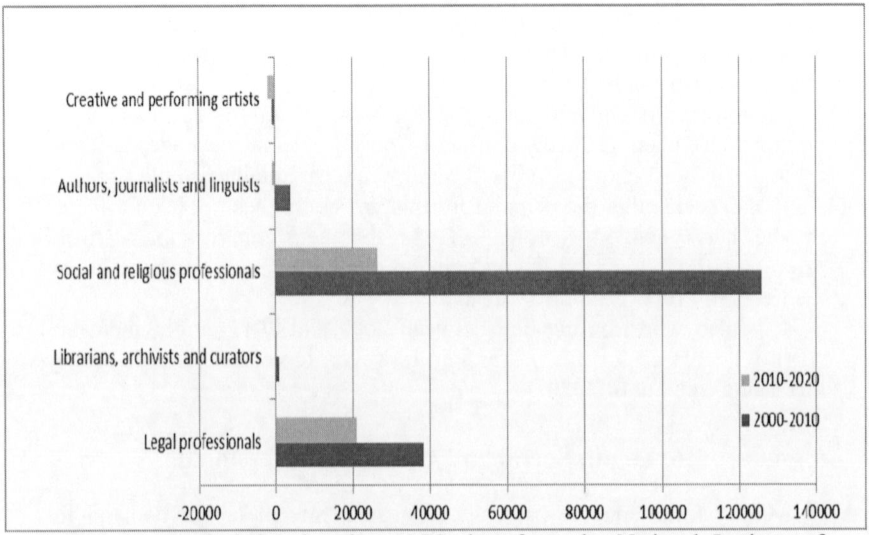

Source: Own calculation based on LFS data from the National Institute of Statistics, Romania.

4. Conclusions

The projection of labour demand plays an important role for policymakers related to the education and training system, and employment policies. Therefore, we investigated past and future employment trends for highly educated professionals in Romania, as we notice overall and structural changes in the employment of highly educated persons during the last decade that presumably will continue in the future. Driven by the economic developments of the last decade, labour demand for professionals has been increasing at a rapid pace.

We employed forecasting techniques in order to cast light on the future evolution of employment for highly educated professionals and the results suggest that the employment trends from the past are going to be continued during the next decade, though at a slower growth rate. We noticed structural changes and non-uniform evolutions among different categories of professionals. While there is still room for the employment of information and technology professionals, the demand for teaching professionals seems to decrease, though slowly. Yet we estimate a moderate increase in the demand of health professionals and science and engineering professionals.

However, employment trends for higher education graduates do not seem to change substantially, at least during the next decade. In the years ahead, our focus should be on labour market imbalances and skills mismatches which affect especially disadvantaged groups such as young people, women, people with disabilities, elderly, etc., even those holding a university degree. It becomes clear that productivity, innovation and competitiveness can be achieved only by using adequate and well trained workforce, so Romania shall concentrate its resources on stimulating employer demand for labour through adequate fiscal policies and enhance knowledge, skills and competence of the labour force through educational and training policies, and sound labour market policies.

References

Adams, P., J. Dixon, J. Giesecke, M. Horridge. 2010. *MONASH Multi Regional Forecasting Model: a Dynamic Multi- Regional Model of the Australian Economy*. Center of Policy Studies: Monash University.

Bhargava, A., F. Docquier, and Y. Moullan. 2010. *Modeling the Effect of Physician Emigration on Human Development,* http://perso.uclouvain.be/frederic.docquier/oxlight.htm (accessed 20 June 2013).

Brinkman, P., C. McIntyre. 1997. "Methods and Techniques of Enrolment Forecasting," *New Directions for Institutional Research* 93, Jossey-Bass Publishers.

Correa, H., J. Tinbergen. 1962. "Quantitative Adaption of Education to Accelerated Growth," *International Review for Social Sciences* 15:776-86.

Dobrescu, E. 2006. *Macromodels of Romanian Market Economy*. Bucharest: Editura Economică.

Edwards D., P. Weldon. 2011. *Student Demand Projections Supporting Analysis: Gippsland Tertiary Education Plan*. Australian Council for Educational Research.

Hanhijoki, I., J. Katajisto, M. Kimari, and H. Savioja. 2008. "Higher Education in 2030," Demographics 1. Paris: OECD.

—. 2008. "Higher Education Enrolment Forecasting: An Analysis Containing Recommendations for Process Improvements," Office for Economic and Demographic Research.

—. 2009. *Education, Training and Demand for Labour in Finland by 2020*. Finnish National Board of Education, Edita Prima Oy.

Harbison, F., C. A. Myers. 1965. *Manpower and Education: Country Studies in Economic Development*. New York: McGraw-Hill.

Korka, M., ed. 2009. *Educaţie de calitate, pentru piaţa muncii*. Bucharest: Editura Universitară.

Meagher, G. A, P. D. Adams, and J. M. Horridge. 2000. *Applied General Equilibrium Modelling and Labour Market Forecasting.* Centre of Policy Studies: Monash University.

Spalletti, S. 2008. "The History of Manpower Forecasting in Modelling Labour Market," Working paper No. 18, University of Macerata.

CHAPTER TWO:

SCHOOL-TO-WORK TRANSITION

THE TRANSITION FROM SCHOOL TO WORK: SOME RECENT CHALLENGES

CRISTINA LINCARU AND DRAGA ATANASIU

1. Introduction

The impact of the financial crisis on Romania's economy is still visible, for sluggish recovery impedes growth. In this sense, some recent developments on the demand side concerning the functioning of the labour market—particularly remuneration and employment —can be seen in the transition between jobs.

Against this background, the overall picture of the population aged 18-24 years can be drawn, taking into account both educational attainments and employment grade.

Many intermediary stages exist between exiting and entering the labour market, which are described as exceptional or undesirable situations. Those who are not in employment, education or training—NEETs—are an egregious example in this connection. The status of NEET for those in the 15-24 age group can be investigated considering the disjunctive character of their labour market participation, being either unemployed or inactive. The transition from school to work obtains when one leaves formal education and accesses employment for the first time.

The school-to-work transition process is assessed considering the median age for exiting formal education and the average time between leaving school and starting the first job, also counting towards the educational attainments. Our discussion will focus on the transition of NEETs aged 15 to 34 years old from inactivity or unemployment to activity and employment.

2. The Demand Side: Some Recent Developments

Romania reported one of the lowest levels of job vacancy growth in EU during the Q1 2008 and Q3 2011, together with the Czech Republic and Latvia.

> These developments are rooted firstly in the relatively poor economic performance in these countries which typically affects private sector employment in the short term and secondly in the impact of austerity measures on public sector employment after some delay.[1]

The stock of job vacancies[2] in 2011 was equal to 26 thousand, decreasing by 66 thousand in 2008 (92.2 thousand). The normalized value of the Index Stock of Job Vacancies (JVS) for Romania was 27 in Q1 2008 and 100 in Q1 2011, indicating a loss of 63 positions and a significant difference with the average loss for the EU15 during the same period (20 positions).[3] A slowdown in the labour market dynamics was evidenced by the 71.6pp decrease of the stock of job vacancies between 2008 and 2011.

2.1. A Moderate Decrease Reported in terms of Job Vacancy Rates

Romania's sluggish recovery and unmet demand are aspects that translate into less job openings and a potential mismatch between supply and demand. In Quarter 1- Q1 and Q4[4] of 2012, the job vacancy rate[5] in Romania was 0.6%—remaining as such for the whole year—that is 3 times lower than the EU27 average, which was equal 1.5% in Q1 and 1.6 in Q4 2012, respectively.

The recent evolution in unmatched demand in 2011 and 2012, which is calculated in annual variations, was the same. In figures, this means that the job vacancies rate[6] was 0.6%, 3 times lower than the job vacancies rate

---

[1] European Commission. *European Vacancy and Recruitment Report 2012.* European Commission Directorate-General for Employment, Social Affairs and Inclusion Unit C.4: Employment Services. Brussels: European Commission, 21.

[2] Job Vacancy Statistics by Occupation and NUTS 2 Regions, Annual Data, NACE Rev. 2 (from 2008 onwards) [jvs_a_NACE2].

[3] European Commission. *European Vacancy and Recruitment Report 2012.* European Commission Directorate-General for Employment, Social Affairs and Inclusion Unit C.4: Employment Services. Brussels: European Commission, 115.

[4] http://epp.EUROSTAT.ec.europa.eu/statistics_explained/index.php/Job_vacancy_statistics (accessed 20 December 2013).

[5] EUROSTAT Metadata: The job Vacancy Rate (JVR) measures the percentage of total posts that are vacant, according to the definition of job vacancy above, as follows: JVR = Number of Job Vacancies / (Number of Occupied Posts + Number of Job Vacancies) * 100.

[6] EUROSTAT. *Job Vacancy Statistics by Occupation and NUTS 2 Regions, Annual Data, NACE Rev. 2 (from 2008 onwards)* [jvs_a_nace2],

in 2008 (1.9%). The annual change in the job vacancy rate was equal to 0% in 2010/2011, increasing from (-1%) in 2008/2009.

2.2. Romania Experienced a Contraction in Demand

The number of job vacancies per 1000 unemployed (the indicator for a bottleneck) in 2008[7] was 160/1000 unemployed persons, decreasing by almost 4.5 times in 2011—35.8 job vacancies/1000 unemployed persons – thus indicating a contraction phase.

> […] the group of countries that registered a short-term decline in job vacancies were mostly newer Member States […] these countries continue to be seriously affected by the economic downturn in terms of recruitment demand and this is partly due to their relatively important manufacturing sectors. Short-term falls in vacancies between the second quarters of 2012 and 2011 in Cyprus, Lithuania, Romania and Slovenia confirm continuation of the trend, to which can be added Spain, which also saw a sharp fall in job vacancies of one-third. In addition, in the second quarter of 2012, vacancies across this group of countries were -30% or less as compared to the second quarter of 2008, with Cyprus and Romania recording aggregate falls of over -70%.[8]

2.3. Public Employment Services (PES) Vacancies Inflows Decreasing in Romania

The inflow of job vacancies to PES experienced a decrease in Romania equal to more than 10% in the last 12 months from the second quarter of 2011. Significantly:

> The inflow of registered job vacancies depends not only on the demand for labour, but also on the extent to which employers notify their job vacancies to the PES […] the decrease in PES vacancies are more likely to reflect a general decline in recruitment demand, as evidenced by the total number of vacancies.[9]

---

http://epp.EUROSTAT.ec.europa.eu/tgm/table.do?tab=table&init=1&language=en &pcode=tps00172&plugin=1 (accessed 20 December 2013).

[7] EUROSTAT: une_nb_a; jvs_a_nace2). Brussels: EUROSTAT.

[8] European Vacancy Monitor. 2013. "Monitoring Labour Market Developments in Europe," DG Employment, Social Affairs and Inclusion of the European Commission, 8:4.

[9] European Vacancy Monitor. 2013. "Monitoring Labour Market Developments in Europe," DG Employment, Social Affairs and Inclusion of the European Commission, 8:5.

2.4. Hiring in Romania Reported Relatively Stable Short-term Growth

The EUROSTAT Labour Force Survey (LFS) states that:

> Job hirings refer to employees in a "reference week" that had started working for the employer at most three months earlier—this excludes contract renewals. For a person who started multiple jobs within the same quarter, only the last hire is counted. Statistical offices often define such persons as job-finders according to different national definitions. EUROSTAT uses the neutral term "time since job started". Job hirings reflect completed recruitment even if no formal vacancies had been posted.[10]

In addition

> […] Job-finders were employees at the moment of the survey employed for at most three months […] "Job-finder" data is used as an approximation for "filled vacancies".[11]

On the basis of such definitions, the number of hirings in the second quarter of 2012 was 134 thousand, the PES inflow job vacancies were 137 thousand, the stock of vacancies was equal to 24 thousand and the stock of unemployed persons amounted to 692 thousand.

The number of job-finders was 394 thousand in Q1 2007, decreasing to 106 thousand in Q1 2010 and slowly increasing to 133 thousand in Q1 2011 (132 thousand in Q3 2011). In Q1 2011, the Index number of job-finders (LFS) in Romania was 34, decreasing by 66 positions in the 1 to 100 scale in 2007, while the EU27 index number of job-finders was 84 in Q1 2011, decreasing by only 16 positions in the 1 to 100 scale in Q1 2007.[12] The job-finders rate[13] in Romania was 2.2% in Q1 2011,

---

[10] *Ibid.*, 7.

[11] European Commission. 2012. *European Vacancy and Recruitment Report 2012.* European Commission Directorate General for Employment, Social Affairs and Inclusion Unit C.4, Employment Services. Brussels: European Commission, 23.

[12] EUROSTAT. 2012. *Labour Force Survey (LFS), Data Extracts Provided by EUROSTAT.* Cited in European Commission. 2012. *European Vacancy and Recruitment Report 2012.* European Commission Directorate General for Employment, Social Affairs and Inclusion Unit C.4, Employment Services. Brussels: European Commission, 116.

[13] European Commission. 2012. *European Vacancy and Recruitment Report 2012.* European Commission Directorate General for Employment, Social Affairs and Inclusion Unit C.4, Employment Services. Brussels: European Commission, 118.

decreasing by 4.3pp from the 6.5% reported in 2007, pointing to an increase in the gap between Romania and the EU27 in Q1 2011 (4.4pp from -0.1pp in 2007).

As for the ratio of the unemployed to job hirings for the EU27, slightly over two people were unemployed for every person hired in the second quarter of 2012 (2:1), whereas in Romania this ratio rose to 5:1 in the same period, indicating relative high levels of competition in hiring.

Compared with the second quarter of 2008, the unemployed-job hirings ratio was significantly lower, with only 1.3 unemployed people for every person hired in the EU27 and 3.5 unemployed people for every person recruited in Romania.

In addition, the ratio of the number of unemployed to job-finders[14] (which is useful to identify potential bottleneck occupations) was 5.6 persons unemployed for every person hired in the Q1 2011 for Romania, increasing by 3.8 unemployed persons for every person hired per quarter from the Q1 2007, where the minimum level was reported (1.8).

As for the EU27, such ratio was 2.5:1 in the Q1 2011 and 1.6:1 in the Q1 2007. The gap between Romania and EU27 increased from 0.2 persons unemployed for every person hired in the Q1 2007 to 3.1 persons unemployed for every person hired in the Q1 2011.[15] In Romania, an increase was reported both in the ratio of the unemployed to the stock of job vacancies and in that of the unemployed to job-finders between Q2 2008 and Q2 2012.

> In eleven countries, for example in Greece, Ireland, Portugal, Romania, Slovakia and Spain, a high labour surplus continued in 2011. In those countries, the burden of unemployment is high with relatively few job opportunities- reflecting again the relatively low labour market developments in those countries identified earlier.[16]

---

[14] While being an indirect measure for labour demand, job-finder data has a further advantage: they include virtually all vacancies even so-called "hidden" vacancies, filled informally without any notification of the vacancy to the public, cited from EVRR 2012, 7, http://ec.europa.eu/social/main.jsp?catId=955&langId=en (accessed 13 June 2013).

[15] EUROSTAT. 2012. *Labour Force Survey (LFS), Data Extracts Provided by EUROSTAT.* Cited in European Commission. 2012. *European Vacancy and Recruitment Report 2012.* European Commission Directorate General for Employment, Social Affairs and Inclusion Unit C.4, Employment Services. Brussels: European Commission, 135.

[16] European Vacancy and Recruitment Report 2012. European Commission Directorate-General for Employment, Social Affairs and Inclusion Unit C.4-Employment Services, EURES Manuscript Completed in November 2012, 10.

3. Occupational Transitions by Employment Status: Some General Considerations

3.1. The Situation of the Population Aged 18-24 years by Educational Level and Employment Status

The transition from school to work is measured from the moment one leaves formal education to when one engages in his first job. A job-training combination (at least 1 hour per week) might take place in between. Yet there are exceptional or undesirable situations that might involve school leavers while in education or employment. Table 1 presents an overview of the population aged 18-24 years by educational levels and employment status in 2009, for both Romania and the EU27.

Table 2-1. Population Aged 18-24 by Educational Levels and Employment Status, 2009.

18 to 24-Year-Olds	Romania	EU27
Total Population (in Thousands)	2297.5	42543.7
Persons Not in Employment	61.4%	54.6%
Exclusively in Education	44.9%	38.5%
Below Tertiary Education (Up to ISCED4)	14%	13%
Tertiary Education (ISCD 5-6)	30.9%	14.5%
Non-Formal Education		1%
Combining Education and Employment (At Least One Hour a Week)	2.6%	16.5%
Other Contracts (Full Time)	2%	4.5%
Other Contracts (Part Time)	0.6%	4%
Temporary Contracts Covering a Period of Training	-	4%
Persons in Employment	31.1%	45%
Exclusively in Employment	28.5%	28.5%
Neither in Employment Nor in Education	16.5%	16.1%
Unemployed	8%	8.2%
Inactive	8.5%	7.9%

Source: http://epp.EUROSTAT.ec.europa.eu/statistics_explained/index.php?title=File:Population_aged_18-24,_by_educational_and_employment_status,_2009.png&filetimestamp=20111024084327.

In Romania, the pattern of distribution of the population aged 18-24 years old in 2009 indicates a propensity to exclusively engage in education (44.9%) which is higher than in the EU27 (38.5%). The employment status is less representative in Romania, where 31.1% of youth are in employment only and 2.6% are involved in employment and education, that is lower than the EU27 mean (13.9 for both status). Regarding NEETs aged 18-24 years, Romania and the EU27 seem to follow the same path.

The odds to become NEET in Romania were 16.5% (there is an 8% probability to become unemployed and an 8.5% probability to remain inactive) and 16.1% in the EU27 (with 8.2% of NEETs in unemployment and 7.9% of NEETs who can be inactive).

3.2. Occupational Transitions by Employment Status

In Romania, occupational transitions[17] in 2010 mainly involved those to employment (97.3%), followed by transitions to unemployment (0.9%) and to inactivity (1.8%). Some variations were reported in 2010 if compared to 2008, particularly an increase in the transition between jobs (+1.4pp) and a decrease in the shift from employment to inactivity (-1.5pp), while the passage from employment to unemployment remained almost constant (+0.2pp). In 2010, the gap between Romania and the EU27 can be summarized as follows:

a) + 5pp regarding the transition from employment to employment;

b) - 2.7pp if the transition from employment to unemployment is taken;

c) - 2.3pp in terms of the transition from employment to inactivity;

Further, the transition from unemployment in 2010 primarily concerned that to unemployment (56.6%), followed by transitions to employment (28.9%) and inactivity (14.5%). From 2008 to 2010, some variations could be seen in the odds to transit from unemployment to unemployment (+5.7pp), from unemployment to employment (-5.3pp) and from unemployment to inactivity (0.4pp). In 2010, the gap between Romania and the EU27 can be summarized as follows:

a) -0.3pp regarding the transition from unemployment to unemployment;

---

[17] EUROSTAT. *Labour Transitions by Employment Status* [ilc_lvhl30]. Brussels: EUROSTAT.

b) + 0.2pp if the transition from unemployment to employment is taken;

c) + 0.1pp in terms of the transition from unemployment to inactivity.

In both Romania and the EU27, this points to hysteresis as a consequence of limited new positions and to an increase of the unemployment spell and long-term unemployment, more generally.

Further, the transition from inactivity in 2010 primarily concerned that to inactivity (93.1%), followed by transitions to employment (5.5%) and unemployment (1.4%). From 2008 to 2010, some variations could be seen in the odds to transit from inactivity to inactivity (+0.9pp), from inactivity to inactivity (-1.1pp) and from inactivity to employment (1.1pp). In 2010, the gap between Romania and the EU27 can be summarized as follows:

a) -2.8pp regarding the transition from inactivity to unemployment;

b) -3.6pp if the transition from inactivity to unemployment is taken;

c) +6.3pp in terms of the transition from inactivity to inactivity.

This indicates that the unemployment status is biased in Romania and it is four times—two times in the EU27—more likely to transit from inactivity to employment than from inactivity to unemployment.

3.3. Occupational Transitions by Employment Status and Pay Level[18]

Compared to 2009, in 2010 some 77.1% of the employed persons in Romania made a transition to the same or higher qualification levels—in terms of employment status and pay—that is 11.4pp higher than 2008 and 4.4pp higher than the EU27 level in 2010. As much as 22.9% of those in employment transited to occupations with lower levels of qualification, corresponding to a decrease of 11.4 pp with respect to 2008 and a 4.4pp decrease if the 2010 EU27 average is taken.

As for the unemployed, 86.1% of them moved to jobs with the same or higher qualification levels over the same period, which means that an increase of 2.1pp was reported compared to 2008, 0.9pp lower than the EU27 level in 2010. As much as 13.9% of those without a job transited to

[18] EUROSTAT. *Labour Transitions by Employment Status and Pay Level - Changes in Qualifications* [ilc_lvhl35]. Brussels: EUROSTAT.

occupations with lower levels of qualifications, which corresponds to a decrease of 2.1pp with respect to 2008 and a 0.9pp decrease if the 2010 EU27 average is taken.

When it comes to students, 0.8% of them move to positions having the same or higher levels of qualifications—(-9.8)pp compared to 2008 and 87.2pp lower than the EU27 average in 2010—while 99.2% of students transit to lower level jobs, which translates into a 95.1pp increase compared to 2008 and an 87.2pp rise with respect to the EU27 average in 2010. The transition between jobs in order to change one's employment status and pay level points to increased segmentation of the labour market on account of:

a) If 2009 is taken, the consolidation of the insiders in the labour market in terms of remuneration, through an increase of 11.4pp of the employed persons transiting to jobs with the same or higher qualification levels; an increase of 2.1pp for the unemployed entering jobs with the same or higher qualification levels, compared to 2009 and the EU27 average;

b) A major capital loss resulting from a blockage of occupational transitions to positions with the same or higher qualification levels, since compared to the previous year, only 0.8% of the total number of students succeeded in these positive transitions. This process is peculiar to Romania and indicates its inability to absorb highly qualified workers.

4. Median Age When Leaving Formal Education

Like in many European countries, compulsory schooling in Romania statutorily ends at 18. Yet this is not always the case.

The median age at which one completes formal education (total ISCED 1997) during the 2006-2009 period was 21.6 years for the EU27 and 20.2 years for Romania. Young people with low educational levels (ISCED 0:2) leave formal education at the age of 14.7 years old, that is 3.2 years earlier than the average EU27. Young people with average levels of education (ISCED, 3:4), leave formal education at 18.7 years old—1.4 years earlier than in the EU27—while higher education graduates (ISCED, 5:6) end school at 24 years (EU27 average: 24.3 years old).

Based on the median age at which one exits formal education, it can be concluded that the low and medium levels of education are the most likely for population aged 15 to 24, including NEETs. As for the goal to "ensure guarantees for young people to access employment, or undergoing education or training",[19] and based on the data for the first quarter of 2012:

- 338.7 thousand people aged 15-24 years old are willing to work, are eligible to be employed or to pursue training programmes and to benefit from active labour market measures programmes aimed at increasing employability and accelerating transitions to employment and training;

- 125.9 thousand people in the 15 to 24 age group, who should be in education, are not in employment, education or training, nor are they willing to work.

5. Leaving Formal Education and Starting the First Job: Average Time by Educational Levels

In Romania, school-to-work transition is slower and more difficult, on account of the severe recession that took place in 2008 through 2009, and partly because of the unsustainable boom lasting until 2008.

The EU27 average duration of the school-to-work transition for those who have left education during 2006 through 2009 (measured in 2009) is 4 months, and 5 months for Romania. Such average duration rises to 6.5 months for the EU27 and 10 months for Romania if those who completed education are considered.

Further, a 1-month gap exists between Romania and EU27 for those who left formal education within 3 years, which increases to 3.5 months for those who completed formal schooling within 5 years.[20]

The transition from school to work in Romania is a serious issue for young people with average levels of education (ISCED 3:4). During the first three years after exiting formal education, it takes 5.9 months to access employment (1.4 months longer than in the EU27), and 12 months during the first 5 years of leaving school (4.7 months longer than in the EU27).

---

[19] European Commission. 2012. "Youth Unemployment: Studies Show that Apprenticeships and Traineeships are Useful but Need to be Improved," Press Release, IP/12/731. Brussels: European Commission.

[20] EUROSTAT. 2009. *Average Time Between Leaving Formal Education and Starting the First Job by Age Group, Sex and Educational Attainment Level for Persons Who Left Within the Last 3 or 5 Years—(Months), LFS Ad-hoc Module 2009—Entry of Young People into the Labour Market (edatt3).* Brussels: EUROSTAT.

As for youth with low levels of education (ISCED 0:2), these figures drop to 6.2 months within three years from leaving formal education (0.5 months longer than in the EU27), and 12.5 months within 5 years from graduating (2.7 months longer than in the EU27).

Finally, higher education graduates (ISCED 5:6) are the quickest to find employment. More specifically, those in their first three years from graduation take 4 months to enter the labour market (+0.8 months compared to the EU27), a period which increases to 7.2 months after 5 years from graduation (+2.2 months with respect to the EU27).

These figures, particularly for poorly educated young people, point to a serious risk of increasing the transition and the unemployment spell to more than 1 year, indirectly increasing the bouts of long-term unemployment.

The Council recommendation to "ensure that all young people are in a job, further education or activation measures within four months of leaving school and to provide this as a form of "Youth Guarantee"" [21] is correlated to the 4 months average duration of school-to-work transition in the EU27 (5 months in Romania).

> In the 2013 Annual Growth Survey (AGS),[22] the Commission stressed that Member States should secure school-to-work transitions for young people, develop and implement Youth Guarantee schemes whereby every young person under 25 receives an offer of employment, continued education, an apprenticeship or a traineeship within four months of leaving formal education or becoming unemployed.[23]

---

[21] European Commission. 2012. "Youth Unemployment: Studies Show that Apprenticeships and Traineeships are Useful but Need to be Improved," Press Release, IP/12/731. Brussels: European Commission.

[22] European Commission. 2012. *Annual Growth Survey 2013. COM(2012) 750 of 28 November 2012.* Brussels: European Commission.

[23] European Commission. 2012. *Proposal for a Council Recommendation on Establishing a Youth Guarantee* {SWD (2012) 409 final} COM(2012) 729 Final, 2012/0351 (NLE). Brussels: European Commission.

6. NEETs Aged 15-34 Years Old and their Transitions to the Labour Market

6.1. NEETs Aged 15-34 Years: Transitions from Education/ Training to Activity by Educational Levels in 2011[24]

In Romania, in 2011, for NEETs aged 15 to 34 with low educational levels (ISCED 0:2), the activity rate is 52.3% after three years from exiting education and training (-14.6pp compared to the EU27) and with this rate which increases by 13.4pp after 5 years from completing education and training (-9.1pp compared to the EU27). For NEETs with average levels of schooling (ISCED 3:4), the activity rate is 84.4% after three years from exiting education and training (-3pp compared to the EU27) with this rate which rises to 96.7% for highly educated NEETs (+3.2pp compared to the EU27).

6.2. NEETs Aged 15-34 Years: Transitions from Education/ Training to Employment by Educational Levels in 2011[25]

In Romania, in 2011, for NEETs aged 15-34 years with low educational levels (ISCED 0:2), the employment rate is 43% after three years from exiting education and training (+6.1pp compared to the EU27) and with this rate which increases by 14.8pp after 5 years from completing education and training (-9.1pp compared to the EU27). For NEETs with average levels of schooling (ISCED 3:4), the employment rate is 56.6% after three years from exiting education and training (-14pp compared to the EU27) with this rate which amounts to 80.4% for highly educated NEETs (-2pp compared to the EU27).

---

[24] EUROSTAT. *Activity Rates of Persons not in Education and Training by Sex and Educational Attainment Level [edat_lfse_26] Activity Rates of Persons not in Education and Training by Sex and Educational Attainment Level, Labour Status of Young People by Years after Leaving Education and Training*. Brussels: EUROSTAT.

[25] EUROSTAT. *Employment Rates of Persons not in Education and Training by Sex and Educational Attainment Level [edat_lfse_24], Labour Status of Young People by Years After Leaving Education and Training (Annual Results From 2000)(edatt2)*. Brussels: EUROSTAT.

6.3. NEETs Aged 15-34 Years: Transitions from Education/ Training to Unemployment by Educational Levels in 2011[26]

In Romania, in 2011, for NEETs aged 15-34 years with low educational levels (ISCED 0:2), the unemployment rate is 13% after three years from exiting education and training (-12.2pp compared to the EU27) with this rate which increases by 1.4 pp after 5 years from completing education and training (-11.3pp compared to the EU27). For NEETs with average levels of schooling (ISCED 3:4), the unemployment rate is 33% after three years from exiting education and training (-11.7% compared to the EU27) and 8.3% after five years from completing education and training (-2.2% compared to the EU27). The unemployment rate amounts to 16.5% for highly educated NEETs (+4.4pp compared to the EU27).

7. Conclusions

Transiting to adulthood and achieving financial independence in order to gain social status and identity is a complex process. As we have seen, many intermediary stages exist between employment and education.

One's interaction with economic and social aspects by means of status variation and labour market participation (inactive/active, unemployed/ employed) can be used as a proxy for evaluating the effectiveness of the school-to-work transition process.

If the pathway to independence coincides with that of employment, progress can be monitored through one's transition from school to work.

Recent developments indicate that the time needed to take up employment after leaving formal education is increasing, yet it might not be enough. This transition is a more objective process, out of the individual control, highly dependent on macroeconomic developments in a globalised world. In considering the current knowledge-based economy, the labour market has two different dimensions:

a) It is strongly dependent[27] on goods generating labour demand. This dimension is closely connected with the evolution of applied technologies in production processes. The new jobs are then the result of a

[26] EUROSTAT. *Unemployment Ratio of Persons not in Education and Training by Sex and Educational Attainment Level [edat_lfse_25]*. Brussels: EUROSTAT.

[27] Raboaca, G. 2003. "Piaţa muncii şi dezvoltarea durabilă," Premiul pentru Economie P.S. Aurelian al Academiei Române pentru anul 2003.

multiplication of pre-existent patterns. In this case, traditional transitions take place within the same sector.

b) As a source for boosting demand, the other dimension is related to technology having an impact on the creation of new economic sectors. The new economic sector enters the global market and impacts the previous ones. The effect on the labour market is radical; job creation that generates skills demand and occupations. The new jobs created result in the diversification or radical innovation of pre-existing patterns. Thus traditional transitions take place from old to emergent sectors, if quick learning is considered.

References

European Commission. 2012. *European Vacancy and Recruitment Report 2012.* European Commission Directorate General for Employment, Social Affairs and Inclusion Unit C.4, Employment Services. Brussels: European Commission.

—. 2012. *Proposal for a Council Recommendation on Establishing a Youth Guarantee* {SWD (2012) 409 final}. COM (2012) 750 of 28 November 2012, Brussels, 5.12.2012, COM (2012) 729 final, 2012/0351 (NLE). Brussels: European Commission.

European Vacancy Monitor. 2013. "Monitoring Labour Market Developments in Europe," DG Employment, Social Affairs and Inclusion of the European Commission, 8.

EUROSTAT. 2009. *Average Time Between Leaving Formal Education and Starting the First Job by Age Group, Sex and Educational Attainment Level for Persons Who Left Within the Last 3 or 5 Years—(Months), LFS Ad-hoc Module 2009—Entry of Young People into the Labour Market (edatt3).* Brussels: EUROSTAT.

—. *Activity Rates of Persons Not in Education and Training by Sex and Educational Attainment Level* [edat_lfse_26] *Activity Rates of Persons not in Education and Training by Sex and Educational Attainment Level, Labour Status of Young People by Years after Leaving Education and Training*. Brussels: EUROSTAT.

—. *Average Age When Leaving Formal Education by Sex, and Educational Attainment Level for Persons Who Left Within the Last 3 or 5 Years, LFS Ad-hoc module 2009*—Entry of Young People into the Labour Market, [edat_lfso_09t2]. Brussels: EUROSTAT.

—. *Employment Rates of Persons Not in Education and Training by Sex and Educational Attainment Level [edat_lfse_24], Labour Status of*

Young People by Years after Leaving Education and Training (Annual Results From 2000)(edatt2). Brussels: EUROSTAT.

—. *Job Vacancy Statistics by Occupation and NUTS 2 Regions, Annual Data*, NACE Rev. 2 (from 2008 onwards) [jvs_a_nace2]. Brussels: EUROSTAT.

—. *Labour Transitions by Employment Status* [ilc_lvhl30]. Brussels: EUROSTAT.

—. *Labour Transitions by Employment Status and Pay Level, Changes in Qualifications [ilc_lvhl35].* Brussels: EUROSTAT. Brussels: EUROSTAT.

—. *The Job Vacancy Rate* (JVR). Brussels: EUROSTAT.

Răboaca, G. 2003. "Piaţa Muncii şi Dezvoltarea Durabilă," Premiul pentru Economie P.S. Aurelian al Academiei Române pentru anul 2003.

THE SCHOOL-TO-WORK TRANSITION OF HIGHER EDUCATION GRADUATES IN ROMANIA

ANA-MARIA ZAMFIR, CRISTINA MOCANU, ELIZA-OLIVIA LUNGU AND SPERANŢA PIRCIOG

1. Introduction

Education is an important factor for allocation and matching in the labour market.[1] On the basis of this assumption, this case study investigates patterns of school-to-work transition and early career of higher education graduates in Romania. The school-to-work transition is a period of profound changes from the social and economic point of view.

Thus, the focus will be on the transition from education to the world of work, placing emphasis on the characteristics of the first work experiences of this category of workers.

The analysis is based on survey data collected among graduates leaving education in 2002, 2005 and 2007, and looks at their employment history by exploring several dimensions: the time it takes to enter the labour market, the methods of finding employment, and the adequacy of insertion and job mobility. Therefore, the first part provides details about the duration of the first job, methods for finding the first job and the education-job mismatch, taking into account self-assessment criteria.

The second part analyzes the major characteristics of higher education graduates' early career, with a focus on job mobility. Research on youth employment shows that job mobility represents one of the most important features for new entrants to the labour market, because propensity towards job swapping declines with age and work experience. Moreover, the

---

[1] Wolbers, M. H. J. 2003. "Job Mismatches and their Labour Market Effects among School Leavers in Europe," in *School-to-Work Transitions in Europe: Analyses of the EU LFS 2000 Ad Hoc Module*, eds. Kogan I., and W. Müller, (Mannheim: Mannheimer Zentrum für Europäische Sozialforschung), 89-121.

human capital theory states that young workers bear lower costs in terms of job mobility due to the fact that they have acquired fewer job-specific skills. Labour economists consider that early career is a period of “shopping” or “trashing stage” characterized by exploring and testing the market. In order to understand the intensity and nature of job mobility among Romanian higher education graduates, the number of jobs held in their early career stage, job search behaviour and employment interruptions will be analysed. Finally, we examine the incidence of desired mobility vs. undesired mobility and desired stability vs. undesired stability, while taking into account some gender differences.

2. Data and Methodology

Our analysis is based on two-wave panel data collected from graduates leaving education in 2002, 2005 and 2007. Our first wave of observation consists of a national survey carried out in November 2008 aimed at investigating labour market entry and first employment experiences of Romanian higher education graduates. The face-to-face questionnaire covered the period from graduation to the time of observation, gathering data regarding personal profiles and characteristics of all the jobs held by school leavers: professional status, occupation, sector, type of contract, job search strategies, and so forth. The sample included 2,194 graduates and was stratified by educational field according to statistical data provided by the National Institute of Statistics.

The second wave of observation took place in November 2012 and surveyed 400 out of the 2,014 graduates from the initial sample. The new sample complied with the previous stratification criterion, namely the educational field. The questionnaire was similar to the one from the first survey and collected employment data from the previous observation to the moment of the data gathering. This case study analysed labour market entry and early career of the 400 graduates included in both surveys.

Therefore, the range of employment experiences of 2002, 2005 and 2007 graduates is investigated, from the moment of graduation until the end of 2012.

3. Labour Market Entry of Romanian Higher Education Graduates

In order to assess how long higher education graduates take to enter the labour market, we applied the Kaplan-Maier estimator which is widely implemented in medical and biological research on lifetime data. The duration of the first job is measured as the conditional probability that school leavers enter their first job within a particular month, given that this has not occurred prior to that month. Leaving education is regarded as the start time. The Kaplan-Maier analysis estimates a “survival” probability for each moment (months) until a “death”/target event takes place. In the context of this study, the target event is entering the first job. We considered the graduates who continued with the job they had while in education, as well as those who found work immediately after leaving school.

The results for Romanian higher education graduates are plotted in Fig. 1, which shows the cumulative share of higher education graduates that took up their first job, by gender. First, almost 30% of graduates were employed at the time of graduation, signifying that they experienced the so-called dual model, in which education and labour are performed simultaneously (thus contrary to the traditional model). Our results show that around half of school leavers found employment in the first three months after graduation. Moreover, a rather quick school-to-work transition is reported, taking into account that after one year since graduation around 80% of graduates found their first job. However, one might note that most of them entered the labour market during favourable economic conditions.

Further, the gender of school leavers influences the pace at which the school-to-work transition takes place. Male graduates report a faster transition to the first job compared to their female counterparts. The speed deficit of female graduates is more visible for those entering the labour market after more than 20 months since graduation.

Around half of them found their first employment through relatives, friends and acquaintances, some 25% using the Internet and responding to newspapers jobs advertisements, and as much as 4% of graduates through public or private employment agencies. The importance of graduates’ social capital in their transition to the world of work is evident.

Our results highlight the modest role of employment services in youth transition to the labour market, especially when it comes to higher education graduates. In general, public employment services are more effective among low and medium qualified workers, while private agencies work better in terms of “head hunting” (talent scouting). As a result, young graduates with higher education looking for employment mostly rely on their social connections (including networks of their family members).

Fig. 2-1. Cumulative Failure Functions of Romanian Higher Education Graduates that Ever Entered a First Job (by Gender).

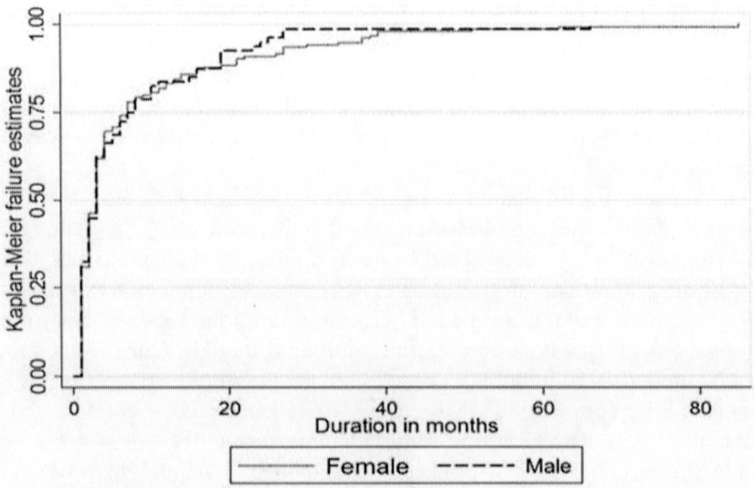

Source: INCSMPS survey data, authors' calculation.

One important indicator for successful school-to-work transition is the share of graduates taking up jobs matching their specialization. Some 36.1% of them entered mismatched jobs, while the rest operated in matched jobs. As already discussed, most graduates accessed the labour market during a period of economic prosperity, but the share of those in mismatched jobs is significant. Such a result confirms the vulnerability of youth leaving education who have to accept jobs in which they do not use the bulk of knowledge and skills acquired in school. From a gender perspective, female graduates experience a lower incidence of education-job mismatch: 34.3% of female graduates have had a first mismatched job, as against 39.7% of males. Research on youth emphasizes that the school-to-work transition is a critical socio-economic period in one's life which includes skills development, job-searching, unemployment, inactivity or unstable employment, and that young people change jobs in the hope of a better match and higher benefits. However, a number of young people remain trapped in mismatched jobs, especially during the years of economic downturn.

Table 2-2. Investigated University Graduates by Education-Job Match/Mismatch and Gender (N=374), in the First Job after Graduation.

	Males	Females	Total
Job Match	60.3%	65.7%	63.9%
Job Mismatch	39.7%	34.3%	36.1%
Total	100.0%	100.0%	100.0%

Source: INCSMPS survey data, authors' calculation.

3. Job Mobility in the Early Career of Romanian Higher Education Graduates

Job mobility in the early career of 374 Romanian graduates has also been surveyed, based on the sample and methodology previously described. We will first have a look at the number of jobs held after graduation and then analyse their job stability and job mobility by year of graduation and gender. The aim here is to emphasize the pattern of career development for higher education graduates in Romania. A significant number of variables influence job mobility, such as age, gender, intergenerational mobility, study or work experiences in other countries, but also the cultural model with respect to career expectations and labour market mobility. Ten years ago, it was assumed that the first job should be held for at least one year in order to be considered "serious" and "responsible" for another occupation.

Now, job mobility is highly encouraged by the business environment but also by cultural beliefs; maintaining a job for more than five years would translate into "it's time to move on."

Table 2-3. Distribution of University Graduates by Number of Jobs Occupied from Graduation to the Time of Investigation (%) (N=374).

	2003	2005	2007	Total
1 Job	20.4%	26.7%	32.1%	27.0%
2 Jobs	30.1%	37.0%	39.4%	36.1%
3 Jobs	20.4%	23.0%	13.1%	18.7%
More than 3 Jobs	29.1%	13.3%	15.4%	18.2%
Total	100.0%	100.0%	100.0%	100.0%

Source: INCSMPS survey data, authors' calculation.

The average number of jobs held by graduates of the 2003, 2005, and 2007 cohort is 2.7, 2.3, and 2.2, respectively. Even if the economy was booming until 2008, the mobility of higher graduates does not seem to vary with the economic conditions. Mobility increases with the time spam after graduation, being the highest for the 2003 cohort, but without any notable differences between the 2005 and 2007 cohorts.

Mobility for men is higher than for women, being more likely to have men in the category of those with more than 3 jobs, and women in the category of those with less than three jobs. Also, as the table below evidences, there are no significant differences for men and women holding only one job after graduation.

Table 2-4. Distribution of University Graduates by the Number of Jobs Occupied from Graduation to the Time of Investigation (%) (N=374).

	Male	Female	Total
1 Job	26.2%	27.4%	27.0%
2 Jobs	33.3%	37.5%	36.1%
3 Jobs	17.5%	19.4%	18.7%
More than 3 Jobs	23.0%	15.7%	18.2%
Total	100.0%	100.0%	100.0%

Source: INCSMPS survey data, authors' calculation.

Later on, we focused our analysis on those that only had one job after graduation, and we considered their job search behaviour in order to assess if their job stability was desired or not. We asked both groups if they were searching for a new job at the time of investigation, and based on their answers we classified their job stability. If in any of the two moments they declared that they were searching for a new job, we classified their job stability as undesired. If for the two moments they declared they were not searching for another job, then we consider their job stability as being desired.

One out of four interviewees experienced undesired job stability after graduation, irrespective of their graduation year or gender. Undesired stability is higher for men, than for women. Thus, it is less likely to find men among graduates holding only one job after graduation, and it is more likely to hold undesired positions among men having the same job.

Respectively, almost three of four graduates that only had one job after graduation experienced desired stability, that being much higher for women than for men. So, we could argue that the labour market and the career patterns for university graduates seem to be stable. When it comes to career patterns for women, then the model is encouraging even more stability.

Table 2-5. Distribution of University Graduates by Type of Stability they experienced over the First Job, by gender (%).

	Males	Females	Total
Desired Stability	66.7%	78.6%	74.8%
Undesired Stability	33.3%	21.4%	25.2%
Total	100.0%	100.0%	100.0%

Source: INCSMPS survey data, authors' calculation.

The labour market conditions after the 2008 socio-economic crisis explains the high share of graduates in the 2007 cohort regarding they experience as undesired stability (up to 1/3). In other words, one third of the 2007 cohort that had one job after graduation was searching for a job at the time of investigation, yet failing to find one.

Table 2-6. Distribution of University Graduates by type of Stability Experienced over the First Job, Taking into Account their Graduation Year (%).

	2003	2005	2007
Desired Stability	76.2%	81.1%	68.9%
Undesired Stability	23.8%	18.9%	31.1%
Total	100.0%	100.0%	100.0%

Source: INCSMPS survey data, authors' calculation.

Some 73% of the graduates surveyed had at least two jobs after graduation. Was their mobility desired or not? In order to categorize the type of job mobility, we considered their entire employment history, month by month. If between two jobs they encountered a period of unemployment, we classified their mobility as undesired. Otherwise, if they transited between jobs, we considered their mobility as desired.

Table 2-7. Distribution of University Graduates by Experienced Mobility from Graduation until the Time of Investigation (%).

	2003	2005	2007	Total
Desired Mobility	59.8%	68.7%	75.3%	68.2%
Undesired Mobility	40.2%	31.3%	24.7%	31.8%
Total	100.0%	100.0%	100.0%	100.0%

Source: INCSMPS survey data, authors' calculation.

Only a minority of university graduates (31.8%) that had two jobs or more after graduation experienced undesired mobility. Respectively, almost two thirds of graduates having two jobs or more experienced desired mobility. As the table above evidences, desired mobility increases from cohort to cohort. If only 59.8% of the 2003 cohort experienced desired mobility after graduation, the share increased to 75.3% for the 2007 cohort. As said before, the cultural model started to encourage more job mobility.

If gender is taken into account, male graduates experienced undesired mobility more often (34% compared with 31% in the case of females).

Even without significant differences between men and women, the changes in the cultural career model for women have to be evidenced.

Also, the transition in Romania was more difficult for men than for women, with more people made redundant in male-dominant sectors than in traditional female-dominant ones.

Table 2-8. Distribution of University Graduates by type of Mobility Experienced from Graduation until the time of Investigation (%).

	Male	Female	Total
Desired Mobility	65.6%	69.4%	68.2%
Undesired Mobility	34.4%	30.6%	31.8%
Total	100.0%	100.0%	100.0%

Source: INCSMPS survey data, authors' calculation.

To conclude, this case study has pointed to a cultural career model, emphasising the importance of university degrees (the speed of labour market entry being quite high), whereas the specialization is seemingly less important (due to a high share of mismatched graduates). Moreover, the model seems to encourage job stability: the number of jobs after graduation is rather low, while most graduates with only one job after graduation experienced desired stability. Finally, the share of graduates experiencing undesired mobility after graduation is relatively high.

References

Gangl, M. 2002. "Changing Labour Markets and Early Career Outcomes: Labour Market Entry in Europe over the Past Decade," in *Work, Employment and Society* 16: 67-90.

Hannan, D. F., D. Raffe and E. Smyth. 1996. *Cross-National Research on School-to-Work Transitions: An Analytical Framework*, http://www.econ.upf.edu/~montalvo/sec1034/school_work_ocde.pdf (accessed 20 June 2013).

Kogan, I., and W.Műller, eds. 2003. *School-to-work Transitions in Europe: Analyses of the EU LFS 2000 Ad Hoc Module*. Mannheim: Mannheimer Zentrum fűr Europäische Sozialforschung http://www.mzes.unimannheim.de/publications/books/school_to_work_2ed.pdf (accessed 20 June 2013).

OECD. 2000. *From Initial Education to Working Life: Making Transitions Work*. Paris: Organisation for Economic Co-operation and Development.

Quintini, G, J. P. Martin, and S. Martin. 2007. "The Changing Nature of the School-to-Work Transition Process in OECD Countries," Discussion Paper Series No. 2582.

Ryan, P. 2001. "The School-to-Work Transition: a Cross-National Perspective," *Journal of Economic Literature* 39:34-92.

Sattinger, M. 1993. "Assignment models of the Distribution of Earnings". *Journal of Economic Literature* 31:851-880.

Shavit, Y., and W. Müller.1998. *From School to Work. A Comparative Study of Educational Qualifications and Occupational Destinations*. Oxford: Claredon Press.

Wolbers, M. H. J. 2003. "Job Mismatches and their Labour Market Effects among School Leavers in Europe," in *School-to-Work Transitions in Europe: Analyses of the EU LFS 2000 Ad Hoc Module*, eds. Kogan, I., and W. Müller, (Mannheim: Mannheimer Zentrum fűr Europäische Sozialforschung), 89-121.

—. 2007. "Pattern of Labour Market Entry: A Comparative Perspective on School-to-Work Transitions in 11 European Countries," *Acta Sociologica* 50:189-210.

SHORT-TERM ANTICIPATION OF DEMAND OF ROMANIAN VET AT NUTS 3 LEVEL*

CRISTINA LINCARU, GABRIELA PREDOŞANU, SPERANŢA PIRCIOG AND VASILICA CIUCĂ

1. Introduction

With path dependence developing at a pace which differs among sectors and industries, the need to anticipate the demand of Vocational Education and Training (hereafter simply as VET), in order to be covered by the statistic indicator "Vocational, complementary or apprenticeship educational level"[1] at region NUTS 3 level is closely related to two dimensions: the development dimension and the growth dimension. We are going to explore the relationship between demand—which measures productivity and competitiveness at the NUTS 3 level—and human capital supply (TVET graduates) by means of spatial analysis instruments.

1.2. Demand Satisfaction of Romanian VET: Some Major Characteristics

The employed people with VET levels were almost 2 million in Quarter IV 2010, that is 22% of the employed population.

In addition, a decreasing tendency was reported among all the age groups (see Fig. 2-2).[2]

[1] As calculated by the INS Romania in Household Labour Force Statistical Survey—AMIGO (indicator presented in the TEMPO database as AMG110W Employment by Group of Occupations, by Educational Level and by Sex), https://statistici.insse.ro/shop/index.jsp?page=tempo3&lang=en&ind=AMG110W.

[2] [Indicator: AMG110I—MIGO—Employment by Educational Level, by Age Group and by Sex) Beginning with 2002*, the data are not comparable with the data series of previous years, because of the revised definitions used. The data are estimated by taking into account the results coming from the Population and Housing Census of March 2002].

Fig. 2-2. Number of Employed People with "Vocational, Complementary or Apprenticeship Educational Level" by Age Group, between 1996 and 2010.

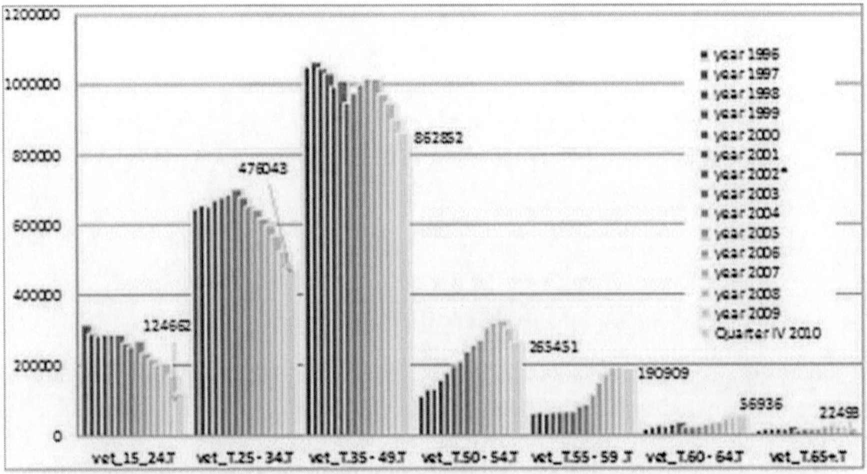

Source: Authors' Own Elaboration, on AMG110I—(AMIGO data)—Employment by educational level by age group and by sex) Tempo INS.

The shortage caused by low intergenerational replacement rates could be estimated from the dynamics of each age group, arrived at by the difference between those entering and exiting the labour market. In terms of labour market dynamics, there is no equilibrium between these fluxes.

The breaking point is 2005 for males and 2007 for females (Fig. 2-3).

Traditionally, the normal levels of occupational segregation and/or specialization are reported by sex for the employed people with VET levels of education.

Fig. 2-3. Difference between the Number of new Entrants and Exits in Employment for Males and Women with Vet levels of Education, between 1996-2010 for the age group 15-24 and age group 55-65 and over.

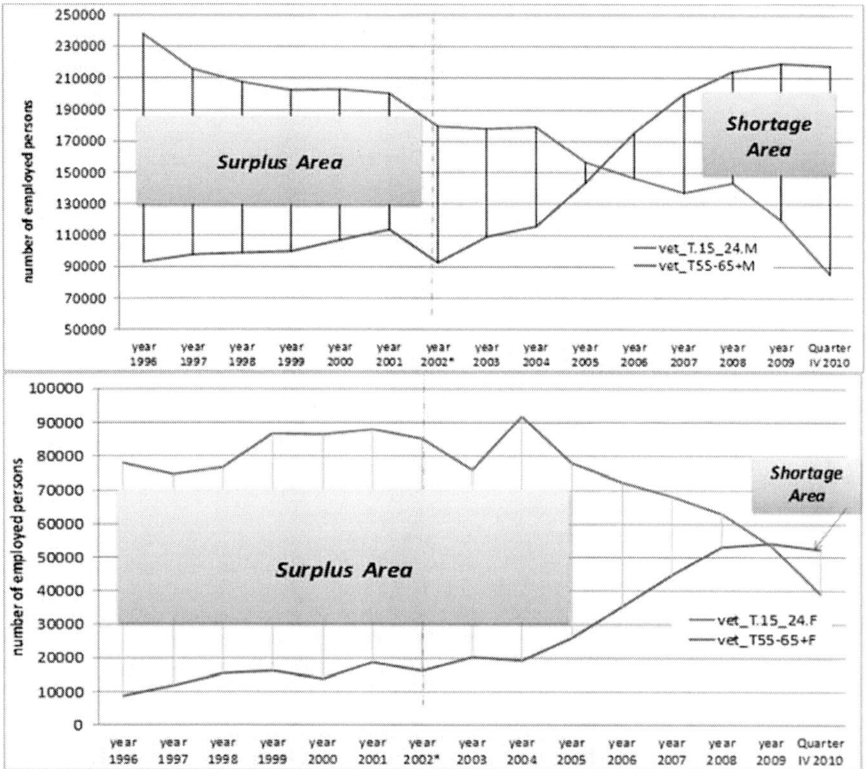

Source: data from AMG110I—AMIGO, Tempo Online, INS Romania.

In 2009, the difference between the share of males and females in the employed population with VET levels of education (Fig. 2-4) was 23pp for the 55-59 age group (6%). This difference dwindles by 12pp (1%) for the 25-34 age group and by 9pp (7%) for the 15-24 age group.

The share of labour market entrants in the same age group is 27% for men or 37% if the 55-59 age group is considered. For women, the difference between entrants and exits is 4pp, still a positive trend if compared to the 15-24 and 55-59 age groups.

Fig. 2-4. Shares of Males and Females in the Employed Population with VET Levels of Education by Age in the Same Group of Age in 2009.

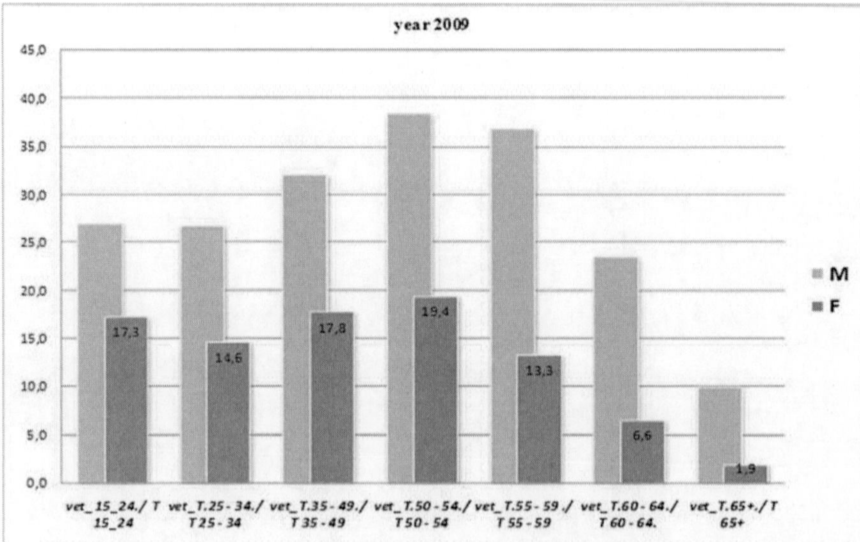

Source of data: AMG110I—AMIGO, Tempo Online, INS Romania.

Further, low rates of substitution have been reported, based on the idea that VET occupations are more specialised by sex. Table No. 1 provides a comparison between the estimated number of shortage caused by low intergenerational replacement rates and the total number of VET level graduates attained at the end of the academic year 2008-2009:

Vet_age_replacement_M = vet_T15_24_M - vet_55-65+M (1);

Vet_age_replacement_F= vet_T15_24_F—vet_55-65+F (2);

Vet_age_replacement_T=Vet_age_replacement_M + Vet_age_replacement_F (3).

The AMIGO Complementary Survey, second Quarter 2009, carried out by The Romanian National Institution of Statistics (INS Romania), provides the major features of the young VET graduates experiencing the transition from school to work. The module "Young People Access to the Labour Market" is used to undertake statistical research on "The Household Survey of the Labour Force—AMIGO".

Table 2-9. Comparing the Estimated Shortage of Intergenerational Replacement with the Total Number of VET Level Graduates at the End of School Year 2008-2009.

		Males estimated number of employed people with VET level shortage deficit of intergenerational replacement = vet_T15_24_M-vet_55-65+M	**Females estimated number of employed people with VET level shortage deficit of intergenerational replacement = vet_T15_24_F-vet_55-65+F**	**Total estimated number of employed people with VET level shortage deficit of intergenerational replacement = (2)+(3)**	**The total number of graduated of VET level attained at the end of school year 2008-2009**	**(5)-(4) delta**
	(1)	*(2)*	*(3)*	*(4)*	*(5)*	*(6)*
(1)	Year 2009	-99630	-822	-100452	100901	449
(2)	Quarter IV 2010	-132408	-13266	-145674		

Observation: For (2), (3) and (4) the values used to calculate using the Indicators are: AMG110I—AMIGO—Employment by educational level by age group and by sex, detail for “Vocational, complementary or apprenticeship educational level”; Column (5) row (1) value is taken from “9m. Numarul Absolventilor Din Invatamantul Profesional, Pe Regiuni, Judete, Pe Forme De Profiluri, Specializari Si Sexe, La Sfarsitul Anului Scolar 2008—2009,” 07/08/20, [Number of Graduates with Vocational, Complementary or Apprenticeship Educational Level Attained at the End of School Year 2008-2009 by Profile, Specialization and Sex], INS, 2010 August.

A main argument for including this control data to our spatial model is given by the methodology of this complementary survey, which has been harmonised with the European standards and regulations and offers comparable data.[3]

In this survey, the target group was made up of people aged 15 to 34 years old who are considered as young. This VET group is homogenous regarding low occupational and geographical mobility levels:

> the gradual increase in the number of years of education has led the recent cohorts of young graduates in Europe to be more mobile than low-skilled workers [...]. Less educated individuals are less mobile, even though they are most exposed to unemployment.[4]

The 2009 AMIGO Complementary Survey points out that the insertion rate into the labour market was 24.8% for males and 20.6% for females after 6 months from leaving education. Being included in the ISCED 3 level, the direct correlation between the educational attainments and the speed of insertion into the labour market is confirmed: the higher the level of education, the higher the rate of insertion in the reference time.

In the second term of 2009, if higher education in urban areas is considered, the insertion rate was 49% 6 months after leaving education, which drops to 5.2% for low educated people in the same period.

According to the relevant literature, the higher the level of education, the higher the propensity to be geographically mobile for people having these characteristics. Among the employed people, those with ISCED 3

---

[3] The European Commission Regulation No. 207/2008 (OJ No L 62/4/6.3.2008) regarding the Module ad hoc “The Young People Entrance on the Labour Market”.

[4] Bassanini, A., A. Booth, M. De Paola, P. Fredriksson, A. Lamo, E. Leuven, J. Messina, and G. Peri. 2007. *Education and Training in Europe*, eds. Brunello, B., P. Garibaldi, and E. Wasmer. http://www.econ.ucdavis.edu/faculty/gperi/non_refereed/Book_Final.pdf, 18.

levels of education are the less mobile (also compared to the persons of lower levels) and

> There are now many studies on mobility based on ECHP. Two recent works use a definition of geographical mobility similar to the one used here, in that it is not based on the change in the macro region of residence. The main reason for this is that, in several countries, macro-regions (which are a group of regions, corresponding to the geographical level NUTS1) are so large that geographical mobility would be strongly underestimated.[5]

Fig. 2-5 ((a), (b) and (c)) shows that the VET group of youth aged 15 to 34 years in 2009 mostly falls under the 7th major group (41.1%), followed by the GM 6 group (Farmers and skilled workers, 17.8%) and the group GM5 (Service workers and shop and market sales workers, 14.1%). Another important group is the GM9 group (Unskilled workers, 14%).

Fig. 2-5 illustrates that there is a tendency on the part of VET graduates to be employed in jobs with low levels of productivity, notwithstanding their high levels of specialisation and significant substitution rates for this category. This could reflect the development of new occupations or the modernisation of existing ones.

---

[5] Bassanini, A., A. Booth, M. De Paola, P. Fredriksson, A. Lamo, E. Leuven, J. Messina, and G. Peri. 2007. *Education and Training in Europe*, eds. Brunello, B., P. Garibaldi, and E. Wasmer. http://www.econ.ucdavis.edu/faculty/gperi/non_refereed/Book_Final.pdf, pg. 49 (accessed 20 December 2013).

Fig. 2-5. (a): VET Employment by Groups of Occupations [Persons], (b): Absolute Variation between Years 2009 and 2002 for Males' Distribution, by Groups of Occupations [Persons], (c): Absolute Variation between Years 2009 and 2002 for Females' Distribution, by Groups of Occupations [persons].

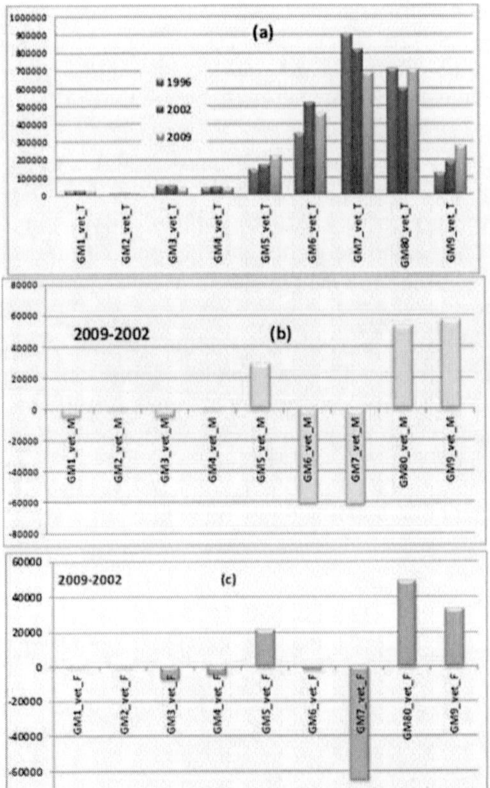

Major groups of occupations COR/ISCO 88 (TEMPO):

GM1: *Members of legislative, executive, senior officials of public administration, managers and clerks of economic, social and political units*

GM2: *Experts in intellectual and scientific occupations*

GM3: *Technicians, foremen and assimilated*

GM4: *Workers in services and trade and assimilated*

GM5: *Service workers and shop and market sales workers*

GM6: *Farmers and skilled workers in agriculture, forestry and fishing*

GM7: *Artisans and skilled workers in handicraft, machinery and equipment regulation and maintenance*

GM8: *Others categories of occupations*

GM9: *Unskilled workers*

Source AMG110W—AMIGO—Employment by group of occupations, by educational level and by sex level, especially at NUTS 3 level.

Fig. 2-5. (d) The Tendency for Graduates of VET to be Employed in Occupations with Low Levels of Productivity.

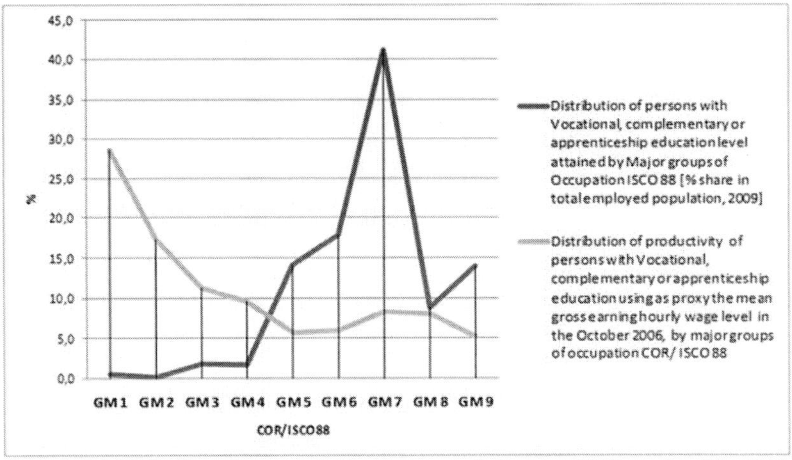

Source: AMIGO Complementary Survey, second Quarter 2009 realised by INS Romania: "The young people access to the Labour Market" as a module of the statistical research "The Household Survey of the Labour Force—AMIGO" (2006—The Salaries Structure Survey: influence factors, INS Romania (National Institute of Statistics).

2. Methodology and Theoretical Background

In the context of this paper, the **development dimension** is represented by the qualitative aspect explained through the variety of demand (the diversity of economic activity at NUTS 3 level) and supply (qualification under the domain of specialisation criteria).

The **growth dimension** is concerned with the quantitative aspect of "potential" demand mainly shaped by the economic potential and strategic perspective of the area surveyed (NUTS 3 level). Significant path dependency is also exhibited because the area is characterised by a specific spectrum of economic activities with a spatial degree of agglomeration/concentration[6] and important effects also on productivity and competitiveness. In accordance with this spectrum, the educational institutions, the VET units in our case, are also developed. Through this methodology, pronounced inertia is reported in the areas with high levels

[6] Marshall, A. 1920. *Principles of Economics*. Prometheus Books.

of specialisation, which translates into higher probabilities to organise initial VET programmes in response to slow economy.

We develop a secondary analysis (Cluster and Outlier Analysis) using the aggregate data at NUTS 3 level offered by the National Institute for Statistics, making use of Anselin Local Moran's I (Spatial Statistics) and the GIS Software programme (Arc Gis 9.0), considering that:

- Calculations are based on the Euclidean distance;

- The model of spatial relationships is the Inverse Distance one, since

> With Inverse Distance the conceptual model of spatial relationships is one of impedance, or distance decay. All features impact/influence all other features, but the farther away something is, the smaller the impact it has.[7]

- The cluster and outlier analysis output gives rise to Local Moran's I index value, Z score, P-value and to a cluster type code for each value of the NUTS 3 distribution of CANE Rev.2 sections (mentioned in Annex 1), by means of which we identify the areas with a high probability to absorb or to reject VET graduates.

a) Data, Variables and Model Specifications

In our research, initial VET is calculated in accordance with the INS statistics methodology used in the annual research (Sc.5.1.a). In this exhaustive survey, initial vocational education training is included in upper secondary education (ISCED 1997 version), that is the 3rd level. The reference year for the data selection is 2008-2009, in order to identify the last generation of graduates for the target group. 5 types of educational units have been singled out:

1. School of arts and trades (vocational),
2. School of arts and trades (year of completion),
3. Specialised school of arts and trades (specialised training, including the specialised school centre),

---

7 http://webhelp.esri.com/arcgisdesktop/9.3/index.cfm?TopicName=Cluster%20and%20Outlier%20Analysis:%20Anselin%20Local%20Moran's%20I%20(Spatial%20Statistics) (accessed 20 December 2013).

4. Special school of re-education,

5. Second chance education.

In our analysis, we intentionally ignored the following criteria:

a. The type of unit (independent or autonomous scholar groups),

b. The type of education (full time, part time or with reduced frequency),

c. The property type (public of national or local interest, private or cooperative),

d. The type of funding (budget, contract, taxes or mixed) or

e. The functioning of the unit (one shift/day, two shifts/day, three shifts/day or multiple shifts/day).

Using the "Conversion matrix" presented in Annex 1, we developed the correspondence between the profiles/specialisations provided by the foregoing types and the corresponding economic activity related to CANE Rev.2. These sketchy statistics are presented in Table 2-10 and Fig. 2-6.

Table 2-10. Distribution of Specializations by VET Schools in 2009 (CANE Rev.2).

NACE Rev.2	A	B	C	D	F	G	H	I	S	Total
Number of specialisations	29	12	193	8	37	7	27	12	2	327
%	9	4	59	2	11	2	8	4	1	100

Source: Authors' Own Elaboration.

The second source of data is the public TEMPO online database, in particular the FOM103D provided by "Labour force balance", which measures the civil employed population[8] by regions at NUTS3 level.

[8] The Civil Employed Population does not include armed forces and similar categories (the personnel of the Ministry of Defence, Ministry of Interior, Romanian Intelligence Office, conscripts), convicts and political and community organisations employees.

Thanks to this indicator, we built the Demand Structure Matrix (MD2009). The Demand Structure Matrix represents the structure at NUTS3 level for the employed people in economic activities at section-level NACE Rev.2.

The third source of data, used to estimate the variety of demand at NUTS3 level, is represented by micro aggregated data at local level for the firms registered with the Statistic Register of Enterprises Romania (number of employees and turnover) concerning data as of July 2010 for 18 counties out of 41 (NUTS 3 level regions). Unlike the NACE Rev.2 classification, we identified 558 classes of economic activities out of 615.

Fig. 2-6. Distribution of Specializations in VET Schools by Profiles/Scientific Domains in 2009.

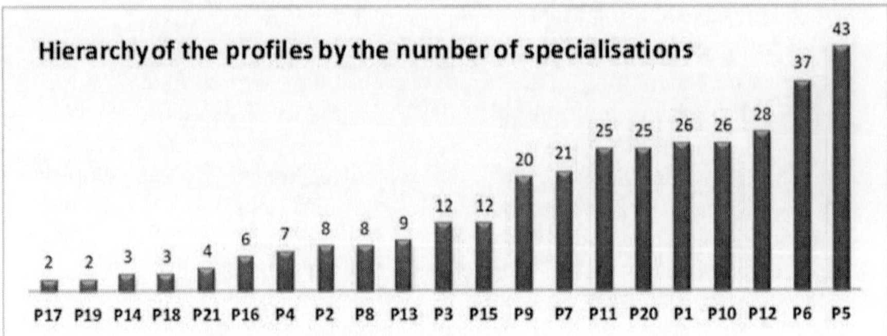

Source: Authors' Own Elaboration.

We may conclude that economic activity as an expression of demand satisfaction covers 90% of the agreed spectrum of the NACE Rev.2 (which is broken down into sections, divisions, groups and classes).

b) Model Specifications

In view to project short-term necessary VET supply (Fig. 2-7), we hypothesized that the conversion matrix is constant so projections only concern the quantitative aspect (i.e. the estimated number of future VET graduates), ignoring the qualitative dimension (the diversification of specialisation provided by schools).

Fig. 2-7. Model for "The Short-Term Anticipation of the Demand of Romanian VET at NUTS 3 level".

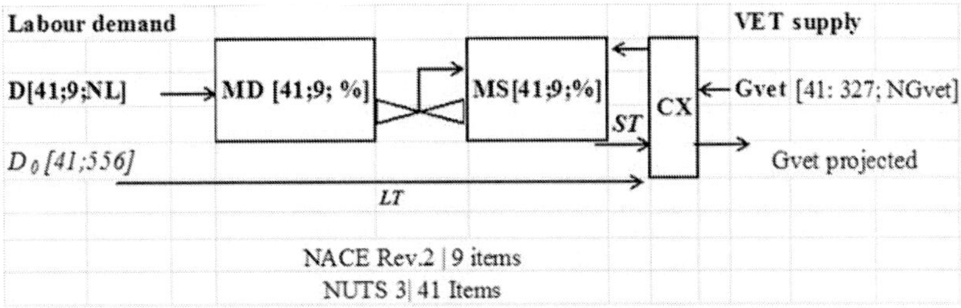

Gvet 2009 graduates with VET level of education
CX Conversion matrix: selection 9/20 section CAEN Rev 2
MS Supply structure matrix
D satisfied demand matrix (employed persons by sections of NACE rev.2 and by counties/at NUTS 3 level)
MD Demand structure matrix
Source: Authors' Own Elaboration.

We had to reconsider the supply structure matrix under the action of new National Education Law that reviewed the entire educational system in Romania, including the VET system.

The aim of this model is to harmonise the spatial pattern of the VET offer with demand. In this perspective, we compared the structure of supply and demand at NACE, Rev.2/ section and at NUTS 3 level. In order to quantify the scope of the VET offer, we considered the main enter variable (the estimated necessary of qualification requested by the intergenerational replacement, EV) using the relations:

$GVET_t$: VET (space, quantity, ……….quality, t)=
= VET (county, number, Profile/Specialisation, t)

$GVET_{t+1}$:VET (county, estimated demand VET, estimated Profile/Specialisation, t+1)

$GVET_{t+1} = EV*MD/MS*CX$ (4)

c) The National Regulation Framework

Since 1996, the TVET reform has been initiated in parallel with the economic restructuring. During the PHARE Projects, the EU provided technical assistance (IMC Consulting Ltd., Cambridge Education Ltd., etc.) to some selected educational units in view of supporting and guiding the modernising of the TVET System and affording the necessary knowledge demanded of the labour market. The TVET system was totally restructured by Education Law No. 268 of 13 June 2003 and the amendments made to Education Law No. 84/1995. The new perspective provided by these provisions changes the finality of TVET, considering it as a contributing factor to the "society and economy development based on knowledge, in the conditions of assurance of a high level of economic and social cohesion".

As a consequence of the reorganisation of the European Higher Education Area, Romania reviewed the entire education system through the new provision of June 2004 (Law No. 288/2004) in accordance with the Bologna process. Regardless of the educational, vocational or lifelong leaning pathway, vertical and horizontal mobility is now possible. In this new context, the certified competences could serve as a chance to be employed but also as an open option to follow up to higher education (in view to obtain the ISCED 5+ level of education). Some shortcomings were identified especially to progressive SAM (the pathway of school of arts and trades). Other laws which have an impact on the TVET development in Romania are: Law No. 53 of 24 January 2003 of the Labour Code and Law No. 279 of 5 October 2005, and the provision on apprenticeships that was modified by newly-issued Law No. 106/2011.

The National Educational Act initiated by the Ministry of Education, Research, Youth and Sports (MECTS) was adopted on 10 January 2011 thanks to Law No. 1/2011 (the National Education Law) which stipulates that VET programmes should last between 6 months and 2 years.

The modernization process of the educational system in Romania is set to review TVET and implicitly VET as Type III (vocational or technical) of the OECD definition,[9] which is oriented towards an immediate transition to the labour market.

---

[9] OECD. "The Scope and Coverage of Internationally Comparative Education Statistics," *Handbook for Internationally Comparative Education Statistics*, Chapter 5, 85: "Type III (Vocational or Technical) covers education that prepares participants for direct entry, without further training, into specific occupations. Successful completion of such programmes leads to a labour-market relevant vocational qualification".

3. Results

With different analysis instruments, some links were created between demand (which measures productivity and competitiveness at the NUTS 3 level) and supply (TVET graduates) that describe:

a) The Development Dimension

The quality/development dimension is presented with partial results. In 2009, we compared the variance of number of VET graduates at NUTS 3 level, by profile and specialisation (Annex 2) and structured the results by NACE Rev.2 sections with the variance of demand (Table 2-11 a and b).

Even this analysis is partial; it only covers 18 counties, without Bucharest, and still offers a starting point in view to evaluate the convergence in the development of demand and supply of VET labour.

The spatial pattern is homogenous and, at county level, a different matching probability between labour demand and supply is visible.

Table 2-11a and 2-11b. Table 2-11a. Partial Estimation of Development Concordance between VET Labour Demand and Supply at county/ NUTS 3 Level in Romania in 2009- Hierarchy by Variance of Demand.

(a)

higer variety of demand ↕ *lower variety of demand*

CAENR2	Variance of offer (number of VET graduates by profile and specialisation in 2009)	Variance of demand (NACE Rev.2 classes level) - hierachy
CT	2007	6490097
AR	1340	6450371
CL	1113	6445762
BV	2209	6443888
GR	465	6362450
BT	4708	6330451
DB	1049	6327226
AG	3286	6310308
BZ	1783	6278954
CS	715	6278639
BC	2446	6268586
CJ	2005	6234654
BR	698	6200557
BH	1891	6184520
CV	431	6159381
BN	668	6141494
AB	752	6122720
TM	1473	6023534

(b)

high probability of concordance between offer and demand ↕ *low probability of concordance between offer and demand*

CAENR2 at NUTS 3 level	Variance of offer (number of VET graduates by profile and specialisation in 2009)	Variance of demand (NACE Rev.2 classes level)	Variance of demand/variance of offer - hierachy of the counties
BT	4708	6330451	1344
AG	3286	6310308	1921
BC	2446	6268586	2563
BV	2209	6443888	2917
CJ	2005	6234654	3109
CT	2007	6490097	3234
BH	1891	6184520	3271
BZ	1783	6278954	3521
TM	1473	6023534	4089
AR	1340	6450371	4812
CL	1113	6445762	5789
DB	1049	6327226	6031
AB	752	6122720	8144
CS	715	6278639	8777
BR	698	6200557	8882
BN	668	6141494	9194
GR	465	6362450	13675
CV	431	6159381	14304
mean	*1613,4*	*6280755,1*	*5865,4*
maxim	*4708*	*6490097*	*14304*
minim	*431*	*6023534*	*1344*

Source: Authors' Own Elaboration, data Tempo INS.

b) The Growth Dimension

In the short term, in order to describe the growth dimension, we deemed it important to estimate and analyze the concordance of the structure of VET labour force demand with the supply in the hypothesis that has a fixed background.

After finalizing the calibration of the model in the short term, another challenge will be to analyze the stability of both structures (MD and MS).

3.1. The Structure Concordance

The concordance of the structure of VET labour force demand with supply in the hypothesis with a fixed background is presented in the Annex 4 (Demand structure matrix (MD2009)—supply structure matrix (MS2009)).

Annex 3 presents the distribution model in two scenarios, as a first iteration:

- Case 1: Projections for 2010 using the supply structure matrix (arrived at with the school types and the number of graduates in 2009).

- Case 2: Projections for 2010 using the demand structure matrix at NUTS2 level for economic activities at section level NACE Rev.2 (using the indicator FOM103D TEMPO/INS, 2009).

The next step is finalizing the calibration of the model in the short term with the MD/MS validated at the end of all procedures.

a) The "Growth" Potential as Externalities of Clusters/Agglomeration Spatial Structures

The results of Cluster and Outlier Analysis applying the Anselin Local Moran's I made by the conversion matrix indicate whether the apparent similarity (or dissimilarity) in values for a feature and its neighbours is greater than one would expect in a random distribution.

- A high positive Z >1.96 score for a feature indicates that the surrounding features have similar values (either high values or low value). The COType field indicates HH for a statistically significant (0.05 level) cluster of high values and LL for a statistically significant (0.05 level) cluster of low values.

- A low negative Z<1.96 score for a feature indicates a statistically significant (0.05 level) spatial outlier. The COType field indicates whether the feature has high value and is surrounded by features with low values (HL), or whether the feature has a low value and is surrounded by features with high values (LH).

The significant identification of clusters is a more laborious work and needs more resources for a better understanding of the dynamics of growth at regional and even at local level. As exhibited in the maps of Annex 7, there are some spatial patterns for each section of interest. For counties identified as outliers, it is necessary to apply corrections in the demand matrix. This objective represents a topic for future research.

4. Final Remarks

Our model reinforces and attempts to prove the argument that it is impossible to plan a VET offer without a spatial perspective for both demand and supply. The connection of two national networks is realised at local level. In this context, the demand at regional level, especially at NUTS 3 level, plays an important role for better anticipation, allocation and insertion into the labour market of this group of people.

Through this model we can estimate the scope (still at NUTS 3 level) and the institutional capacity of VET, as well as the prospects for labour market integration. The other two essential and very real dimensions, "quality" and "time" should be considered in our future research.

References

AMIGO Complementary Survey. 2009. "The Young People Access to the Labour Market," Statistical Research The Household Survey of the Labour Force—AMIGO, INS Romania.

Anselin, L. 2005. *Exploring Spatial Data with GeoDaTM: A Workbook Spatial Analysis Laboratory*. Department of Geography, University of Illinois, Urbana-Champaign Urbana, IL 61801. http://sal.uiuc.edu/Pg.6. Center for Spatially Integrated Social Science. http://www.csiss.org/Revised Version, March 6, 2005, 106.

ArcGIS Desktop Help 9.3, including 9.3.1, http://webhelp.esri.com/arcgisdesktop/9.3/index.cfm?TopicName=How%20Spatial%20Autocorrelation:%20Moran's%20I%20(Spatial%20Statistics)%20works.

Bassanini, A., A. Booth, M. De Paola, P. Fredriksson, A. Lamo, E. Leuven, J. Messina and G., Peri. 2007. *Education and Training in Europe*, eds. Brunello, B., P. Garibaldi, and E. Wasmer. http://www.econ.ucdavis.edu/faculty/gperi/non_refereed/Book_Final.pdf, pg. 18, 47, 49.

Ciuca, V., C. Lincaru, and L., Grecu. 2010. "Vocational Training in Romania and the Training Fields Variety—Starting Point for a New Methodology of a Projection of the Human Capital Development," Abstract ID 914, Virtual Modality, ICERI 2010 (International Conference of Education, Research and Innovation) held in Madrid (Spain) on the 15th, 16th and 17th of November, 2010 (Technology in Teaching and Learning: WEB 2.0. and Social Networking: Blogs, Wikis…); ICERI2010 Proceedings CD ISBN:978-84-614-2439-9. http://www.iated.org/inted2010/publications, http://library.iated.org/view/CIUCA2010VOC: 2961-2966.

European Commission. 2008. *The European Commission Regulation no.207/2008* (*OJ No L 62/4/6.3.2008*) regarding the module ad hoc "the Young People Entrance on the Labour Market".

INS Romania. 2006. *The Salaries Structure Survey: Influence Factors.*

Lincaru, C., M. Ghenţa, D. Atanasiu, V. Ciucă, C. Drăgoiu, and B., Chiriac. 2010. "The Regions Development Characterization by Diversity/Variety of the Firms—Study case for Romania," *Regional Science Inquiry Journal*, 2, No.2:119-132.

OECD. "The Scope and Coverage of Internationally Comparative Education Statistics," *Handbook for Internationally Comparative Education Statistics,* chapter 5, 85.

Saviotti, P. P. 2009. "Is There a Direction in Economic Development?," presented in the DIMETIC Summer School Pech 2009, first version for INRA GAEL, Grenoble, and CNRS GREDEG I2C, Sophia Antipolis, France.

Saviotti, P. P., and A., Pyka. 2003. "Economic Development, Variety and Employment," Working Paper No. 35, Working Papers Series: Growth and Employment in Europe: Sustainability and Competitiveness.

Varga, A. 2009. "Introduction to Applied Spatial Econometrics," course presentation, DIMETIC Pécs.

The INS's Annual Exhaustive National Research Sc.5.1.a. The Initial Vocational Education Training is included in secondary superior—ISCED1997 version, the 3rd level (statistics of education).

The Statistic Register of Enterprises Romania 2010 INS/Enterprises Statistics Direction.

Tempo Online https://statistici.insse.ro/shop/?lang=en.

Annex One: Conversion Matrix

CANE Rev.2 activities of the national economy					Type 1 of school	
	Section		Divison	Group	Code	Profile
1	**A**	Agriculture, hunting and forestry	**01**	*011, 012, 013, 014, 015, 016*	**P14**	Agriculture
			02	*021, 021, 022, 023, 024*	**P15**	Forestry
3	**B**	Mining and quarring	**06**	*061, 062*	**P3**	Petrolium
4	**C**	Manufacturing	**24, 26, 27, 28**	*243, 265, 266, 267, 268, 271, 281, 282, 283, 284*	**P1**	Machine manufacture / machine construction
			26, 27	*261, 262, 263, 264, 271, 272*	**P2**	Electrotechnics and electronics
			20	*201*	**P5**	Industrial chemistry
			23	*231, 233, 235*	**P6**	Materials for construction
			16	*161, 162*	**P8**	Wood procesing and exploitation
			10, 11	*101, 102, 103, 104, 105, 106, 107*	**P10**	Alimentar industry
			13, 14, 15	*131, 132 , 133, 139, 141, 142, 143, 151, 152*	**P11**	Light industry
			18	*181*	**P12**	Poligraphy
			93, 96	*930, 960*	**P19**	Small industry and services
5	**D**	Electricity, gas and water supply	**35**	*351*	**P4**	Energetic
7	**F**	Construction	**41, 43**	*412, 432, 433, 439*	**P7**	Construction-montage
			42, 49	*421, 491, 492*	**P9**	Transports
			43	*433*	**P8**	Wood procesing and exploitation
8	**G**	Wholesale and retail trade; repair of vehicles, motorcycles and personal and household goods	**45, 46, 47**	*451, 452, 453, 454, 461, 462, 463, 464, 465, 466, 467, 469, 471, 472, 473, 474, 475, 476, 477, 478, 479,*	**P16**	Commerce
9	**H**	Transport and storage	**50**	*501, 502*	**P9**	Transports
10	**I**	Hotels and restaurants	**56**	*561, 562*	**P17**	Public alimentation
			55	*551, 552, 553, 559*	**P18**	Tourism
20	**S**	Others activities of national economy	**94**	*9131, 9491*	**P13**	Theological

Annex 2: Variance of Number of VET Graduates by Profile and Specialisation at NUTS 3 Level, in 2009 – Hierarchy by Total Variance

Profile	P1	P2	P3	P4	P5	P6	P7	P8	P9	P10	P11	P12	P13	P14	P15	P16	P17	P18	P19	P20	P21	*Total*
SV	20240	18491					444	2342	61	250	14921			1237	,	,	4287	800				***7556***
IS	9340	859		5	,	,	1122	1307	13101	1085	25961	,		13207		365	6466	1	1693			***7289***
PH	4798	6588	1	,	,	,	837	7688	7531	1194	7575			445	,	670	36121	,	1796			***5914***
B	**8543**	**15250**		**37**	**648**	**108**	**339**	**597**	**10428**	**186**	**1733**	**207**	,	**72**		**848**	**13239**	,	**2145**			***5369***
BT	25400	174					100	5081	1405	272	10501			2343		162	7745		246			***4708***
AG	5181	2985	25		,		729	856	20209	2	1924			591	,	32	2459		317			***3286***
SJ	11920	25			,		148	120	,		1390			52			516		18			***3209***
SM	3103	607				5	193	5802	20402	42	8947			1660	,	761	5248	,	,			***3188***
MM	2810	957		,	,	,	134	1820	8536	29	5054	13		17	,	200	15681		113			***2964***
BC	5719	152	,				1171	2309	925	121	2387			5373		1408	10082		10			***2446***
BV	1368	1661					42	429	38	357	119			1201	,	2245	12318	2	860			***2209***
VS	5521	78	,				1750	392	3042	1344	2899			3109		1102	3740	,	146			***2209***
DJ	2901	1288			,		76	57	2	109	10			1260	,	1682	2842		142			***2020***
VL	3943	1372			,	,	113	25	9408	174	1825		,	44	,	128	3968		1301		,	***2014***
CT	3797	1037		549	,	,	910	13	606	958	321		5	403	,	2450	6607	,	81			***2007***
CJ	3497	602		,	,	,	1305	173	7089	325	1198	,		82		61	5519	,	2232	,	,	***2005***
NT	1848	409			,	1	638	1207	7580	166	2876		1	237	,	,	7565	925	4			***1971***
BH	4169	1270	,				444	762	3601	279	731			468	,	648	7249	481	1744		,	***1891***
GL	2689	1311		,			1422	85	2823	797	664		,	563		6050	6796	98	177			***1836***
BZ	2963	2081			,	1	24	610	10584	239	444		39	127		2144	4471		0			***1783***
TR	1832	1386	,				1237		2813	313	351			4244		145	3145		,			***1519***
MS	4906	469	8		,	24	750	1591	1682	256	362	,		190	,	2813	3521	,	0			***1512***
GJ	3439	1155	145		,		1030	32	2813	492	37			13		72	192	648	33			***1480***
TM	2881	640	5	113	,		1010	368	3872	486	678	,		91	,	2048	3587		496			***1473***
HD	2557	1004		14	,		400	9	10225	365	888	8		38	,	5	1938	,	,			***1434***
SB	2684	740	258			2	543	265	2465	343	752	,		16	,	41	5369		346		,	***1383***
AR	1789	429	,				1291	409	4379	,	390			48		98	1893		377			***1340***
IL	2557	456					288		223	602	1101			3948		481	12		30			***1334***
OT	838	1245			,		539	40	1191	449	3688			139		421	709		166			***1239***
CL	487	882		,			111	,	3208	,	401		0	1995		,	2511		207			***1113***
DB	1095	3136	27			,	434	242	481	16	2451		5	1453	,	5	1557	,	61	,		***1049***
VN	2805	61					66	98	1310	161	387			104	,	338	1752	,				***817***
HR	291	25					268	1810	143	26	53	,		204	,	50	2923	,	98			***789***
TL	112	216			,	,	228	5	14	304	304			558	,	,	301	,	25			***762***
AB	736	428			,	14	374	175	427	,	137			78	,	4418	3430	,	61			***752***
CS	1251	527		,			964	1966	1861	0	12			276	,	32	756	181	5			***715***
MH	534	972			,		4	134	,	2	33		,	15	,	5	181				,	***712***
BR	468	145	,				185	64	1512	567	577			2611		2356	758	,	56			***698***
BN	1584	117		,	,	,	382	382	,	21	405			650	,	18	258	32	,			***668***
IF	365	108					25		,	,	,			39	,	91	2020	,				***529***
GR	192	489	,				90	,	481	12	34			44		145						***465***
CV	3872	225					19	658	,	18	234	,		133		1	117	,	169			***431***

Annex 3

Profile	P1	P2	P3	P4	P5	P6	P7	P8	P9	P10	P11	P12	P13	P14	P15	P16	P17	P18	P19	P20	P21	*Total*
SV	20240	18491					444	2342	61	250	14921			1237			4287	800				*7556*
IS	9340	859		5			1122	1307	13101	1085	25961			13207		365	6466	1	1693			*7289*
PH	4798	6588	1				837	7688	7531	1194	7575			445		670	36121		1796			*5914*
B	8543	15250		37	648	108	339	597	10428	186	1733	207		72		848	13239		2145			*5369*
BT	25400	174					100	5081	1405	272	10501			2343		162	7745		246			*4708*
AG	5181	2985	25				729	856	20209	2	1924			591		32	2459		317			*3286*
SJ	11920	25					148	120			1390			52			516		18			*3209*
SM	3103	607				5	193	5802	20402	42	8947			1660		761	5248					*3188*
MM	2810	957					134	1820	8536	29	5054	13		17		200	15681		113			*2964*
BC	5719	152					1171	2309	925	121	2387			5373		1408	10082		10			*2446*
BV	1368	1661					42	429	38	357	119			1201		2245	12318	2	860			*2209*
VS	5521	78					1750	392	3042	1344	2899			3109		1102	3740		146			*2209*
DJ	2901	1288					76	57	2	109	10			1260		1682	2842		142			*2020*
VL	3943	1372					113	25	9408	174	1825			44		128	3968		1301			*2014*
CT	3797	1037		549			910	13	606	958	321		5	403		2450	6607		81			*2007*
CJ	3497	602					1305	173	7089	325	1198			82		61	5519		2232			*2005*
NT	1848	409				1	638	1207	7580	166	2876		1	237			7565	925	4			*1971*
BH	4169	1270					444	762	3601	279	731			468		648	7249	481	1744			*1891*
GL	2689	1311					1422	85	2823	797	664			563		6050	6796	98	177			*1836*
BZ	2963	2081				1	24	610	10584	239	444		39	127		2144	4471		0			*1783*
TR	1832	1386					1237		2813	313	351			4244		145	3145					*1519*
MS	4906	469	8			24	750	1591	1682	256	362			190		2813	3521		0			*1512*
GJ	3439	1155	145				1030	32	2813	492	37			13		72	192	648	33			*1480*
TM	2881	640	5	113			1010	368	3872	486	678			91		2048	3587		496			*1473*
HD	2557	1004		14			400	9	10225	365	888	8		38		5	1938					*1434*
SB	2684	740	258			2	543	265	2465	343	752			16		41	5369		346			*1383*
AR	1789	429					1291	409	4379		390			48		98	1893		377			*1340*
IL	2557	456					288		223	602	1101			3948		481	12		30			*1334*
OT	838	1245					539	40	1191	449	3688			139		421	709		166			*1239*
CL	487	882					111		3208		401		0	1995			2511		207			*1113*
DB	1095	3136	27				434	242	481	16	2451		5	1453		5	1557		61			*1049*
VN	2805	61					66	98	1310	161	387			104		338	1752					*817*
HR	291	25					268	1810	143	26	53			204		50	2923		98			*789*
TL	112	216					228	5	14	304	304			558			301		25			*762*
AB	736	428				14	374	175	427		137			78		4418	3430		61			*752*
CS	1251	527					964	1966	1861	0	12			276		32	756	181	5			*715*
MH	534	972					4	134		2	33			15		5	181					*712*
BR	468	145					185	64	1512	567	577			2611		2356	758		56			*698*
BN	1584	117					382	382		21	405			650		18	258	32				*668*
IF	365	108					25							39		91	2020					*529*
GR	192	489					90		481	12	34			44		145						*465*
CV	3872	225					19	658		18	234			133		1	117		169			*431*

Annex 4

NUTS2	NUTS3	Demand structure matrix at NUTS2 level for economic activities at section level NACE Rev.2 (using the indicator FOM103D TEMPO/INS, 2009) - variant 1										Demand structure matrix (MD2009) - supply structure matrix (MS2009)									probabilities	
		Section NACE R2										Section NACE R2									Matching MD-MS	Substitution C with A
		A	B	C	D	F	G	H	I	S	Total	A	B	C	D	F	G	H	I	S		
	BC	1,02	0,05	0,54	0,03	0,34	0,43	0,12	0,03	0,06	2,61	0,84	0,03	-1,00	0,03	-0,02	0,28	0,03	-0,24	0,06	0,01	**-0,16**
	BT	1,14	0,00	0,30	0,01	0,07	0,22	0,07	0,02	0,03	1,85	0,70	0,00	-1,14	0,01	-0,03	0,12	-0,08	-0,39	0,03	-0,77	**-0,44**
	IS	1,43	0,00	0,62	0,04	0,38	0,54	0,18	0,06	0,07	3,30	0,94	0,00	-1,94	0,01	-0,02	0,35	-0,18	-0,34	0,07	-1,10	
	NT	1,27	0,01	0,45	0,02	0,13	0,38	0,10	0,03	0,03	2,41	0,99	0,01	-1,02	0,02	-0,13	0,36	-0,16	-0,43	0,00	-0,37	**-0,03**
	SV	1,64	0,02	0,47	0,02	0,15	0,42	0,15	0,06	0,07	3,00	1,22	0,02	-2,23	0,02	-0,06	0,34	0,10	-0,59	0,07	-1,09	**-1,01**
N-E	VS	0,87	0,04	0,44	0,04	0,20	0,33	0,10	0,04	0,03	2,09	0,47	0,02	-0,88	0,04	-0,02	0,22	-0,05	-0,26	0,03	-0,44	**-0,41**
	BR	0,59	0,01	0,39	0,02	0,18	0,25	0,08	0,03	0,03	1,56	0,47	-0,01	-0,40	0,02	0,09	0,04	-0,06	-0,18	0,03	0,01	**0,07**
	BZ	1,11	0,02	0,47	0,02	0,12	0,32	0,10	0,02	0,04	2,23	0,96	0,02	-0,73	0,02	0,02	0,16	-0,17	-0,27	0,01	0,01	**0,23**
	CT	0,97	0,03	0,62	0,07	0,52	0,68	0,41	0,12	0,12	3,54	0,73	0,03	-0,90	-0,02	0,28	0,37	0,14	-0,35	0,10	0,37	**-0,17**
	GL	0,92	0,01	0,47	0,04	0,25	0,36	0,16	0,05	0,04	2,29	0,68	0,01	-0,91	0,02	-0,06	0,18	-0,17	-0,39	0,03	-0,60	**-0,23**
	TL	0,48	0,01	0,22	0,01	0,07	0,11	0,06	0,02	0,03	1,00	0,16	0,01	-0,34	0,01	-0,07	0,07	0,01	-0,13	0,03	-0,25	**-0,18**
S-E	VN	0,96	0,00	0,35	0,01	0,11	0,23	0,09	0,01	0,03	1,79	0,86	0,00	-0,34	0,01	0,05	0,16	-0,08	-0,20	0,03	0,51	**0,52**
	AG	1,06	0,03	0,94	0,03	0,28	0,43	0,16	0,04	0,04	3,02	0,80	-0,01	-1,09	0,03	-0,01	0,25	-0,25	-0,16	0,04	-0,41	**-0,29**
	CL	0,73	0,00	0,19	0,01	0,06	0,12	0,06	0,01	0,00	1,18	0,50	0,00	-0,36	-0,02	0,01	0,10	-0,23	-0,19	-0,01	-0,20	**0,14**
	DB	1,07	0,05	0,62	0,02	0,10	0,39	0,17	0,02	0,02	2,47	0,78	-0,02	-0,56	0,02	-0,11	0,34	0,01	-0,16	-0,01	0,30	**0,22**
	GR	0,70	0,02	0,09	0,01	0,10	0,10	0,06	0,01	0,00	1,08	0,64	0,00	-0,26	0,01	0,00	-0,08	0,00	0,01	0,00	0,32	**0,38**
	IL	0,68	0,00	0,20	0,01	0,08	0,17	0,06	0,02	0,03	1,24	0,35	0,00	-0,55	0,01	0,02	0,09	-0,02	-0,06	0,03	-0,14	**-0,20**
	PH	0,98	0,09	1,03	0,04	0,40	0,62	0,26	0,07	0,06	3,56	0,78	0,04	-1,29	0,01	-0,05	0,46	0,00	-0,81	0,06	-0,78	**-0,51**
S	TR	1,31	0,03	0,26	0,01	0,05	0,21	0,07	0,01	0,02	1,98	0,99	0,00	-0,48	0,01	-0,11	0,08	-0,04	-0,18	0,02	0,29	**0,51**
	DJ	1,65	0,02	0,53	0,05	0,25	0,54	0,17	0,03	0,04	3,26	1,21	0,02	-1,26	0,05	0,10	0,26	0,12	-0,25	0,04	0,29	**-0,05**
	GJ	0,59	0,23	0,23	0,06	0,21	0,20	0,08	0,03	0,02	1,66	0,55	0,19	-1,11	0,06	0,07	0,09	-0,12	-0,17	0,02	-0,42	**-0,56**
	MH	0,75	0,01	0,19	0,04	0,12	0,15	0,07	0,01	0,01	1,35	0,63	0,01	-0,51	0,04	0,07	0,04	-0,09	-0,14	0,00	0,06	**0,13**
	OT	1,17	0,02	0,41	0,01	0,12	0,20	0,08	0,02	0,02	2,06	0,98	0,02	-0,87	0,01	-0,14	-0,08	-0,07	-0,10	0,02	-0,23	**0,11**
S-W	VL	1,04	0,00	0,32	0,01	0,06	0,20	0,07	0,01	0,02	1,73	0,97	0,00	-0,86	0,01	-0,08	0,13	-0,20	-0,24	0,00	-0,26	**0,11**
	AR	0,71	0,01	0,87	0,02	0,17	0,45	0,17	0,05	0,08	2,53	0,54	0,01	0,14	0,02	-0,08	0,22	-0,09	-0,20	0,08	0,63	
	CS	0,63	0,01	0,36	0,02	0,11	0,18	0,09	0,03	0,02	1,44	0,42	0,01	-0,48	-0,03	-0,10	0,12	-0,02	-0,14	0,02	-0,19	**-0,06**
	HD	0,64	0,17	0,55	0,05	0,18	0,44	0,13	0,04	0,03	2,24	0,40	0,17	-0,78	-0,01	-0,12	0,23	-0,06	-0,21	0,03	-0,34	**-0,38**
W	TM	1,10	0,02	1,12	0,04	0,31	0,70	0,25	0,08	0,11	3,72	0,96	-0,01	-0,46	0,02	-0,05	0,43	0,13	-0,19	0,11	0,92	**0,50**
	BH	1,32	0,03	0,91	0,04	0,22	0,54	0,20	0,07	0,05	3,38	1,07	0,02	-0,25	0,04	-0,12	0,43	-0,07	-0,55	0,05	0,62	**0,82**
	BN	0,67	0,00	0,40	0,01	0,13	0,24	0,09	0,02	0,04	1,59	0,31	0,00	-0,69	-0,01	-0,05	0,10	-0,01	-0,12	0,04	-0,43	**-0,38**
	CJ	1,10	0,02	0,90	0,04	0,42	0,78	0,27	0,07	0,11	3,73	1,01	0,02	-0,54	0,00	-0,01	0,63	-0,07	-0,42	0,11	0,74	**0,47**
	MM	1,12	0,01	0,65	0,01	0,17	0,33	0,14	0,04	0,04	2,50	0,97	0,01	-0,97	-0,01	-0,03	0,22	-0,08	-0,54	0,04	-0,38	**0,00**
	SM	0,85	0,00	0,49	0,01	0,14	0,24	0,09	0,02	0,03	1,87	0,60	0,00	-0,86	0,01	-0,02	0,16	-0,15	-0,30	0,03	-0,53	**-0,26**
N-W	SJ	0,54	0,00	0,32	0,01	0,06	0,19	0,08	0,01	0,02	1,23	0,49	0,00	-0,50	0,01	-0,02	0,19	-0,13	-0,12	0,02	-0,07	**-0,01**
	AB	0,76	0,01	0,61	0,02	0,10	0,32	0,13	0,03	0,04	2,02	0,63	0,01	-0,46	0,02	-0,05	0,15	0,06	-0,23	0,04	0,17	**0,17**
	BV	0,48	0,01	0,80	0,03	0,38	0,60	0,22	0,11	0,07	2,71	0,33	0,01	-0,79	0,03	0,30	0,45	0,16	-0,56	0,07	0,02	**-0,45**
	CV	0,36	0,00	0,32	0,00	0,06	0,19	0,05	0,02	0,01	1,02	0,23	0,00	-0,23	0,00	-0,04	0,15	-0,02	-0,19	0,01	-0,08	**0,00**
	HR	0,64	0,01	0,46	0,01	0,09	0,26	0,09	0,04	0,02	1,62	0,47	0,01	-0,40	0,01	0,01	0,13	0,01	-0,31	0,02	-0,06	**0,07**
	MS	1,06	0,05	0,72	0,04	0,20	0,45	0,19	0,05	0,06	2,83	0,72	0,00	-0,57	0,04	-0,01	0,28	0,01	-0,25	0,06	0,27	**0,15**
C	SB	0,42	0,03	0,71	0,02	0,18	0,37	0,16	0,06	0,06	2,02	0,31	-0,06	-0,59	0,02	-0,08	0,13	-0,04	-0,27	0,06	-0,52	**-0,27**
	IF	0,52	0,00	0,50	0,01	0,12	0,50	0,18	0,04	0,02	1,90	0,36	0,00	0,22	0,01	0,10	0,46	0,16	-0,19	0,02	1,15	
B-IF	B	0,03	0,04	1,89	0,18	2,24	3,14	0,97	0,35	0,51	9,36	-0,03	0,04	-2,57	0,08	1,80	2,98	0,44	-0,28	0,49	2,95	**-2,59**

Total employment 2009 *6499700*

Annex 5

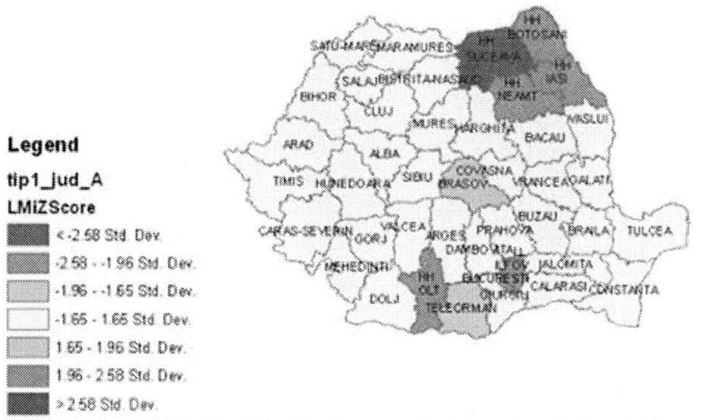

tip1_jud_CAENRev2: A. Agriculture, hunting and forestry

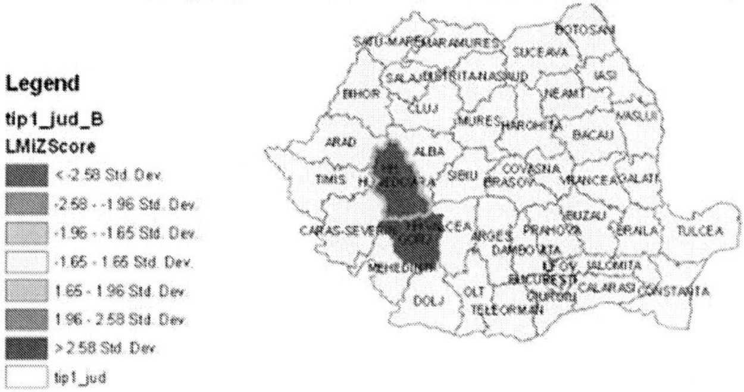

tip1_jud_CAENRev2: B. Mining and quarring

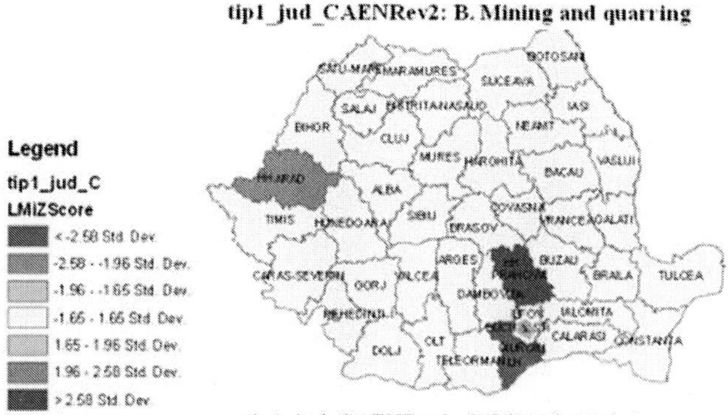

tip1_jud_CAENRev2: C. Manufacturing

tip1_jud_CAENRev2: D. Electricity, gas and water supply

tip1_jud_CAENRev2: F. Construction

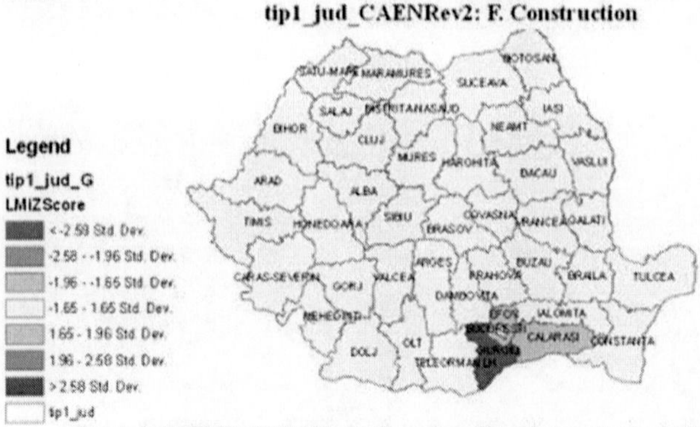

tip1_jud_CAENRev2: G. Wholesale and retail trade; repair of vehicles, motorcycles and personal and household goods

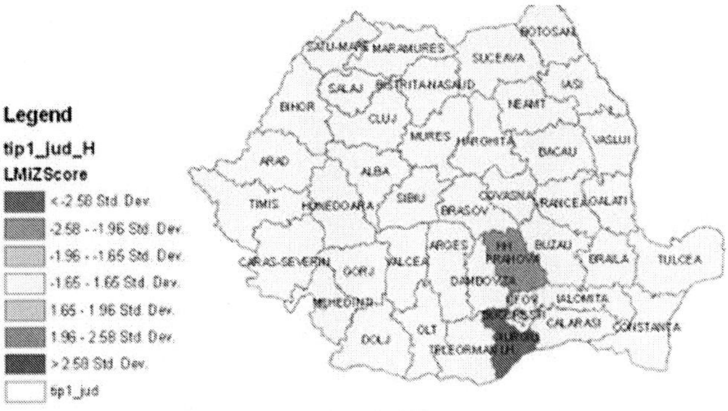

tip1_jud_CAENRev2: H. Transport and storage

tip1_jud_CAENRev2: I. Hotels and restaurants

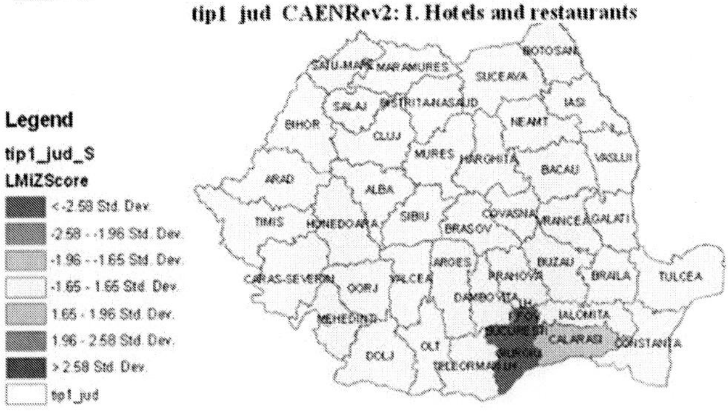

tip1_jud_CAENRev2: S. Others activities of national economy

Modelling Transitions to Employment, their Impact on Labour Market Performance and Some Estimations of Ideal Regulatory Levels for Youth Aged 15-24: Reconstruction and Simulation (EUROSTAT Data)

Cristina Lincaru and Draga Atanasiu

1. Introduction

This paper focuses on the analysis of the absolute transitions from inactivity to employment, from unemployment to employment and from inactivity to unemployment, drawing on the marginal variations of main labour market aggregates (inactivity, unemployment and employment) calculated using aggregate micro data in quarterly and annual variations.

Leaving aside at this stage the risk of underestimations in absolute transitions evaluations as well as the changes in the workforce structure (i.e. hiring and termination of employment) in the labour market, the advantage of calculations based on core indicators is that they enable constant monitoring of transitions, making it possible to determine what is required to increase employment rates, providing additional information to par. 7.3.

Not only is it necessary to increase the number of transitions (flows), but it is also essential to increase the overall employment rate (employment stocks) through positive transitions. For this reason, this paper addresses the following question: “How much should employment rate grow?” with a view to determining the impact of policies on youth employment. The purpose is to analyse short-term “simulated” absolute positive transitions, marginal variations of main labour market aggregates, ideal normative levels for simultaneous absolute positive transitions, as well as to provide an assessment of the ex-ante impact on labour market performance.

Drawing on the theory of "transitional labour markets" (Transitional Labour Markets TLMs) initiated in the early 1990s by G. Schmid[1] and the Social Science Research Center in Berlin (WZB), mention should be made of the fact that:

> The concept of transitional labour markets (TLMs) serves as the theoretical background for taking a policy-oriented view on labour markets (cf. Schmid 1998; Schmid 2002; Schmid and Schömann 2004; Schmid 2006; Schmid 2008). Given the increasing demand for flexibility and the need to preserve social security in times when traditional full-employment is no longer feasible, this concept encourages policy-makers to address labour market transitions through institutional regulations and policies that safeguard and motivate both employers and employees.[2]

This aspect should be considered on the assumption that:

> The objective was to create a comprehensive framework for labour market analysis based on normative foundations and empirical findings in order to promote coordinated efforts of labour market reforms.[3]

The purpose is to respond to the challenges that labour market operators have to face. In particular, TLMs introduce a "life course approach", i.e. an integrated approach that provides an overall assessment of policies and actions that benefit individuals, their relationship with institutions as well as their impact on society and environment. This approach offers new opportunities for the development of methodologies meeting the new requirements imposed by the use of longitudinal micro data. Measurements are carried out over a period of time to track the necessary changes to assess the impact as well as the desired and undesired effects of actions/events. Yet this methodology is time-consuming and can be applied in Romania only to a limited extent.

The transition from education to employment relates to the notion of "transitional labour markets" and goes hand in hand with an anthropological development: the transition from youth to adulthood, a complex process accompanied by specific policies aimed at fostering positive transitions. We consider here as positive transitions the changes in

---

[1] Handbook of Labour Market Policy and Evaluation (Schmid et al. 1996).

[2] Brzinsky-Fay, C. 2010. "The Concept of Transitional, Labour Markets," A Theoretical and Methodological Inventory Discussion Paper SP I, 1.

[3] *Ibid.*, 2.

one's status within the labour market, including transitions from inactivity to unemployment, from inactivity to employment, and from unemployment to employment.

1.1. Data and Methodology to Measure Key Labour Market Indicators

The data used for the purpose of this analysis come from the International Labour Office (ILO). The research study draws on employment statuses in the labour market as a key factor, and therefore it is based on the main labour market aggregates—employment, unemployment and inactivity—as interdependent units. The latest methodological updates reveal the importance of comparing labour and income to define one's employment status and whether or not employment is provided in a company or a family-run business, yet excluding productions for self-consumption.

According to the new methodology adopted in 2011 by the National Statistics Institute (INS) to measure employment rates in Romania, new criteria need to be met for unpaid family workers to be considered as employed:

> Since 2011, self-employed and unpaid family workers who work in the agricultural sector have been considered employed if they own the agricultural production (not necessarily the land) they produce and meet one of the following conditions:
>
> a) The agricultural production is intended, at least in part, for sale or exchange in kind (barter);
>
> b) The agricultural production is intended exclusively for their own consumption whether it represents a substantial part of household consumption (at least 50% of overall household consumption).
>
> Excluded from the employed population are persons:
>
> - Carrying out minor agricultural activities (equal or less than 10 hours/week) for recreational purposes, as a hobby or to get additional food, but not accounting for an important part of total household consumption;
>
> - Agricultural activities (of more than 10 hours/week) where production is intended for personal consumption but does not account for a substantial share of total household consumption.[4]

[4] Ocuparea şi şomajul în trimestrul I. 2012. "*Cercetarea statistică asupra forţei de muncă în gospodării (AMIGO)*," Comunicat de presă Nr. 143 din 26 iunie 2012 http://www.insse.ro/cms/files/statistici/comunicate/somaj/somaj_Ir_12.pdf (accessed 20 December 2013).

It should be noted that "employed person" also refers to people who:

> on a weekly basis carry out paid or income generating work even if still in education, retired or registered at the National Agency for Employment (ANOFM), receiving or not unemployment benefits, as well as apprentices and paid interns working full or part-time.[5]

2. Aggregate Population by Employment Status and Absolute Positive Transitions

A dynamic approach to the labour market requires the use of both stock and flow data. Stock data provide a snapshot of the situation at a given time, and are measured at predefined intervals usually on a quarterly and monthly basis. Flow data describe the number of persons who enter or exit a specific status in the relevant time span. The relationship between stock and flow data could be modelled (Fig. 2-8) depending on main population aggregates in the labour market and connected to each other through transitions between statuses:

Fig. 2-8. Population Aggregates Linked to Each Other through Status Transitions.

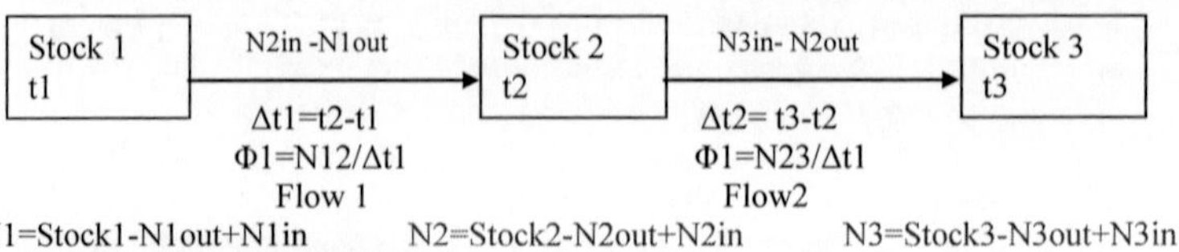

Stock- stock data (maintain the status)
N - flow data (changes the status)
t - moment / time
Φ - transitions flow of individuals changing their status over a period of time

Our model (Fig. 2-9) estimates the flow variations between statuses calculated as absolute variations of the stock using aggregate micro data (EUROSTAT source). The main purpose is to estimate the flows required to meet employment targets. The approach is only a first step towards the estimation of Nin (number of persons changing status in the relevant

[5] Ocuparea şi şomajul în trimestrul I. 2012. *Cercetarea statistică asupra forţei de muncă în gospodării (AMIGO)*, Comunicat de presă Nr. 143 din 26 iunie 2012 http://www.insse.ro/cms/files/statistici/comunicate/somaj/somaj_Ir_12.pdf (accessed 20 December 2013).

period) and flows are higher than absolute variations (see the chapter on worker flows).

We refer to positive transitions to indicate changes in labour market status with a view to finding employment or increasing employability.

Fig. 2-9. Population Aggregates by Employment Status and Absolute Positive Transitions between Statuses: Inactivity, Unemployment and Employment.

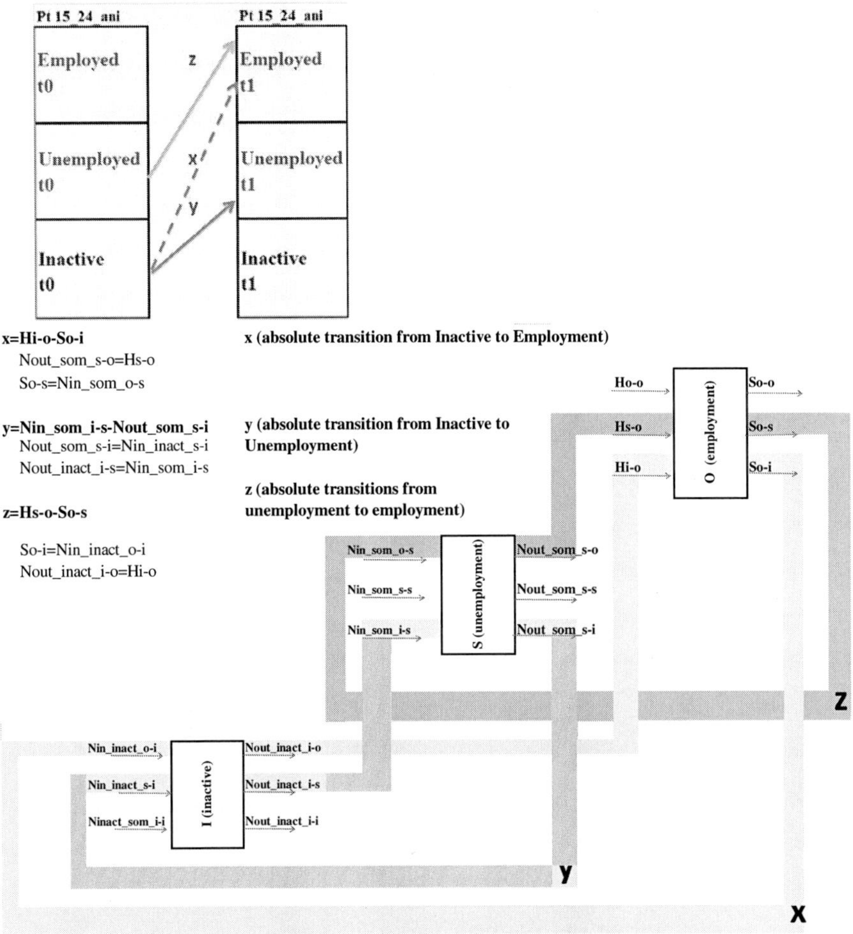

Ho-o *entry to employment/ hiring of already employed people*
Hs-o *entry to employment/ hiring of previously unemployed people*
Hi-o *entry to employment/ hiring of inactive people*
So-o *exit from employment/ termination of employment and entry to*

	employment / employment-employment transitions
So-s	*exit from employment/ termination of employment and entry to unemployment / employment-unemployment transitions*
So-i	*exit from employment/ termination and entry to inactivity/ employment-inactive transitions*
Nin_som_o-s	*entry to unemployment from employment*
Nin_som_s-s	*maintaining unemployment status*
Nin_som_i-s	*exit from inactivity and entry to unemployment*
Nout_som_s-o	*exit from unemployment and entry to employment*
Nout_som_s-s	*maintaining unemployment status*
Nout_som_s-i	*exit from unemployment and entry to inactivity*
Nin_inact_o-i	*exit from employment and entry to inactivity*
Nin_inact_s-i	*exit from unemployment and entry to inactivity*
Nin_inact_i-i	*maintaining inactivity status*
Nout_inact_i-o	*exit from inactivity and entry to employment*
Nout_inact_i-s	*exit from inactivity and entry to unemployment*
Nout_inact_i-i	*maintaining inactivity status*

In Fig. 2-9, the following notations (regardless of time) were used:

"x" is the difference between the number of people who have transited from inactivity and taken up employment and the number of persons transited from employment to inactivity = absolute transition from inactivity to employment, therefore:

The "+" sign means that the prevailing flow is from inactivity to employment, that is the desired transition subject of specific policies;

The "-" sign means that the prevailing flow is from employment to inactivity, that is the undesired transition that is also subject to specific policies (e.g. youth activation policies);

"y" is the difference between the number of people who have transited from inactivity to unemployment and the number of persons who transited from unemployment to inactivity = absolute transition from inactivity to unemployment, therefore:

The "+" sign means that the prevailing flow is from inactivity to unemployment, that is the desired transition which is the subject of specific policies (e.g. youth activation policy);

The "-" means that the prevailing flow is that from inactivity to unemployment, that is the undesired transition which is the subject of specific policies;

"z" is the difference between the number of people who have transited from unemployment to employment and the number of those who have transited from employment to unemployment = absolute transition from unemployment to employment;

The "+" sign means that the prevailing flow is that from

unemployment to employment, that is the desired transition which is dealt with by specific policies;

The "-" sign means that the prevailing flow is that from employment to unemployment, that is the undesired transition that is the subject of specific policies (e.g. youth activation policy).

3. The Reconstruction of Real Absolute Transitions Based on Marginal Variations of the Main Labour Market Aggregates (Algorithm 1)

Based on Algorithm 1 (Fig. 2-10) we performed x, y and z calculations, using quarterly data for youth aged 15 to 24 in Romania. The example refers to the period between 2008Q2-2008Q1, representing the final and initial moment, respectively. The purpose of this calculation is to "reconstruct" absolute transitions through recent labour market history.

These indicators enable simultaneous readings of absolute variations of active, employed and unemployed population.

Fig. 2-10. Calculation of Algorithm 1: x, y, z, Calculation of Absolute Transitions Using Real Quarterly Data for Youth Aged 15 to 24 in Romania. *(The Example refers to the period 2008Q2 - 2008Q1 representing the final time-baseline).*

				2008Q1	2008Q2
			H_15_24	40,3	51,2
				2008Q1	2008Q2
	input	[lfsq_pganws]	Pt1_15-24	3.150,4	3.150,4
	input		Pal_15_24	914,9	989,6
	input		Pol_15_24	733,9	817,1
	input		Ps1_15_24	180,9	172,5
	input		Pil_15_24	2.235,6	2.160,8
calculated-fixed		***Pal/Pt1*100***	*ral_15_24*	*29,0*	*31,4*
		Pol/Pt1*100	*rol_15_24*	*23,3*	*25,9*
		Ps1/Pa1*100	*rs1_15_24*	*19,8*	*17,4*
		Pil/Pt1*100	*ril_15_24*	*71,0*	*68,6*

				2008Q2	2008Q3
	input	[lfsq_pganws]	**Pt2**	3.150,4	3.120,4
	input	**Pa1+x+y**	**Pa2**_*15*_*24*	989,6	1.020,6
	input	**Po1+x+z**	**Po2**_*15*_*24*	817,1	824,1
	input	**Ps1+y-z**	**Ps2**_*15*_*24*	172,5	196,4
	input	**Pi1-x-y**	**Pi2**_*15*_*24*	2.160,8	2.099,9
calculated-fixed		***Pa2/Pt2*100***	***ra2***_*15*_*24*	*31,4*	*32,7*
		Po2/Pt2*100	***ro2***_*15*_*24*	*25,9*	*26,4*
		Ps2/Pa2*100	***rs2***_*15*_*24*	*17,4*	*19,2*
		Pi2/Pt*100	***ri2***_*15*_*24*	*68,6*	*67,3*
output		**dPa**	**Pa2-Pa1**	74,7	31,0
output		**dPo**	**Po2-Po1**	83,2	7,0
output		**dPs**	**Ps2-Ps1**	-8,4	23,9
x= tr_I_O		**(dPa+dPo-dPs)/2**	**X**	83,2	7,1
y= tr_I_S		**(dPa-dPo+dPs)/2**	**Y**	-8,5	24,0
z= tr_S_O		**(-dPa+dPo+dPs)/2**	**Z**	0,0	0,0
				2008Q2	*2008Q3*
verification		output –verification	**Pa1+x+y**	989,6	1.020,6
		output –verification	**Po1+x+z**	817,1	824,1
		output –verification	**Ps1+y-z**	172,4	196,5
		output –verification	**Pi1-x-y**	2.160,9	2.129,8

output		*Pa2_15_24*	*0,0*	*0,0*
output		*Po2_15_24*	*0,0*	*0,0*
output		*Ps2_15_24*	*0,1*	*-0,1*
output	*error /Out from system*	*Pi2_15_24*	*-0,1*	*-29,9*

x *(absolute transitions from inactivity to employment)*

y *(absolute transitions from inactivity to unemployment)*

z (absolute transitions from unemployment to employment)

Data source: EUROSTAT, LFS.

Pt1_15-24 total population aged 15-24 at the initial moment, before the transition

Pt2_15-24 total population aged 15-24 at the final moment, after the transition

Pt = Pa + Pi

Pa1_15-24 active population aged 15-24 at initial moment, before the transition

Pa2_15-24 active population aged 15-24 years at the final moment, after the transition

ra1_15-24 activity rate of population aged 15-24 years at initial moment, before the transition

ra2_15-24 activity rate of population aged 15-24 years at the final moment, after the transition

ra = Pa / Pt * 100

Pa = Po + Ps

dPa = Pa2- Pa1, absolute variation in the number of active persons during the reference period, absolute variations of the active population

Po1_15-24 employed population aged 15-24 at the initial moment, before the transition Po2_15-24 employed population aged 15-24 at the final moment, after the transition ro1_15-24 employment rate of the population aged 15-24 at the initial moment, before the transition

ro2_15-24 employment rate of the population aged 15-24 at the final moment, after the transition

ro=Po/Pt*100

dPo=Po2-Po1 absolute variation in the number of employed persons during the reference period, the absolute variations of the employed population

Ps1_15-24 unemployed population aged 15-24 at the initial moment, before the transition; Ps2_15-24 unemployed population aged 15-24 at the final moment, after the transition; rs1_15-24 unemployment rate of the population aged 15-24 at the initial moment, before the transition

rs2_15-24 unemployment rate of the population aged 15-24 at the final moment, after the transition

rs=Ps/Pa*100

dPs=Ps2-Ps1 absolute variation in the number of unemployed persons during the reference period, the absolute variations of the unemployed population

Pi1_15-24 inactive population aged 15-24 at the initial moment, before the transition

Pi2_15-24 inactive population aged 15-24 at the final moment, after the transition ri1_15-24 inactivity rate of population aged 15-24 at initial moment, before the transition

ri2_15-24 inactivity rate of population aged 15-24 at the final moment, after the transition

The main purpose of this model is to provide information on the labour market effect of the combined action of employment and labour market policies designed to stimulate positive transitions, increase employment, reduce unemployment and lower inactivity rates.

Fig. 2-11a. Estimating Absolute Transitions (x, y, z) following their Quarterly Evolution during 1999Q1-2012Q1 in Romania, their Impact on Active, Employed, Unemployed and Inactive Population, and Population Variations for people aged 15-24.

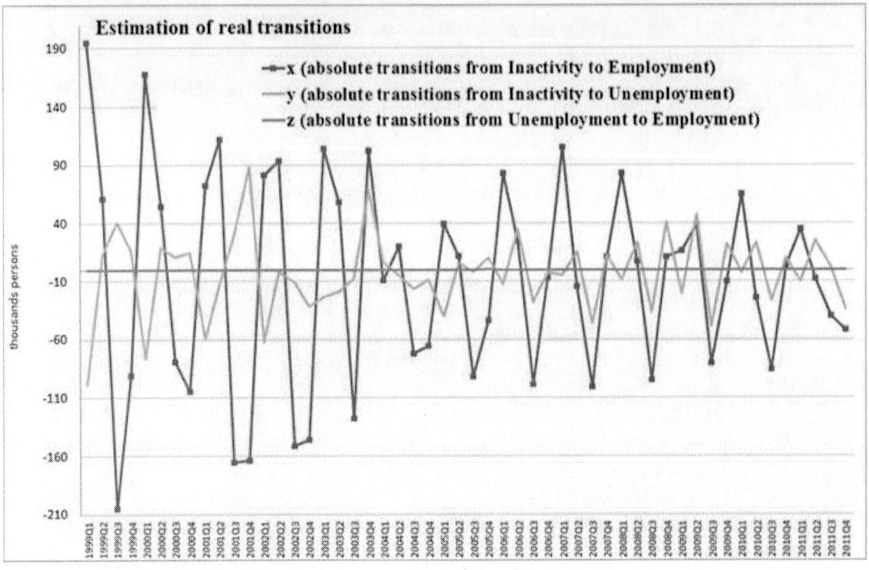

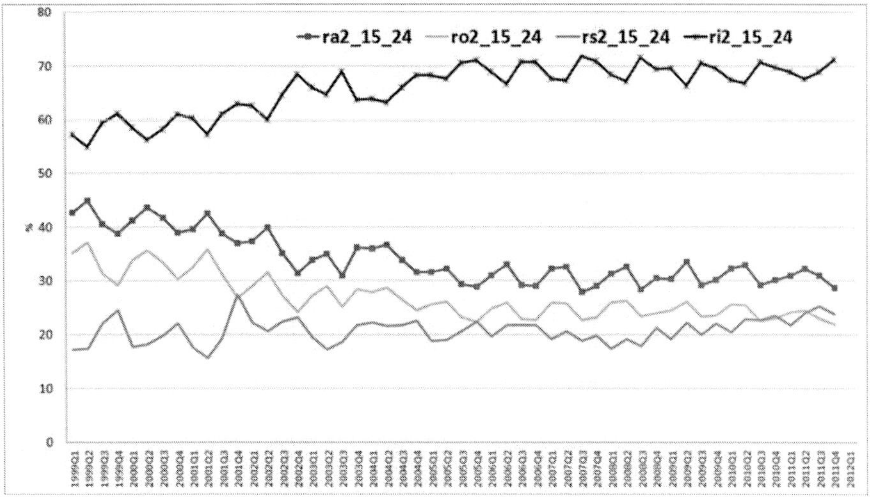

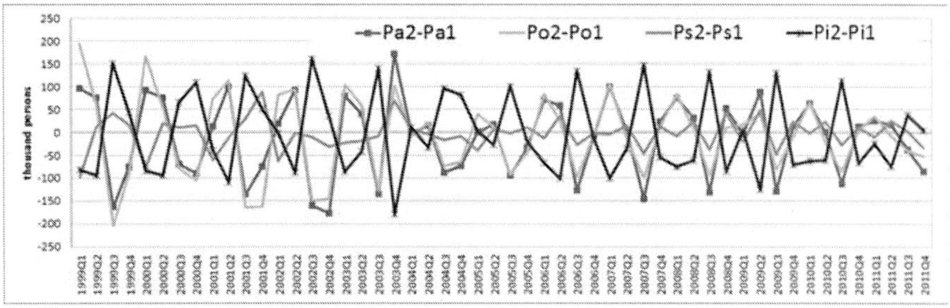

Source: Authors' Own Elaboration.

Fig. 2-11b. Estimating the Absolute Transitions (x, y, z) and the Annual Evolution during 1997-2011 in Romania, their Impact on Active, Employed, Unemployed and Inactive Population and Population Variation for People Aged 15-24.

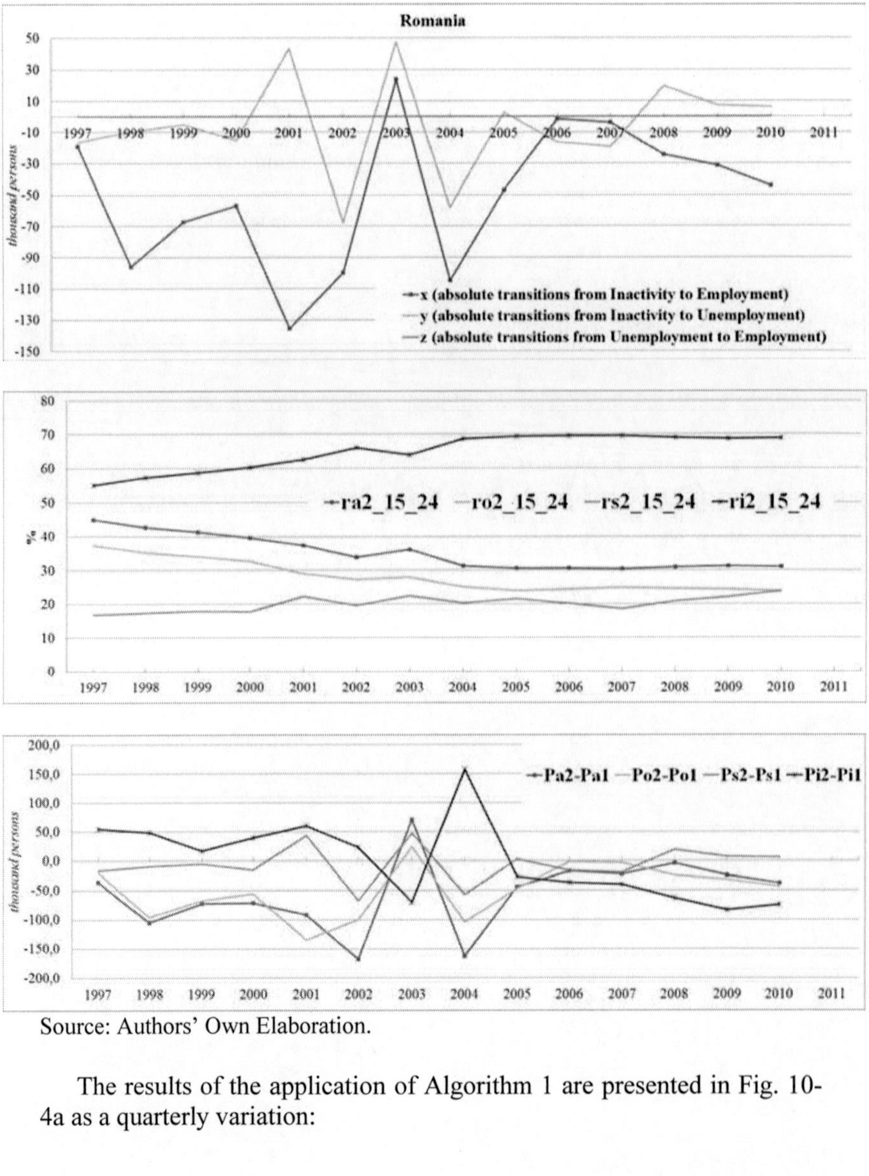

Source: Authors' Own Elaboration.

The results of the application of Algorithm 1 are presented in Fig. 10-4a as a quarterly variation:

• Trends of continuous improvement in absolute transitions. The 1999Q1-2003Q4 period was characterized by major absolute transitions from inactivity to employment for over 200,000 people in 1999Q1, as well as by transitions from unemployment to employment.

4. Short-term "Simulated" Absolute Transitions—Marginal Variations of the Main Labour Market Aggregates (Algorithm 2)

The simulations of the absolute positive transitions and their impact on labour market performance computing are carried out by applying Algorithm 2 (Figure 5), that simulates absolute transitions on the basis of x, y and z, by referring to the first quarter of 2012 and using real quarterly data for youth aged 15-24 in Romania through the following procedure:

Notation for the indicators used in the algorithm by entry order into the calculation procedure:

input data

Q12012:Pt1_15-24 total population aged 15-24 at the initial moment Q12012 before the transition

Q12012:Pa1_15_24 active population aged 15-24 at the initial moment Q12012 before the transition

Q12012:Po1_15_24 employed population aged 15-24 at the initial moment Q12012 before the transition

Q12012:Ps1_15_24 unemployed population aged 15-24 at the initial moment Q12012 before the transition

Q12012:Pi1_15_24 inactive population aged 15-24 at the initial moment Q12012 before the transition

Q12012:ra1_15_24 activity rate of the population aged 15-24 at the initial moment Q12012 before the transition

Q12012:ro1_15_24 employment rate of population aged 15-24 at the initial moment Q12012 before the transition

Q12012:rs1_15_24 unemployment rate of population aged 15-24 at the initial moment Q12012 before the transition

Q12012:ri1_15_24 inactivity rate of the population aged 15-24 at the initial moment Q12012 before the transition

Q12012:**Pt2=Pt1=** Pt2_15-24=Pt1_15_24, total population aged 15-24 at the final moment, after the transition: model hypothesis.

Simulated output data:

Pa2_*15_24*=**Pa1+x+y** active population aged 15-24, simulated at the final moment t +1 = Q2 2012, after the simulated positive transition;

Po2_*15_24*=**Po1+x+z** employed population aged 15-24, simulated at the final moment t +1 = Q2 2012, after the simulated positive transition;

Ps2_*15_24*=**Ps1+y-z** unemployed population aged 15-24, simulated at the final moment t +1 = Q2 2012, after the simulated positive transition;

Pi2_*15_24*=**Pi1-x-y** inactive population aged 15-24, simulated at the final moment t +1 = Q2 2012, after the simulated positive transition;

ra2_*15_24*=**Pa2/Pt2*100** activity rate of population aged 15-24, simulated at the final moment t +1 = Q2 2012, after the simulated positive transition;

ro2_*15_24*=**Po2/Pt2*100** employment rate of population aged 15-24, simulated at the final moment t +1 = Q2 2012, after the simulated positive transition;

rs2_*15_24*=**Ps2/Pa2*100** unemployment rate of population aged 15-24, simulated at the final moment t +1 = Q2 2012, after the simulated positive transition;

ri2_*15_24*=**Pi2/Pt*100** inactivity rate of population aged 15-24, simulated at the final moment t +1 = Q2 2012, after the simulated positive transition;

Fig- 2-12. Algorithm 2: Calculation of Simulated Absolute Transitions x, y and z, Using as Reference Q1 2012, Quarterly Data for Youth Aged 15-24 in Romania.

Total population 15-24 years [thousand persons]						2846,4	year
By employment status							*2011*
Number of persons that are not in employment [thousand persons]					**17,4**	**495,3**	
Unemployed persons [thousand persons]					6,8	193,6	
Inactive persons [thousand persons]					10,5	298,9	
Inactive persons with intention to work [thousand persons]						142,3	**3 .a.**
By disponibility to work							
Persons with intention to work (either are looking or not for a job) [thousand pe					11,9	338,7	
Persons withowt intention to work [thousand persons]					5,5	156,6	
calculated				***rs2_15_24***	23	23	
3 .b.	(x+y) maximum	**maximum transition inactive-active**			142,3	142,3	
	from 0 to 1				1	0,9	
year 2011	(x+y) **simulated**	142,3 *(0,1;1)	maxim	**x+y**	**142,3**	**128,1**	
3 .c.	**3**		x= tr_I_O	*x*	-77,3	-68,9	
	2	rsPa2-Ps1+z	y+tr_I_S	*y*	219,6	197,0	
year 2011	193,6	**maximum transiton unemployment -employment**		**zmax**	193,6	193,6	
				input 1	1	0,9	
	Z simulated		z=tr_S_O	*z*	193,6	174,2	
		reference	Q12012	Pt1_15-24	2.736,2	2.736,2	
			Q12012	Pa1_15_24	786,6	786,6	
			Q12012	Po1_15_24	598,9	598,9	
			Q12012	Ps1_15_24	187,6	187,6	
			Q12012	Pi1_15_24	1.949,6	1.949,6	
			Q12012	ra1_15_24	28,7	28,7	
			Q12012	ro1_15_24	21,9	21,9	
			Q12012	rs1_15_24	23,8	23,8	
			Q12012	ri1_15_24	71,3	71,3	
			Q12012	**Pt2=Pt1**	2.739,2	2.740,2	
	1		**Pa1+x+y**	**Pa2**_*15_24*	928,9	914,7	
	4		**Po1+x+z**	**Po2**_*15_24*	715,2	704,2	
	5		**Ps1+y-z**	**Ps2**_*15_24*	213,6	210,4	
	6		**Pi1-x-y**	**Pi2**_*15_24*	1.807,3	1.821,3	
	7		**Pa2/Pt2*100**	**ra2**_*15_24*	33,9	33,4	
	8		**Po2/Pt2*100**	**ro2**_*15_24*	26,1	25,7	
	simulated	input2	**Ps2/Pa2*100**	**rs2**_*15_24*	23	23	
	9		**Pi2/Pt*100**	**ri2**_*15_24*	66,0	66,5	
		reference	Q12012	Pt1_15-64	14.938,5	14.938,5	
			Q12012	Pa1 15-64	9.399,9	9.399,9	
			Q12012	Po1 15-64	8.660,1	8.660,1	
			Q12012	Ps1 15-64	739,8	739,8	
			Q12012	Pi1_15_64	5.538,6	5.538,6	
			Q12012	ra1_15_64	62,9	62,9	
			Q12012	ro1_15_64	58,0	58,0	
			Q12012	rs1_15_64	7,9	7,9	
			Q12012	ri1_15_64	37,1	37,1	
			Q12012	Pt2_15-64	14.938,5	14.938,5	
			Pa1+x+y	Pa2 15-64	9.542,2	9.528,0	
			Po1+x+z	Po2 15-64	8.776,4	8.765,4	
			Ps1+y-z	Ps215-64	765,8	762,6	
			Pi1-x-y	Pi2_15_64	5.396,3	5.410,5	
			Pa2/Pt2*100	ra2_15_64	63,9	63,8	
			Po2/Pt2*100	ro2_15_64	58,7	58,7	
			Ps2/Pa2*100	rs2_15_64	8,0	8,0	
			Pi2/Pt*100	ri2_15_64	36,1	36,2	
		ceteris paribus		**Relative estimated impact**			
				ra2-ra1_*15_24*	5,2	4,6	
				ro2-ro1_*15_24*	4,2	3,8	
				rs2-rs1_*15_24*	-0,8	-0,8	
				ri2_-ri1_*15_24*	-5,3	-4,8	
				ra2-ra1_15_64	1,0	0,9	
				ro2-ro1_15_64	0,8	0,7	
				rs2-rs1_15_64	0,2	0,1	
				ri2_-ri1_15_64	-1,0	-0,9	
				Pa2-Pa1_*15_24*	142,3	128,1	
				Po2-*Po1_15_24*	116,3	105,3	
				Ps2-Ps1_*15_24*	26,0	22,8	
				Pi2-Pi1_*15_24*	-142,3	-128,1	
				Pa2-Pa1 15-64	*142,3*	*128,1*	
				Po2-Po1_15-64	*116,3*	*105,3*	
				Ps2-Ps1_15-64	*26,0*	*22,8*	
				Pi2-Pi1_15_64	*-142,3*	*-128,1*	

***x** (absolute transitions from Inactivity to Employment)*
***y** (absolute transitions from Inactivity to Unemployment)*
z (absolute transitions from Unemployment to Employment)

Input data:

Q12012:Pa1_15_64 active population aged 15_64 at the initial moment Q1 2012, before the transition

Q12012:Po1_15_64 employed population aged 15_64 at the initial moment Q1 2012, before the transition

Q12012:Ps1_15_64 unemployed population aged 15_64 at the initial moment Q1 2012, before the transition

Q12012:Pi1_15_64 inactive population aged 15_64 at the initial moment Q1 2012, before the transition

Q12012:ra1_15_64 activity rate of population aged 15_64 at the initial moment Q1 2012, before the transition

Q12012:ro1_15_64 employment rate of population aged 15_64 at the initial moment Q1 2012, before the transition

Q12012:rs1_15_64 unemployment rate of population aged 15_64 at the initial moment Q1 2012, before the transition

Q12012:ri1_15_64 inactivity rate of population aged 15_64 at the initial moment Q1 2012, before the transition

Simulated output data:

Positive transitions *ceteris paribus* conditions x, z, y, of people aged 15-24. Transitions in other age groups are not considered

x=x_15-24

y= y_15-24

z= z_15-24

Pt2_15-64=Q12012, constant;

Pa2 15-64=**Pa1+x+y** active population aged 15-64 at the final moment simulated t +1 = Q2 2012, after the simulated positive transition x, z, y for the age group 15-64;

Po2 15-64=**Po1+x+z** employed population aged 15-64 at the final moment simulated t +1 = Q2 2012, after the simulated positive transition x, z, y for the age group 15-64 years;

Ps215-64=**Ps1+y-z** unemployed population aged 15-64 at the final moment simulated t +1 = Q2 2012, after the simulated positive transition simulated x, z, y for the age group 15-64;

Pi2_15_64=**Pi1-x-y** inactive population aged 15-64 at the final moment simulated t +1 = Q2 2012, after the simulated positive transition x, z, y for the age group 15-64;

ra2_15_64=**Pa2/Pt2*100** activity rate of population aged 15-64 at the final moment simulated t +1 = Q2 2012, after the simulated positive transition x, z, y for the age groups 15-64;

ro2_15_64=**Po2/Pt2*100** employment rate of population aged 15-64 at the final moment simulated t +1 = Q2 2012, after the simulated positive transition x, z, y for the age group 15-64;

rs2_15_64=**Ps2/Pa2*100** unemployment rate of population aged 15-64 at the final moment simulated t +1 = Q2 2012, after the simulated positive transition x, z, y for the age group 15-64;

ri2_15_64=**Pi2/Pt*100** inactivity rate of population aged 15-64 at the final moment simulated t +1 = Q2 2012, after the simulated positive transition x, z, y for the age group 15-64;

Estimated relative impact determined by the positive transitions model: ex ante evaluation through simulation of the impact on youth employment performance in Q2 2012 of the 15-24 age group

ra2-ra1_*15_24* absolute variation of activity rate for young people aged 15-24 from Q1 2012, the absolute activity rate variation due to changes in activity transitions simulated x, y and z for the 15-24 age group modelled under *ceteris paribus* – the transitions in other age groups are not considered;

ro2-ro1_*15_24* absolute variation of employment rate for young people aged 15-24 from Q1 2012, the absolute employment rate variation due to changes in activity transitions simulated x, y and z for the 15-24 age group modelled under *ceteris paribus* – the transitions in other age groups are not considered;

rs2-rs1_*15_24* absolute variation of unemployment rate for young people aged 15-24 from Q1 2012, the absolute unemployment rate variation due to changes in activity transitions simulated x, y and z for the 15-24 age group modelled under *ceteris paribus* – the transitions in other age groups are not considered;

ri2_-ri1_*15_24* absolute variation of inactivity rate for young people aged 15-24 from Q1 2012, the absolute inactivity rate variation due to changes in activity transitions simulated x, y and z for the 15-24 age group modelled under *ceteris paribus* – the transitions in other age groups are not considered;

Ex ante evaluation through simulation of the impact on employment performance of positive transitions of people aged 15-64 in Q2 2012

ra2-ra1_15_64 absolute variation of activity rate for people aged 15-64 from Q1 2012, absolute variation of activity rate for people aged 15-64 due to transitions simulated with x, y and z for the 15-24 age group modelled under *ceteris paribus*- the transitions in other age groups are not considered;

ro2-ro1_15_64 absolute variation of employment rate for people aged 15-64 from Q1 2012, absolute variation of employment rate for people aged 15-64 due to transitions simulated with x, y and z for the 15-24 age group modelled under *ceteris paribus*—the transitions in other age groups are not considered;

rs2-rs1_15_64 absolute variation of unemployment rate for people aged 15-64 from Q1 2012, absolute variation in unemployment rate for people aged 15-64 due to transitions simulated with x, y and z for the 15-24 age groups modelled under *ceteris paribus* – the transitions in other age groups are not considered;

ri2_-ri1_15_64 absolute variation of inactivity rate for people aged 15-64 from Q1 2012, the absolute variation in inactivity rate of people aged 15-64 due to transitions simulated with x, y and z for the 15-24 age groups modelled under *ceteris paribus* – the transitions to other age groups are not considered;

The Impact estimated through simulations determined by positive transitions x, z, y of 15-24 age group, modelled under *ceteris paribus* restrictions:

Pa2-Pa1_*15_24*= dPa=Pa2-Pa1, absolute variation in active population in the reported period, absolute variation in the active population aged 15-24 = 15-64 years

Po2-*Po1_15_24*= dPo=Po2-Po1 absolute variation in the number of employed population in the reported period, absolute variation in the number of employed population 15-24 years= 15-64 years

Ps2-Ps1_*15_24*= dPs=Ps2-Ps1 absolute variation in the unemployed population in the reported period, absolute variation in the unemployed population aged 15-24 = 15-64 years

Pa2-Pa1_*15_24*= dPa=Pa2-Pa1, absolute variation in the inactive population in the reported period, the absolute variation in the inactive population aged 15-24 = 15-64 years

Fig. 2-13. Absolute Distribution of Simulated Transitions Using as Input the Youth Unemployment Rate Variable (Simulated Variable) with Values Increasing According to the Employment Rate for Young People Aged 15-24.

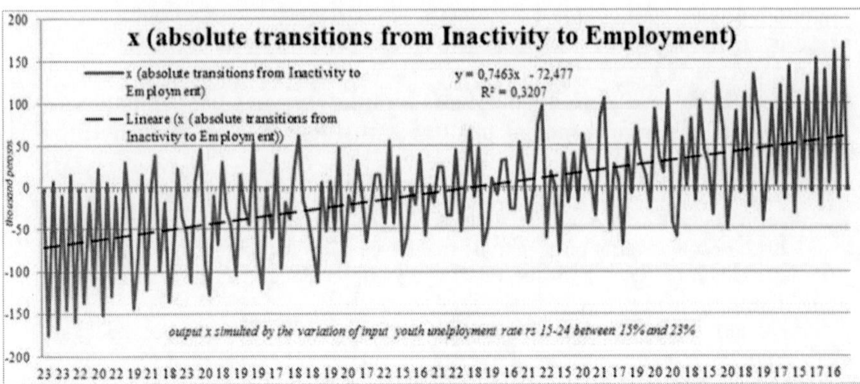

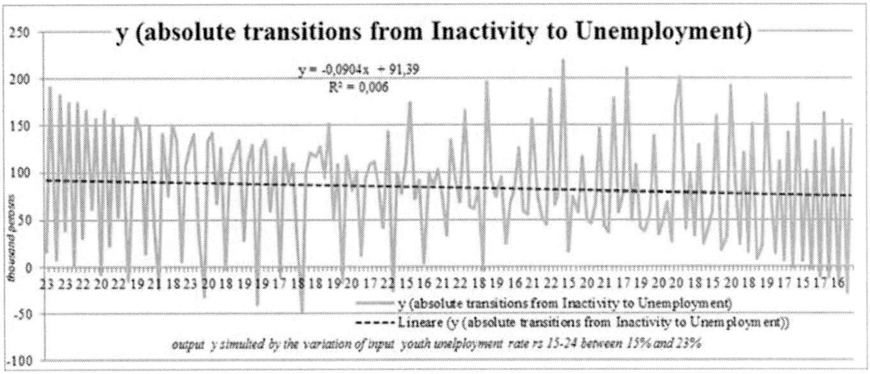

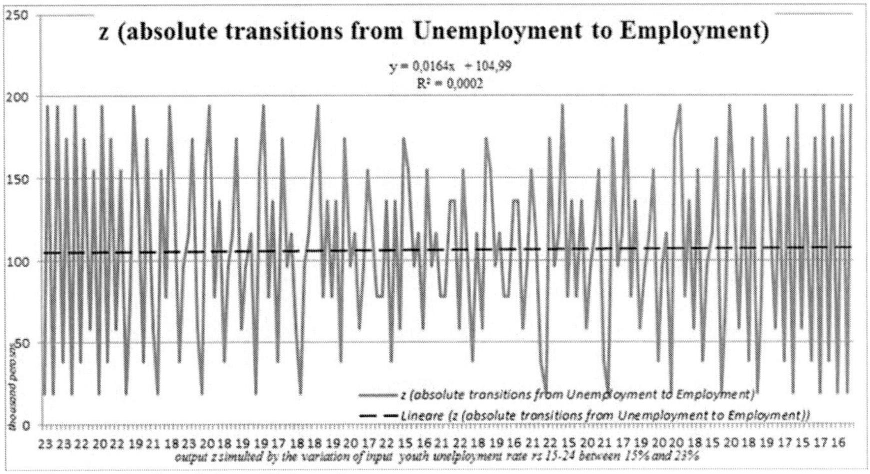

Source: Authors' Own Elaboration.

Fig. 2-14. Simulated Absolute Transitions and their Impact on Employment, Unemployment and Inactivity Rates using as Input Variable the Youth Unemployment Rate (Simulated Variable) with Values Increasing According to the Employment Rate for Young People aged 15-24.

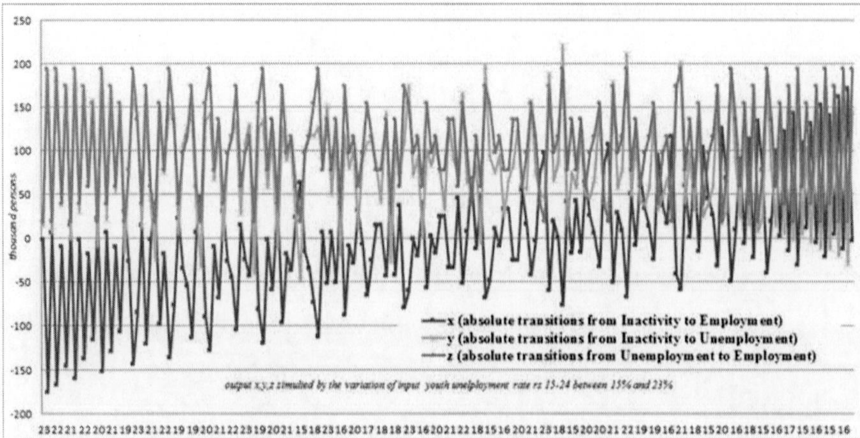

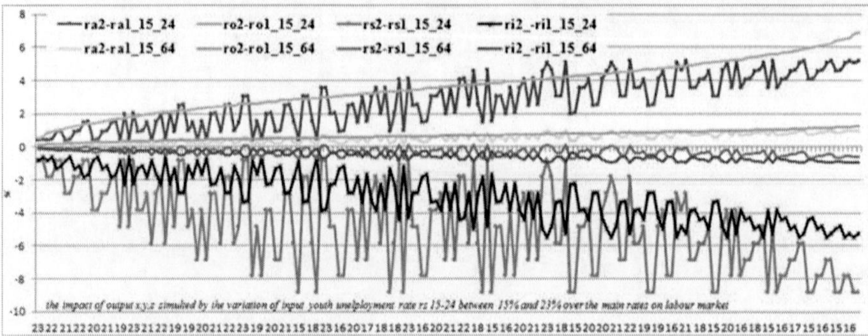

Source: Authors' Own Elaboration.

Fig. 2-15 – see over. Simulated Absolute Positive Transitions Aggregated to Estimate the Effort Required to Increase Employment and Unemployment Rate - Multiple Solutions.

The impact of x,y,z simulated output by the variation of input considering the youth unemployment rate for the 15-24 age group is between 15% and 23%.

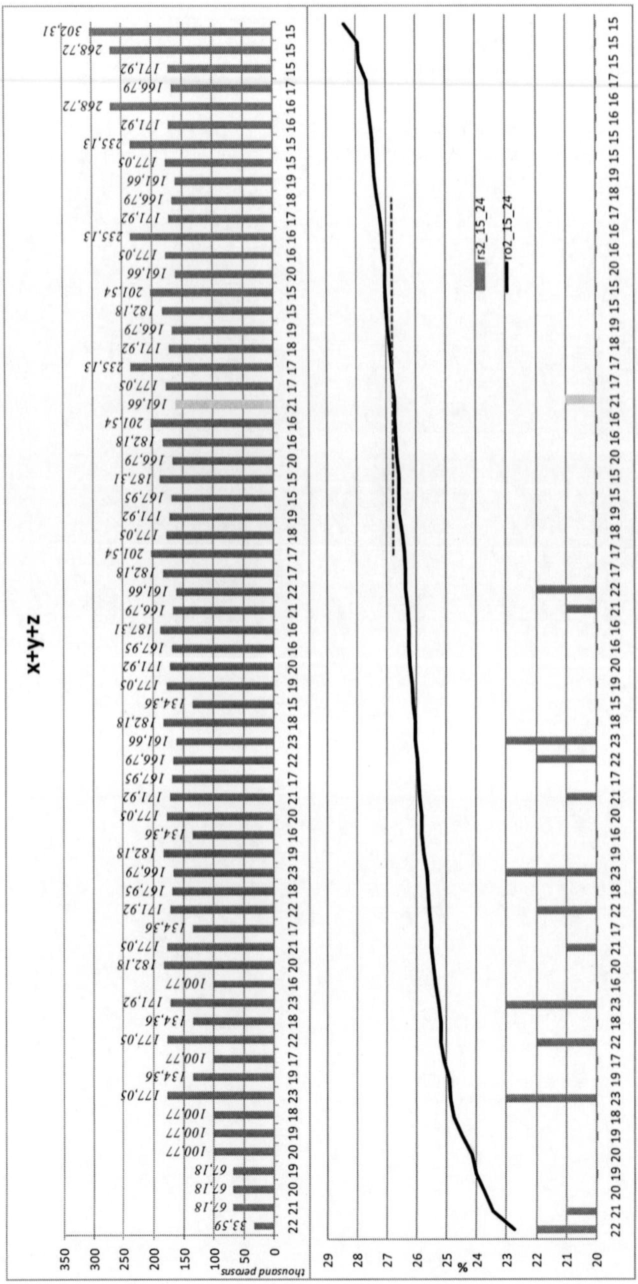
x+y+z
thousand persons
%
rs2_15_24
ro2_15_24

Table 2-12a. Simulated Positive Absolute Transition Results and their Impact on Labour Market Performance.

						thousand persons					%				thousand persons					%															
						Pt1_15-24	Pa1_15_24	Po1_15_24	Ps1_15_24	Pi1_15_24	ra1_15_24	ro1_15_24	rs1_15_24	ri1_15_24	Pt1_15-64	Pa1 15-64	Po1 15-64	Ps115-64	Pi1_15_64	ra1_15_64	ro1_15_64	rs1_15_64	ri1_15_64												
						2736	787	599	188	1950	28,7	21,9	*23,8*	71,3	14939	9400	8660	740	5539	62,9	58,0	7,9	37,1	%				%				thousand persons			
	rs2_15_24	x+y+z	x (absolute transitons from Inactive to Employment)	y (absolute transitons from Inactive to Unemployment)	z (absolute transitons from Unemployment to Employment)	Pt2=Pt1	Pa2_15_24	Po2_15_24	Ps2_15_24	Pi2_15_24	ra2_15_24	ro2_15_24	*rs2_15_24*	ri2_15_24	Pt2_15-64	Pa2 15-64	Po2 15-64	Ps215-64	Pi2_15_64	ra2_15_64	ro2_15_64	rs2_15_64	ri2_15_64	ra2-ra1_15_24	ro2-ro1_15_24	rs2-rs1_15_24	ri2_-ri1_15_24	ra2-ra1_15_64	ro2-ro1_15_64	rs2-rs1_15_64	ri2_-ri1_15_64	Pa2-Pa1_15_24	Po2-Po1_15_24	Ps2-Ps1_15_24	Pi2-Pi1_15_24
	15	134	41	16	77	2745	844	717	127	1893	30,7	26,1	*15*	68,9	14939	9457	8778	679	5482	63,3	58,8	7,2	36,7	2,0	4,2	-8,8	-2,3	0,4	0,8	-0,7	-0,4	57	118	-61	-57
	15	168	33	38	97	2744	858	729	129	1878	31,3	26,6	*15*	68,5	14939	9471	8790	681	5467	63,4	58,8	7,2	36,6	2,5	4,7	-8,8	-2,8	0,5	0,9	-0,7	-0,5	71	130	-59	-71
	15	187	14	57	116	2743	858	729	129	1878	31,3	26,6	*15*	68,5	14939	9471	8790	681	5467	63,4	58,8	7,2	36,6	2,5	4,7	-8,8	-2,8	0,5	0,9	-0,7	-0,5	71	130	-59	-71
	15	182	45	40	97	2744	872	741	131	1864	31,8	27,0	*15*	67,9	14939	9485	8802	683	5453	63,5	58,9	7,2	36,5	3,0	5,1	-8,8	-3,3	0,6	1,0	-0,7	-0,6	85	142	-57	-85
	15	202	26	59	116	2743	872	741	131	1864	31,8	27,0	*15*	68,0	14939	9485	8802	683	5453	63,5	58,9	7,2	36,5	3,0	5,1	-8,8	-3,3	0,6	1,0	-0,7	-0,6	85	142	-57	-85
	15	177	77	23	77	2745	886	753	133	1850	32,3	27,4	*15*	67,4	14939	9500	8814	685	5439	63,6	59,0	7,2	36,4	3,5	5,5	-8,8	-3,9	0,7	1,0	-0,7	-0,7	100	154	-55	-100
	15	235	19	81	136	2742	886	753	133	1850	32,3	27,5	*15*	67,5	14939	9500	8814	685	5439	63,6	59,0	7,2	36,4	3,6	5,6	-8,8	-3,8	0,7	1,0	-0,7	-0,7	100	154	-55	-100
	15	172	108	6	58	2746	900	765	135	1836	32,8	27,9	*15*	66,8	14939	9514	8826	687	5425	63,7	59,1	7,2	36,3	4,0	6,0	-8,8	-4,4	0,8	1,1	-0,6	-0,8	114	166	-53	-114
	15	269	11	102	155	2741	900	765	135	1836	32,8	27,9	*15*	67,0	14939	9514	8826	687	5425	63,7	59,1	7,2	36,3	4,1	6,0	-8,8	-4,3	0,8	1,1	-0,6	-0,8	114	166	-53	-114
max Ro15-24	15	302	4	124	174	2740	915	777	137	1822	33,4	28,4	*15*	66,5	14939	9528	8839	689	5411	63,8	59,2	7,2	36,2	4,6	6,5	-8,8	-4,8	0,9	1,2	-0,6	-0,9	128	178	-50	-128
	16	101	40	3	58	2746	829	697	133	1907	30,2	25,4	*16*	69,4	14939	9443	8758	685	5496	63,2	58,6	7,3	36,8	1,4	3,5	-7,8	-1,8	0,3	0,7	-0,6	-0,3	43	98	-55	-43
	16	134	32	25	77	2745	844	708	135	1893	30,7	25,8	*16*	68,9	14939	9457	8770	687	5482	63,3	58,7	7,3	36,7	2,0	3,9	-7,8	-2,3	0,4	0,7	-0,6	-0,4	57	110	-53	-57
	16	168	25	46	97	2744	858	720	137	1878	31,3	26,3	*16*	68,5	14939	9471	8782	689	5467	63,4	58,8	7,3	36,6	2,5	4,4	-7,8	-2,8	0,5	0,8	-0,6	-0,5	71	122	-50	-71
	16	187	5	66	116	2743	858	720	137	1878	31,3	26,3	*16*	68,5	14939	9471	8782	689	5467	63,4	58,8	7,3	36,6	2,5	4,4	-7,8	-2,8	0,5	0,8	-0,6	-0,5	71	122	-50	-71
	16	182	37	49	97	2744	872	732	140	1864	31,8	26,7	*16*	67,9	14939	9485	8794	692	5453	63,5	58,9	7,3	36,5	3,0	4,8	-7,8	-3,3	0,6	0,9	-0,6	-0,6	85	133	-48	-85
	16	202	17	68	116	2743	872	732	140	1864	31,8	26,7	*16*	68,0	14939	9485	8794	692	5453	63,5	58,9	7,3	36,5	3,0	4,8	-7,8	-3,3	0,6	0,9	-0,6	-0,6	85	133	-48	-85
	16	177	68	32	77	2745	886	744	142	1850	32,3	27,1	*16*	67,4	14939	9500	8806	694	5439	63,6	58,9	7,3	36,4	3,5	5,2	-7,8	-3,9	0,7	1,0	-0,6	-0,7	100	145	-46	-100
	16	235	10	90	136	2742	886	744	142	1850	32,3	27,1	*16*	67,5	14939	9500	8806	694	5439	63,6	58,9	7,3	36,4	3,6	5,3	-7,8	-3,8	0,7	1,0	-0,6	-0,7	100	145	-46	-100
	16	172	99	15	58	2746	900	756	144	1836	32,8	27,5	*16*	66,8	14939	9514	8817	696	5425	63,7	59,0	7,3	36,3	4,0	5,7	-7,8	-4,4	0,8	1,1	-0,6	-0,8	114	157	-44	-114
	16	269	2	111	155	2741	900	756	144	1836	32,8	27,6	*16*	67,0	14939	9514	8817	696	5425	63,7	59,0	7,3	36,3	4,1	5,7	-7,8	-4,3	0,8	1,1	-0,6	-0,8	114	157	-44	-114
	17	101	31	11	58	2746	829	688	141	1907	30,2	25,1	*17*	69,4	14939	9443	8749	693	5496	63,2	58,6	7,3	36,8	1,4	3,2	-6,8	-1,8	0,3	0,6	-0,5	-0,3	43	89	-47	-43
	17	134	24	33	77	2745	844	700	143	1893	30,7	25,5	*17*	68,9	14939	9457	8761	696	5482	63,3	58,6	7,4	36,7	2,0	3,6	-6,8	-2,3	0,4	0,7	-0,5	-0,4	57	101	-44	-57
	17	168	16	55	97	2744	858	712	146	1878	31,3	25,9	*17*	68,5	14939	9471	8773	698	5467	63,4	58,7	7,4	36,6	2,5	4,1	-6,8	-2,8	0,5	0,8	-0,5	-0,5	71	113	-42	-71
	17	182	28	57	97	2744	872	724	148	1864	31,8	26,4	*17*	67,9	14939	9485	8785	700	5453	63,5	58,8	7,4	36,5	3,0	4,5	-6,8	-3,3	0,6	0,8	-0,5	-0,6	85	125	-39	-85
	17	202	9	77	116	2743	872	724	148	1864	31,8	26,4	*17*	68,0	14939	9485	8785	700	5453	63,5	58,8	7,4	36,5	3,0	4,5	-6,8	-3,3	0,6	0,8	-0,5	-0,6	85	125	-39	-85
	17	177	59	40	77	2745	886	735	151	1850	32,3	26,8	*17*	67,4	14939	9500	8797	703	5439	63,6	58,9	7,4	36,4	3,5	4,9	-6,8	-3,9	0,7	0,9	-0,5	-0,7	100	137	-37	-100
	17	235	1	99	136	2742	886	735	151	1850	32,3	26,8	*17*	67,5	14939	9500	8797	703	5439	63,6	58,9	7,4	36,4	3,6	4,9	-6,8	-3,8	0,7	0,9	-0,5	-0,7	100	137	-37	-100
	17	172	90	24	58	2746	900	747	153	1836	32,8	27,2	*17*	66,8	14939	9514	8808	705	5425	63,7	59,0	7,4	36,3	4,0	5,3	-6,8	-4,4	0,8	1,0	-0,5	-0,8	114	148	-35	-114
	17	167	121	7	39	2747	915	759	155	1822	33,3	27,6	*17*	66,3	14939	9528	8820	708	5411	63,8	59,0	7,4	36,2	4,5	5,7	-6,8	-4,9	0,9	1,1	-0,4	-0,9	128	160	-32	-128
	18	101	23	20	58	2746	829	680	149	1907	30,2	24,8	*18*	69,4	14939	9443	8741	701	5496	63,2	58,5	7,4	36,8	1,4	2,9	-5,8	-1,8	0,3	0,5	-0,4	-0,3	43	81	-38	-43
	18	134	15	42	77	2745	844	692	152	1893	30,7	25,2	*18*	68,9	14939	9457	8753	704	5482	63,3	58,6	7,4	36,7	2,0	3,3	-5,8	-2,3	0,4	0,6	-0,4	-0,4	57	93	-36	-57
	18	168	8	64	97	2744	858	703	154	1878	31,3	25,6	*18*	68,5	14939	9471	8764	707	5467	63,4	58,7	7,5	36,6	2,5	3,7	-5,8	-2,8	0,5	0,7	-0,4	-0,5	71	104	-33	-71
	18	182	19	66	97	2744	872	715	157	1864	31,8	26,1	*18*	67,9	14939	9485	8776	709	5453	63,5	58,7	7,5	36,5	3,0	4,2	-5,8	-3,3	0,6	0,8	-0,4	-0,6	85	116	-31	-85
	18	177	50	49	77	2745	886	727	160	1850	32,3	26,5	*18*	67,4	14939	9500	8788	712	5439	63,6	58,8	7,5	36,4	3,5	4,6	-5,8	-3,9	0,7	0,9	-0,4	-0,7	100	128	-28	-100
	18	172	81	33	58	2746	900	738	162	1836	32,8	26,9	*18*	66,8	14939	9514	8799	714	5425	63,7	58,9	7,5	36,3	4,0	5,0	-5,8	-4,4	0,8	0,9	-0,4	-0,8	114	139	-26	-114
	18	167	112	16	39	2747	915	750	165	1822	33,3	27,3	*18*	66,3	14939	9528	8811	717	5411	63,8	59,0	7,5	36,2	4,5	5,4	-5,8	-4,9	0,9	1,0	-0,3	-0,9	128	151	-23	-128

Table 2-12b. Simulated Positive Absolute Transition Results and their Impact on Labour Market Performance

						thousand persons					%				thousand persons					%															
						Pt1_15-24	Pa1_15_24	Po1_15_24	Ps1_15_24	Pi1_15_24	ra1_15_24	ro1_15_24	rs1_15_24	ri1_15_24	Pt1_15-64	Pa1 15-64	Po1 15-64	Ps115-64	Pi1_15_64	ra1_15_64	ro1_15_64	rs1_15_64	ri1_15_64												
						2736	787	599	188	1950	28,7	21,9	23,8	71,3	14939	9400	8660	740	5539	62,9	58,0	7,9	37,1	%				%				thousand persons			
	rs2_15_24	x+y+z	x (absolute transitons from Inactive to Employment)	y (absolute transitons from Inactive to Unemployment)	z (absolute transitons from Unemployment to Employment)	Pt2=Pt1	Pa2_15_24	Po2_15_24	Ps2_15_24	Pi2_15_24	ra2_15_24	ro2_15_24	rs2_15_24	ri2_15_24	Pt2_15-64	Pa2 15-64	Po2 15-64	Ps215-64	Pi2_15_64	ra2_15_64	ro2_15_64	rs2_15_64	ri2_15_64	ra2-ra1_15_24	ro2-ro1_15_24	rs2-rs1_15_24	ri2_-ri1_15_24	ra2-ra1_15_64	ro2-ro1_15_64	rs2-rs1_15_64	ri2_-ri1_15_64	Pa2-Pa1_15_24	Po2-Po1_15_24	Ps2-Ps1_15_24	Pi2-Pi1_15_24
	19	67	22	6	39	2747	815	660	155	1921	29,7	24,0	19	69,9	14939	9428	8721	707	5510	63,1	58,4	7,5	36,9	0,9	2,1	-4,8	-1,3	0,2	0,4	-0,4	-0,2	28	61	-33	-28
	19	101	15	28	58	2746	829	672	158	1907	30,2	24,5	19	69,4	14939	9443	8733	710	5496	63,2	58,5	7,5	36,8	1,4	2,6	-4,8	-1,8	0,3	0,5	-0,4	-0,3	43	73	-30	-43
	19	134	7	50	77	2745	844	683	160	1893	30,7	24,9	19	68,9	14939	9457	8744	712	5482	63,3	58,5	7,5	36,7	2,0	3,0	-4,8	-2,3	0,4	0,6	-0,3	-0,4	57	84	-27	-57
	19	182	11	75	97	2744	872	706	166	1864	31,8	25,7	19	67,9	14939	9485	8767	718	5453	63,5	58,7	7,6	36,5	3,0	3,8	-4,8	-3,3	0,6	0,7	-0,3	-0,6	85	107	-22	-85
	19	177	41	58	77	2745	886	718	168	1850	32,3	26,1	19	67,4	14939	9500	8779	721	5439	63,6	58,8	7,6	36,4	3,5	4,3	-4,8	-3,9	0,7	0,8	-0,3	-0,7	100	119	-19	-100
	19	172	72	42	58	2746	900	729	171	1836	32,8	26,6	19	66,8	14939	9514	8790	723	5425	63,7	58,8	7,6	36,3	4,0	4,7	-4,8	-4,4	0,8	0,9	-0,3	-0,8	114	130	-17	-114
	19	167	103	25	39	2747	915	741	174	1822	33,3	27,0	19	66,3	14939	9528	8802	726	5411	63,8	58,9	7,6	36,2	4,5	5,1	-4,8	-4,9	0,9	0,9	-0,3	-0,9	128	142	-14	-128
	19	162	134	8	19	2748	929	752	176	1807	33,8	27,4	19	65,8	14939	9542	8814	729	5396	63,9	59,0	7,6	36,1	5,1	5,5	-4,8	-5,5	1,0	1,0	-0,2	-1,0	142	153	-11	-142
	20	67	14	14	39	2747	815	652	163	1921	29,7	23,7	20	69,9	14939	9428	8713	715	5510	63,1	58,3	7,6	36,9	0,9	1,8	-3,8	-1,3	0,2	0,4	-0,3	-0,2	28	53	-25	-28
	20	101	6	36	58	2746	829	663	166	1907	30,2	24,2	20	69,4	14939	9443	8725	718	5496	63,2	58,4	7,6	36,8	1,4	2,3	-3,8	-1,8	0,3	0,4	-0,3	-0,3	43	64	-22	-43
	20	182	2	84	97	2744	872	697	174	1864	31,8	25,4	20	67,9	14939	9485	8759	727	5453	63,5	58,6	7,7	36,5	3,0	3,5	-3,8	-3,3	0,6	0,7	-0,2	-0,6	85	99	-13	-85
	20	177	33	67	77	2745	886	709	177	1850	32,3	25,8	20	67,4	14939	9500	8770	729	5439	63,6	58,7	7,7	36,4	3,5	3,9	-3,8	-3,9	0,7	0,7	-0,2	-0,7	100	110	-10	-100
	20	172	63	51	58	2746	900	720	180	1836	32,8	26,2	20	66,8	14939	9514	8781	732	5425	63,7	58,8	7,7	36,3	4,0	4,3	-3,8	-4,4	0,8	0,8	-0,2	-0,8	114	121	-8	-114
	20	167	94	34	39	2747	915	732	183	1822	33,3	26,6	20	66,3	14939	9528	8793	735	5411	63,8	58,9	7,7	36,2	4,5	4,7	-3,8	-4,9	0,9	0,9	-0,2	-0,9	128	133	-5	-128
	20	162	125	18	19	2748	929	743	186	1807	33,8	27,0	20	65,8	14939	9542	8804	738	5396	63,9	58,9	7,7	36,1	5,1	5,1	-3,8	-5,5	1,0	1,0	-0,1	-1,0	142	144	-2	-142
	21	67	6	22	39	2747	815	644	171	1921	29,7	23,4	21	69,9	14939	9428	8705	723	5510	63,1	58,3	7,7	36,9	0,9	1,5	-2,8	-1,3	0,2	0,3	-0,2	-0,2	28	45	-16	-28
	21	177	24	76	77	2745	886	700	186	1850	32,3	25,5	21	67,4	14939	9500	8761	738	5439	63,6	58,6	7,8	36,4	3,5	3,6	-2,8	-3,9	0,7	0,7	-0,1	-0,7	100	101	-1	-100
	21	172	54	60	58	2746	900	711	189	1836	32,8	25,9	21	66,8	14939	9514	8772	741	5425	63,7	58,7	7,8	36,3	4,0	4,0	-2,8	-4,4	0,8	0,8	-0,1	-0,8	114	112	1	-114
	21	167	85	43	39	2747	915	722	192	1822	33,3	26,3	21	66,3	14939	9528	8784	744	5411	63,8	58,8	7,8	36,2	4,5	4,4	-2,8	-4,9	0,9	0,8	-0,1	-0,9	128	124	4	-128
	21	162	115	27	19	2748	929	734	195	1807	33,8	26,7	21	65,8	14939	9542	8795	747	5396	63,9	58,9	7,8	36,1	5,1	4,8	-2,8	-5,5	1,0	0,9	0,0	-1,0	142	135	7	-142
min Ro 15-24	22	34	6	8	19	2748	801	625	176	1935	29,1	22,7	22	70,4	14939	9414	8686	728	5524	63,0	58,1	7,7	37,0	0,4	0,8	-1,8	-0,8	0,1	0,2	-0,1	-0,1	14	26	-11	-14
	22	177	15	85	77	2745	886	691	195	1850	32,3	25,2	22	67,4	14939	9500	8752	747	5439	63,6	58,6	7,9	36,4	3,5	3,3	-1,8	-3,9	0,7	0,6	0,0	-0,7	100	92	7	-100
	22	172	45	69	58	2746	900	702	198	1836	32,8	25,6	22	66,8	14939	9514	8763	750	5425	63,7	58,7	7,9	36,3	4,0	3,7	-1,8	-4,4	0,8	0,7	0,0	-0,8	114	103	10	-114
	22	167	76	52	39	2747	915	713	201	1822	33,3	26,0	22	66,3	14939	9528	8775	753	5411	63,8	58,7	7,9	36,2	4,5	4,1	-1,8	-4,9	0,9	0,8	0,0	-0,9	128	114	14	-128
	22	162	106	36	19	2748	929	724	204	1807	33,8	26,4	22	65,8	14939	9542	8786	757	5396	63,9	58,8	7,9	36,1	5,1	4,5	-1,8	-5,5	1,0	0,8	0,1	-1,0	142	126	17	-142
	23	177	6	94	77	2745	886	682	204	1850	32,3	24,9	23	67,4	14939	9500	8743	756	5439	63,6	58,5	8,0	36,4	3,5	3,0	-0,8	-3,9	0,7	0,6	0,1	-0,7	100	83	16	-100
	23	172	36	78	58	2746	900	693	207	1836	32,8	25,2	23	66,8	14939	9514	8754	759	5425	63,7	58,6	8,0	36,3	4,0	3,4	-0,8	-4,4	0,8	0,6	0,1	-0,8	114	94	20	-114
	23	167	67	61	39	2747	915	704	210	1822	33,3	25,6	23	66,3	14939	9528	8765	763	5411	63,8	58,7	8,0	36,2	4,5	3,7	-0,8	-4,9	0,9	0,7	0,1	-0,9	128	105	23	-128
	23	162	97	45	19	2748	929	715	214	1807	33,8	26,0	23	65,8	14939	9542	8776	766	5396	63,9	58,7	8,0	36,1	5,1	4,1	-0,8	-5,5	1,0	0,8	0,2	-1,0	142	116	26	-142
min_ro>26,7	20	34	2	8	19	2744	801	625	166	1807	29,1	22,7	20	65,8	14939	9414	8686	718	5396	63,0	58,1	7,6	36,1	0,4	0,8	-3,8	-5,5	0,1	0,2	-0,3	-1,0	14	26	-22	-142
max_ro>26,7	23	182	125	94	97	2748	929	743	214	1935	33,8	27,0	23	70,4	14939	9542	8804	766	5524	63,9	58,9	8,0	37,0	5,1	5,1	-0,8	-0,8	1,0	1,0	0,2	-0,1	142	144	26	-14
min_tr_x_y_z>0	15	34	1	3	19	2736	787	599	127	1807	28,7	21,9	15	65,8	14939	9400	8660	679	5396	62,9	58,0	7,2	36,1	0,4	0,8	-8,8	-5,5	0,1	0,2	-0,7	-1,0	14	26	-61	-142
max_tr_x_y_z>0	23	302	134	124	174	2748	929	777	214	1950	33,8	28,4	24	71,3	14939	9542	8839	766	5539	63,9	59,2	8,0	37,1	5,1	6,5	-0,8	-0,8	1,0	1,2	0,2	-0,1	142	178	26	-14

Fig. 2-16. Absolute Transitions Calculated for the Period 1999Q1-2012Q1 in Romania Matched with Labour Market Performance and with the Set of Possible Solutions to Identify Ideal Regulation to Increase Absolute Positive Transitions.

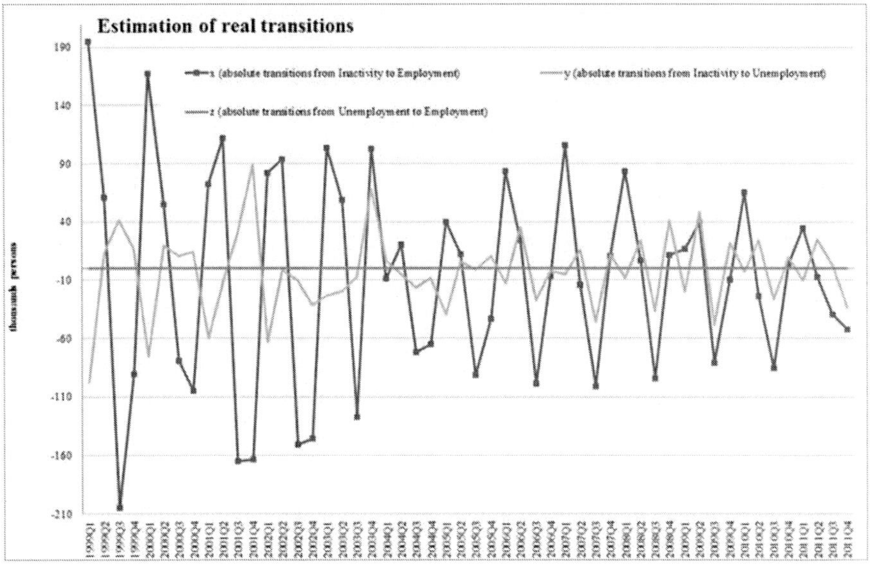

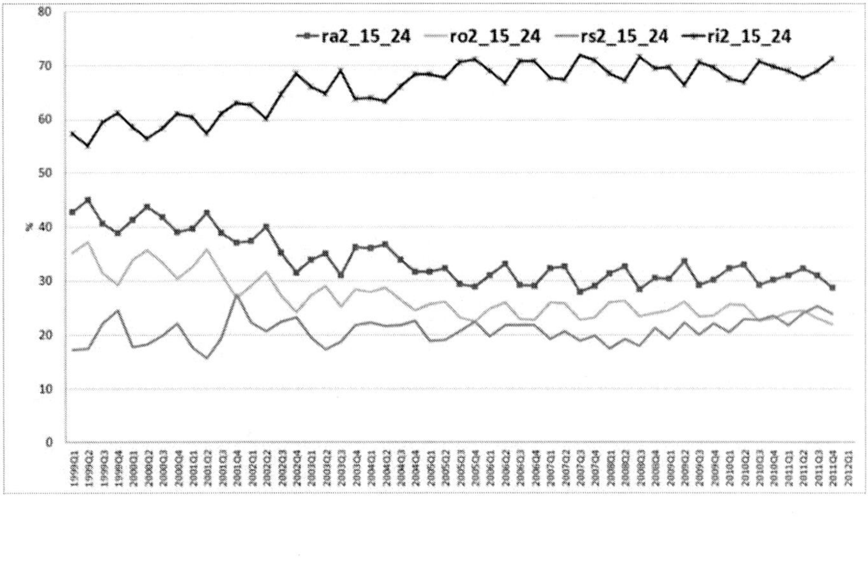

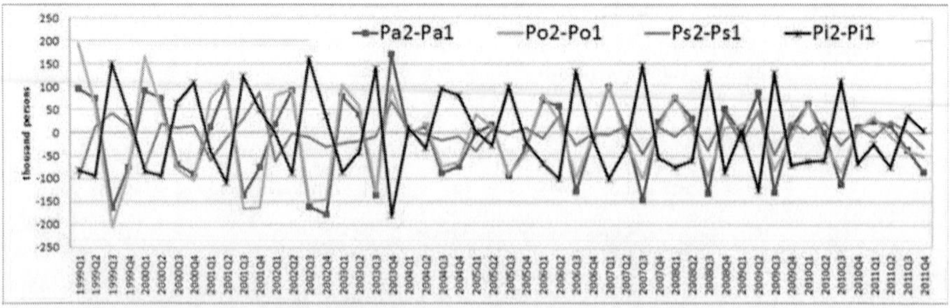
Pa2-Pa1
Po2-Po1
Ps2-Ps1
Pi2-Pi1
thousand persons

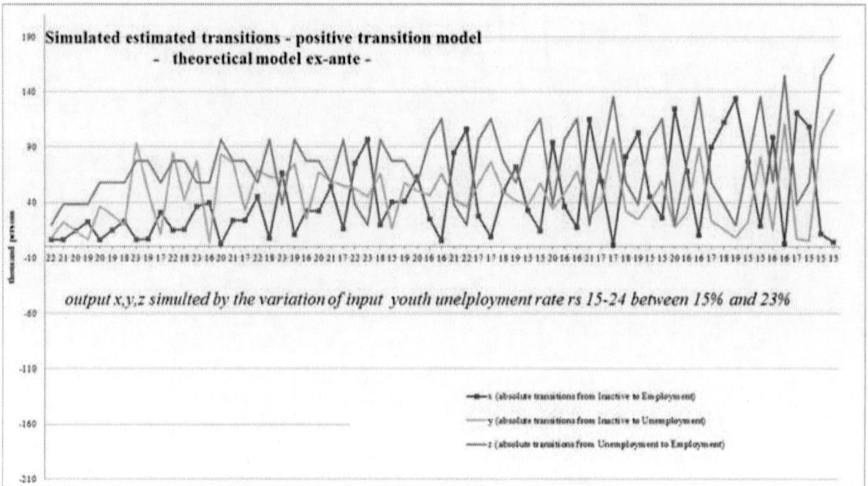
Simulated estimated transitions - positive transition model
- theoretical model ex-ante -
output x,y,z simulted by the variation of input youth unelployment rate rs 15-24 between 15% and 23%
x (absolute transitions from Inactive to Employment)
y (absolute transitions from Inactive to Unemployment)
z (absolute transitions from Unemployment to Employment)

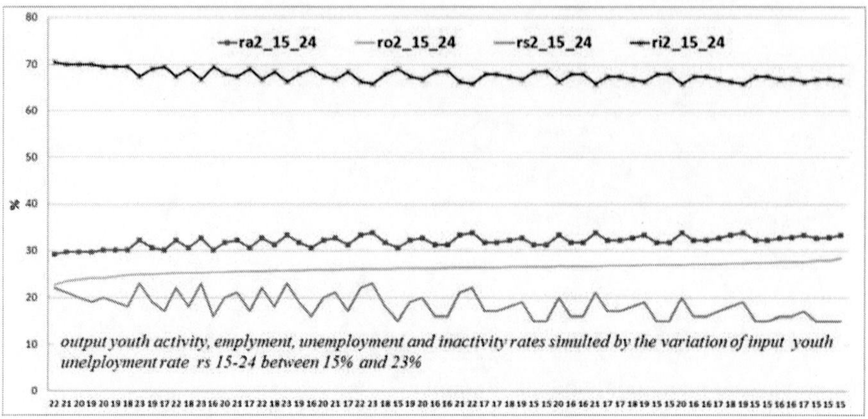
ra2_15_24
ro2_15_24
rs2_15_24
ri2_15_24
%
output youth activity, emplyment, unemployment and inactivity rates simulted by the variation of input youth unelployment rate rs 15-24 between 15% and 23%

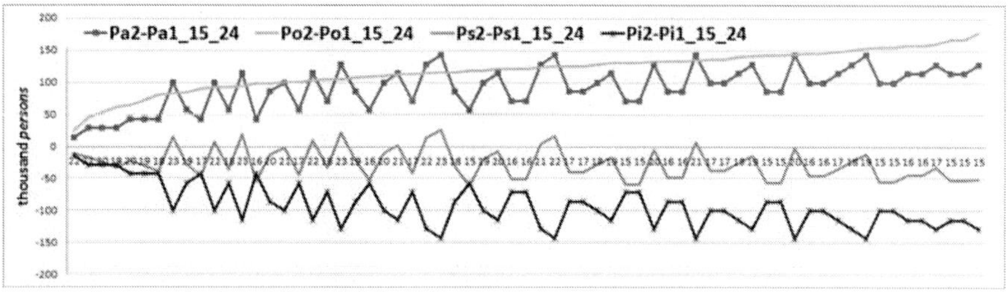

Source: Authors' Own Elaboration.

5. Ideal Regulatory Levels for Absolute Positive Transitions and Expected Impact on Labour Market Performance

In the **minimum effort scenario,** positive absolute transitions for young people aged 15-24 could be achieved only if 33.6 thousand persons take up employment (6.3 thousand persons should transit from inactivity to employment, 7.9 thousand persons from inactivity to unemployment and 19.4 thousands persons from unemployed to employment) and if the youth unemployment rate falls by 1.8pp and employment increases by 0.8 pp. This transition requires an increase in the active population of 14.2 thousand people, an increase in employment of 25.6 thousand people, a decline in unemployment of 11.4 thousand people and a decline in active population of 14.2 thousand people. The estimated impact of these transitions on the employment rate for people aged 15-64 is an increase in the activity rate by 0.1pp, an increase in the employment rate by 0.2pp and a decrease in the unemployment and inactivity rates by 0.1pp.

In the maximum effort scenario, positive absolute transitions for young people aged 15-24 could be achieved if 302.3 thousand persons access employment (4.2 thousand from inactivity to employment, 123.8 thousand from inactivity to unemployment and 174.2 thousand from unemployment to employment), if the youth unemployment rate decreases by 8.8pp and if the youth employment rate increases by 6.5pp. This would result in an increase in the working population of 128 thousand people, an increase in employment of 178.5 thousand people, a decrease of 50.4 thousand people among unemployed youth and a decline in youth inactive population of 128.1 thousand people. The estimated impact of these transitions on the employment rate for people aged 15-64 is an increase in the activity rate by 0.9pp, in the employment rate by 1.2pp and a decrease in the unemployment and inactivity rates by 0.6pp.

Table 2-13. Ideal Regulatory Levels to Ensure Absolute Positive Transitions and Youth Employment Growth.

Assuming normative levels designed to ensure positive transitions		
	minimum effort	**maximum effort**
unemployment rate 15-24 years [%] simulated	22	15
x+y+z [thousand persons]	**33,59**	**302,3**
x (absolute transitons from Inactive to Employment)	6,3	4,2
y (absolute transitons from Inactive to Unemployment)	7,9	123,8
z (absolute transitons from Unemployment to Employment)	19,4	174,2
Pa2_15_24 [thousand persons]	800,8	914,7
Po2_15_24 [thousand persons]	624,5	777,4
Ps2_15_24 [thousand persons]	176,2	137,2
Pi2_15_24 [thousand personse]	1935,4	1821,5
ra2_15_24 [thousand persons]	29,1	33,4
ro2_15_24 [%]	**22,7**	**28,4**
rs2_15_24 [%]	22,0	15,0
ri2_15_24 [%]	70,4	66,5
ra2-ra1_15_24 [%]	0,4	4,6
ro2-ro1_15_24 [%]	**0,8**	**6,5**
rs2-rs1_15_24 [%]	-1,8	-8,8
ri2_-ri1_15_24 [%]	-0,8	-4,8
ra2-ra1_15_64 [%]	0,1	0,9
ro2-ro1_15_64 [%]	0,2	1,2
rs2-rs1_15_64 [%]	-0,1	-0,6
ri2_-ri1_15_64 [%]	-0,1	-0,9
Pa2-Pa1_15_24 [thousand persons]	14,2	128,1
Po2-Po1_15_24 [thousand persons]	25,6	178,5
Ps2-Ps1_15_24 [thousand persons]	-11,4	-50,4
Pi2-Pi1_15_24 [thousand persons]	-14,2	-128,1

Source: Authors' Own Elaboration.

6. Conclusions

This paper analysed the aggregate population considering employment status and absolute positive transitions between statuses (inactivity, unemployment and employment) using an absolute transition estimation following a reality-based and regulatory approach. Comparing the real situation with simulated absolute transitions could provide an estimate of the achievable potential. This approach offers complementary information in a comparative perspective (using EUROSTAT core indicators of employment policy) that is useful to monitor, analyse and implement employment processes.

This approach highlights the recent trends occurring in Romania after 2008 affecting the population aged between 15 and 24:

- A loss of dynamism of the Romanian labour market demonstrated by the reduction in the number of positive absolute transitions to employment with regard to both quarterly and annual variations;
- An increase in labour market stability demonstrated by the reduction in absolute negative transitions (i.e. out of employment) with regard to both quarterly and annual variations;
- An increase in absolute transitions from inactivity and employment to unemployment caused by the recent economic crises, and an increase in the recourse to public support provided by labour market institutions. This trend is also reflected in the absolute variation of labour market aggregates.

In light of the recent economic crises, negative transitions out of employment have simultaneously increased, as have unemployment and inactivity. In order to stimulate and accelerate positive transitions to employment, it is necessary now more than ever to focus on active policy measures.

References

Elder, S. 2009. *ILO School-to-work Transition Survey: A Methodological Guide. Key Indicators of Youth Labour Markets: Concepts, Definitions and Tabulations.* Geneva: Youth Employment, Programme International Labour Office.

Brzinsky-Fay, C. 2010. *The Concept of Transitional, Labour Markets, A Theoretical and Methodological Inventory Discussion.*

INS. 2012. Ocuparea şi şomajul în trimestrul I 2012, Cercetarea statistică asupra forţei de muncă în gospodării (AMIGO), Comunicat de presă Nr. 143 din 26 iunie 2012 http://www.insse.ro/cms/files/statistici/comunicate/somaj/somaj_Ir_12.pdf.

EUROSTAT. *Population by sex, age, nationality and labour status* (1 000) [lfsa_pganws]. Brussels: EUROSTAT.

—. *Population by sex, age, nationality and labour status* (1 000) [lfsq_pganws]. Brussels: EUROSTAT.

—. 2008. *Employment by Sex, Age, Time since Job Started and Economic Activity (from 2008, NACE rev.2) (1 000)* [lfsq_egdn2]. Brussels: EUROSTAT.

Schmidt et. al. 1996. *Handbook of Labour Market Policy and Evaluation.*

CHAPTER THREE:

RECENT POLICIES AND INITIATIVES TO STIMULATE YOUTH LABOUR MARKET ENTRY

RECENT POLICIES AND INITIATIVES TO STIMULATE YOUTH LABOUR MARKET ENTRY: THE EUROPEAN PERSPECTIVE

CRISTINA LINCARU AND VASILICA CIUCĂ

1. Introductory Remarks

Youth are one of the most important target groups of European policies, increasingly designed to address a number of relevant issues in a range of key areas – including employment – through an integrated approach.

> […] the subject of employment should not be confined solely to the domains of education and training, but should also include social inclusion, health, well-being, participation, gender equality and diversity. […] The European Commission document makes links across the full range of policy domains: education and training; employment and entrepreneurship; health and well-being; participation; voluntary activities; social inclusion; creativity and culture; and youth and the world. The Council of Europe sets out the case for a similar vision of policy integration. This vision is animated, moreover, by a complementary set of organizing principles: human rights and democracy; the celebration of diversity; and social inclusion. In the final analysis there is consensus on the need to broaden the parameters of youth employment policy to include these wider issues.[1]

The White Paper: *A New Impetus for European Youth and the European Youth Pact (2005)* and the Lisbon Strategy put in place a strategic approach targeted at young people in the European Union. These experiences are based on the idea that:

---

[1] Text drafted by Jonathan Evans as part of the Partnership for youth between the European Commission and the Council of Europe, http://youth-partnership-eu.coe.int/youth-partnership/ekcyp/BGKNGE/Employment.

> The notion that employment policy needs to be embedded in an integrated European youth policy is expressed well in two key European mission statements: the European Commission's "An EU Strategy for Youth-Investing and Empowering" and the Council of Europe's Agenda 2020.[2]

2. EU Youth Strategy: A Renewed Framework for European Cooperation in the Youth Field (2010-2018)

Youth employment is a high-priority issue in the EU agenda. The EU Youth Strategy and Europe 2020 laid the foundation for coordinated European action aimed at tackling youth employment in the current decade. Yet, further efforts are needed to increase access to apprenticeships and traineeships and to improve youth employability.

> The Council Resolution on the renewed framework for European cooperation in the youth field (2010- 2018)[3], also known as "EU Youth Strategy", requires that an *EU Youth Report is drawn up at the end of each three-year cycle*, with a twofold objective: assess progress, and serve as a basis for establishing priorities for the future.[4]

The renewed framework for European cooperation for youth is action-based and addresses a number of issues such as employment and entrepreneurship:

> In 2009, the Council endorsed a renewed framework for European cooperation in the youth field (2010-2018), based on the Communication "EU Youth Strategy: Investing and Empowering".[5] By reinforcing

---

[2] Text drafted by Jonathan Evans for the Partnership between the European Commission and the Council of Europe in the field of youth, http://youth-partnership-eu.coe.int/youth-partnership/ekcyp/BGKNGE/Employment.

[3] OJ C 311, 19.12.2009, 1.

[4] European Union. 2012. *Joint Report of the Council and the Commission on the Implementation of the Renewed Framework for European Cooperation in the Youth Field* (2010-18) (2012/C 394/03), Notice from European Union Institutions, Bodies, Offices and Agencies Council European Commission, 20.12.2012 Official Journal of the European Union C 394/5. Brussels: European Commission.

[5] European Commission. 2009. *Communication from the Commission to the Council, the European Parliament, the European Economic and Social Committee and the Committee of Regions. An EU Strategy for Youth— Investing and Empowering. A Renewed Open Method of Coordination to Address Youth Challenges and Opportunities.* {SEC(2009) 545}, {SEC(2009) 546}, {SEC(2009)

cooperation and sharing good practices, the renewed framework's objectives include:
(i) The improvement of equal opportunities for all young people in education and in the labour market,
(ii) The promotion of active citizenship, social inclusion and solidarity among young people.

Fig. 3-1. Tree Diagram Representing the Fields of Action.

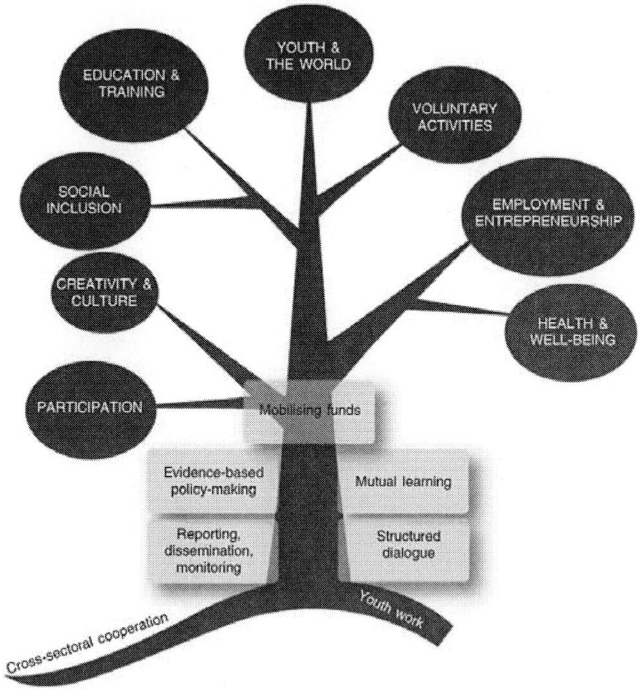

Source: Author's Own Elaboration.

As illustrated by the tree diagram above, the programme branches out into eight policy areas (called "fields of action"): education and training; employment and entrepreneurship; social inclusion; health

548}, {SEC(2009) 549}, 27.4.2009 COM(2009) 200 final. Brussels: European Commission, 4.

and well-being; participation; culture and creativity; volunteering, youth and the world.[6]

2.1. Youth Employment and Entrepreneurship Policy

All policy areas, including youth employment and entrepreneurship, draw on some common principles: evidence-based policy-making; mutual learning; regular progress reporting, dissemination and monitoring of results; structured dialogue with young people and youth organizations and mobilisation of EU programmes and funds. Despite the differences in terms of objectives, all policy measures are aimed at tackling the issue of youth employment[7] through cross-sectoral cooperation.

Youth employment was set as a priority by the Council, which adopted a number of resolutions to ensure young people's active inclusion[8] into the labour market and to increase employability.[9]

The active inclusion of young people was ensured through the adoption of a number of measures, which differed from country to country: labour reforms, tax incentives to foster youth labour market entry; the promotion of work experiences abroad; targeted counselling (offered by educational bodies, employment services or youth information services), as well as courses, placement and support to the unemployed or vulnerable groups, traineeships during education, or the implementation of dual systems which combine classroom learning with apprenticeship.[10]

Actions to promote employability included increased access to labour market information, non-formal learning, a quality framework for internships, a focus on flexicurity and equal access to mobility. Following these Council recommendations, the Commission launched the Youth Opportunities Initiative.

---

[6] European Union. 2012. *Joint Report of the Council and the Commission on the Implementation of the Renewed Framework for European Cooperation in the Youth Field* (2010-18) (2012/C 394/03), Notice from European Union Institutions, Bodies, Offices and Agencies Council European Commission, 20.12.2012 Official Journal of the European Union C 394/5. Brussels: European Commission.

[7] "Youth work covers a large scope of social, cultural, educational or political activities by, with and for young people. It is about 'out-of-school' education and leisure time activities managed by professional or voluntary youth workers and youth leaders. It is based on non-formal learning and voluntary participation". Cited from (2012/C 394/03).

[8] OJ C 137, 27.5.2010, 1.

[9] (2012/C 394/03).

[10] Doc. 13707/12 ADD 1, 27. cited by (2012/C 394/03).

Entrepreneurship education is ensured at different levels through a number of actions[11] which are not only limited to lifelong learning strategies across Europe, and as such include country-specific strategies (8 countries), policies in terms of youth and growth (13 countries), ongoing initiatives (3 countries), as well as dedicated events such as the European Youth Week.

3. Europe 2020: Supporting Youth during the Crisis

The Europe 2020 Strategy launched in 2010 sets out a vision for Europe's social market economy for the 21st century:

> A strategy to help us come out stronger from the crisis and turn the EU into a smart, sustainable and inclusive economy delivering high levels of employment, productivity and social cohesion.[12]

Youth are explicitly mentioned in the Europe 2020 strategy as a specific headline target: the share of early school leavers should fall below 10% and at least 40% of younger generations should have a tertiary degree.

Moreover, youth are targeted as part of so-called "mutually reinforcing priorities":

Smart growth:[13] the *EU* flagship initiative "Youth on the Move"[14] is aimed at enhancing the performance of the education systems and increasing international attractiveness of Europe's higher education promoting youth mobility.

Inclusive growth: the EU flagship initiative "An agenda for new skills and jobs"[15] focusing on employment and skills, and the EU flagship initiative "European platform against poverty"[16] set out to tackle poverty.

---

[11] European Commission. 2012. *Entrepreneurship Education at School in Europe*, http://eacea.ec.europa.eu/education/Eurydice/documents/thematic_reports/135EN.pdf (accessed 20 June 2013).

[12] European Union. 2010. *Communication from the Commission. Europe 2020, A Strategy for Smart, Sustainable and Inclusive Growth*. Brussels: European Commission.

[13] *Ibid.*

[14] COM (2010), 477.

[15] COM (2010), 682.

[16] COM (2010), 758.

On 26 November 2012, the Council also reached political agreement on a Council Recommendation on the validation of non-formal and informal learning.[17]

3.1. Youth on the Move: Unleashing the Potential of Young People to Achieve Smart, Sustainable and Inclusive Growth in the EU

This complex policy initiative provides a long-term response to strategic demand, but also a number of solutions to short-term issues brought about by the crisis. It also contributes to increasing the flexibility of the European single market in synergy with the flagship initiative "Agenda for New Skills and Jobs" aimed at responding to the challenges of the knowledge economy.

> The Europe 2020 flagship initiative "Youth on the Move" puts young people at the centre of the EU's agenda to create an economy based on knowledge, research and innovation, high levels of education and skills in line with labour market needs, adaptability and creativity, inclusive labour markets and active participation in society.[18]

It also stimulates worldwide responsiveness to recommendations, addressing the issues related to decent employment for young people:

> Youth employment has come even further to the fore of the global political debate in response to the crisis and recovery, underlining a convergence of policy priorities and stimulating policy exchange. This was highlighted by the ILO Global Jobs Pact, recommendations from the G20 Employment and Labour Ministers, the G20 Global Training Strategy or the OECD Youth Forum. [COM (2010) 477 final]

---

[17] European Union. 2012. *Joint Report of the Council and the Commission on the Implementation of the Renewed Framework for European Cooperation in the Youth Field (2010-18)* (2012/C 394/03). Notice from European Union Institutions, Bodies, Offices and Agencies Council European Commission, 20.12.2012 Official Journal of the European Union C 394/5. Brussels: European Commission.

[18] European Commission. 2010. *Communication from the Commission to the European Parliament, the Council, the European Economic and Social Committee and the Committee of the Regions. Youth on the Move.* Brussels: European Union, 19.

In addition, it aims at filling existing vacancies, which represent an unused potential and could be an opportunity for young people to make the most of geographical mobility.

This initiative promotes an integrated approach supporting youth in education and employment. This approach is based on four main lines of action:

- developing modern education and training systems to deliver key competences and excellence;
- promoting the attractiveness of higher education for the knowledge economy;
- supporting a strong development of transnational learning and employment mobility for young people;
  - promoting learning mobility;
  - promoting employment mobility;
- providing a framework for youth employment to
  - help to obtain one's first job and start a career;
  - support youth at risk;
  - provide adequate social safety nets for young people;
  - support young entrepreneurs and self-employment.

3.2 Key Actions to Stimulate Youth Employment

The actions undertaken have multiple aims. First, they promote employment mobility,[19] as provided in the third line of action. In this connection, the initiative "Your first EURES job" provides advisory, job-searching, recruitment and financial support to young jobseekers willing to work abroad and companies (in particular SMEs) recruiting young European mobile workers by means of comprehensive integration programmes for the newcomers. This new mobility instrument should be managed by the European job mobility network of Public Employment Services (EURES). Moreover, in 2010 the "European Vacancy Monitor" was set up with the aim to "improve transparency and information on available jobs for young jobseekers by developing an intelligence system on labour and skills demand all over Europe". At the national level, some measures need to be adopted to effectively implement EU legislation on workers' freedom of movement, by identifying areas for action to promote youth mobility.

---

[19] European Union. 2010. *Communication from the Commission. Europe 2020 A Strategy for Smart, Sustainable and Inclusive Growth.* Brussels: European Commission, 11.

In addition, they promote a framework for youth employment, as laid down in the fourth line of action. The purpose of the initiative is to assist youth in obtaining their first job and starting a career.

This new paradigm aims at fostering the transition of young people to employment. After graduating from secondary school, young people should look for a job or attend an educational programme, otherwise they must receive appropriate support through active employment measures or social measures, even if they are not entitled to benefits. It is important, especially in those Member States with few new jobs available for young people, not to exclude them from the labour market at an early stage.
Key actions are implemented as follows:

Table 3-1. Active Measures Adopted by the Public Employment Services (PES)

A new perspective: individualised services for youth.
Target group: young people entering the labour market.

Active Measures and Services	Objectives
The provision of information services on employment opportunities.	Young people should obtain a permanent job as quickly as possible.
The provision of professional consulting services.	Young people should obtain a permanent job as quickly as possible.
The conclusion of local and regional partnerships with educational and vocational institutions, social support services, unions and employers institutions.	Young people should obtain a permanent job as quickly as possible.

Table 3-2. Active Measures Provided by Enterprises/Employers.

A new perspective: support offered by companies as part of their Corporate Social Responsibility (CSR) policy.
Target group: young people entering the labour market.

Active measures and services	Objectives
The provision of information services regarding employment opportunities.	Young people should obtain a permanent job as quickly as possible.
The provision of assistance for persons looking for a job.	Young people should obtain a permanent job as quickly as possible.
Differentiated entry wage levels, as laid down by collective bargaining, additional benefits and access to training for young new employees.	Supporting young people in job retention.

Table 3-3. Youth Employment Incentives for Employers Target group: young people entering the labour market.

Active Measures and Services	Objectives
The introduction of tax incentives for businesses hiring youth on permanent contracts.	Combating youth labour market segmentation.
The introduction of tax incentives to transform temporary contracts into permanent ones.	Combating youth labour market segmentation.
The provision of incentives applying to employers to hire inexperienced workers.	Combating youth precarious income by reducing wage and non-wage labour costs through collective agreements.

Policies should also provide support to youth at risk. These measures address youth aged 15 to 24 years old who are neither in employment, education or training (NEET) as well as young people who are at risk of permanent exclusion from the labour market and dependency on benefits.

In this connection, it is necessary to provide targeted measures for these groups, with a view of allowing them to access education and training.

In addition, measures should pay particular attention to the needs of young people with disabilities or health problems. In this connection, the aim of these measures is that of improving as much as possible the transition to employment for young people with disabilities or health conditions in order to minimise their inactivity and risk of social exclusion.

Table 3-4. Active Measures Adopted by Public Employment Services.

Active Measures and Services	Objectives
Concluding partnerships and agreements with employers who are granted special support to recruit youth at risk.	NEETs and young people aged 20 to 24 years old could benefit from training.
Concluding partnerships and agreements with employers who are granted special support to recruit youth at risk.	NEETs aged 20 to 24 years old could gain work experience as well as a first contact with the labour market.
Developing partnerships and agreements with employers who are granted special support to recruit youth at risk.	The employment of a large number of young people with disabilities or health problems could minimize their risk of inactivity and social exclusion.

Adequate social safety nets for young people are directed towards the most vulnerable groups and those who are unemployed without any work experience.

Activation measures	Objectives
Activation measures and conditionality as a combination of adequate income support, inclusive labour market and access to quality services.[20]	Engaging youth in active job searching or encouraging them to enter further education or training. Avoiding dependence on benefits and reducing risks. Designing and implementing efficient and effective activation policies: programmes should be tailored according to one's skills.

Table 3-5. Supporting Entrepreneurship and Self-employment.

Active Measures and Services	Objectives
Creating opportunities for young people to gain entrepreneurship experience through public-private partnerships.	Boosting independent employment and fostering entrepreneurship. Creating new jobs especially in the service sector.

[20] Commission Recommendation on the active inclusion of people excluded from the labour market of 03.10.2008 (OJ L 307, 18.11.2008), endorsed by the Council on 17 December 2008 and by the European Parliament in its Resolution of 6 May 2009.

Table 3-6. Measures Adopted by Public Employment Services.

Active Measures and Services	Objectives
Counseling on business plans, access to capital and advice on business startups.	Youth are encouraged to create their own jobs by setting up SMEs and micro-enterprises.
Counseling to people willing to become self-employed.	Boosting cooperative opportunities in the knowledge economy.

Table 3-7. Tools to Stimulate Youth Employment.

Youth on the Move: Objectives	Programmes
Education and training.	Lifelong Learning Erasmus, Leonardo da Vinci, Comenius and Grundtvig, Youth in Action, Erasmus Mundus, Tempus and Marie Curie Actions.
Entrepreneurship and youth mobility.	"Erasmus for young entrepreneurs" initiative.
Youth employment, educational opportunities and higher education infrastructure.	European Regional Development Fund, PROGRESS and the new European Micro-finance Facility.
Supporting youth employment, entrepreneurship and learning mobility of young workers, preventing school drop-out and increase skills.	The European Social Fund (ESF).

4. The Youth Opportunities Initiative (YOI)

In 2011, the Commission adopted the Youth Opportunities Initiative (YOI)[21] calling for a stronger partnership between the Commission and national governments, with a focus on the 8 Member States[22] with the

[21] http://ec.europa.eu/social/main.jsp?catId=1006&langId=en.

[22] Greece, Ireland, Italy, Latvia, Lithuania, Portugal, Slovakia and Spain.

highest youth unemployment rates. It has been estimated that the amount of money spent on supporting measures in 2011 to reduce youth unemployment accounted for around 2 billion every week, i.e. over 1% of EU-27 GDP.[23]

The Youth Opportunities initiative aimed at boosting youth employment, labour market entry, apprenticeships and internships [COM(2011) 815] in line with EU targets regarding growth potential and indicative timelines.[24]

The European Commission proposed a dedicated Youth Opportunities Initiative (YOI),[25] with a view to mobilising resources and increasing efforts "to drive down youth unemployment and develop employability of young people". In this context, the Commission urged Member States to make better use of the European Social Fund to support young people.

The YOI identifies some major causes of youth unemployment:[26]

- Early school leaving without qualifications.
- Lack of relevant skills and lack of work experience.
- Precarious employment followed by spells of unemployment.
- Limited training opportunities.
- Insufficient/inappropriate active labour market programmes.

The primary responsibility for tackling youth unemployment lies with Member States, which are required to implement the relevant measures also at regional and local level.[27]

The YOI [COM (2011) 933] is intended to:

- Mobilise the ESF to support skills development and school-to-work transitions;
- Support the transition from education to work;
- Support labour market mobility;
- Strengthen policy delivery as part of the European Semester.

[23] European Commission. 2010. *EU Calls for Immediate Action to Drive Down Youth Unemployment.* Press release. Brussels: European Commission.

[24] European Commission. Action Required: Commission proposal by end 2011, agreement by Council and EP by end June 2012.

[25] COM(2011), 933.

[26] *Ibid.*

[27] European Commission. 2011. *Communication from the Commission to the European Parliament, the Council, the European Economic and Social Committee and the Committee of the Regions. Youth Employment Initiative.* COM(2011), 933 Brussels: European Commission, 6.

The expected impact of this initiative[28] is to establish a partnership between the Commission, national authorities, social partners and civil societies to help young people move into jobs through targeted funding. At least 5,000 young people will benefit from the "Your First EURES Job" initiative if they want to find a job in another EU country. EU countries will set up schemes to ensure that young people are either at work, in education or training within four months after leaving school. The Commission will establish a framework for high-quality traineeships to improve information on which opportunities are available throughout the EU, how to get them and what to offer to trainees.

5. The Annual Growth Survey

The annual growth survey was launched in 2012 to support youth employment as a response to the unacceptable high rate of youth unemployment.[29] It focused on supporting employment, especially that of young people, following the persistence and increase of young people failing to enter the labour market, and in the light of the increasing number of NEETs and of rampant labour market segmentation.

Among the priorities for action established at EU and national levels to boost growth and jobs to support youth employment, four recommendations out of five take a youth employment perspective:

- Identifying the most urgent needs and proposing concrete actions, targeting NEETs as well as commitments to promote quality apprenticeships and traineeship contracts and entrepreneurial skills. Particular attention should be paid to the vocational training dimension in tertiary education systems and getting work experience.
- Engaging with social partners to implement commitments to promote quality apprenticeships and traineeship contracts, especially in sectors with bottlenecks in filling vacancies, so that young people gain real work experience and quickly enter the job market.
- Reforming employment protection legislation in consultation with social partners, reducing the excessive rigidities of permanent contracts and providing protection and easier access to the labour market to those left outside, in particular young people.
- Further adapting education and training systems to reflect labour market conditions and skills demand, while reinforcing their efficiency and quality, and focusing on sectors and occupations that experience the most pronounced skills or labour shortages; for instance, the

[28] Citizens' summary "Youth Opportunities Initiative".
[29] COM(2011), 815.

> number of IT graduates has not increased since 2008 and if this persists, the EU may lack 700,000 IT professionals by 2015".[30]

Country-specific recommendations[31] have been adopted taking into account the specific condition of each Member State.

The EU Communication of 5 December 2012, *Moving Youth into Employment*,[32] describes the actions taken at the EU and national level to implement the YOI, providing an overview of country-specific recommendations concerning youth.

6. The Youth Employment Package

The Europe 2020 Strategy develops an idea of the labour market as the place where synergies to support smart, sustainable and inclusive growth are created. Strategic implementation is based on new economic governance addressing both demand and supply within the labour market.

Employment and social policies are related to policies in other fields, including macro-economic stability and growth. Consequently, the labour market reform needs to be properly coordinated at national and EU level.

Following the Annual Growth Survey of 18 April 2012, the mid-term policy Commission Communication[33] "Towards a job-rich recovery" was issued with a medium-term policy guidance perspective regarding the Europe 2020 implementation process. Its objective is to build trust among all actors and generate confidence for the necessary reforms put in place through an integrated and complex project, known as the "Employment Package".[34]

---

[30] European Commission. 2011. *Annual Growth Survey 2012*. COM(2011), 815 final, VOL. 1/5. Brussels: European Commission.

[31] COM(2012), 299.

[32] European Commission. 2012. Moving Youth into Employment. Commission Staff Working Document accompanying the document: Communication from the Commission to the European Parliament, the Council, the European Economic and Social Committee and the Committee of the Regions,{COM(2012) 727 final} SWD(2012), 406 final. Brussels: European Commission.

[33] COM(2012), 173.

[34] COM(2012), 173, SWD(2012), 98, SWD(2012), 99.

6.1. Towards a Job-rich Recovery[35] [COM(2012) 173 final]

Besides contributing to short-term recovery, employment policies also constitute a social investment to prevent an increase in social and tax costs in the long term. The EU 2012 Annual Growth Survey calls for resolute action to step up job creation and ensure a job-intensive recovery, and this message was forcefully echoed by the Heads of State and Government at the 2012 Spring European Council.

This policy Communication seeks to complement the employment priorities laid down in the Annual Growth Survey, providing medium-term policy guidance to achieve the Europe 2020 employment objectives. It builds upon the Employment Guidelines, aiming to build up trust between all actors with a view to make the necessary reforms. In doing so, it also responds to the call from the European Council to back up the new economic governance with a closer monitoring of employment and social policies, particularly where these can have an impact on macro-economic stability and growth.

The Communication is accompanied by a series of Staff Working Documents, elaborating on how employment policies intersect with a number of other policy fields in supporting smart, sustainable and inclusive growth. Altogether, not only does the "Employment Package" make progress as regards the EU 2020 flagship initiative on "New skills and jobs", but it also helps promote, through better synergies, flagship initiatives such as the "Digital Agenda for Europe", "Innovation Union", "Youth on the move", "Resource-efficient Europe", "An Industrial Policy for the Globalisation Era" and "European Platform against Poverty and Exclusion".

The Employment Package also shows how EU funding, in particular the European Social Fund, can be mobilised in support of labour market reform to help deliver the necessary investments in case of an economic downturn.

While the labour market dynamics will need to be generated mainly at national level, this Communication lays the foundation for a job-rich recovery, addressing both the demand and supply side of the labour

---

[35] European Commission. 2012. *Communication from the Commission to the European Parliament, the Council, the European Economic and Social Committee and the Committee of the Regions, Towards a Job-rich Recovery.* {SWD (2012) 90 final}, {SWD (2012) 92 final}, {SWD (2012) 93 final}, {SWD (2012) 95 final}, {SWD (2012) 96 final}, {SWD (2012) 97 final}, {SWD (2012) 98 final}, {SWD (2012) 99 final}, {SWD (2012) 100 final}, COM (2012) 173 final. Strasbourg: European Union.

market and taking further steps towards creating a genuine EU labour market.

Table 3-8. Youth Employment. Problems and Remedies Laid Down in the Youth Employment Package.[36]

Problem	Possible Remedy	EU Level Tools/Actions
Young people, particularly disadvantaged groups, dropping out of education or work; rising long-term unemployment and inactivity.	Setting up Youth Guarantee schemes; effective use of ESF funding.	The Commission is proposing a Council Recommendation to Establish a Youth Guarantee scheme.
Difficult school-to-work transitions.	Increasing the quality of traineeships and apprenticeships.	The Commission is launching an additional social partner consultation on a Quality Framework for Traineeships; The Commission will set up a European Alliance for Apprenticeships.
Vacancies coexist with high unemployment rates, growing skills and geographical mismatches.	Reducing obstacles to mobility to allow companies to recruit workers, apprentices and trainees from other EU countries.	The Commission will develop an integrated mobility plan specifically directed to young people (EURES).

The Youth Employment Package proposed by the Commission is aimed at fostering a smooth transition between school and work through youth guarantee schemes. Within 4 months after leaving school or after

[36] European Commission, MEMO/12/938. Event Date: 05/12/2012 http://europa.eu/rapid/press-release_MEMO-12-938_en.htm.

losing a job, youth under 25 years old should receive a quality job offer, or the opportunity to stay on in education, or an apprenticeship or a traineeship.

It is also aimed at ensuring that "traineeships are high-quality work experiences under safe conditions; that apprenticeships are of good quality; and that youth are given more opportunities to work and study abroad".[37]

The role of the EU is to provide both financial means – in particular through the European Social Fund–[38] and policy guidance to Member States to fight high youth unemployment.

Actions to be taken at the national level are laid down in the Council Recommendation (Annex 1) to Member States regarding the Youth Guarantee scheme:

> The proposed recommendation urges Member States to establish strong partnerships with stakeholders, ensure early intervention by employment services and other partners supporting young people, take supportive measures to enable labour integration, make full use of the European Social Fund and other structural funds to that end, assess and continuously improve the Youth Guarantee schemes and implement them rapidly.

Actions to be taken by the Commission (Annex 1) include:

- Supporting Member States through EU funding;
- Promoting exchanges of good practices;
- Monitoring the implementation of Youth Guarantees in the European Semester exercise; and
- Raising awareness.[39]

Further developments and deadlines:

By February 2013,[40] national governments were expected to have adopted the recommendation and begun implementing a Youth Guarantee scheme. Employers' and employees' organisations might begin negotiating a quality framework on traineeships.

In summer 2013, the European Alliance for Apprenticeships has started promoting successful apprenticeship schemes and developing

---

[37] Citizens' summary EU Commission proposes Youth Employment Package.
[38] http://ec.europa.eu/social/main.jsp?langId=en&catId=325.
[39] http://ec.europa.eu/social/main.jsp?langId=en&catId=89&newsId=1731.
[40] Citizens' summary EU Commission proposes Youth Employment Package.

common curricula for professions, with a view to recognising apprenticeships undertaken abroad. Depending on the outcome of negotiations, the Commission could propose a quality framework for traineeships.

7. The Youth Guarantee Scheme

The Youth Guarantee scheme is a tool aimed at ensuring smoother transitions from school to work. It requires stakeholders to engage in strong partnerships to increase its effectiveness (Annex 1 and 2). The Youth Guarantee scheme should:

> ensure that all young people up to the age of 25 years receive a good-quality offer of employment, continued education, an apprenticeship or a traineeship within four months of becoming unemployed or leaving formal education.[41]

The target group is constituted by NEETs between 15 and 24 years old, as well as persons that could fall within the categories identified by Eurofound.[5] The following factors contribute to increasing the likelihood of becoming a NEET: i) a disability; ii) immigration background; iii) low education; iv) living in remote areas; v) coming from a low-income household vi) having parents who experienced unemployment; vii) having parents with a low level of education and viii) coming from divorced families.[42]

> Funding sources of Youth Guarantees are the EU Structural Funds and in particular the European Social Fund.[43]
>
> The costs of a Youth Guarantee scheme were calculated in a number of ways. In July 2012, the International Labour Organisation (ILO) estimated the costs of implementing a Youth Guarantee scheme in the Eurozone. Their total cost estimate for the Eurozone stood at 0.45% of the Eurozone's GDP, equal to approximately 21 billion Euros. Their analysis is based on the Swedish model of the "special job-search support", estimated to have an annual cost of €6,000 per unemployed young person plus administrative

[41] European Union. *Proposal for a Council Recommendation on Establishing a Youth Guarantee* {SWD(2012) 409 final}, COM(2012) 729 final, 2012/0351 (NLE). Brussels: European Commission.

[42] Eurofound. 2011. *Young People and NEETs in Europe: First Findings*. Dublin: Eurofound.

[43] European Commission. 2012. MEMO/12/938, Event Date: 05/12/2012 http://europa.eu/rapid/press-release_MEMO-12-938_en.htm.

> costs (in terms of resources needed for Public Employment Services to serve the programme) amounting to €600 per participant. As the Commission's proposal for a Youth Guarantee scheme goes beyond the Swedish model, this is only an indication of the potential cost of a Youth Guarantee initiative.[44]

Cost estimates are extremely important, especially when considering that many authors warned that they could be very high. However, it is necessary to adopt a different perspective to assess whether the investment is worth doing. In this respect, a European press release points out that:

> these costs should be compared with the costs of unemployment, inactivity and lost productivity. The costs of benefits paid out to unemployed young people, foregone earnings and taxes, are estimated by Eurofound to be the equivalent of 1.21 % of GDP, i.e. an annual loss of €153 billion for the EU. In addition, for young people themselves, being unemployed at a young age can have a long-lasting negative "scarring effect".
>
> These young people face not only higher risks of future unemployment, but also higher risks of exclusion, of poverty and of health problems.[45]

> The reason for the adoption of a Youth Guarantee scheme is that the youth unemployment rate (under 25 years old) in the EU is twice as high as the adults' unemployment rate in most Member States (22.7 % as against 9.2 % in the third quarter of 2012) and has dramatically increased over the last four years.[46]

---

[44] European Commission. 2012. *Commission Staff Working Document accompanying the document Proposal for a Council Recommendation on Establishing a Youth Guarantee* {COM(2012) 729 final}, SWD(2012) 409 final. Brussels: European Commission.

[45] http://europa.eu/rapid/press-release_MEMO-12-938_en.htm.

[46] European Commission, MEMO/12/938. Event Date: 05/12/2012 http://europa.eu/rapid/press-release_MEMO-12-938_en.htm.

Table 3-9. Examples of Youth Guarantee Activities/Interventions Potentially Supported by the ESF.[47]

Measures	Examples of Activities/Interventions
Outreach strategies and focal points [YG rec 8-9]	School visits by PES; Training sessions for teachers by PES; Development of specialised youth services as part of PES or contracted private providers; Distribution of printed material at youth centres or youth events; Use of internet and social media; Data gathering systems; Road-shows.
Providing individual action planning [YG rec 10]	PES staff training; Contract with specialised partners.
Offering early school leavers and low-skilled young people routes to re-enter education and training or second-chance education programmes, addressing skills mismatches and improving digital skills [YG rec 11-13]	Training and second chance programmes; Language training provision; Counselling and extra teaching support to keep or bring youth back into education or training; Supporting at-risk youth in the acquisition of relevant qualifications and the completion of upper secondary qualification; Work-based learning and apprenticeships; Providing digital skills training; Training vouchers.
Encouraging schools and employment services to promote and provide continued guidance on entrepreneurship and self-employment for young people. [YG rec 14]	Training sessions of employment services' staff and teachers; Development and implementation of entrepreneurship courses in secondary education; Training sessions for unemployed young people.

[47] European Commission. 2012. MEMO/12/938. Event Date: 05/12/2012 http://europa.eu/rapid/press-release_MEMO-12-938_en.htm.

Using targeted and well-designed wage and recruitment subsidies to encourage employers to provide young people with an apprenticeship or a job placement, and particularly for those furthest from the labour market.[YG rec 17]	Hiring credits targeted at the new hiring of young people via jobs as well as apprenticeships (ESF support for the subsidies credits should be accompanied by activation measures, such as practical training etc.).
Promoting employment/labour mobility by making young people aware of job offers, traineeships and apprenticeships and available support in different areas and providing adequate support for those who have moved [YG rec 18]	Operations of EURES points (the ESF support to EURES focuses on recruitment and related information, advice and guidance services at national and cross border level). Awareness-raising campaigns Support to voluntary organisations providing mentors. Support to youth organisations reaching out to migrant young workers.
Ensuring greater availability of start-up support services [YG rec 19]	Cooperation between employment services, business support and finance providers (e.g. regional employment fairs and networking events). SME start-up support. Self-employment support. Training in business skills, e.g. for unemployed persons, accompanied by entrepreneurship grants.
Enhancing mechanisms for supporting young people who drop out from activation schemes and no longer access benefits. [YG rec 20]	Supporting youth organisations and youth services. Cooperating with other organisations that are in contact with youth. Establishing tracking systems. Supporting employment and school career support services.

Monitoring and evaluating all actions and programmes contributing to a Youth Guarantee initiative, so that more evidence-based policies and interventions can be developed on the basis of what works, where and why[YG rec 23]	Identifying cost-effective initiatives. Using controlled trials. Setting up centres for analysis. Developing policy models, pilot actions, testing and mainstreaming of policies (social innovation and experimentation)
Promoting mutual learning activities at national, regional and local level between all parties fighting youth unemployment in order to improve design and delivery of future Youth Guarantee schemes. [YG rec 24]	Using the European Network on Youth Employment (ESF supports transnational cooperation activities on exchange of good practice among organisations at EU level through ESF Technical Assistance funding at Commission level)
Strengthening the capacities of all stakeholders, including the relevant employment services, involved in designing, implementing and evaluating Youth Guarantee schemes, in order to eliminate any internal and external obstacles related to policy and to the way these schemes are developed. [YG rec 25]	Providing training and workshops; Establishing exchange programmes and secondments between organisations through transnational cooperation activities.

8. Conclusions

The persistence of the crisis and its consequences deterred the Commission from adopting in 2010 the Youth Opportunities Initiative, an aspect which called for a stronger partnership between the Commission and national governments to boost youth employment, in particular youth labour market entry, apprenticeships and internships. The Annual Growth

Survey 2012 focused on increasing youth employment to reduce youth unemployment rates, to support youth labour market entry, reduce the number of NEETs and market segmentation in order to boost growth and increase jobs. Following the Annual Growth Survey of 18 April 2012, the intermediary policy Communication[48] "Towards a job-rich recovery" was issued, providing medium-term policy guidance on the Europe 2020 implementation process. The purpose of the Communication is to build trust between all the actors involved, with a view to adopting the necessary reforms through an integrated set of solution, known as the "Employment Package". This package contains a series of tools such as:

- The Youth Guarantee scheme aimed at responding to the increasing number of school dropouts and job losses, rising long-term unemployment and inactivity levels, particularly among disadvantaged groups, such as NEETs aged between 15 and 24 years old;
- The Quality Framework for Traineeships and the European Alliance for Apprenticeships aimed at improving the quality of traineeships and apprenticeships to accelerate positive transitions from school to work;
- An integrated mobility plan for young people (EURES) to reduce obstacles to mobility, to allow companies to recruit workers and apprentices and trainees from other EU countries, with a view to filling existing vacancies and reducing mismatch.

The Communication "Moving Youth into Employment"[49] of 5 December 2012 described the actions taken at EU and at national level to implement the YOI, also providing an overview of country-specific recommendations laid down in dedicated fact sheets.

The present analysis shows the dynamism and variety of policies and initiatives aimed at stimulating labour market entry which were developed over the last 4 years, the enforcement of which poses now a number of challenges. Analyses regarding future prospects provide for the possibility to design diversified solutions taking into account the specific characteristics of target groups. This procedure is essential to ensure a smoother transition to employment in a context characterised by multiple policies that need to be harmonised in a coordinate manner at European, national, regional and local level. Under these circumstances, the role of the labour market institutions and in particular of Public Employment

---

[48] COM (2012), 173.

[49] European Commission. 2012. *Moving Youth into Employment. Commission Staff Working Document, Accompanying the Communication from the Commission to the European Parliament, the Council, the European Economic and Social Committee and the Committee of the Regions,* {COM(2012) 727 final}, SWD(2012) 406 final. Brussels: European Commission.

Services becomes crucial for the implementation of the policies at the national level.

References

Council of the European Union and European Commission. 2012. *Joint Report of the Council and the Commission on the Implementation of the Renewed Framework for European Cooperation in the Youth Field (2010-18) (2012/C 394/03).* Official Journal of the European Union C 394/5.

Council of the European Union. 2010. *Council Decision 2010/707/EU of 21 October on Guidelines for Employment Policies of the Member States.* Council of the European Union.

Eurofound. 2011. *Young People and NEETs in Europe: First Findings.* Dublin: Eurofound.

—. 2012. *Recent Policy Developments Related to those not in Employment, Education and Training (NEETs).* Dublin: Eurofound.

European Commission. 2001. *The White Paper on Youth—A New Impetus for European Youth.* Brussels: European Commission.

—. 2005. *European Youth Pact.* Brussels: European Commission.

—. 2008. *Commission Recommendation on the Active Inclusion of People Excluded from the Labour Market of 03.10.2008 (OJ L 307, 18.11.2008), endorsed by the Council on 17 December 2008 and by the European Parliament in its Resolution of 6 May 2009.* Brussels: European Commission.

—. 2009. *Communication from the Commission to the Council the European Parliament, the European Economic and Social Committee and the Committee of the Regions. An EU Strategy for Youth—Investing and Empowering. A Renewed Open Method of Coordination to Address Youth Challenges and Opportunities.* {SEC(2009) 545}, {SEC(2009) 546}, {SEC(2009) 548}, {SEC(2009) 549}, COM(2009) 200 final. Brussels: European Commission.

—. 2010. *Communication from the Commission to the Council the European Parliament, the European Economic and Social Committee and the Committee of the Regions. A strategy for Smart, Sustainable and Inclusive Growth,* COM(2010) 2020. Brussels: European Commission.

—. 2010. *Communication from the Commission to the Council the European Parliament, the European Economic and Social Committee and the Committee of the Regions. Youth on the Move.* COM(2010) 477, SEC(2010) 104719. Brussels: European Commission.

—. 2010. *Communication from the Commission to the Council the European Parliament, the European Economic and Social Committee and the Committee of the Regions. An Agenda for New Skills and Jobs: A European Contribution towards Full Employment,* COM(2010), 682. Brussels: European Commission.

—. 2010. *Communication from the Commission to the Council the European Parliament, the European Economic and Social Committee and the Committee of the Regions. The European Platform against Poverty and Social Exclusion: A European Framework for Social and Territorial Cohesion,* COM(2010), 758. Brussels: European Commission.

—. 2010. *EU Calls for Immediate Action to Drive Down Youth Unemployment.* Press release. Brussels: European Commission.

—. 2011. *Communication from the Commission to the Council the European Parliament, the European Economic and Social Committee and the Committee of the Regions. Annual Growth Survey 2012,* COM(2011), 815 final, VOL. 1/5. Brussels: European Commission.

—. 2011. *Communication from the Commission to the Council the European Parliament, the European Economic and Social Committee and the Committee of the Regions.* Youth Opportunities Initiative, COM(2011), 933 final. Brussels: European Commission.

—. 2011. *Communication from the Commission to the Council the European Parliament, the European Economic and Social Committee and the Committee of the Regions. Towards a Job-rich Recovery,* {SWD(2012) 90 final}, {SWD(2012) 92 final}, {SWD(2012) 93 final}, {SWD(2012) 95 final}, {SWD(2012) 96 final}, {SWD(2012) 97 final}, {SWD(2012) 98 final}, {SWD(2012) 99 final}, {SWD(2012) 100 final}, 18.4.2012, COM(2012), 173 final. Strasbourg: European Union.

—. 2011. *Youth Guarantees: PES Approaches and Measures for Low-skilled Young People, Thematic Synthesis Paper, Chapter 4.* Brussels: European Commission.

—. 2011. Citizens' Summary. Youth Opportunities Initiative. Brussels: European Union.

—. 2012. *Proposal for a Council Recommendation on Establishing a Youth Guarantee,* COM(2012), 729 final. Brussels: European Commission.

—. 2012. *Communication from the Commission to the Council the European Parliament, the European Economic and Social Committee and the Committee of the Regions and the European Investment Bank. Action for Stability, Growth, and Jobs,* COM(2012), 299. Brussels: European Commission.

—. 2012. *Entrepreneurship Education at School in Europe.* Brussels: European Commission. http://eacea.ec.europa.eu/education/Eurydice/documents/thematic_reports/135EN.pdf.

—. 2012. *Moving Youth into Employment, Commission Staff Working Document Accompanying the document, Communication from the Commission to the Council the European Parliament, the European Economic and Social Committee and the Committee of the Regions,* COM (2012), 727 final. Brussels: European Commission.

—. 2012. Citizens' Summary. EU Commission Proposes Youth Employment Package. Brussels: European Union.

Evans, J. 2012. *Synoptic Chapter on Employment, drafted for the Partnership between the European Commission and the Council of Europe in the Field of Youth.* http://youth-partnership-eu.coe.int/youth-partnership/ekcyp/BGKNGE/Employment.

Finnish Ministry of Employment and Economy. 2013. *Youth Guarantee 2013.* Finnish Ministry of Employment and Economy.

Annex 1: The Proposal for a COUNCIL RECOMMENDATION to Establish a Youth Guarantee 2012/0351 (NLE)[50]

RECOMMENDS THAT MEMBER STATES:

(1) Ensure that all young people up to the age of 25 years receive a good-quality offer of employment, continued education, an apprenticeship or a traineeship within four months of becoming unemployed or leaving formal education.

Building up Partnership-based Approaches

(2) Identify the public authority in charge of establishing and managing the Youth Guarantee scheme and coordinating partnerships across all levels and sectors.

(3) Ensure that young people have full information about available services and support by strengthening cooperation between employment services, career guidance providers, education and training institutions and youth support services, and by making full use of all relevant information channels.

(4) Strengthen partnerships between employers and relevant labour market players (employment services, various levels of government, trade unions and youth services) in order to boost employment, apprenticeship and traineeship opportunities for young people.

(5) Develop partnerships between public and private employment services, career guidance services, and other specialised youth services (NGOs, youth centres and associations) that help smooth the transition from unemployment, inactivity or education to work.

(6) Ensure the active involvement of social partners at all levels in designing and implementing policies targeted at young people; promote synergies under their initiatives to develop apprenticeship and traineeship schemes.

(7) Ensure the involvement of representatives of young people and/or youth organisations in designing and implementing the Youth

[50] European Union. 2012. *Proposal for a Council Recommendation on Establishing a Youth Guarantee* {SWD (2012) 409 final}, COM(2012) 729 final 2012/0351 (NLE). Brussels: European Union.

Guarantee scheme to tailor services to the needs of beneficiaries and to have them act as multipliers in awareness-raising activities.

Early Intervention and Activation

(8) Develop effective outreach strategies towards young people with a view to catchment and registration with employment services, focusing on young vulnerable people facing multiple barriers (such as social exclusion, poverty or discrimination) and NEETs, and taking into consideration their diverse backgrounds (due in particular to poverty, disability, low educational attainment or ethnic minority/migrant background).

(9) In order to support young people better and to address the potential lack of awareness of existing offers, consider establishing 'focal points', i.e. organisations that would ensure coordination between all the institutions concerned, in particular with the public authority responsible for managing the Youth Guarantee scheme, so that information could be shared about young people leaving school, in particular about those at risk of not securing a job or further education.

(10) Enable employment services, together with other partners supporting young people, to provide personalised guidance and individual action planning, including tailor-made individual support schemes, based on the principle of mutual obligation at an early stage.

Supportive Measures for Labour Market Integration

Enhancing skills

(11) Offer early school-leavers and low-skilled young people routes to re-enter education and training or second-chance education programmes which provide learning environments responding to their specific needs and enabling them to gain the qualification they missed.

(12) Ensure that any action delivered in the context of a Youth Guarantee scheme aimed at boosting skills and competences helps to address existing mismatches and service labour-demand needs, particularly in relation to the green economy, ICT and health care sectors.

(13) Ensure that efforts to boost skills and competences include ICT/digital skills. Likewise important is the promotion of professional

knowledge and competences, ensuring that ICT curricula and certifications conform to standards and are internationally comparable.

(14) Encourage schools (primary and secondary), including vocational training centres, and employment services to promote and provide continued guidance on entrepreneurship and self-employment for young people, also by means of entrepreneurship courses.

(15) Ensure the validation of the skills, knowledge and competences acquired through non-formal and informal learning experiences, by acknowledging the skills, knowledge and competences acquired in these activities and recognising that they boost jobseekers' chances in the labour market.

Labour market related measures

(16) Reduce non-wage labour costs in order to boost recruitment prospects amongst young people.

(17) Use targeted and well-designed wage and recruitment subsidies to encourage employers to create new opportunities for young people, such as an apprenticeship, a traineeship or a job placement, particularly for those furthest from the labour market, in line with the applicable State aid rules.

(18) Promote labour mobility by making young people aware of job offers, traineeships and apprenticeships and available support in different areas, regions and countries, e.g. through services and schemes, such as EURES, thus encouraging people to move and work within the EU. Likewise important is ensuring that adequate support is available to help young people who find work in another area or Member State adapt to their new environment.

(19) Make start-up support services available, through a closer cooperation between employment services, business support and (micro) finance providers.

(20) Enhance mechanisms for supporting young people who drop out of activation schemes and no longer access benefits.

The Use of EU Structural Funds

(21) Make full and optimal use of the Cohesion Policy funding instruments, in the 2014—2020 period to support the establishment of Youth Guarantee schemes.

To this end, it is pivotal to ensure that the necessary priority is given and corresponding resources are allocated for supporting the conception and the implementation of the foregoing measures, including the possibilities for financing targeted recruitment subsidies from the European Social Fund. The use of funding which is still available from the 2007-2013 period should be maximised.

(22) In the context of the planning of the 2014-2020 period, it is important to pay the necessary attention in the Partnership Contract to the specific objectives related to the implementation of Youth Guarantee schemes and to describe in the operational programmes the actions to be supported under the relevant investment priorities of the European Social Fund, in particular those concerning the sustainable integration of young NEETs into the labour market and support for young entrepreneurs and social enterprises and their respective contribution to the specific objectives.

Assessment and Continuous Improvement of Schemes

(23) Monitor and evaluate all Youth Guarantee actions and programmes, so that more evidence-based policies and interventions can be developed on the basis of what works, where and why, thus ensuring the efficient use of resources and positive returns on investment; maintain an up-to-date overview of how much funding has been allocated for the setting-up and implementation of the Youth Guarantee scheme, in particular under the Cohesion Policy operational programmes.

(24) Promote mutual learning activities at national, regional and local level between all parties involved in combating youth unemployment, in order to improve the establishment and delivery of future Youth Guarantee schemes; make full use of the results of projects supported during the preparatory works of Youth Guarantee schemes.

(25) Strengthen the capacities of all stakeholders, including the relevant employment services, involved in designing, implementing and evaluating Youth Guarantee schemes, in order to eliminate any internal and external obstacles related to policy and to the way these schemes are developed.

Implementing the Youth Guarantee Schemes

(26) Implement Youth Guarantee schemes as soon as possible and ensure that they are properly integrated into possible EU co-financed programmes, preferably from the start of the 2014-2020 Multiannual Financial Framework.

THE PROPOSAL ALSO NOTES THAT THE COMMISSION IS CONCERNED WITH:

Funding

(27) In accordance with the relevant investment priorities of the European Social Fund for the 2014-2020 programming period, the Commission will encourage Member States to make the best use of the European Social Fund to support the setting-up and implementation of Youth Guarantee schemes as a policy instrument for combating and preventing youth unemployment and social exclusion.

(28) The Commission will also support programming work under the EU Common Strategic Framework Funds (European Social Fund, European Regional Development Fund, Cohesion Fund, European Agricultural Fund for Rural Development, European Maritime and Fisheries Fund), including through peer learning, networking activities and technical assistance.

Good Practices

(29) The Commission will make full use of the new Programme on Social Change and Innovation to gather examples of good practice on Youth Guarantee schemes at national, regional and local level.

(30) The Commission will make use of the European Employment Strategy Mutual Learning Programme to encourage Member States to share their experiences and exchange good practices.

Monitoring

(31) The Commission will continue to monitor and report regularly on developments concerning the design, implementation and results of Youth Guarantee schemes as part of the annual programmes of work of the European Network of Public Employment Services.

(32) The Commission will monitor the implementation of this recommendation, and establish through the Employment Committee a multilateral surveillance of the implementation of Youth Guarantee schemes within the framework of the European Semester, analysing the impact of the policies in place and addressing, where appropriate, country-specific recommendations to the Member States.

Awareness-raising

(33) The Commission will support awareness-raising activities on the setting-up of the Youth Guarantee schemes across the Member States, using the European Youth Portal and liaising in particular with its information campaigns.

(32) The Commission will monitor the implementation of this recommendation, and establish through the Employment Committee a multilateral surveillance of the implementation of Youth Guarantee schemes within the framework of the European Semester, analysing the impact of the policies in place and addressing, where appropriate, country-specific recommendations to the Member States.

Annex 2: Principles to Consider when Establishing Youth Guarantee Schemes

I. Young people are not a homogeneous group and are from different social environments; furthermore a particular focus will be needed on those young people particularly at risk of becoming or staying as NEET.

II. Principles of mutual obligation: it could be conceivable that the condition to receive an offer under the Youth Guarantee Scheme would be to register at an employment service.

III. The potential cycles of inactivity should be addressed. The scheme should include mechanisms or action plans to break and avoid cycles of inactivity for young people, as these can lead to a further lack of motivation and destruction of their human capital.

IV. The risk of moral hazard might arise if young people rely on an external organization, such as an employment service, to deliver an offer of employment.

V. The regional or even the local level can be relevant in terms of implementation while it would be important to ensure a mechanism of national coordination with a national ministry, body or organisation to take the lead.

VI. These principles might include rules on timing as part of a Youth Guarantee Scheme. The Commission proposes that Member States should offer the Youth Guarantee to all young people within four months of unemployment or leaving education. Rules on timing of interventions are already foreseen in many PES.[51] Besides this, in many countries,

---

[51] AT (guarantee for training within 3 months), BE - FOREM (within 4 weeks of registering, the need arises to be linked with the labour market), BE - VDAB (within 4 months of registering, Youth Action Plan), DK (interviews within 3 months for young people under 30; within 3 months for anyone entitled to ALMPs), DE (legal provisions for those under 25, who will be immediately placed), FI (all young people under 30 are provided with safeguards), PL (they will receive an offer for activation within 6 months), ES (there is a guarantee for either training or experience), SE (90 days after registering, they are offered a range of activities), NL and LT have relevant guidelines in place, SI, BG, CZ, EE, MT and FR offer supportive measures with youth regarded as a priority group. European

unemployed young people are already a priority group for early PES intervention.

Commission (Mobility Laboratory). 2012. *PES Crisis Response Questionnaire 2012*, 16.

RECENT POLICIES AND INITIATIVES TO STIMULATE YOUTH LABOUR MARKET ENTRY: THE NATIONAL PERSPECTIVE

DRAGA ATANASIU AND CRISTINA LINCARU

1. Youth Policy and Youth Employment Policy in Romania

There is no single national youth strategy in Romania at the moment, except for Youth Law No. 350 of 21 June 2006 addressing the needs and rights of young people.

The Ministry of Youth and Sports, the Ministry of National Education (education and training), the Ministry of Economy (entrepreneurship), the Ministry of Agriculture and Rural Development (young farmers' programmes) and the Ministry of Labour, Family, Social Protection and Elderly (employment, social inclusion, and equal opportunities) are responsible for the development of youth policies. The Interdepartmental Council for Education, Culture, Research, Youth, Sports and Minorities was created following the Government Decision No. 750/2005 which lays down the establishment of permanent inter-ministerial commissions. The Consultative Council for Youth Issues[1] is made up of representatives of national youth organizations and has the function of disseminating the EU Youth Strategy to the relevant stakeholders.

The Ministry of Youth and Sports (MTS) was set up on 19 January 2013, when a new provision was introduced repealing GD No. 141/2010 and subsequent amendments, and provided for the setting-up of a National Authority for Sports and Youth. Since then, the MTS, a legal entity, has been organized and operates as a specialized body of the central public administration, with a view to implementing governmental youth and sports strategies and policies. In this context, the MTS plays a fundamental

[1] LEGE nr. 351/ 2006 din 21 iulie 2006 privind infiintarea, organizarea si functionarea Consiliului National al Tineretului din Romania publicat in M.Of. nr. 643/26 iul. 2006 http://www.anst.gov.ro/politici/programe/13_consiliul-tineretului-din-romnia.html.

role in developing, elaborating and implementing youth and sports policies. It supervises the activities of the County Departments of Sports and Youth, including that of the city of Bucharest, and it also coordinates the activities of so-called "houses of culture", sports clubs, national sports facilities, and so on. To accomplish its mission, the MTS (according to GD No.11/2013) is intended to fulfill the following tasks:

a) Ensuring the proper and full use of EU funds for Youth and Sports;
b) Accessing structural funds aimed at supporting activities in the field of youth and sports performing the role of manager, beneficiary or partner;
c) Managing public funds and funds collected by national and international bodies, which are allocated to support youth initiatives and NGO structures in line with relevant legislation;
d) Collaborating with the National Agency for community programmes in the field of Education and training within the framework of the "Youth in Action"[2] Programme.

The work of the MTS focuses on sports, recreational activities and NGOs[3] and aims at ensuring the implementation of Youth Policies in Romania,[4] paying special attention to:

- Priority issues, as laid down in EU White Papers including Better understanding of Youth (2008); Participation (2011); Voluntary activities (2011); Information (2008).
- Transversal youth policy issues, including the "Living conditions and Lifestyles of young people" initiative, and the "Youth Attitude" initiative.
- Seminars and studies developed by the EU-CoE partnership, such as the "Country report on Youth employment in Romania", carried out within the socio-economic study on youth employment.

---

[2] Government Decision 11 of 19.01.2013 regarding the Ministry of Youth and Sports organizing and functioning, MONITORUL OFICIAL AL ROMÂNIEI, PARTEA I, Nr. 42/19.I. 2013.

[3] European Steering Committee for Youth (CDEJ). 2000. *Romanian National Youth Policy,* 26th meeting Budapest, 25-27 October 2000, Strasbourg, 2 September, 2000, CDEJ. 2000. *Evaluation Report by the International Group of Experts,* Council of Europe, Council of Europe country reviews on national youth policy in Romania.

[4] Mitulescu, S. *Youth Policy in Romania*, European Knowledge Centre for Youth Policy Correspondent in Romania http://youth-partnership-eu.coe.int/youth-partnership/ekcyp/By_country/Romania.html (accessed 20 December 2013).

With regard to "transversal" youth policy issues, the Ministry of Economy[5] is in charge of issues concerning entrepreneurship and SMEs.

> 1. The Ministry of Economy fulfills the following functions:
> f) State authority:
> 2. In the domains of economy, energy, trade, SMM, business, environment and tourism, it monitors and enforces regulations, serving as the managing body for the Sectoral Programme "Increase Economic Competitiveness";
> 3. It performs coordination and control functions of territorial offices for SMEs and Cooperatives to ensure they fulfill their duties and obligations and representing their interests towards other bodies, organizations, institutions and authorities".[6]

The Ministry of Education[7] (ME) develops, coordinates and implements national policies on education. The ME establishes procedures for the recognition of diplomas, certificates and titles issued abroad in compliance with national legislation as well as international agreements and conventions.

The CNDIPT is a specialized body working under the authority of the ME, which following Government Decision No. 855 of 26 November 1998, has now become a legal entity. The CNDIPT was established with the aim of reforming vocational education and training (TVET) started within the framework of the European Union initiative called *Phare VET RO 9405*. Through subsequent amendments, the institution has gradually been assigned new functions in the field of VET.[8]

The Ministry of Labour, Family Social Protection and Elderly[9] plays an important role with regard to youth employment policies and social

---

[5] Ordonanta de urgenta nr. 96 din 22 decembrie 2012 privind stabilirea unor masuri de reorganizare in cadrul administratiei publice centrale si pentru modificarea unor acte normative, Emitent: Guvernul, PUBLICAT ÎN: MONITORUL OFICIAL nr. 884 din 22 decembrie 2012.

[6] Hotarare nr. 47 din 19 februarie 2013 privind organizarea si functionarea Ministerului Economiei EMITENT: GUVERNUL PUBLICAT ÎN: MONITORUL OFICIAL nr. 102 din 20 februarie 2013 Data intrarii in vigoare: 20 Februarie 2013

[7] Ordonanta de Urgenta nr. 96 din 22 decembrie 2012 privind stabilirea unor masuri de reorganizare in cadrul administratiei publice centrale si pentru modificarea unor acte normative, EMITENT: GUVERNUL, PUBLICAT ÎN: MONITORUL OFICIAL nr. 884 din 22 decembrie 2012.

[8] http://www.tvet.ro/index.php/ro/despre-noi.html (accessed 20 December 2013).

[9] Ordonanta de Urgenta nr. 96 din 22 decembrie 2012 privind stabilirea unor masuri de reorganizare in cadrul administratiei publice centrale si pentru modificarea unor acte normative, EMITENT: GUVERNUL, PUBLICAT ÎN: MONITORUL OFICIAL nr. 884 din 22 decembrie 2012.

inclusion/equal opportunities. In particular, it contributes to the functioning of the labour market in Romania with particular regard to employment protection legislation (EPL) and flexicurity strategies (Labour Code, Law No. 76/2002, Law of Social Assistance No. 292/2011). It enforces national employment legislation in line with EU strategic documents, for instance through the 2011-2013 National Reform Programme (NRP), the National Strategy for Sustainable Development, the National Development Plan 2007-2013, the National Strategic Reference Framework 2007-2013, the Sectoral Operational Programme for Human Resources Development 2007-2013, and the Employment Strategy.

Youth employment is at the centre of all the actions undertaken by this Ministry, such as:

a) Developing policies, strategies, plans and draft laws in the field of employment and continuing vocational training (employment legislation, training legislation, legislation on the classification of occupations in Romania, and the law on qualifications);
b) Establishing, maintaining and monitoring the National Strategy for Employment and the Vocational Training strategy;
c) Monitoring vocational training and managing apprenticeship opportunities;
d) Collaborating with other ministries and institutions in the development of a national qualifications system in Romania;
e) Proposing and implementing technical projects financed by European funds or other sources, as well as bilateral cooperation projects in the field of employment and vocational training;
f) Examining and approving changes to the National Employment Programme and the National Training Plan, proposed by the National Agency for Employment (ANOFM);
g) Establishing performance indicators for the National Agency for Employment (ANOFM);
h) Reviewing the classification of occupations and qualifications in Romania that serves as a point of reference for training programmes issuing qualification certificates;
i) Providing technical support to the National Commission for the Promotion of Employment;
j) Monitoring and Updating the National Registry of authorized temporary work agencies;
k) Coordinating the National Observatory of Employment and Vocational Training.[10]

---

10 http://www.mmuncii.ro/nou/index.php/ro/munca/programe-si-strategii/51-munca/ocuparea-formarea-profesionala-si-mibilitatea-fortei-de-munca/2637-

The Employment Department

> According to the Government Decision No. 10/2013 on the organization and functioning of the Ministry of Labour, Social Protection and Elderly, the Employment Department is responsible for a wide range of activities relating to the identification, development and promotion of policies and strategies in the field of employment, training and mobility in line with national legislation and in compliance with the obligations imposed by the EU in collaboration with other ministries and public institutions in the country and in other EU Member States, as well as social partners' representatives, civil societies and other stakeholders.[11]

The Ministry of Labour, Social Protection and Elderly[12] develops EU-funded projects specifically targeted at young people, such as: "An inclusive labour market in rural areas"; "Synthesis: a partnership for social inclusion"; "Equilibrium: a new work-life balance approach" which are activated through the European Social Fund.

The Order[13] of the Ministry of Labour, Family and Social Protection MMFPSPV No. 1804/03.07.2012 and that of the Ministry of Education, Youth and Sports No. 4469/12.06.2012 have established the use of the Youthpass and Europass and have adopted a framework methodology towards counselling and lifelong career guidance.

1.1. ANOFM: The Public Employment Services Institution

The National Agency for Employment (NAE)[14] is responsible for the implementation of employment services, as well as active and passive labour market policies funded through the budget allocated to labour market initiatives. The institution supervises the activities of the Bucharest Agency, and of other 41 county agencies (including 70 local agencies and

---

%202013-02-04-directia-ocupare-prezentare-si-atributii%20 (accessed 20 December 2013).

[11] http://www.mmuncii.ro/nou/index.php/ro/munca/programe-si-strategii/51-munca/ocuparea-formarea-profesionala-si-mibilitatea-fortei-de-munca/2637-%202013-02-04-directia-ocupare-prezentare-si-atributii%20 (accessed 20 December 2013).

[12] Ordonanta de Urgenta nr. 96 din 22 decembrie 2012 privind stabilirea unor masuri de reorganizare in cadrul administratiei publice centrale si pentru modificarea unor acte normative, EMITENT: GUVERNUL, PUBLICAT ÎN: MONITORUL OFICIAL nr. 884 din 22 decembrie 2012.

[13] http://www.edu.ro/index.php/articles/c967/ (accessed 20 December 2013).

[14] http://www.anofm.ro/prezentare-generala-actualizat (accessed 20 December 2013).

141 help desks), 8 district training centres for unemployed people, 8 regional centres for adult training and the National Center for Vocational Training (NCOSVT) in Rasnov. Its services are mainly directed to the unemployed (see also Law No. 76/2002)[15] to increase their employability.

The objectives of ANOFM are:
• The institutionalization of social dialogue in the field of employment and vocational training;
• The implementation of strategies in the field of employment and vocational training;
• The development of social protection measures for the unemployed.
In addition, the National Agency for Employment has the following main responsibilities:
• Organising, funding and providing training services for the unemployed in compliance with relevant legislation;
• Providing guidance to the unemployed and as well as services to connect workers and employers aimed at reducing the mismatch between labour supply and demand;
• Proposing a draft budget for unemployment insurance;
• Managing the Unemployment Insurance Fund, supervising the activity of the Ministry of Labour and Social Solidarity and supplying quarterly and annual reports on budgetary issues;
• Proposing draft laws in the field of employment and vocational training, as well as social protection of the unemployed together with the Ministry of Labour and Social Solidarity;
• Establishing and organising services, as well as providing financial support in the form of unemployment insurance;
• Implementing programmes financed through the European Social Fund;
• Developing annual programmes on the basis of the social performance indicators laid down by the Ministry of Labour, Family, Social Protection and Elderly.[16]

1.2. The Managing Authority for the Human Resources Development Programme (AMPOSDRU)

The Ministry of Labour is also in charge of the Human Resources Development Programme AMPOSDU/AM SO PHRD and supervises the European Social Fund through the AMPOSDRU. Following Article no.

[15] Legea 76 2002 privind sistemul asigurărilor pentru şomaj şi stimularea ocupării forţei de muncă, publicată în Monitorul Oficial nr. 103 din 6 februarie 2002. “Legea şomajului”.

[16] http://www.anofm.ro/prezentare-generala-actualizat (accessed 20 December 2013).

59(2) of the General Regulation 1083/2006, the AMPOSDRU delegates certain functions to a number of intermediary organisms (OIs) with a view to implementing the POSDRU programme made up of 8 regional OIs (BI, S, SE, SW, W, NE, NW, C) and 3 national intermediary organisms: MEN, CNDIPT, ANOFM.[17]

Functions that are delegated to OI by the AMPOSDRU

The OIPOSDRU-MEN is responsible for the implementation of the following initiatives:

- AP 1 (AP Principal Axe) "Education and vocational training to support growth and development in the knowledge society, according to the following main directions of Intervention: 1.1. "Access to quality education and initial vocational training", 1.2. "Quality in Higher Education", 1.3. "Human resources development in education and training", 1.4. "Quality in CVT", 1.5. "Doctoral and postdoctoral Research Support Programmes";
- AP 2 "Lifelong learning and the labour market" and 2.2. "Preventing and reducing early school leaving".

As for the OIPOSDRU-NEA, it is in charge of the implementation of:

- AP 4 "Modernizing Public Employment Service," 4.1. "Strengthening employment services" 4.2. "Providing training to PES staff".

The OIPOSDRU-CNDIPT monitors the implementation of the following actions:

- AP 2 "Lifelong learning and the labour market", 2.1. "School-to-work transition" 2.3. "Access and participation in CVT"

The 8 regional OIs HRD-MMFPs are responsible for the implementation of the following initiatives:

- AP 3 "Increasing the adaptability of workers and enterprises", and in particular 3.1. "Entrepreneurial culture", 3.2. "Training and support for enterprises and employees to promote adaptability" and 3.3.

[17] http://www.fseromania.ro/index.php/posdru/informatii-generale/autoritatea-de-management (accessed 20 December 2013).

"Developing partnerships and encouraging initiatives for social partners and civil societies";
- AP 5 "Promoting active employment measures", DMI 5.1. "Developing and implementing active employment measures" 5.2. "Promoting the long-term sustainability of rural areas in terms of human resources development and employment";
- AP 6 "Promoting social inclusion", namely 6.1. "The development of social economy", 6.2. "Improving access and participation of vulnerable groups in the labour market" and 6.1. "Promoting equal opportunities in the labour market".

The AMPOSDRU coordinates the implementation of the following initiatives:

- AP 6 "Promoting social inclusion", 6.4. "Transnational initiatives for an inclusive labour market";
- AP 7 "Technical support", 7.1. "Support for the implementation, overall management and evaluation of the SOPHRD/POSDRU" and 7.2. "Support for the SOPHRD/POSDRU promotion and communication".

Further responsibilities of the AMPOSDRU

Pursuant to Article 60 of Regulation (EC) No. 1083/2006 of July 11, 2006 laying down general provisions regarding the European Regional Development Fund, the European Social Fund and the Cohesion Fund and repealing Regulation (EC) No. 1260/1999 and subsequent amendments, AMPOSDRU:

- Contributes to the development of the National Strategic Framework of Reference 2007-2013 (CSNR), a document approved by the European Commission Decision No. 2594 of. June 25, 2007. The CSNR represents the national strategic document setting down the priorities for structural instruments (European Regional Development Fund, European Social Fund and the Cohesion Fund). It connects the national development priorities laid down in the National Development Plan 2007-2013 and the priorities established at the European level (Community Strategic Guidelines on Cohesion 2007-2013) and the revised Lisbon Strategy.
- Is responsible for the efficient, effective and transparent use of funds financing the Human Resources Development Programme 2007-2013, approved by the European Commission Decision No. 5811 of 22

November 2007, with the aim of promoting the human resources development strategy, within the framework of the programme "development and efficient use of human capital in Romania". Drawing on the principles of lifelong learning, increased adaptability and entrepreneurship, the main purpose of the HRD programme is to contribute to the strategic objectives of the CSNR, particularly by providing high quality education, higher qualifications and improved management capacity to satisfy the education and training needs of the modern and expanding economy.

- Additionally, the AMPOSDRU is responsible for transferring money made available by the State and by the European Union to cover VAT costs for ESF projects and to pay contractors who provide technical assistance. The European Social Fund ESF is the main instrument through which the EU finances strategic objectives of employment policy. For the programming period 2007-2013, the purpose of the ESF is to support Member States to anticipate and effectively manage economic and social changes.

The National Research Institute for Labour and Social Protection (INCSMPS) is the government body that carries out surveys and cross-disciplinary research related to young people and their living conditions in line with the Council resolution on active inclusion, taking into account the socio-economic conditions, as well as the opportunities available and the obstacles to social inclusion and employability of young people.

> The INCSMPS carries out surveys and studies on a theoretical and practical level in fields of national interest including human resources management, social development and social protection in Romania, acting in coordination with the Ministry of Labour, Family, Social Protection and Elderly. In this respect, the Institute regularly conducts research in relation to:
>
> 1. "Determining factors of labour market entry of graduate students";
> 2. "The relationship between educational curricula and labour market demand in Romanian TIC field-Horizon 2015";
> 3. "Discrimination, discouragement and disadvantage in the labour market";
> 4. The "I want to work!" project (Lifelong learning and the labour market-POSDRU/55/1.1/S/37932);
> 5. "Connecting vocational and technical education to labour market needs" (POSDRU/22/2.1/G/40427).[18]

---

[18] http://ec.europa.eu/youth/documents/national_youth_reports_2012/romania.pdf (accessed 20 December 2013).

The National Authority for Persons with Disabilities DPPH[19]

The DPPH is the specialized entity that coordinates at central level the activities designed to promote the rights of disabled people, developing policies, strategies and standards to ensure that the rights of people with disabilities are protected and that regulations are properly implemented.[20]

Youth are also considered in this respect. In this connection, mention should be made of some relevant provisions such as Law No. 448/2006 regarding the Protection and Promotion of the Rights of Disabled Persons; the National Strategy for Social Protection, Integration and Inclusion of People with Disabilities for the period 2006-2013, the Government Decision No. 1175/2005 to increase the number of jobs for disabled persons and ensure the full development of their potential; and G.D. No. 39/2009, Governmental Programme (Chapter 9).

2. Romania's National Report: First cycle of the EU Youth Strategy 2010-2012. Fields of Action: Employment, Entrepreneurship and Social Protection

Fields of action concerning "Employment and Entrepreneurship": Some proposed initiatives (Renewed framework) (2012/C 394/03):

> Youth employment was the overall priority of the first Presidency after the entry into force of the renewed framework. During this period, the Council adopted a number of resolutions focusing on the active inclusion of young people[21] and on the promotion of youth employability. (2012/C 394/03)

2.1. The National Report: First cycle of the EU Youth Strategy 2010-2012, SECTION 2a regarding the Response to the Presidency Priorities on Youth Employment and Entrepreneurship[22]

Flexicurity strategies need to take into account the specific conditions of young people. To improve youth labour market entry and increase flexibility, the Labour Code was amended on 1 May 2011 to streamline

---

[19] http://www.anph.ro/eng/ (accessed 20 December 2013).

[20] http://www.anph.ro/anph.php?m=anph (accessed 20 December 2013).

[21] OJ C 137, 27.5.2010, 1.

[22] http://ec.europa.eu/youth/documents/national_youth_reports_2012/romania.pdf (accessed 20 December 2013).

the recourse to fixed-term contracts. However, no specific measure was taken with regard to lifelong learning strategies by the Ministry of Labour, Family, Social Protection and Elderly, although active policies were introduced for youth aged 16 to 25 providing individualised services in the form of vocational guidance, labour mediation and support to enter the labour market. For students under 30 years old applying for subsidized loans from the unemployment insurance fund, courses are organised to ensure the provision of tertiary education either in the public or private sector, provided that the institution complies with the relevant standards established at the national level. Further, business consultancy is made available to young entrepreneurs, and job fairs are organised for graduates, with subsidies offered to employers hiring young graduates for at least 12 months (18 months for young people with disabilities). In addition, exemptions from the payment of the unemployment fund contribution for 12 months have also been introduced. These measures have proved to be an efficient way to help youth enter the labour market.[23]

2.1.1. Promoting Cross-border Professional Experiences and Vocational Opportunities for Young People

Government Ordinance No. 129/2000 on adults' vocational training establishes the right of young people to access social protection while carrying out vocational training ensuring "no discrimination with regard to age, gender, race, ethnic origin, political or religious affiliation". The Ordinance also expressly establishes the obligation on all employers to take appropriate measures to make sure that employees have access to vocational training, pointing at the same time to the right of jobseekers to attend free vocational training programmes organised by the National Agency for Employment/ NEA (ANOFM) or by other licensed providers of vocational training services. Vocational Education and Training (VET) was also given priority in the national development plan 2007-2013 (PND), the National Reform Programme (PNR) and the sectoral operational programme for human resources development (POS DRU).

VET specific objectives can be explicitly found in a number of strategic documents, such as the national employment strategy 2004-2010 (MMSSF, 2004), the short and medium-term strategy for lifelong vocational training 2005-2010 (MMSSF, ANOFM, MEC, CNFPA with the support of Sectoral Committees, 2005), the strategic guidelines of the

---

[23] http://ec.europa.eu/youth/documents/national_youth_reports_2012/romania.pdf (accessed 20 December 2013).

Minister of Education and Research for the period 2006-2008 (2005), and the Development strategy for pre-university education.[24]

2.1.2. Developing Career Guidance and Guidance Services

In order to ensure sustainable labour market entry, guidance services for jobseekers (including young people) are provided through the ANOFM Employment Programme. In this respect, in 2002, ANOFM implemented the programme "From school to professional life and career", designed for future graduates and for youth in pre-university education, which provides information and counselling. Moreover, 32 offices were established within the Child Protection Directorate's structure, to provide specific counselling to teenagers. At present, at the national level, there are 50 offices and a number of related projects, directed to teenagers and young people and operating in 22 counties. These include counselling services and are designed to provide teenagers with the necessary skills to be independent in the future.[25]

2.1.3. Promoting Quality Internships and Apprenticeships to Facilitate Labour Market Entry and Future Careers

According to the Romanian Labour Code (Art. 210), the organization, the development and the supervision of apprenticeship have to be regulated by a special provision. Law No. 106 of 15 June 2011 amending Law No. 279/2005 on apprenticeships was adopted for this purpose. In order to stimulate the development of vocational training through apprenticeship as well as the access to the labour market for young people aged between 16 and 25 years old, employers who hire people through an apprenticeship contract, according to this law, receive a monthly gross subsidy of 300 RON for each apprentice from the employment agencies. In this way, the Government has improved the legal framework on apprenticeship, in line with national legislation on education, so that after grade nine, one can choose to enter either vocational education or employment through apprenticeship.[26]

---

24 http://ec.europa.eu/youth/documents/national_youth_reports_2012/romania.pdf (accessed 20 December 2013).

25 http://ec.europa.eu/youth/documents/national_youth_reports_2012/romania.pdf (accessed 20 December 2013).

26 http://ec.europa.eu/youth/documents/national_youth_reports_2012/romania.pdf (accessed 20 December 2013).

2.1.4. Promoting the Sharing of Household Chores to Facilitate Work-life Balance for Both Young Women and Young Men

In 2010, the Ministry of Labour, Family, Social Protection and Elderly implemented a project through some EU funding named "Equilibrium: a new approach towards work-life balance".[27]

2.1.5. Promoting Entrepreneurship in the Field of Sustainable Development

A number of projects were set up in this field to introduce entrepreneurship in school curricula. Moreover, the Erasmus for Young Entrepreneurs was developed which provides support to young entrepreneurs.[28]

2.2. National Report: First Cooperation Cycle of the EU Youth Strategy 2010-2012, Section C Regarding the Response to the Presidency Priorities for Social inclusion

The project focuses on a cross-sectoral approach to improve community cohesion and solidarity to reduce the social exclusion of young people. It analyses the connection between young people's education and employment outcomes, and their social inclusion. Social inclusion is a principle promoted by Law No. 116 of 15 March 2002 aimed at preventing and combating social marginalization. The initiative promotes the recourse to special "solidarity contracts" concluded with local employment agencies and intends to help young people in difficult situations. Law No. 292 of 20 December 2011 on Social Assistance, published in the *Official Romanian Journal* No. 905 of 20 December 2011 makes reference to the issue of social inclusion. Before January 2010, an important initiative was launched to foster labour market entry of young graduates through job fairs. The initiative was organised at national level by the Agency. Incentives and subsidies were also provided to improve graduates' access to employment.

Youth unemployment is a key issue in terms of social inclusion among young people. In this respect, one of the NEA programmes, called the

---

[27] http://ec.europa.eu/youth/documents/national_youth_reports_2012/romania.pdf (accessed 20 December 2013).

[28] http://ec.europa.eu/youth/documents/national_youth_reports_2012/romania.pdf (accessed 20 December 2013).

Employment Programme for Socially Excluded People, is designed for both socially excluded people and those at risk of exclusion: orphans; youth with children; young ex-offenders. The objectives of the programme were to improve access to employment for disadvantaged people; promote social inclusion and social security, protect young people from labour market exclusion; make youth aware of the risk of social exclusion and prepare them for an active life in the community in formal and non-formal education systems.[29]

2.2.1. Homelessness, Housing and the Financial Exclusion of Young People

Law No. 116 of 15 March 2002 aims at preventing and combating social marginalization as well as facilitating access to housing for youth under 35 years old who cannot afford to buy a house.[30]

3. Romania's Country Sheet Presented in the Staff Working Document that Accompanies the Communication "Moving Youth into Employment"

In the Commission Staff Working Document accompanying the Communication "Moving Youth into Employment"[31] detailed information is provided on the implementation of the Youth Opportunities Initiative (YOI) one year after its adoption as well as an overview of youth specific country recommendations.

Annex II [SWD (2012) 406 final] provides an overview of country-specific recommendations (CSRs) adopted by the Council on 10 July 2012 hereby pointing out that Romania should take action within the period 2012-2013 to:

> Implement the measures laid down in Decision 2009/459/EC, as amended by Decision 2010/183/EU, together with the measures laid down in

---

[29] http://ec.europa.eu/youth/documents/national_youth_reports_2012/romania.pdf (accessed 20 December 2013).

[30] http://ec.europa.eu/youth/documents/national_youth_reports_2012/romania.pdf (accessed 20 December 2013).

[31] European Commission. 2012. *Moving Youth into Employment, Commission Staff Working Document Accompanying the document, Communication from the Commission to the Council the European Parliament, the European Economic and Social Committee and the Committee of the Regions,* COM (2012), 727 final. Brussels: European Commission.

Decision 2011/288/EU and further specified in the Memorandum of Understanding of 23 June 2009 and its subsequent supplements, and in the Memorandum of Understanding of 29 June 2011 and its subsequent supplements.[32]

In Annex III [SWD (2012) 406 final] some current trends in youth unemployment are presented, and commitments are made to combat and prevent youth unemployment (mostly under the YOI). Progress was reported in the implementation of these commitments and in the mobilisation of funds, whereas amendments were made following a questionnaire sent to MS in July 2012.

3.1. Commitments made by Romania to Combat and Prevent Youth Unemployment in 2012

€216 million were reallocated within the ESF Human Resources Development Operational Programme (HRD OP) to support 329,000 young people. Furthermore, changes to the Employment Stimulation Law No.76/2002 were made aiming to introduce more flexible conditions in case of subsidies granted to employ young graduates, e.g. an increase of the age threshold and a review of those eligible for subsidized contracts.

Finally, a National Jobs Plan was adopted concerning youth.

3.1.1. Progress in the Implementation of the Commitments

Youth Guarantee Schemes and Other Measures Targeting Youth Not in Employment, Education or Training (NEET) and Other Groups at Risk

The National Employment Agency (ANOFM) provides customized services (in line with Law 76/2002) through "solidarity contracts" for young people aged 16 to 25 years old at risk of social exclusion.

Employers hiring youth at risk can receive subsidies up to 75% of the average wage for a period of up to 2 years. They can also receive a monthly allowance equal to 50% of the full amount of the unemployment

[32] European Council. 2012. *Council Recommendation on the National Reform Programme 2012 of Romania and delivering a Council opinion on the Convergence Programme of Romania,* 2012-2015, UEM 221, ECOFI 595, SOC 572, COMPET 440, ENV 536, EDUC 213, RECH 276, ENER 305, Brussels: European Council. (OR. en) http://register.consilium.europa.eu/pdf/en/12/st11/st11270.en12.pdf (accessed 20 December 2013).

benefit if they hire youth with an open-ended contract. Between January and July 2012, almost 500 young people facing social exclusion were employed (budget: EUR 130,000).

Within the ESF HRD OP programme, a number of projects are being implemented aiming at promoting social inclusion, social economy and labour market access of vulnerable groups. Currently, 23,222 youth aged 15-24 (24% of all participants) are taking part in these projects. In addition, a series of measures were implemented to prevent and reduce early school leaving involving 2,014 people between the ages of 15 and 24.

Youth Traineeships and Apprenticeships

Young people can be hired from 1 to 3 years through an apprenticeship contract. In this case, the employer has the duty to provide theoretical and/or practical training. So far, 43 apprenticeship contracts have been concluded.

ESF projects aim at ensuring a smoother transition from school to work and contributing to the development of skills for apprentices, students and young graduates during their first work experience. Almost 70,000 people under the age of 25 participated in education and training projects. It has been estimated that in 2011-2013 about 2,700 students took part in traineeships in other EU Member States, through the Leonardo da Vinci Programme and 16,000 young people have been involved in projects implemented within the Youth in Action initiative. Finally, in the academic year 2011/2012, 1,215 Romanian Erasmus students benefited from placement grants in organisations and companies in other EU countries.

Support to Job Creation (Including Entrepreneurship and Self-employment Schemes)

Job subsidies are offered for a period of 12 months to employers who hire young graduates, with the obligation to maintain the contractual relation for a further 2 years after the funded period. The number of graduates employed in January-July 2012 was 1,960.

Special allowances are granted to those graduates registered as unemployed if they enter into an employment relationship longer than 12 months while receiving the unemployment benefit. The number of young people who have benefited from this measure so far has been 543.

A special programme for students and pupils to help them obtain a fixed-term job during the holiday period was also implemented. By the end of July 2012, 325 people had benefited from it.

In 2011, the Government created about 5,500 jobs by developing and implementing a programme to stimulate the creation of start-up micro-enterprises by young entrepreneurs.

By the end of July 2012, 86,331 young people participated in projects financed through the ESF aimed at promoting active employment and entrepreneurial culture.

The Mobilisation of Funds

Under the ESF HRD OP, at the end of July 2012, the total amount of money allocated to the programme "Developing and implementing active employment measures" (mainly directed to young people) was EUR 298.46 million, with a further ESF contribution of EUR 257.49 million.

The total amount initially allocated was EUR 259.74 million (ESF contribution: EUR 207.96 million), while the total amount provided was EUR 131.35 million. In addition, the Managing Authority reallocated EUR 216 million to the project "Lifelong learning and the labour market", although no call for proposals has been launched at the time of writing.

Romania plans to use the ESF to support mobility programmes under the lifelong learning programme. A special Technical Working Group for Youth has recently been set up within the framework of the HRD OP.

Almost some €130,000 were spent in the first seven months of 2012 for so-called "solidarity contracts".

Funds allocated under the Leonardo da Vinci and the Youth in Action programmes amounted to a total of €19.8 million, while €2.6 million were supplied for Erasmus grants.

The total amount of (both ESF and national) resources spent for job creation policies as described under section 3.3 was €320.86 million.

Amendments to the Legislative Framework to Facilitate the Labour Market Entry of Young People

In 2011, the Law on apprenticeship was amended and supplemented with a view of establishing an adequate framework to increase employment opportunities for youth with low or no qualifications and realize investments promoting regional development by using IC technologies to create at least 200 jobs.

4. Romania's Youth-related Measures in the Staff Working Document accompanying the Proposal for a Council Recommendation on Establishing a Youth Guarantee Scheme

Table 3-10. Youth-related measures introduced on 5 December 2012 in Romania[33]

Vocational Training, Apprenticeship Traineeship Measures	Early Intervention and Activation Measures	Labour Market Integration Measures, Including Subsidies to Employers
Young people can get a job from 1 to 3 years through an apprenticeship contract and the employer has the duty to provide theoretical and/or practical training. ESF projects allow for a smoother transition from school to work by contributing to the development of job-specific skills of apprentices, students and young graduates in their first job.	The National Employment Agency provides personalised services through solidarity contracts for young people (16-25) at risk of social exclusion. ESF HRD OP includes measures to prevent and reduce early school leaving of young people (15-24).	The National Employment Agency provides personalised services through solidarity contracts for young people (16-25) at risk of social exclusion. ESF HRD OP includes measures to prevent and reduce school dropout of young people (15-24).

6. Labour Market Policy Expenditure in Romania

6.1. Labour Market Policy Expenditure in Romania in 2010: a European Comparison

In 2010 in Romania, LMP expenditure as reported by EUROSTAT represented 0.6% of GDP. Fig. 11-1 presents the share of GDP allocated to LMP across Europe. Ireland and Spain, with an expenditure of about 4% of GDP, rank first within the EU27, whereas Romania (0.62%) is just

[33] Commission Staff Working Document. 2012. *Accompanying the document Proposal for a Council Recommendation on Establishing a Youth Guarantee* {COM(2012) 729 final} Brussels, 5.12.2012, SWD(2012) 409 final. Brussels: European Commission.

ahead of Bulgaria (0.58%) and Malta (0.51%) which are bringing up the rear.

Fig. 3-2. Labour Market Policies Expenditure in Romania as % of GDP in 2010.

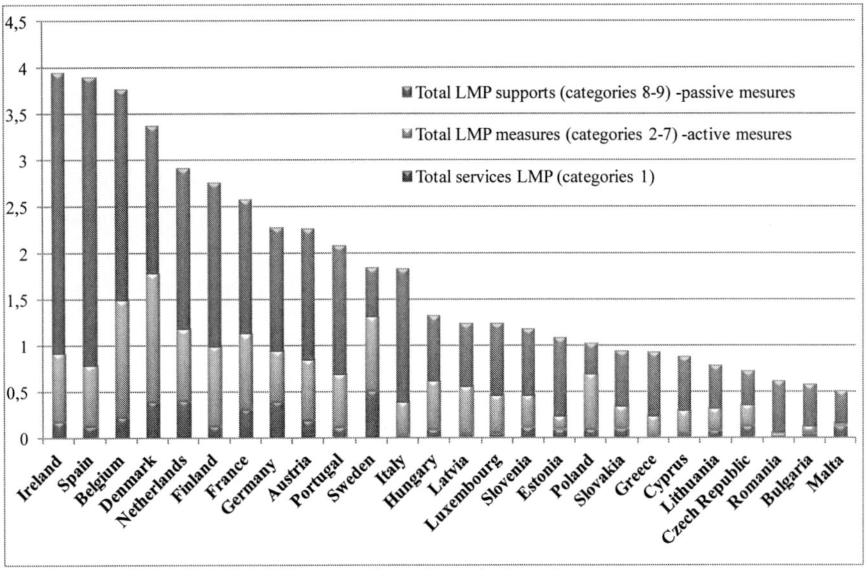

Source: EUROSTAT, LMP expenditure [lmp_ind_exp].

The public expenditure structure in 2010 in Romania was uneven in comparison with other European countries. As Fig. 3-3 points out, expenditure on active measures was only 4.8% of overall LMP expenditure, whereas that on passive measures was about 90.3% of the overall LMP expense, the highest share European-wide.

By contrast in Sweden and Poland, the expenditure concerning active measures exceeded that related to passive measures. In Sweden, active measures expenditure was 43.8%, i.e. 14.6 percentage points higher than the expenditure rate on passive measures. In Poland, active measures expenditure accounted for about 58.3%, i.e. 25.3 percentage points higher than passive measures expenditure.

Fig. 3-3. The Structure of Public Expenditure on LMP by Intervention Type in 2010.

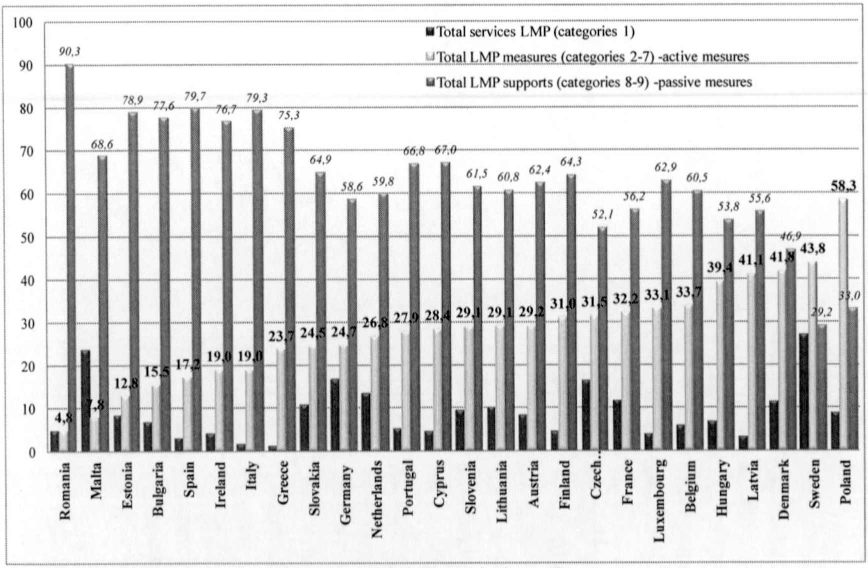

Source: EUROSTAT, LMP expenditure [lmp_ind_exp].

The values reported by official sources for Romania and EUROSTAT do not reflect all efforts made to introduce active measures to increase employment. One important cause of these major inconsistencies could be related to the different national methodologies of reporting LMP expenditure. With regard to 2010, for instance, the reported data for Romania[34] (*749.13 million Euros*) covered exclusively the LMP funded by the public administration (*34.75 million Euros for active measures and 714.36 million Euros for passive measures)*, and did not include active measures funded by ESF programmes (*in 2011, 57.07 million Euros, more than 573.92 million Euros*[35] *in 2010*). This makes it possible to understand the different structure of LMP expenditure across countries, and the good performance of some countries such as Poland.

---

[34] Expenditure by LMP interventions in Romania [lmp_expme_ro].

[35] Guvernul României, Ministerul Muncii, Familiei şi Protectiei Sociale, autoritatea de management Pentru Programul Operaţional Sectorial Dezvoltarea Resurselor Umane Programul Operaţional Sectorial "dezvoltarea Resurselor Umane 2007-2013", Raportul Anula de Implementare 1 ianuarie—31 decembrie 2011, 11.

6.2. Main Labour Market Interventions Directed to Young People Reported by Romania in the EUROSTAT LMP Database: The 2010 Database on Labour Market Policies in 2010 as Implemented by ANOFM

In 2010, 69.6% of the 626,960 people registered as unemployed benefited from LMPs. Some 7.4% of the total number of people registered as unemployed (without double counting) benefited from active measures and 62.3% benefited from passive ones. In 2010, the registered unemployed under the age of 25 accounted for almost 16% of the total number of unemployed people (99,142 registered unemployed persons were under the age of 25). This means that the percentage of young people registered as unemployed benefiting from active measures was 1.6 percentage points higher than average and that people benefiting from passive measures were 28.9 percentage points lower than average. The average unitary cost of passive measures was 2.3 times higher than the cost of the active measures.

In 2010, among a total of 436,544 people who have benefited from LMP measures, 9.6% were young people under the age of 25. The total LMP expenditure reported by EUROSTAT accounted for *749.13 million Euros,* funded through the LMP administrative fund (as part of the labour market budget) and had an average cost per year per beneficiary of about €1,716.

With regard to young beneficiaries, 21.3% benefited from active measures, twice as many as those who benefited from active measures.

Among the total active measures beneficiaries, 19.3% were young people, i.e. twice the number of those benefiting from passive measures (8.5%). In 2010, the budget allocated to active measures was *34.75 million Euros,* with an average cost per year/beneficiary of €753.6. for LMP active measures.

With regard to the distribution of young beneficiaries of LMP, 78.7% of them benefited from active measures as against 89.4% who benefited from passive measures. The budget allocated to passive measures in 2010 was *714.36 million Euros*, with an average cost per year/beneficiary of €1,740.6.

The typical active measure (Table 3-11) applied in Romania for young people in 2010 was the one falling within "category 6" of the EUROSTAT codification "Direct job creation" through so-called "solidarity contracts" for young people at risk of exclusion. The number of beneficiaries was 1,067, 89.1% of whom were young people under the age of 25, with expenditure amounting to 2 million Euros and an average cost per year/beneficiary of €1,874.

Identification code: 6 RO25[36]

Country: Romania, Year 2010, Category: 6, Direct job creation Intervention No/name: 25 solidarity contracts for young people at risk of exclusion. Type of action: 6 "direct job creation".

Description:
Aim: Integration/reintegration at work of young people aged between 16 and 25 years old.

Beneficiaries / participants:
Young people between the age of 16 and 25 facing difficulties and who are at risk of professional exclusion:
- Young people coming from placement centres;
- Young single parents;
- Young people with family and children;
- Young people with family but no children;
- Young ex-offenders with family.

Other young people facing special difficulties:

Whereas available, the remaining funds can be allocated to initiatives directed to people below 35 years old facing similar difficulties, provided that they are registered with the ANOFM.

Action/Instrument: Promoting employment through solidarity contracts;
Financing/support: Unemployment insurance fund (plus administrative costs);
Responsible institution: Public employment services;
Eligibility:
- Compliance with the foregoing conditions;
- Registration with the ANOFM;
- The existence of an agreement between the beneficiary and the ANOFM for a maximum period of 2 years granted to find a job.

Legal basis: Law No. 116/2002 regarding the prevention of social exclusion;

[36] Romania 2010, EUROSTAT, Labour market policy statistics, Qualitative report.

Recent changes: None;
Supplementary information: None;
Expenditure breakdown: Transfers to employers (in the form of periodic cash payments and reduced social contributions);
Target groups: Registered unemployed (All, Youth);
Unemployment spells: Continuous;
Receipt of benefits: None;
Planned duration: Maximum 24 Months;
Implementation: started in 2002 (ongoing);

Additionally, other interventions falling within category 4 of "employment incentives" were planned for youth:

- 7 people under the age of 25 benefited from subsidies provided to create jobs for disabled graduates. The allocated budget was not reported;
- 4,059 people under the age of 25 (accounting for 82.3% of the total number of beneficiaries) received s*ubsidies allocated for initiatives directed to graduate recruitment*, accounting for an expenditure of 1.03 million Euros and with an average cost per year/person of €208.8.
- 43 people under the age of 25 (accounting for 80.9% of the total beneficiaries) benefited from *Income support measures for graduates*, accounting for an expenditure of 0.06 million Euros with an average cost per year/person of €937.5.

In 2010, the passive measure was the "out-of-work income support/unemployment allowance 2": 50% allowance with an expenditure of 24.54 million Euros and an average cost per year/person of €1304.1.

Table 3-11. Main Labour Market Interventions Directed to Young People Reported by Romania in the EUROSTAT LMP Database, in the 2010 Labour Market Policies Database Implemented by ANOFM.

LMP policy code	LMP intervention type	Expenditure by LMP intervention, Romania [lmp_expme_at], million euros	Participants by LMP intervention, Romania[lmp_partme_at], persons	Participants by LMP intervention under 25, Romania [lmp_partme_at], persons	Share of young people [%]	Average unit expenditure /intervention / person/year [euros]	
6_RO25	"Solidarity contracts" for young people with difficulties and at risk of professional exclusion	2,00	1.067	951	89,1	1874,4	6_RO25
41_RO16	Subsidiesto create jobs for disabled graduates	0,00	8	7	87,5	0,0	41_RO16
41_RO14	Subsidies to promote recruitment of graduates	1,03	4.933	4.059	82,3	208,8	41_RO14
81_RO2_1	[Component] Unemployment allowance 2 - allowance (50%)	24,54	18.817	15.217	80,9	1304,1	81_RO2_1
41_RO41	Income support for graduates	0,06	64	43	67,2	937,5	41_RO41

Source LMP EUROSTAT, 2010.

6.3. Main Labour Market Interventions Directed to Young People reported by Romania to the ESF SOP HRD 2007-2013 Monitoring Systems, Intermediary Situation as of 31 December 2011

As of 31 December 2011, 589,324 people had been included in the SIM ESF SOP HRD information system and their participation in ESF programmes had been validated. This accounted for 35.71% of the total number of people hired within the SOP HRD 2007-2013 initiative (1,650,000).

This figure is particularly important with regard to the further development of the HRD programme, since as of 31 December 2011, 24.21% of recipients had received benefits (pre + ESF contribution) within the framework of the ESF 2007-2013 programme, and 5.47% had been reimbursed from the European Commission.

Table 3-12 shows that as of 31 December 2011, 163,983 people out of a total number of 589,324 were aged 15-24 years old.

If we consider that one person could benefit from more than one incentive, we can conclude that the most successful initiative for young people was the AP2 "Lifelong learning and the labour market". Some 52,426 people were involved in the programme accounting for 53.2% of the total number of beneficiaries and for 32% of the overall number of ESF beneficiaries funding under the age of 25. The SOP total financing[37] (ESF + State Budget) was 991.3 million Euros with a total expenditure of 20.9 million Euros plus a public contribution of 20.3 million Euros, pointing to a 2.05% implementation rate. AP2 projected budget accounted for 24.2% of the total projected budget, with the realised percentage amounting to 8.8%, with an expense to beneficiary ratio of 206 Euros.

The AP5 initiative "Promoting active employment measures" involved 175,623 participants; among them, 47,612 were young people, accounting for 27.1% of the total number of participants in AP5, i.e. 29% of ESF funding directed to youth. SOP total financing (ESF + State Budget) accounted for 543.3 million Euros, 59.6 million of which were paid to the beneficiaries. Of these, 57.5 million Euros accounted for public contributions, indicating a low level of implementation rate (10.6%). The budget allocated to the AP5 initiative was equal to 13.3% of the total projected budget; the realised percentage was 25% with an expense to beneficiary ratio of 328 Euros.

[37] Accounts related to payment request No. 11, updated and retransmitted to the European commission by the Certification and Payment Authority (ACP) on 13 April 2012 including the accounts provisionally closed on 31 December 2011.

Table 3-12. Total Number of Participants at ESF Financed Initiatives until 31 December 2011 and Accounts Related to Payment Request No. 11, Updated and Retransmitted to the European Commission by the Certification and Payment Authority (ACP) on 13 April 2012 Including the Accounts Provisionally Closed on 31 December 2011.

ESF funding by principal axes	Age group: 15-24			Total participants at ESF operations			Young participants (15-24) as a % of the total particpants			Structure of ESF beneficiaries by AP		SOP total financing (ESF+State Budget)= calc. base for EU contribution	Total expenses paid to eligible beneficiaries [euros]	Corresponding public contribution [euros]	Structure of ESF expenses by AP		Execution rate (%)	Expenses/ beneficiary [euro]
	men	women	*total*	men	women	*total*	men	women	*total*	*young*	*total*	a	c	d	a	d	e=d/a*100	d/total
AP 1 "Education and vocational training in support for growth and development of the knowledge society	1806	4090	***5896***	10027	21721	***31748***	18,0	18,8	18,6	3,6	3,9	991788814	37625969	36816629	24,3	15,8	3,71	1160
AP 2 "Linking lifelong learning and labor market"	**24088**	**28338**	**52426**	**46715**	**51914**	**98629**	**51,6**	**54,6**	**53,2**	32,0	18,3	**991397184**	**20986362**	**20308886**	24,2	8,8	**2,05**	**206**
AP 3 "Increasing adaptability of workers and enterprises	13870	20937	***34807***	79917	99874	***179791***	17,4	21,0	19,4	21,2	31,3	519565411	77364678	75275901	12,7	32,5	14,49	419
AP 4 "Modernizing Public Employment Service"	12	15	***27***	2059	4600	***6659***	0,6	0,3	0,4	0,0	0,8	235541719	1325232	1078312	5,8	0,6	0,46	162
AP 5 "Promoting active employment measures"	23946	23666	***47612***	86319	89304	***175623***	27,7	26,5	27,1	29,0	33,8	543356044	59615845	57542308	13,3	25,0	10,59	328
AP 6 "Promoting social inclusion	8437	14780	***23217***	29993	66881	***96874***	28,1	22,1	24,0	14,2	11,8	644007986	40978116	39993829	15,7	17,2	6,21	413
Ap 7 Technical assitance												163610556	414609	414609	4,0	0,2	0,25	0,7
Total	**72159**	**91826**	***163985***	***255030***	***334294***	***589324***	**28,3**	**27,5**	**27,8**	**100,0**	**100,0**	**4089267714**	**238310811**	**231430473**	**100,0**	**100,0**	**5,66**	**393**

Source: Guvernul României, Ministerul Muncii, Familiei şi Protectiei Sociale, autoritatea de management Pentru Programul Operaţional Sectorial Dezvoltarea Resurselor Umane Programul Operaţional Sectorial "dezvoltarea Resurselor Umane 2007-2013", Raportul Anula de Implementare 1 ianuarie—31 decembrie 2011, 11.

7. Conclusions

In Romania, youth policies are under the responsibility of the Ministry of Youth and Sports, the Ministry of National Education, the Ministry of Economy, the Ministry of Agriculture and Rural Development and the Ministry of Labour, Family, Social Protection and Elderly.

The Ministry of Labour, Family, Social Protection and Elderly (MMFPSPV)[1] is responsible for a number of issues related to youth policies such as youth employment, social inclusion and equal opportunities for young people.

Employment protection and flexicurity strategies are regulated by the Labour Code and by Law No. 76/2002 and subsequent amendments, as well as Social Assistance Law No. 292/2011. The National Agency for Employment (ANOFM) is responsible for the implementation of LMP and as the main public employment services provider, it promotes active and passive measures financed through the labour market budget or other public sources.

National employment policies are connected to EU strategic documents through a series of measures, including the 2011-2013 National Reform Programme (NRP), the National Strategy for Sustainable Development, the National Development Plan 2007-2013, the National Strategic Reference Framework 2007-2013 and the Sectoral Human Resources Development 2007-2013 programme, and the Employment Strategy (draft) as implemented by the Managing Authority for Sectoral Operational Programme on Human Resources Development (AMPOSDRU) which also manages the Mission for the European Social Fund.

Public expenditure structure in 2010 in Romania was unbalanced in comparison with other European countries. The LMP expenditure, as reported by EUROSTAT, accounts for 0.6% of GDP (third from last in the EU27). Active measures account for 4.8% of total LMP expenditure, the lowest level in the EU27, whereas passive measures account for 90.3% of total expenses for LMP, the highest value within the EU27. In times of crisis, the demand for active measures increases, but resources are limited because of the increasing need for passive measures. The present analysis is limited because the methodology adopted does not make it possible to estimate the efficiency and effectiveness of the measures applied.

---

[1] Ordonanta de Urgenta nr. 96 din 22 decembrie 2012 privind stabilirea unor masuri de reorganizare in cadrul administratiei publice centrale si pentru modificarea unor acte normative, EMITENT: GUVERNUL, PUBLICAT ÎN: MONITORUL OFICIAL nr. 884 din 22 decembrie 2012.

Structural funds, however, have provided relatively positive results. As of 31 December 2011, 589,324 people had been included in the SIM ESF SOP HRD information system and participated in ESF programmes. This accounted for 35.71% of the total number of people (1,650,000) hired within the SOP HRD 2007-2013 initiative.

Public and structural funds are complementary and contribute to sustaining employment growth. Despite the difficulties in producing results, it is still possible to draw some tentative conclusions:

Youth registered as unemployed account for 15.8% of the total unemployed. Young people accounted for 19.3% of the beneficiaries of active measures provided by PES, twice as much as the percentage of youth benefiting from passive measures (8.5%). In this case, active measures were the main tool to stimulate the transition to employment.

The share of young people aged 15-24 years among the total number of participants in programmes financed through the ESF was 27.3% from 2007 to 31 December 2011. Under the ESF SOP HRD programme, which is comprised of a series of different interventions (such as main interventions, tools, active measures), percentages are comparable with those related to the results of the initiatives carried out through the SPO system.

The diversification of policies, the increasing capacity of analysis, and powerful institutional networks are an attempt to implement, in a coordinated and efficient manner, measures to address the needs of youth.

The greatest challenge to achieve this goal relates to the lines of action and intervention, especially in terms of active measures. This poses the question of whether the system is able to use active measures to solve the issue without experiencing problems related to system dependency for beneficiaries or, in the worst scenario, without losing the generation of people who failed to enter the system.

References

Council of the European Union. 2012. Council Recommendation on the National Reform Programme 2012 of Romania and delivering a Council opinion on the Convergence Programme of Romania, 2012-2015, UEM 221, ECOFI 595, SOC 572, COMPET 440, ENV 536, EDUC 213, RECH 276, ENER 305, (OR. en) http://register.consilium.europa.eu/pdf/en/12/st11/st11270.en12.pdf. Brussels: European Union.

European Commission. 2012. Commission Staff Working Document accompanying the Document Proposal for a Council Recommendation on Establishing a Youth Guarantee {COM (2012) 729 final}, 5.12.2012, SWD (2012) 409 final. Brussels: European Commission.

—. 2012. *Moving Youth into Employment,* {COM(2012) 727 final}, 5.12.2012, SWD (2012) 406 final. Brussels: European Commission.

European Steering Committee for Youth. 2000. *Romanian National Youth Policy,* (CDEJ), 26th meeting Budapest, 25-27 October 2000, Strasbourg, 2nd September , 2000, CDEJ (2000) 5, Evaluation report by the International Group of Experts, Council of Europe, Council of Europe country reviews on national youth policy in Romania.

EUROSTAT, Expenditure by LMP interventions: Romania [lmp_expme_ro]. Brussels: EUROSTAT.

—. 2010. *Labour Market Policy Statistics Qualitative Report,* Romania. EUROSTAT, 31.

—. 2010. *Romania 2010, Labour Market Policy Statistics, Qualitative Report.* Brussels: EUROSTAT.

Government of Romania. 2013. Government Decision 11 of 19.01.2013 regarding the organization and functioning of the Ministry of Youth and Sports. Monitorul Oficial al României, Partea 1, Nr. 42/19.I.2013.

Guvernul României, Ministerul Muncii, Familiei şi Protectiei Sociale, autoritatea de management Pentru Programul Operaţional Sectorial Dezvoltarea Resurselor Umane Programul Operaţional Sectorial "dezvoltarea Resurselor Umane 2007-2013", Raportul Anula de Implementare 1 ianuarie—31 decembrie 2011, 11.

Guvernul României, Ministerul Muncii, Familiei şi Protectiei Sociale. Hotarare nr. 47 din 19 februarie 2013 privind organizarea si functionarea Ministerului Economiei EMITENT: GUVERNUL PUBLICAT ÎN: MONITORUL OFICIAL nr. 102 din 20 februarie 2013 Data intrarii in vigoare: 20 Februarie 2013.

Lege nr. 351/2006 din 21 iulie 2006 privind infiintarea, organizarea si functionarea Consiliului National al Tineretului din Romania publicat in M.Of. nr. 643/26 iul. 2006 http://www.anst.gov.ro/politici/programe/13_consiliul-tineretului-din-romnia.html.

Legea 76 2002 privind sistemul asigurărilor pentru şomaj şi stimularea ocupării forţei de muncă, publicată în Monitorul Oficial nr. 103 din 6 februarie 2002 "Legea şomajului".

Mitulescu, S. 2012. *Youth Policy in Romania.* European Knowledge Centre for Youth Policy Correspondent in Romania http://youth-partnership-eu.coe.int/youth-partnership/ekcyp/By_country/Romania.html.

Ordonanta de Urgenta, nr. 96 din 22 decembrie 2012 privind stabilirea unor masuri de reorganizare in cadrul administratiei publice centrale si pentru modificarea unor acte normative, EMITENT: GUVERNUL, PUBLICAT ÎN: MONITORUL OFICIAL nr. 884 din 22 decembrie 2012.

YOUTH LABOUR TAXATION AND PROJECT FINANCING IN ROMANIA

GHENADIE CIOBANU

1. Introduction

The aim of this paper is twofold. On the one hand, it seeks to investigate budgetary and fiscal policy, pointing out issues such as inequalities, possible deficits and the provision of a solid tax base in order to fulfill the requirements in relation to public expenditure. On the other hand, it will make an attempt to concentrate on youth and their difficulties to find a job with a decent salary. Accordingly, this work will consider the relationship between young people and questions concerning fiscal policy that is youth labour taxation and the scope to support this category of workers through tax breaks and the funding of a number of projects. This is because youth are deemed to be a catalyst for quick recovery and economic growth, both at a local and national level. Evidently, managing the imbalances resulting from certain market mechanisms cannot be solved only by looking at the relationship between labour demand and supply.

Whereas in developed countries variations between labour demand and supply from one year to another are reported to be irrelevant (1% to 3%), such difference in Romania is more pronounced and leads to some serious consequences.

2. Labour Taxation

Labour taxation in Romania has experienced high fluctuations, from 48.2% in 1999 to 40.9% in 2008, when the highest growth was reported since the 1990s. In addition to a 16% personal income tax rate, statistics also show that the rate of aggregated social security contributions is equal to 20.8%, to which a further 10.5% contribution paid by the employer should be added (31.3% and 24.3% of the gross salary and wage costs, respectively). The rate for contributions to healthcare corresponds to 5.2%

on the part of the employer and 5.5% which is paid by the employee (10.7% and 4.3% of the gross salary and wage costs, respectively).

Unemployment translates into further costs for both employers (0.5%) and employees (0.5%), amounting to 1% and 0.8% of the gross salary and wage costs, respectively. Some contributions cover medical expenses (0.85%), ITM (0.75%), the Risks and Accidents Fund (0.4%), and special funds established in case of wage claims (0.25%), corresponding to 2.25% of the gross salary and 1.7% of wage costs.

Law No. 76/2002[1] entitles employers to pay a monthly sum of money for each graduate recruited. More specifically:

- An amount equal to the reference social indicator applicable on the date of employment, for graduates in lower secondary schools or schools of arts and crafts;

- An amount corresponding to 1.2 times the reference social indicator applicable at the time of employment, for graduates in upper secondary or post-secondary education;

- An amount equal to 1.5 times the reference social indicator applicable at the time of employment for graduates in higher education.

Pursuant to the Tax Code, employers are required to calculate, withhold and transfer contributions for each hire to the unemployment insurance fund on a monthly basis, the rate of which is statutorily provided and shall apply considering the calculation of the single contribution to the unemployment fund.

Section (1), Article 52 of the Tax Code,[2] which entered into force on 1 July 2012 established that income generating from one the following by any legal entity should be regarded as taxable:

a) Income from intellectual property rights;

b) Income from activities conducted under employment contracts or civil agreements concluded pursuant to the Civil Code, as well as income generating as a result of temporary agency contracts;

---

[1] LEGE Nr. 76 din 16 ianuarie 2002 privind sistemul asigurărilor pentru somaj si stimularea ocupării forŃei de muncă no. 76 / / 2002.

[2] Tax Code, Codul Fiscal cu normele metodologice de aplicare, Legea 571/2003 coroborată cu HG 44/2004.

c) Income from accounting and tax advice, either for judicial and extrajudicial documentation.

Also, employers are required to keep track of payment of social contributions, income taxes, and nominal records for each insured workers.

Unemployed people are entitled to some benefits concerning travelling.

More specifically, following the amendments made to Law No. 76/2002,[3] they are granted a "jobseeker" allowance to contribute to their active search for employment.

The measure aims at increasing participation of jobseekers and adds to a number of services already in place (information and counselling, employment agencies, guidance and support to work as a self-employed or to start a business). It can also be seen as an instrument to motivate the long-term unemployed to seek work.

3. Tax Breaks for Young Entrepreneurs

The Government gives youth under 35 years old the opportunity to set up a business, relieving them of fiscal obligations. In order to be considered a "rookie" entrepreneur, the following conditions shall be met:

a) A maximum age of 35 years;

b) No commitment in terms of shareholding, ownership, and membership of any governing bodies or undertaking based in the European Economic Area.

c) A limited liability company (LLC) should be set up pursuant to Law No. 31/1990[4] and Emergency Ordinance No. 6/2011.[5]

As seen, if these conditions are met, a LLC should be established and young entrepreneurs will be exempt from paying registration fees and the expenses associated with the Trade Registry. Finally, and most importantly, booking and establishing the LLC will be free of charge.

---

[3] LEGE Nr. 76 din 16 ianuarie 2002 privind sistemul asigurărilor pentru somaj si stimularea ocupării forŃei de muncă no. 76 / / 2002.

[4] Company Law no. 31/1990.

[5] The Emergency Ordinance no. 6/2011.

At times, establishing a Limited Liability Partnerships is possible, provided that prospective partners meet at least conditions a) and b).

Some major benefits are granted to LLC owners. By way of example, they will not pay social security contributions on the income generated by employees if they are more than four. After three years, entrepreneurs will no longer be considered as "rookies", yet they would maintain such status if an annual turnover of €500,000 is produced at the end of the third year of establishment of the LLC. LLC owners can apply for a number of state-run programmes supporting youth entrepreneurship. In place since 2011, these programmes allocate grants up to €10,000 in case of eligibility, provided that no other funding is received. In order to be eligible, applicants should submit a business plan, specifying the budget.

Successful applicants are allocated the sum, which is paid partly by the state and partly by external partners who might be interested in the project.

If the business can start with €20,000, potential partners fund €10,000, while the government allocates €10,000. For example, if the sum needed is €50,000, external partners fund €40,000 and the government provides €10,000. Further, in order to stimulate the establishment of microenterprises and pursuant to the Emergency Ordinance, youth less than 35 years old who want to start a business are entitled to certain benefits, provided that some conditions are met. They must be 35 years and over, not have acquired shares in other companies or authored business plans. The maximum number of associates in microenterprises is 5.

Another condition to make use of funds is that the employer must hire at least two workers and reinvest not less than 50% of the profits from the previous year. Benefits shall not be granted where turnover will reach €500,000.

In some countries, high debt levels had consequences in terms of solvency, which translated into higher interest rates of sovereign bonds and credit rating agency declassification, and negative effects on economic growth and public finances. Yet one might note that spending cuts—which also concerned the remuneration of government officials—and social transfers are more effective than attempts to increase revenues.

Consequently, consolidation in most countries has been accompanied by a reduction of costs rather than revenue reform.

4. Personal and Household Income in Rural Areas

The problems affecting rural youth deserve further consideration. The Ministry of Labour and Social Welfare carried out field research on rural youth, the outcomes of which were published in the document *An*

Inclusive Labour Market in Rural Areas.[6] According to this survey, young people's major source of income in rural areas is remuneration for their work, which is usually paid on a monthly basis and concerns 37% of population aged 16 to 35 years old, and 41% if 19-year-olds and older are considered on an exclusive basis. Youth reporting the highest wages live in Transylvania and Banat (63% are to be found in western and more developed regions, 49% in central areas and 46% in North-west regions), compared with Moldova, Muntenia, and Dobrogea (below 30%).

Occasional work is another source of income for people in working age (usually those over 23 years old), yet they have fewer opportunities to access employment because of their lower levels of education or other disadvantageous economic factors.

Almost half of them have completed at least secondary school. Social benefits (1%), which include minimum guaranteed income, childcare allowances, "social insertion" income in case of unemployment benefits and other scholarships (1%) represent the main source of income for 5.2% of youth. The share of those whose main source of income consists in the sale of agricultural products is 2%. The majority of them (54%) have owned more than half hectare and very few have the necessary capital to purchase agricultural machinery or implement modern farming practices.

Finally, 70% of youth who have at least one source of revenue in July 2011 reported an average income of 830 Ron. Some 37% reported a personal income equal to 510 Ron, which corresponded to the 2011 minimum wage.

Table 3-13. Personal Income.

36.9 %	30%	21.1 %	11.9%
less than 510 RON	510-840 RON	840—1455 RON	over 1.455 RON

Source: An Inclusive Labour Market in Rural Areas (64).

---

6 *An inclusive labour market in rural areas*, national research on poverty, social exclusion and labour market opportunities of young people (16-35 years) in rural areas, Research Report, Sectoral Operational Programme Human Resources Development 2007-2013.

Table 3-14. Household Income Relative to Poverty Thresholds.

Household Income Relative to Poverty thresholds	
below the absolute poverty line	20.2
below the relative poverty	22.6
below median income	26
over median income	31.2

Source: An Inclusive Labour Market in Rural Areas (64).

About half of those falling within this category are people under 21 years old who rely on social benefits: children benefits, income guaranteed minimum income in case of unemployment, scholarships. A significant minority (40%, mostly Roma older than 23 years old) generates income from salaried employment in the informal sector and occasional labour.

Most of them have just graduated. Being their first job, remuneration is very low, at times equalling the minimum wage. For about 21% of young people, the income is between 830 RON and 1,455 RON, which corresponds to the average net salary in August 2011 (when data were collected). Over 82% of them are employees aged over 26 years.

As a result of the economic slowdown, only 10% of those unemployed or inactive received a job offer while not working or soon after having completed their education. Of these, 72% are men. The main reasons for rejecting the job are low pay or few benefits provided (43%). Other important reasons include problems with personnel (22%) and long-distance commuting (15%).

On average, the value of net minimum wage for which young people aged 19 and older would accept a rural job is between 1,150 RON and 1,000 RON. Less than 5% would be willing to work even under the net minimum wage (510 RON in 2011), and a significant minority (31%) under 1,000 RON. If many would accept a salary between 1,000 and 1,200 RON, very few (10%) are those who aspire to more than 1,500 RON per month, which was the average net salary in August 2011 (the period when the survey data were collected). About two thirds of those who would not accept to work for a salary lower than 1,200 RON are men. Perhaps the strongest factor influencing the minimum wage for young people who would accept a job is the welfare of the household of origin. Some 54% of those who would work for 500 RON per month belong to households under the absolute poverty line.

Table 3-15. Minimum Wage for which Young People Would Accept a Job.

under 500 RON	501-999 RON	1000-1200 RON	1201-1500 RON	over 1500 RON
4.4	30.9	40	14.6	10.1

Source: An Inclusive Labour Market in Rural Areas, 124.

The creation of new jobs must be a national priority. Considerable public investments, tax incentives for employers that hire young people and training and retraining programmes are among the most necessary measures to combat this issue, which otherwise will have devastating effects on the medium and long term. If young people remain outside of the labour market for too long, lose their skills, motivation and efficiency, and will take more time to integrate when they eventually find suitable offers. Law No. 350/2006[7] governing the public funding mechanisms for youth and financing methods of non-governmental youth structures establishes the following:

SECTION 1: public funding of youth activities (Article 27).

(1) The county councils and the General Council of Bucharest, local councils and county capital will fund youth activities taking into consideration their annual budget.

(2) Funds for youth activities referred to in paragraph (1) should be used to finance the activities of non-governmental structures for youth, and youth-related activities of local interest established in consultation with the county sports departments (based in Bucharest), and non-governmental youth organizations.

SECTION 2: governmental bodies regulating the funding of youth and for youth (Article 28):

(1) Non-economic and non-governmental revenues generated from structures for youth are non-taxable.

[7] Law No. 350/2006 (the "Young" Law).

(2) Youth and non-governmental facilities, and those of public utility shall be subject to minimum local taxation, pursuant to Law No. 571/2003[8] regarding the Tax Code, as amended and supplemented.

(3) Non-governmental structures for youth benefit from tax exemptions when using at least 80% of revenues from any source to achieve the purposes for which they were established, including capital expenditure and facilities as well as operating expenses.

5. Opportunities to Support Youth: Some Financial Mechanisms

This section analyzes the effects of two major tax exemptions on wages for young workers included in the last reforms. In general, the estimated effects of job access, hours and wages in the retail industry are not worth mentioning. However, taking into account minimum wage workers, the estimated effects suggest more serious consequences in terms of access to the labour market. This result is consistent with the view that higher minimum wages are a serious obstacle to accessing the labour market for young people. Given that a number of evaluations of payroll tax cuts in the literature indicate that the reforms were costly if compared to the jobs created, these results may be useful for reviewing such reforms.

In addition to a necessary overhaul of legislation, the effective functioning of the funding mechanisms depends on other variables.

In this last part, we focus on the proposal to introduce financial management tools to run youth programmes by implementing budget programmes for youth while developing management strategies. Among the steps to be taken are:

a) Budget planning for the development of youth programmes.[9] Specific programmes allow analyzing the link between the strategic and budget planning activities, providing an opportunity to identify differences between the main medium-term policy priorities, while adjusting the actions needed to achieve the main objectives.

b) We propose a provision regulating the categories of expenditure for the organization and the activities, programmes and projects for youth that

---

[8] Law No. 571/2003.

[9] Ciobanu, G., P. Veverita, L. Padure, and Chişinău. 2000. *Studii şi analize financiar-bugetare,* Parlamentul Republicii Moldova, Centrul analiză bugetară şi financiară.

will govern the costs to be borne by the organization, youth programmes and projects financed by public institutions from the national budget and the use of budget funds and special allocation.

c) Making sure that youth programmes are implemented in accordance with Decision No. 259[10] of 22 February 2006 on the approval of the expenditure of the National Youth programmes. One of the best ways to reduce the tax burden on labour and its impact on employment is through the reform of the social security system.

d) Supporting the private sector that creates decent jobs for young people. An inadequate legal framework (in terms of business registration, licensing, taxation, access to credit means), lack of protection of property rights, and judicial inefficiency may hinder the development of sustainable businesses and discourage job creation. During the transition period, some reforms have been put in place to develop the private sector and promote job creation. Fiscal stimulus measures, infrastructure development and a proper regulatory framework are pivotal for young people and can lead to opportunities in terms of labour demand in the medium and long term.

e) Employers can play an important role in ensuring decent work for young people. They can participate in the development of educational measures which are responsive to labour market needs to help youth to acquire professional experience and facilitate access to capital markets and connections.

f) Youth development investment credit as a direct effect of unemployment results in stagnant credit and consumption. No bank will loan money to people without a job. This aspect is visible among youth as they have limited financial resources, so their purchasing power is affected and, therefore, consumption will decrease. In order to finance and facilitate youth entrepreneurial activity in rural areas, investments are required to support business expansion (purchase of machinery, equipment, raw materials).

[10] Decision No. 259 of 22 February 2006.

References

Barrett, S. 2005. "Youth Work Must Lift its Sights," *Young People Now*, 7-13 December.

Ciobanu, G., P. Veverita, L. Padure, and Chişinău. 2000. *Studii şi analize financiar-bugetare,* Parlamentul Republicii Moldova, Centrul analiză bugetară şi financiară.

Government of Romania, published in the Official Gazette No. 194 March 1, 2006 Pursuant to Art. 108 of the Romanian Constitution, republished, and Art. 13 of the Government Ordinance No. 80/2001.

Law No. 247/2002, Law No. 247/2002 pentru aprobarea Ordonanţei Guvernului nr. 80/2001 privind stabilirea unor normative de cheltuieli pentru autorităţile şi instituţiile publice.

Ministry of Labour, Family and Social Protection. 2012. "An Inclusive Labour Market in Rural Areas," National research on poverty, social exclusion and labour market opportunities of young people (16-35 years) in rural areas 2007-2013.

Ordinance to stimulate the creation and development of micro enterprises by young entrepreneurs and its implementing rules, *OUG6/2011pentru stimularea infiintarii si dezvoltarii microintreprinderilor de catre intreprinzatorii tineri. Ordonanta de urgenta 6/2011.*

Resolution No. 259 of 22 February 2006 approving the Norms of expenditure for implementation of the National Youth programmes in the field of youth.

CHAPTER FOUR:

ACTIVE MEASURES AND THE LABOUR MARKET: A COMPARATIVE ANALYSIS OF ALMPS IMPLEMENTED IN EUROPE IN 2012

ALMPs for Young People: Good Practices, Analyses and Typologies from the EUROSTAT LMP Database

CRISTINA LINCARU AND DRAGA ATANASIU

1. Introduction

In the context of this paper, in order to compare the main Labour Market Policy (LMP) interventions, reference will be made to the methodology and notions provided by the database set up by the European Commission and EUROSTAT.[1] As we will see, the response to the same problem—rampant youth unemployment—on the part of European governments has been diverse and dealt with under specific circumstances. For this reason, LMP methodology is concerned with a wide range of interventions, based on general criteria, such as the regulatory framework and the implementing mechanisms of youth employment policies. Among the latter, priority has been given to:

- The institutions in charge of the planning of employment strategies;

- Funding schemes and their relation with employment policy interventions;

- An overview of the intervention characteristics: name, type of action, description (target groups, objectives, actors, duration, expected results), purpose, beneficiaries/participants, eligibility;

- Benefits and tax systems interactions, spending breakdown, unemployment spells, planned duration;

---

[1] European Commission, and EUROSTAT, Directorate F—Unit F/2: Labour Market Statistics. 2006. *Labour Market Policy Database Methodology Revision of June 2006.* Brussels: European Commission.

- Reporting and monitoring activities (start and end dates of the intervention, indicators from the LMP EUROSTAT database).

2. Comparing Methodological and Conceptual Issues: Labour Market Interventions in Europe[2]

With regard to scopes and types of intervention and based on the partnership between EUROSTAT and the Directorate General for Employment and Social Affairs, this methodology has been regularly developed since 1998, after which the LMP data collection was jointly launched with the OECD. This methodology offers a monitoring instrument for the European Employment Strategy in an international and comparative perspective.

The scope of the LMP database covers the labour market interventions defined as "government measures" involving expenditure, either as actual payments or income losses (reductions in taxes, social or other fees normally paid), most notably:

> Public interventions in the labour market aimed at reaching its efficient functioning and correcting disequilibria, so they can be distinguished from other general employment policy interventions in that they act selectively to favour particular groups in the labour market.[3]

According to the LMP methodology, emphasis is placed on the target group, which is defined as a group of persons sharing a common characteristic: the difficulty to enter the labour market. This selection criterion generates the specific action requested to compensate a difficulty or a disadvantage and effectively contribute to supporting participants while entering the labour market.

Beneficiaries mainly include the unemployed, vulnerable workers and inactive people, including the relating subgroups. As a result of public funding allocated by different entities (service providers, employers, and participants) it is possible to carry out activities benefitting the recipients of the funds. Three main types of interventions have been agreed on, based on their impact on both participants and the labour market:

---

[2] European Commission, and EUROSTAT, Directorate F—Unit F/2: Labour Market Statistics. 2006. *Labour Market Policy Database Methodology Revision of June 2006.* Brussels: European Commission.

[3] *Ibid.*

§5 Services refer to labour market interventions where the main activity of participants is job-search related and where participation usually does not result in a change of labour market status[4].

§6 Services also cover functions of the PES that are not directly linked to participants. This includes placement and other services for employers, administrative functions, general overheads and other activities depending on the responsibilities of the PES (see §44 to §51).

§7 Measures refer to labour market interventions where the main activity of participants is other than job-search related and where participation usually results in a change in labour market status. An activity that does not result in a change of labour market status may still be considered as a measure if the intervention fulfils the following criteria:

- The activities undertaken are not job-search related, are supervised and constitute a full-time or significant part-time activity of participants during a significant period of time; and
- The aim is to improve the vocational qualifications of participants; or
- The intervention provides incentives to take-up or to provide employment (including self-employment).

§8 LMP measures primarily cover government interventions that provide temporary support for groups that are disadvantaged in the labour market (see §13-§15). Most measures are aimed at activating the unemployed, helping people move from involuntary inactivity to employment, or maintaining the jobs of persons threatened by unemployment.

§9 The only measures included in the database that do not provide temporary support relate to the provision of ongoing support for persons with permanently reduced working capacity (see §84).

In this case it is recognized that public support may be needed to counteract the reduced productivity or other overheads associated with such persons, who would otherwise be uneconomic to employ.

§10 Supports refer to interventions that provide directly or indirectly financial assistance to individuals for labour market reasons, or interventions that compensate individuals for disadvantage caused by labour market circumstance.

§11 The participants (see §20) are usually persons who are out of work and actively seeking work but also persons who retire early from the labour market.

§12 Support may be payable to persons who benefit from services but financial assistance paid to persons participating in measures should be

[4] As for "services", a participant who is registered as unemployed always continues to be counted as registered unemployed. Concerning "measures", in most countries a participant who is registered as unemployed usually ceases to be counted as registered unemployed.

considered as part of the costs of the measure and not as a form of support (see §176)."[5]

In terms of type of action, the LMP measures employed in this analysis are standardized as follows:

3.2 LMP MEASURES[6]

Table B, C, D: Classification of interventions by type of action
1 Labour market services
1.1 Client services
1.1.1 Information services
1.1.2 Individual case management
1.2 Other activities of the PES
1.2.1 Administration of LMP measures
1.2.2 Administration of LMP supports
1.2.3 Other services/ activities
2 Training
2.1 Institutional training
2.2 Workplace training
2.3 Alternate training
2.4 Special support for apprenticeships
3 Job rotation and job sharing
3.1 Job rotation
3.2 Job sharing
4 Employment incentives
4.1 Recruitment incentives
4.1.1 Permanent
4.1.2 Temporary
4.2 Employment maintenance incentives
5 Supported employment and rehabilitation
5.1 Supported employment
5.2 Rehabilitation
6 Direct job-creation
7 Start-up incentives
8 Out-of-work income maintenance and support
8.1 Unemployment benefits
8.1.1 Unemployment insurance

[5] European Commission, and EUROSTAT, Directorate F—Unit F/2: Labour Market Statistics. 2006. *Labour Market Policy Database Methodology Revision of June 2006,* European Commission: 6-7.

[6] European Commission, and EUROSTAT, Directorate F—Unit F/2: Labour Market Statistics. 2006. *Labour Market Policy Database Methodology Revision of June 2006,* European Commission, 13.

8.1.2 Unemployment assistance
8.2 Partial unemployment benefits
8.3 Part-time unemployment benefits
8.4 Redundancy compensation
8.5 Bankruptcy compensation
9 Early retirement
9.1 Conditional
9.1.1 Full
9.1.2 Partial
9.2 Unconditional
9.2.1 Full
9.2.2 Partial

Using this standardization, the interventions with code 1 are services; those with code 2 to 7 fall within the "active measures" categories and the intervention with code 8 to 9 are regarded as passive measures.

2.1. The Interaction between Labour Market Status and Interventions Benefitting Jobseekers

In employment-related studies, the notion of "status" describes the type of active participation in the labour market. It has some specific characteristics, as pointed out by the ILO:

> Status in employment describes the type of economic risk and authority which workers have in their jobs, as reflected in their explicit or implicit contract of employment.[7]

The essential characteristics that define the employment status concern the economic activity in a job and some organizational duties. In employment, this means generating income from such economic activity by performing duties resulted from making use of the individual capacity according to his/her knowledge, skills and abilities.

> Knowledge, Skills, and Abilities (KSAs) are the attributes required to perform a job and are generally demonstrated through qualifying experience, education, or training. Knowledge is a body of information applied directly to the performance of a function. Skill is an observable

[7] The 14th ICLS adopted the Resolution concerning the International Classification of Status in Employment (ICSE), known as ICSE-93 .http://www.ilo.org/global/statistics-and-databases/statistics-overview-and-topics/status-in-employment/lang--en/index.htm.

> competence to perform a learned psychomotor act. Ability is the competence to perform an observable behaviour or a behaviour that results in an observable product.[8]

According to Maslow's theory, the interaction between labour market status and needs-related behaviour priorities results in a hierarchical order of satisfying priorities (Table 4-1) related to the need for survival, safety, belonging, esteem and self-actualization:

> In accordance with Maslow's theory, which was not specifically developed to explain behavior in the workplace, employees strive to satisfy their needs in a hierarchical order.[9]

By means of active measures and in considering the transition to employment, labour income and the capacity to perform duties corresponding to the first priority are assured ("survival needs" in this case generate labour income), while "esteem" obtains through improved employability. The 5 Levels of needs theorized by Maslow are somehow similar to Alderfer's ERG theory of existence, relatedness and growth:

> Aldefer said that when needs in a higher category are not met then individuals redouble the efforts invested in a lower category need. For example, if self-actualization or self-esteem is not met then individuals will invest more effort in the relatedness category in the hopes of achieving the higher need.[10]

Out of the employment status, the individual is placed in the position to redouble the efforts to invest especially in existence and relatedness, with objective limits to invest in growth level.

---

[8] http://www.opm.gov/policy-data-oversight/classification-qualifications/general-schedule-qualification-policies/.

[9] Jex, S. M., and T. W., Britt. 2008. *Organizational Psychology*. Hoboken, New Jersey: John Wiley & Sons, Inc.

[10] Alderfer, Clayton P. 1969. "An Empirical Test of a New Theory of Human Needs," *Organizational Behaviour and Human Performance* 4, No. 2:142-175.

Table 4-1. Interaction between Labour Market Status and Behaviour Priorities by Need.

Behaviour priorities			Initial status	Action	Desired status
Priority	Maslow's Hierarchy of Needs	Alderfer's ERG theory	Out of work	Evaluation	In work
1	Survive : food	Existence	Substituting work income	Income independence—in-work subsidies	Work income
			Health problems (temporary or permanent)	Special working condition needs	Work capacity
2	Safety: dwelling		Housing, dwelling access, paying rent	Isolation Access to workplace, housing affordability, geographical mobility support	Housing affordability
3	Belonging	Relatedness Personal Relatedness Interpersonal relationships	Working motivation / availability to work	Dependant family members (children, aged people, persons with disability) Social network	Flexible working programme and life balance
4	Esteem: competence and mastery	Growth	Work experience Competence	Employability improving Training/ measures that support occupational mobility	Carrier development The Need for Achievement
5	Self-actualization:		Skills lack/ skills depreciation	Skills development Learning to know	Developing knowledge, skills and abilities

Source: Authors' Own Elaboration.

Consequently, especially since the setting-up of the ambitious objectives of Europe 2020, active measures need to be reviewed in order to achieve "smart growth". In this sense, individuals should be allowed to invest in self-actualization that is developing knowledge, skills and abilities in order to enhance self-development. In this context, to be in employment means to have and use the attributes to perform a paid job, and, in our view, to generate income in order to contribute to the tax and social contribution system.

This view of employment is consistent with that of EUROSTAT and the OECD concerning the interaction between labour market status and interventions benefitting jobseekers:

> The unemployment spell is broken: participation in an active labour market measure breaks the unemployment spell and automatically resets the counter of duration to zero. A participant is not counted as registered unemployed during a measure. In the case that a person returns to unemployment after completing a measure then a new unemployment spell is started.
>
> The unemployment spell is suspended: periods of activation do not contribute to the duration of the unemployment spell but the counter is not reset and if the person returns to unemployment afterwards then unemployment spell continues from where it left off before activation. A participant is not counted as registered unemployed during a measure.
>
> The unemployment spell is continuous and registration is continuous: participants in active measures continue to be counted as registered unemployed and the duration of the spell includes periods of activation.
>
> The unemployment spell is continuous but registration is discontinuous: participants are not counted as registered unemployed (on an instantaneous observation) during active measures but the unemployment spell is not interrupted and includes periods of activation.[1]

Fig. 4-1 shows how these different approaches can impact on the observed duration of unemployment. To have greater consistency among countries, the EMCO group of indicators recommended that all temporary interruptions of more than 28 days be treated as an interruption in the length of unemployment followed by resetting and starting new periods of unemployment. Yet today most countries are not able to apply this rule as national procedures cannot be easily amended.

---

[1] European Commission, and EUROSTAT, Directorate F—Unit F/2: Labour Market Statistics. 2006. *Labour Market Policy Database Methodology Revision of June 2006.* Brussels: European Commission, 31.

Fig. 4-11. Treatment of Breaks in Unemployment and Registered Unemployment Status, during and after periods of active measures.

Treatment of breaks in the unemployment spell:

	Unemployed				Active measure				Unemployed			
Broken												
Duration at the end of each month	1	2	3	4	0	0	0	0	1	2	3	4
Person is counted as registered unemp.	Y	Y	Y	Y	N	N	N	N	Y	Y	Y	Y
Suspended												
Duration at the end of each month	1	2	3	4	4	4	4	4	5	6	7	8
Person is counted as registered unemp.	Y	Y	Y	Y	N	N	N	N	Y	Y	Y	Y
Continuous/Continuous												
Duration at the end of each month	1	2	3	4	5	6	7	8	9	10	11	12
Person is counted as registered unemp.	Y	Y	Y	Y	Y	Y	Y	Y	Y	Y	Y	Y
Continuous/Discontinuous												
Duration at the end of each month	1	2	3	4	5	6	7	8	9	10	11	12
Person is counted as registered unemp.	Y	Y	Y	Y	N	N	N	N	Y	Y	Y	Y

Source: Labour Market Policy Database- Methodology- Revision June 2006, EUROSTAT, 32.

2.2. Cluster Delimitation according to Youth Performance and Labour Market Integration

The identification of good practices among EU policy strategies for labour market insertion was performed through:

- The delimitation of clusters based on labour market performance (Fig. 4-2 and 4-3);

- The delimitation of clusters according to the diversity of active measures programmes for young people (Fig. 4-4);

- The identification of active measures to help youth access the labour market by target group (see Table 4-2).

The delimitation of clusters based on labour market performance is presented in Fig. 14-2. An inverse correlation is visible between employment and unemployment and inactivity rates, and the agglomerations delimiting the clusters based on youth labour market performance and integration, expressed through synthetic indicators: employment and unemployment rates for 15 to 24-year-olds. The selected countries include

Germany, Austria, The Netherlands, Denmark, while the deriving clusters according to the diversity of active measures programmes for young people also factored in the values for France, Spain and Portugal. The cluster delimitation based on youth labour market performance (employment rate by unemployment rate in 2012Q1 in Europe, data source: EUROSTAT) is presented in Fig. 14-3.

Although not evident in this representation, it should be noted that the levels of performance in lower unemployment—not directly and simultaneously increasing the employment rate, influencing the system—are arrived at by the rate of inactivity (idle status).

The delimitation of clusters according to the diversity of active measures for young people is presented in Fig. 4-4. Some country variations among France, Germany, Austria, Malta and Portugal point to diversified active measures for young people.

3. Good Practices and Active Measures in the Labour Market: High Degrees of Implementation among European Youth

In this paper, the general characteristics of 48 best practices from 7 EU27 countries are presented (Austria; Denmark; France; Germany; The Netherlands; Portugal; Spain), selected from the LMP database (Table 4-2).

Fig. 4-2. EU Good Practices for Youth Labour Market Entry: Cluster Delimitation based on Labour Market Performance.

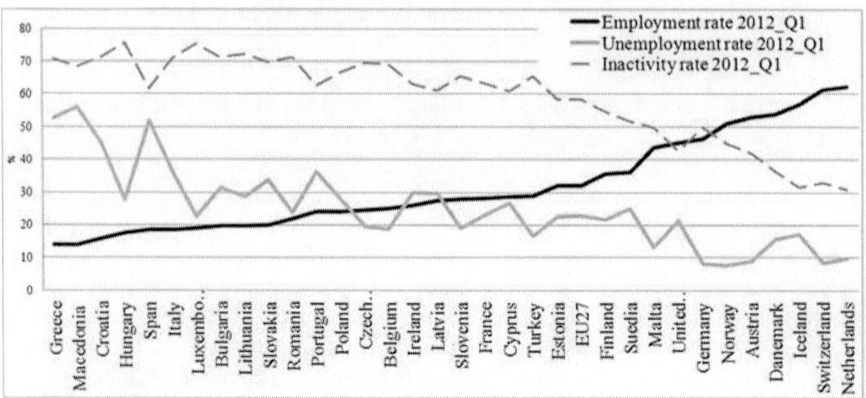

Source: Authors' Own Elaboration for EUROSTAT data.

Legend for Fig. 4-2.

	Employment rate 2012_Q1	**Unemployment rate 2012_Q1**	**Inactivity rate 2012_Q1**	**(4)=(1)-(3)**
	(1)	(2)	(3)	(4)
Greece	13.9	52.7	70.7	-56.8
Macedonia	14.0	55.9	68.4	-54.4
Croatia	15.8	45.1	71.2	-55.4
Hungary	17.5	27.8	75.7	-58.2
Span	18.4	52.0	61.6	-43.2
Italy	18.6	35.9	70.9	-52.3
Luxembourg	19.1	22.7	75.3	-56.2
Bulgaria	19.7	31.4	71.2	-51.5
Lithuania	19.8	28.7	72.3	-52.5
Slovakia	20.0	33.7	69.8	-49.8
Romania	**21.9**	**23.9**	**71.3**	**-49.4**
Portugal	24.0	36.2	62.5	-38.5
Poland	24.1	27.7	66.7	-42.6
The Czech Republic	24.6	19.4	69.5	-44.9
Belgium	25.1	18.8	69.1	-44.0
Ireland	25.9	29.8	63.1	-37.2
Latvia	27.4	29.7	61.1	-33.7
Slovenia	28.0	18.9	65.5	-37.5
France	28.3	23.0	63.3	-35.0
Cyprus	28.6	26.7	60.9	-32.3
Turkey	28.8	16.6	65.5	-36.7
Estonia	32.1	22.7	58.5	-26.4
EU27	***32.1***	***22.9***	***58.4***	***-26.3***
Finland	35.6	21.7	54.5	-18.9
Sweden	36.2	25.0	51.7	-15.5
Malta	43.6	13.1	49.8	-6.2
United Kingdom	**45.0**	**21.5**	**42.6**	**2.4**
Germany	**46.3**	**8.0**	**49.7**	**-3.4**
Norway	50.9	7.7	44.9	6.0
Austria	**52.9**	**8.9**	**41.9**	**11.0**
Denmark	**53.8**	**15.5**	**36.4**	**17.4**
Iceland	56.7	17.1	31.5	25.2
Switzerland	61.4	8.3	33.0	28.4
The Netherlands	62.4	9.9	30.8	31.6

Fig. 4-3. Cluster Delimitation based on Youth Labour Market Performance.

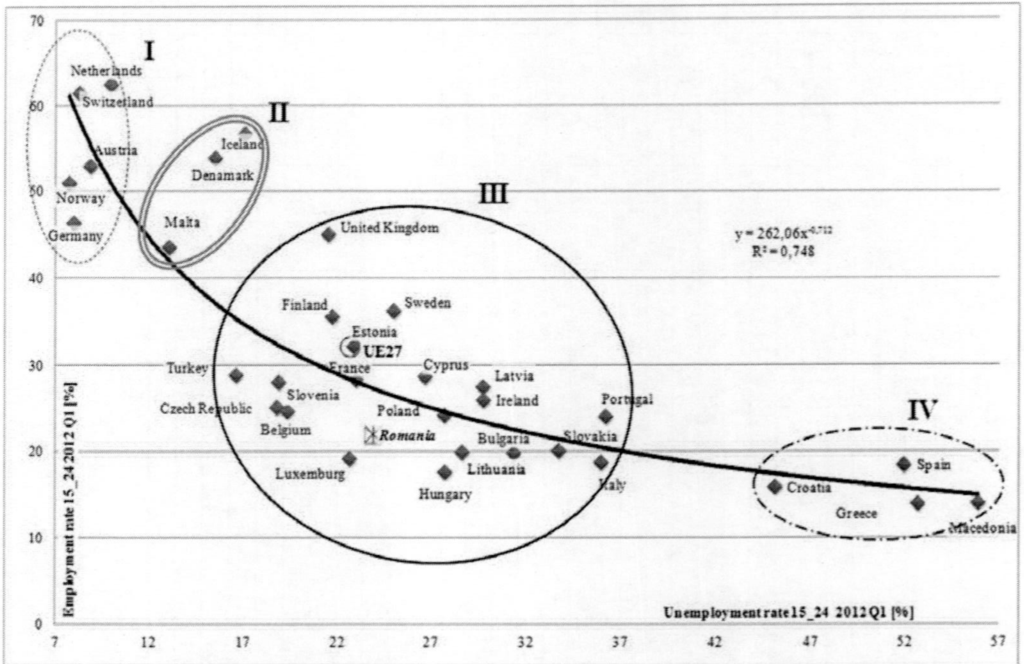

Source: Authors' Own Elaboration, data EUROSTAT (employment rate by unemployment rate in 2012Q1 in Europe).

Legend for the Fig. 4-3:

	Unemployment rate 15_24 2012 Q1 [%]	**Employment rate 15_24 2012 Q1 [%]**	**Cluster**
Norway	7.7	50.9	I
Germany	8.0	46.3	
Switzerland	8.3	61.4	
Austria	8.9	52.9	
The Netherlands	9.9	62.4	
Malta	13.1	43.6	II
Denmark	15.5	53.8	
Turkey	16.6	28.8	
Iceland	17.1	56.7	
Belgium	18.8	25.1	III
Slovenia	18.9	28.0	
The Czech Republic	19.4	24.6	
The United Kingdom	21.5	45.0	
Finland	21.7	35.6	
Estonia	22.7	32.1	
Luxembourg	22.7	19.1	
UE 27	**22.9**	**32.1**	
France	23.0	28.3	
Romania	***23.9***	***21.9***	
Sweden	25.0	36.2	
Cyprus	26.7	28.6	
Poland	27.7	24.1	
Hungary	27.8	17.5	
Lithuania	28.7	19.8	
Latvia	29.7	27.4	
Ireland	29.8	25.9	
Bulgaria	31.4	19.7	
Slovakia	33.7	20.0	
Italy	35.9	18.6	
Portugal	36.2	24.0	
Croatia	45.1	15.8	IV
Spain	52.0	18.4	
Greece	52.7	13.9	
Macedonia	55.9	14.0	

Fig. 4-4. Cluster Delimitation according to the Diversity of Active Measures for Youth.
Country Demarcation for France, Germany, Austria, Malta and Portugal offering Diversified Active Measures.

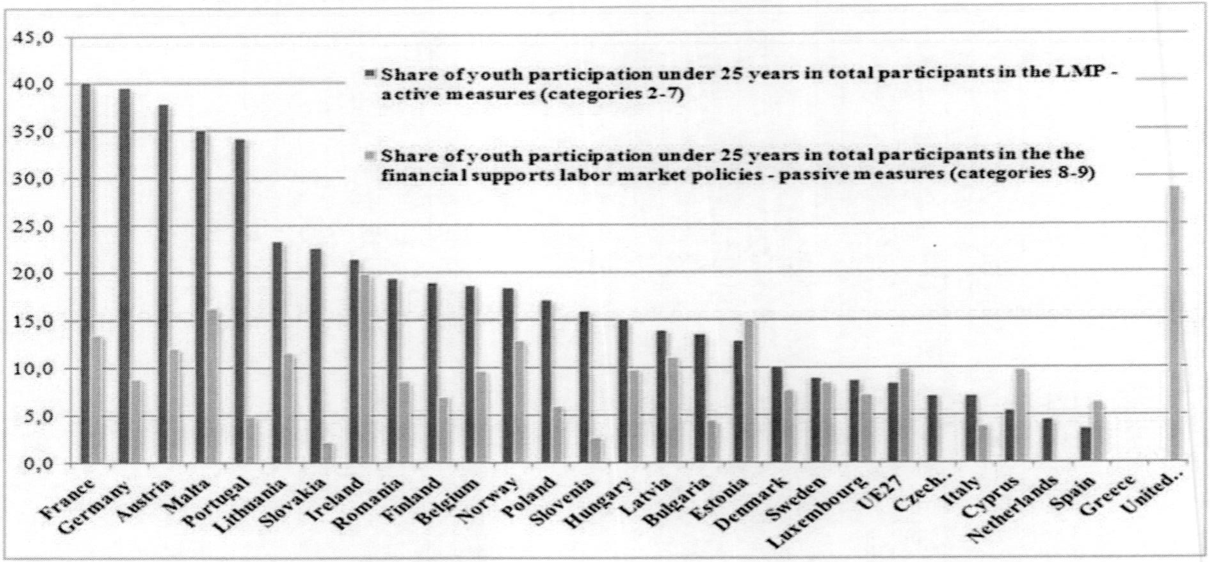

Source: Authors' Own Elaboration, data EUROSTAT.

Both the case studies and statistics reported enforcement rates equal to 19% for youth aged 15 to 24 years old. Of these, 16 initiatives address the 15-24 age group, with a degree of application of 82% (44.7% of the total). The average number of participants is 50,000 people, with the odds that they will involve youth reported to be at 85%. The average unit cost per intervention/person/year was €9,246. The case studies covered the details of the intervention, in accordance with the 2010 LMP Country Qualitative Report produced by EUROSTAT: Name; Type of action; Description; Purpose; Beneficiaries/participants; Action/tool; Funding/support; Responsible Institution; Eligibility; Legal base; Recent Changes; Additional Information.

In Table 2 a selection of good practices concerning labour market services and active measures with a high degree of application among youth is presented, developed in 2010 in several European countries and based on the EUROSTAT methodology and the LMP database. The selection is provided considering the following EUROSTAT criteria: Intervention name, Action/tool and the share of young beneficiaries out of total recipients.

Table 4-2. Good Practices of Labour Market Services and Active Measures with a High Degree of Application among Youth (higher than 30.3% and maximum 100%) developed by European Countries and based on the 2010 EUROSTAT Methodology and LMP Database.

	CODE (EUROSTAT)	Intervention	Type of action	%
		Austria		
1	24_AT32	Apprenticeship-type training at supra-company level	2.4. Special support for apprenticeship training	100.0
2	24_AT11	Promote apprenticeship and training	2.4. Special support for apprenticeship training	98.7
3	22_AT35	Training for people with disabilities	2.2. On-the-job training	76.8
4	6_AT 27	Childcare institutions	6 Direct job creation	76.0
5	11_AT34	Match the types of work and assistance in seeking employment for people with disabilities	1.1.2 individual case management	68.2

6	41_AT5	Promotion of regional mobility and entry into employment, travel allowance	4.1.1. permanent	55.4
Denmark				
7	52_DK28	Pre-rehabilitation	5.2. Rehabilitation	43.4
8	81_DK2	Social assistance (unemployment)	8.1.2 Unemployment Assistance	29.3
France				
9	21_FR101	Voluntary integration contract (CVI)	2.1. Institutional training	100.0
10	24_FR22	Exemptions and subsidies for recruitment of apprentices	2.4. Special support for apprenticeship	99.4
11	11_FR79	Individual coaching youth (CIVIS)	1.1. Individual case management	98.9
12	41_FR67	Contract-type young in business	4.1.1. Permanent	95.0
13	41_FR76	Professionalization contract	4.1.2 Temporary	79.0
14	41_FR81	Employment initiative contract (CIE-PCS)	4.1.1. Permanent	49.7
15	41_FR112	Single contract for inclusion (CUI-CIE)	4.1.1. Permanent	42.2
16	21_FR85	Training courses organized by regions	2.1. Institutional training	40.2
17	6_FR 46	Employment contracts for young	6. Direct job training	37.5
18	2_FR 63	Return to work support-training allowance (AREF)	2. Formation	32.3
19	41_FR61	Companies offering temporary jobs to integrate	4.1.2 Temporary	30.7
20	2_FR 107	Training allowances of Pôle Emploi-Governmental Agency for Employment (RFPE)	2 Training	30.3
Germany				
21	21_DE 110	Support career entry programmes	2.1. Institutional training	100.0
22	21_DE11	Support preparation training measures for young	2.1. Institutional training	99.5
23	22_DE98	Training for young workers compensation	2.2. On-the-job training	99.2

24	24_DE71	First integration qualification for young people	2.4. Special support for apprenticeship training stage	98.6
25	11_DE99	Socio-pedagogical accompaniment	1.1. Individual case management	97.7
26	21_DE93	Training outside the workplace	2.1. Institutional training	97.4
27	24_DE87_3	[Component] Support for training of disabled people-training allowance for the disabled persons	2.1. Institutional training; 2.4. Special support for apprenticeship training following a	97.0
28	22_DE94	Allowances during apprenticeship	2.2. On-the-job training	96.5
29	41_DE101	Bonus apprenticeship	4.1.2 Temporary	94.7
30	22_DE23_1	[Component] Incentives for training and recruitment/ employment of severely disabled- work training grants for disabled persons	2.2. On-the-job training	93.4
31	21_DE81	Training allowance	2.1. Institutional training	88.2
32	24_DE34	Training allowance	2.4. Special support for apprenticeship training stage	82.8
33	21_DE100	Enabling Support	2.1. Institutional training	78.1
34	22_DE111	Qualified individual in the occupation businesses assisted	2.2. On-the-job Training	77.6
35	52_DE90	Interventions to support the introduction of the training in a sheltered workshop	5.2. Rehabilitation	74.7
36	2_DE 27	Independent action = eligible incentives for free	2. Formation	74.6
37	22_DE95	Transitional assistance	2.2. On-the-job training	53.8
The Netherlands				
38	5_NL 59	Act (re) integration into employment of people with occupational disabilities (REA)	5. Employment support and rehabilitation	19.1
Portugal				
39	21_PT99	PROFIJ - training programmes to include young people (Azores)	2.1. Institutional training	100.0

40	24_PT7	Apprenticeships for young people	2.4. Special support for apprenticeship training following a	98.4
41	52_PT84	Training and occupational integration of young people and adults with disabilities (Madeira)	5.2. Rehabilitation	97.5
42	52_PT34	Vocational training schemes for people with disabilities	5.2. Rehabilitation	59.5
43	51_PT33	Supported employment / supported	5.1. Supported employment	58.1
44	41_PT29	Creating jobs for young people by exempting or reducing the mandatory social security contributions	4.1.1. Permanent	55.9
45	22_PT22	Practice Vocational Training	2.2. On-the-job training	50.1
		Spain		
46	22_ES14	Incentives for training contracts	2.2. On-the-job training	62.8
47	22_ES63	Incentives for training contracts (measure ES_14 regions)	2.2. On-the-job training	49.5
48	23_ES9	On-the-job training (employment and training - ET, CO and TE)	2.3. alternative training place	41.1

Source Authors' Own Elaboration, EUROSTAT, Labour market policy statistics Qualitative report by countries.

4. Active Measures Funded through Structural Funds (ESF) targeting Young Inactive Persons

Among the foregoing 48 interventions to increase youth employment through active measures, a sub-selection of 10 measures is presented in Table 4 which are financed through FES-European Structural Funds and concern target groups from 5 countries: Austria (2 groups), Spain (1 group), Portugal (6 groups) and France (1 groups). The eligibility criteria of each target group are described by employment status: formal inactivity (4 groups), informal inactivity (15 groups), unemployment (8 groups) and employment (8 groups).

The selection pointed out two models of good practices implemented in Portugal and addressing target groups of inactive youth (Table 4-3).

Table 4-3. Resources Funding Active Measures, Including the European Social Fund.

Measures for Young People Inactive / ESF Funding Source	Code	
Description of the measure assets	**51_PT33**	**22_PT22**
Intervention	PROFIJ - training programmes to include young people (Azores)	Training and occupational integration of young people and adults with disabilities (Madeira)
Type of action	2.1. Institutional training	5.2. Rehabilitation
Degree of application to youth	100	97.5
Number of participants aged 15 to 24 years old	2705	118
Average unit cost per intervention/ person/ year [Euro]	610	1074
ESF funding	yes	yes
Source of funding	Regional or state government budget and ESF	Regional or state government budget and ESF
Responsible institution	State or regional government	State or regional government

Characteristics of target groups/ target group description		
The apprenticeship programme is developed for young people aged 15 to 21 years old who participated in vocational training, (the Azores) who finished class 9 and do not intend to access secondary education, who are more than 15 years old but have not completed the 9 levels of compulsory education, have completed level I or II of vocational training;	x	
The qualification programme is for young people aged 15 to 23 years old who have no qualifications, have completed class 9 or equivalent and do not intend to continue regular education - failed to complete the 9 years of compulsory education.	x	
People with disabilities (motor, sensory, visual, hearing or intellectual) aged 16 years or older		x
Unregistered/ inactive	x	
Unregistered (disabled)		x

Source: Authors' Own Elaboration.

Institutional development (cat. 2.1) covers measures where most of training (75% or more) is performed in a training institution (schools/colleges, training centers or similar).

Rehabilitation (cat. 5.2) covers rehabilitation for people with reduced working capacity (temporary or permanent) and aims at helping participants adapt their disability or medical condition and develop skills that prepare them for the working world (including subsidized employment measures) or regular training. Rehabilitation only refers to vocational rehabilitation. Social and medical rehabilitation are outside the scope of the LMP database and should not be included.

Table 4-4. Selected Active Measures by Type of Intervention to support Youth Employment: Reported FES Initiatives as Financing Sources, by Target Group (Part A, First Variant).

		caracteristics							
	code	Intervention [1]	Action type [2]	[3]	[4]	[5]	[6]	Financing source [7]	Responsible Insitution [8]
1	24_AT11	Promote apprenticeship and training	2.4. Special support for apprenticeship training stage	98,7	11485	2776	yes	Social security funds - the labor market budget (federal contributions, employer and employee contributions to the unemployment insurance fund) - and European Social Funds	Public Employment Service (AMS Österreich)
2	22_AT35	Training for people with disabilities	2.2. Training at work place	76,8	1555	20079	yes	Tax Compensation Fund (ATF), ESF funding, AMS and government central budget	Federal welfare offices (Bundessozialämter, MSM).
10	23_ES9	Training at work place (employment and training - ET, CO and TE)	2.3. Alternative training	41,1	16240	13136	yes	Budget, ESF	Local government, public employment services
5	24_PT7	Apprenticeships for young people	2.4. Special support for apprenticeship training stage	98,4	14337	4728	yes	The regional (Regional Directorate for Vocational Training - DRFP) and ESF	**State administration and regional Public Employment Services**
3	41_FR81	Employment initiative contract (CIE-PCS)	4.1.1. Permanent	49,7	18009	6439	yes	Central government budget and the European Social Fund	Local Government
4	21_PT99	Vocational training schemes for people with disabilities	5.2. Rehabilitation	59,5	851	38825	yes	IEFP and ESF	Public employment services
6	52_PT84	Supported employment / supported	5.1. Supported employment	58,1	225	4755	yes	IEFP and ESF	Public employment services
7	52_PT34	Practice Vocational Training	2.2. Training at work	50,1	8524	6172	yes	IEFP, the regional (Regional Employment Institute) and ESF	**State administration and regional Public Employment Services**
8	51_PT33	PROFIJ - training program to include young people (Azores)	2.1. Institutional training	100,0	2705	610	yes	Regional or state government budget and ESF	State or regional government administration
9	22_PT22	Training and occupational integration of young people and adults with disabilities (Madeira)	5.2. Rehabilitation	97,5	118	1074	yes	Regional or state government budget and ESF	State or regional government administration

Source: Author's Own Elaboration.

Table 4-5. Selected Active Measures by Type of Intervention to Support Youth Employment: Reported FES Initiatives as Financing Sources, by Target Group (Part A, Second Variant).

		Characteristics							
	de	Intervention [1]	Action type [2]	[3]	[4]	[5]	[6]	Financing source [7]	Responsible Institution [8]
1	**24_AT11**	Promote apprenticeship and training	2.4. Special support for apprenticeship training stage	**98,7**	**11485**	**2776**	**yes**	Social security funds - the labour market budget (federal contributions, employers' and employees' contributions to the unemployment insurance fund) - and European Social Funds	Public Employment Service (AMS *Österreich*)
2	**22_AT35**	Training for people with disabilities	2.2. On-the-job training	**76,8**	**1555**	**20079**	**yes**	Tax Compensation Fund (ATF), ESF funding, AMS and government central budget	Federal welfare offices (*Bundessozialämter*, MSM).
10	**23_ES9**	On-the-job Training (employment and training - ET, CO and TE)	2.3. Alternative training	**41,1**	**16240**	**13136**	**yes**	Budget, ESF	Local government, public employment services
5	**24_PT7**	Apprenticeships for young people	2.4. Special support for apprenticeship training stage	**98,4**	**14337**	**4728**	**yes**	The regional (Regional Directorate for Vocational Training - DRFP) and ESF	**State administration and regional Public Employment Services**

3	**41_FR81**	Employment initiative contract (CIE-PCS)	4.1.1. Permanent	**49,7**	**18009**	**6439**	**yes**	Central government budget and the European Social Fund	Local Government
4	**21_PT99**	Vocational training schemes for people with disabilities	5.2. Rehabilitation	**59,5**	**851**	**38825**	**yes**	IEFP and ESF	Public employment services
6	**52_PT84**	Supported employment / supported	5.1. Supported employment	**58,1**	**225**	**4755**	**yes**	IEFP and ESF	Public employment services
7	**52_PT34**	Practice Vocational Training	2.2. On-the-job training	**50,1**	**8524**	**6172**	**yes**	IEFP, the regional (Regional Employment Institute) and ESF	**State administration and regional Public Employment Services**
8	**51_PT33**	PROFIJ - training programmes to include young people (Azores)	2.1. Institutional training	**100,0**	**2705**	**610**	**yes**	Regional or state government budget and ESF	State or regional government administration

9	22_PT22	Training and occupational integration of young people and adults with disabilities (Madeira)	5.2. Rehabilitation	97,5	118	1074	yes	Regional or state government budget and ESF	State or regional government administration

Source Authors' Own Elaboration, EUROSTAT, Labour market policy statistics Qualitative report by countries.

Table 4-6. Selected Active Measures by Type of Intervention to support Youth Employment: Reported FES Initiatives as Financing Sources, by Target Group (Part B).

		inactive																			unemployed								empl	
	code	[9]	[10]	[11]	[12]	[13]	[14]	[15]	[16]	[17]	[18]	[19]	[20]	[21]	[22]	[23]	[24]	[25]	[26]	[27	[28]	[29]	[30]	[31]	[32]	[33]	[34]	[35]	[36]	[37]
1	24_AT11																				x					x				
2	22_AT35															X					X									X
10	23_ES9																				X						X			
5	24_PT7	X													X							X								
3	41_FR81								X	X			X	X					X							X		X		
4	21_PT99				X											X		X								X				
6	52_PT84					X										X		X								X				X
7	52_PT34																			X			X	X	X	X		X		
8	51_PT33		X	X											X															
9	22_PT22							X								X														

Source Authors' Own Elaboration, EUROSTAT, Labour market policy statistics Qualitative report by countries

LEGEND

Code	Content	
[1]	Intervention	characteristics
[2]	Type of action	
[3]	Degree of application to young	
[4]	Number of participants aged less than 25 years after LMP interventions	
[5]	Average unit cost per intervention/ person/ year [Euro]	
[6]	ESF funding	
[7]	Source of funding	
[8]	Institution responsible	
[9]	Young people less than 25 who have successfully completed the 9 years of the basic educational level (9 years of school) or equivalent and have no secondary school qualification or equivalent.	inactive
[10]	Apprenticeship is developed for young people aged 15 to 21 who participated in vocational training, (the Azores) who finished class 9 and do not intend to enter secondary level- have more than 15 years but not the 9 classes- have completed Level I or II vocational forms;	
[11]	Qualification programmes for young people aged 15 to 23 who have not yet qualified: have completed class 9 or equivalent and do not intend to continue regular education; failed to complete the 9 years of school.	
[12]	Persons with disabilities aged 12 years and over.	
[13]	Persons with disabilities: people whose work capacity is less than 1/3 of normal working capacity of a person without disabilities in the same job.	
[14]	Youth (unemployed) disabled (with a handicap of over 33%).	
[15]	Persons with disabilities (motor, sensory, visual, hearing or intellectual) aged 16 years or older- Madeira.	
[16]	Public priorities.	
[17]	Single parents.	
[18]	Youth aged 16-22 years with low qualifications or no qualifications.	
[19]	Young and low-skilled adults.	
[20]	Young people less than 26 years without a diploma and social benefits.	
[21]	Young people aged 16-25 who have left school early.	
[22]	Unregistered/ inactive.	
[23]	Unchecked (disabled).	
[24]	Immigrants.	
[25]	Other persons seeking employment (disabled).	
[26]	Youth in search of a job.	
[27	Persons seeking work registered.	
[28]	Registered unemployed.	unemployed
[29]	Young Registered unemployed.	
[30]	Young people between 16 and 30 who seek employment (first job).	
[31]	Young people between 16 and 30 years with medium or high levels of education that are unemployed and have not performed any professional activity for more than a year, are unemployed and looking for their first job, and have taken occupation for not more than one year.	

[32]	Young people between 16 and 30 years who have a certain level of skills and through which they access to another skills level and have not worked in a certain field for more than a year, are unemployed and looking for their first job, and have not been occupied for more than one year.	
[33]	Registered unemployed (people with disabilities).	
[34]	Low-skilled unemployed youth.	
[35]	Long-term unemployed.	
[36]	Employed persons.	empl
[37]	Employed persons (persons with disabilities).	

5. Conclusions

The heterogeneous nature of youth is reflected in the all-important LMP interventions, especially in the diversified and specialized range of active measures devoted to them which have been developed in the European common framework with a view to implementing the Employment and the Europe 2020 strategy. European experience and progress made in developing LMP initiatives in a structured framework enabled the amplification of learning and transferability processes, the diminution of risks, and the use of resources in a sustainable, efficient and effective manner. The special interest towards active measure arose from the relevance of these adaptable instruments to fulfill youth employment policy objectives, particularly since the setting-up of Europe 2020 objectives.

References

Alderfer, Clayton P. 1969. "An Empirical Test of a New Theory of Human Needs," *Organizational Behaviour and Human Performance* 4, No. 2:142–175.

Jex, S. M., and T. W., Britt. 2008. *Organizational Psychology*. Hoboken, New Jersey: John Wiley & Sons, Inc.

European Commission, and EUROSTAT, Directorate F - Unit F/2: Labour Market Statistics. 2006. *Labour Market Policy Database Methodology Revision of June 2006,* European Commission.

EUROSTAT. 2010. *Labour Market Policy Statistics Qualitative Report, Austria.* Brussels: EUROSTAT.

—. 2010. *Labour Market Policy Statistics Qualitative Report, Denmark.* Brussels: EUROSTAT.

—. 2010. *Labour Market Policy Statistics Qualitative Report, France.*

—. 2010. *Labour Market Policy Statistics Qualitative Report, Germany.* Brussels: EUROSTAT.

—. 2010. *Labour Market Policy Statistics Qualitative Report, Denmark.* Brussels: EUROSTAT.

—. 2010. *Labour Market Policy Statistics Qualitative Report, France.*

—. 2010. *Labour Market Policy Statistics Qualitative Report, Germany.* Brussels: EUROSTAT.

TARGET GROUPS AND ALMPS TO BOOST YOUTH EMPLOYMENT: AN OVERVIEW OF THE EUROPEAN GOOD PRACTICES

CRISTINA LINCARU, CODRUŢA DRĂGOIU AND BEATRICE CHIRIAC

1. Introduction

Drawing on the results of the previous paper, the next step is to analyse the active measures designed to increase youth employment, taking into account specific European best practices. To this end, a number of initiatives from seven EU27 countries were selected. Most notably: Austria (6 initiatives), Denmark (2 initiatives), France (11 initiatives), Germany (16 initiatives), The Netherlands (1 initiatives), Portugal (7 initiatives) and Spain (3 initiatives).

The foregoing types of action correspond to different active measures which are described considering certain characteristics: the 8 codes of intervention provided by EUROSTAT (using the EUROSTAT LMP2_7 active measures and LMP8_9 passive measures), the degree of application to young people out of the total number of beneficiaries, the number of participants aged less than 25 years old after LMP interventions, the average unit cost per intervention/ person/ year [Euro] and the dummy variable "Funded from the ESF" (with a yes/no value). The main criterion to classify the target groups was the labour market status of the active measure beneficiaries, resulting in 44 target groups with the status of inactive or unregistered unemployed, 10 target groups having the unemployment status and 4 target groups regarded as employed.

As exhibited in Table 1, the typology of the target groups addressed by the main labour market interventions to increase youth employment, presents the following characteristics:

- Target groups are extremely detailed;

- They are extensive and include young inactive and unregistered unemployed youth;

- Inactive young people can apply for several measures originally developed for people registered as unemployed (whether or not they are entitled to unemployment benefits);

- Young people with a disability, even those with a working capacity below 33%, and those with severe mental or behavioural disorders are eligible for active measures to access employment;

- Several target groups could be eligible for only one active measure, which is almost always the case, and there are also active measures dedicated to only one target group (see case 81_Dk2 case No. 47);

- Their applicability rate for young people under 25 years old out of a total number of beneficiaries reflects the special nature of these initiatives, which are intended to favour the transition to employment. In Table 2, the cases surveyed are hierarchically indexed considering such applicability. There are 21 active measures targeting young people, with an applicability rate higher than 82%, where all selected cases have an applicability rate higher than 19%. These figures confirm the specificity of these measures;

- Our working definition for the target group has resulted from the following analysis: a person could be a beneficiary of an active measure and implicitly a member of a corresponding target group if his/her relation with the labour market is affected by one of these factors: age, working capacity, education, work experience, regional and socio-economic development, citizenship, and belonging to some ethnic minorities;

- The diversity of the target groups identified in the cases of good practice illustrates the tendency to adapt these measures to individual needs during the transition towards employment. This approach is crucial, especially at the time of designing active measures. The objective is above all to support beneficiaries of these measures to change their position in the labour market, not only to adjust them to pre-established and rigid sets of initiatives;

- Thus, priority is given to the setting-up of the procedures to identify the target group.

Table 4-7. Typology of Target Groups in the Main Labour Market Interventions to Increase Youth Employment.

Part I

	A	b	C	d	e	f	g
1	**24_AT32**	Apprenticeship-type training at supra-company level	2.4. Special support for apprenticeships	**100**	**9751**	**11914**	
2	**21_FR101**	Voluntary integration contract (CVI)	2.1. Training at the institutional level	**100**	**1985**	**24438**	
3	**21_PT99**	PROFIJ - Training programmes to include young people (Azores)	2.1. Training at the institutional level	**100**	**2705**	**610**	**Y**
4	**21_DE110**	Programmes supporting career entry	2.1. Training at the institutional level	**100**	**21567**	**2566**	
5	**21_DE11**	Support for vocational training measures for young	2.1. Training at the institutional level	**99,5**	**64757**	**9062**	
6	**24_FR22**	Exemptions and subsidies for the recruitment of apprentices	2.4. Special support for apprenticeship	**99,4**	**266859**	**6904**	
7	**22_DE98**	Training allowances for young workers	2.2. On-the-job training	**99,2**	**240**	**7190**	
8	**11_FR79**	Individual coaching youth (CIVIS)	1.1. Management of individual cases	**98,9**	**254704**	**422**	
9	**24_AT11**	Promoting apprenticeship and training	2.4. Special support for apprenticeships	**98,7**	**11485**	**2776**	**Y**
10	**24_DE71**	The first qualification of integrating youth	2.4. Special support for apprenticeships	**98,6**	**19527**	**3809**	
11	**24_PT7**	Apprenticeships for young people	2.4. Special support for apprenticeships	**98,4**	**14337**	**4728**	**Y**
12	**11_DE99**	Socio-pedagogical accompaniment	1.1. Management of individual cases	**97,7**	**85**	**8046**	

13	**52_PT84**	Training and occupational integration of young people and adults with disabilities (Madeira)	5.2. Rehabilitation	**97,5**	**118**	**1074**	**Y**
14	**21_DE93**	On-the-job training	2.1. Training at the institutional level	**97,4**	**76265**	**12681**	
15	**24_DE87_3**	[Component] Support for training of disabled people - training allowance for the disabled	2.1. Training at the institutional level; 2.4. Special support for apprenticeships	**97,0**	**6126**	**2855**	
16	**22_DE94**	Allowances during apprenticeships	2.2. On-the-job training	**96,5**	**42562**	**2163**	
17	**41_FR67**	Contract type-young in business	4.1.1. Permanent	**95,0**	**1815**	**3485**	
18	**41_DE101**	Bonus apprenticeship	4.1.2 Temporary	**94,7**	**28226**	**1221**	
19	**22_DE23_1**	[Component] Incentives for training and recruitment / employment of severely disabled - work training grants for disabled	2.2. On-the-job training	**93,4**	**3223**	**5921**	
20	**21_DE81**	Training compensation	2.1. Training at the institutional level	**88,2**	**65846**	**2563**	
21	**24_DE34**	Training allowance	2.4. Special support for apprenticeships	**82,8**	**103526**	**3349**	
22	**41_FR76**	Professionalization contract	4.1.2 Temporary	**79,0**	**127219**	**629**	
23	**21_DE100**	Enabling Support	2.1. Training at the institutional level	**78,1**	**1049**	**12211**	
24	**22_DE111**	Individual Qualification in the occupation businesses assisted	2.2. On-the-job training	**77,6**	**1569**	**9980**	

25	**22_AT35**	Training for people with disabilities	2.2. On-the-job training	**76,8**	**1555**	**20079**	**Y**
26	**6_AT27**	Childcare institutions	6. Direct job creation	**76,0**	**320**	**6152**	
27	**52_DE90**	Interventions to support the introduction of vocational training in a sheltered workshop	5.2. Rehabilitation	**74,7**	**20045**	**25178**	
28	**2_DE27**	Independent action = free incentives	2. Formation	**74,6**	**1720**	**1414**	
29	**11_AT34**	Matching the types of work and assistance in seeking employment for people with disabilities	1.1.2 Individual case management	**68,2**	**7830**	**4525**	
30	**22_ES14**	Incentives for training contracts	2.2. On-the-job training	**62,8**	**26019**	**562**	
31	**52_PT34**	Vocational training schemes for people with disabilities	5.2. Rehabilitation	**59,5**	**851**	**38825**	**Y**
32	**51_PT33**	Employment support / supported	5.1. Supported employment	**58,1**	**225**	**4755**	**Y**
33	**41_PT29**	Creating jobs for young people by the exemption or reduction of compulsory social security	4.1.1. Permanent	**55,9**	**21590**	**2378**	
34	**41_AT5**	Promotion of regional mobility and access to employment - travel allowances	4.1.1. Permanent	**55,4**	**871**	**2053**	
35	**22_DE95**	Transitional Assistance	2.2. On-the-job training	**53,8**	**7**	**20000**	
36	**22_PT22**	Practice Vocational Training	2.2. On-the-job training	**50,1**	**8524**	**6172**	**Y**
37	**41_FR81**	Employment initiative contract (CIE-PCS)	4.1.1. Permanent	**49,7**	**18009**	**6439**	**Y**
38	**22_ES63**	Incentives for training contracts (measure ES_14 regions)	2.2. On-the-job training	**49,5**	**667**	**2227**	
39	**52_DK28**	Pre-Rehabilitation	5.2. Rehabilitation	**43,4**	**875**	**37463**	

40	**41_FR112**	Contract, single inclusion (CUI-CIE)	4.1.1. Permanent	**42,2**	**26744**	**7224**	
41	**23_ES9**	On-the-job training (employment and training - ET, CO and TE)	2.3. Alternative training	**41,1**	**16240**	**13136**	**Y**
42	**21_FR85**	Training courses organized by the regions	2.1. Training at the institutional level	**40,2**	**83028**	**8083**	
43	**6_FR46**	Contracts of employment for youth	6. Direct job training	**37,5**	**300**	**4650**	
44	**2_FR63**	Support to return to work-training allowance (AREF)	2. Formation	**32,3**	**33586**	**10094**	
45	**41_FR61**	Companies offering temporary jobs to integrate	4.1.2 Temporary	**30,7**	**3182**	**2251**	
46	**2_FR107**	Training allowances of Pôle Emploi - Governmental Agency for Employment (RFPE)	2 Training	**30,3**	**2135**	**8304**	
47	**81_DK2**	Social assistance (unemployment)	8.1.2 Unemployment Assistance	**29,3**	**7845**	**64801**	
48	**5_NL 59**	Law (re) integration into employment of people with occupational disabilities (REA)	5. Employment support and Rehabilitation	**19,1**	**9320**	**6453**	

Source: Authors' Own Elaboration, EUROSTAT, Labour market policy statistics Qualitative report by countries.

Table 4-7. Typology of Target Groups in the Main Labour Market Interventions to Increase Youth Employment.

Part II		Types of target groups - young persons																																																							
	a	1	2	3	4	5	6	7	8	9	10	11	12	13	14	15	16	17	18	19	20	21	22	23	24	25	26	27	28	29	30	31	32	33	34	35	36	37	38	39	40	41	42	43	44	45	46	47	48	49	50	51	52	53	54	55	56	57	58
		inactiv / nonregistered																																												unemployment									empl			
1	24_AT32																																					X	X		X				X			X					X						
2	21_FR101																																		X					X					X		X												
3	21_PT99		X	X																																				X																			
4	21_DE110																				X																			X																			
5	21_DE11																	X	X	X																				X	X						X	X					X						
6	24_FR22																										X													X					X		X												
7	22_DE98																																														X	X							X			X	
8	11_FR79																																	X						X					X		X												
9	24_AT11																																														X						X						
10	24_DE71																X																		X											X		X											
11	24_PT7	X																																						X								X											
12	11_DE99																																							X								X											
13	52_PT84								X																																X																		
14	21_DE93														X																																												
15	24_DE87_3																																								X			X									X						
16	22_DE94														X																															X													
17	41_FR67																							X					X			X								X					X		X								X				
18	41_DE101																X																																										
19	22_DE23_1																																											X									X						
20	21_DE81									X																															X			X									X						
21	24_DE34				X						X	X													X																					X													
22	41_FR76																														X														X														
23	21_DE100													X																										X							X	X											
24	22_DE111				X																																				X			X									X						

Part III		Types of target groups - young persons																																																							
	a	1	2	3	4	5	6	7	8	9	10	11	12	13	14	15	16	17	18	19	20	21	22	23	24	25	26	27	28	29	30	31	32	33	34	35	36	37	38	39	40	41	42	43	44	45	46	47	48	49	50	51	52	53	54	55	56	57	58
		inactiv / nonregistered																																													unemployment									empl			
25	22_AT35																																								X						X										X		
26	6_AT27																																														X												
27	52_DE90																																								X			X									X						
28	2_DE27																X																							X					X		X												X
29	11_AT34																																								X												X				X		
30	22_ES14							X					X																																								X						
31	52_PT34					X																																			X			X									X						
32	51_PT33						X																																		X			X									X				X		
33	41_PT29																																															X	X										
34	41_AT5																																											X			X									X			
35	22_DE95												X																																X														
36	22_PT22																																													X			X	X	X		X		X				
37	41_FR81																					X				X				X	X														X								X		X				
38	22_ES63							X					X																																								X						
39	52_DK28																					X																		X	X	X	X																
40	41_FR112																																X							X						X	X												
41	23_ES9																																														X							X					
42	21_FR85																											X													X					X	X												
43	6_FR46																																			X	X			X					X	X							X						
44	2_FR63																																													X						X							
45	41_FR61																					X	X																							X	X								X				
46	2_FR107																																														X								X				
47	81_DK2																																														X												
48	5_NL 59																																																				X				X		

Source: Authors' Own Elaboration, EUROSTAT, Labour market policy statistics Qualitative report by countries.

Legend: Typology of Target Groups in the Main Labour Market Interventions to Increase Youth Employment.

<table>
<tr><td>a</td><td>EUROSTAT Code</td><td></td></tr>
<tr><td>b</td><td>Intervention</td><td></td></tr>
<tr><td>c</td><td>Type of action</td><td></td></tr>
<tr><td>d</td><td>The degree of application to young people</td><td></td></tr>
<tr><td>e</td><td>Number of participants aged less than 25 years after LMP interventions</td><td></td></tr>
<tr><td>f</td><td>Average unit cost per intervention/ person/ year [Euro]</td><td></td></tr>
<tr><td>g</td><td>Funded from the ESF</td><td></td></tr>
<tr><td>1</td><td>Young people aged under 25 years who have successfully completed the 9 years of basic education (9 years of school) or equivalent and have a secondary school qualification or equivalent</td><td rowspan="14">Inactive/ unregistered</td></tr>
<tr><td>2</td><td>Apprenticeship for young people aged 15-21 years who participated in vocational training, (the Azores) who have completed 9 years and have no intention to move to the secondary level, have more than 15 years but not the required 9 years of schooling; have completed Level I or II Vocational form;</td></tr>
<tr><td>3</td><td>Qualification programmes for youth aged 15 to 23 years who have no qualifications, have completed 9th grade or equivalent and do not intend to continue regular education, failed to complement the 9-year school.</td></tr>
<tr><td>4</td><td>People with disabilities, with a potential to be employed in the labour market and for whom other services to support the loan (e.g., preparation for vocational training, vocational training or additional training) are not adequate. Persons with intellectual disabilities, borderline learning disability, people with severe mental disorders and/ or behavioural disorders, persons with learning disabilities, people with intellectual disabilities, with severe mental and/ or behavioural disorder.</td></tr>
<tr><td>5</td><td>Disabled people aged 12 years and over.</td></tr>
<tr><td>6</td><td>Persons with disabilities: people whose work capacity is less than 1/3 of normal working capacity of persons with disabilities in the same job.</td></tr>
<tr><td>7</td><td>Young people (unemployed) and the disabled (with a 33% disability)</td></tr>
<tr><td>8</td><td>Persons with a disability (be it motor, sensory, visual, hearing or intellectual) aged 16 years or older, Madeira</td></tr>
<tr><td>9</td><td>People with disabilities who are in the preparatory school for apprenticeships or training</td></tr>
<tr><td>10</td><td>Youth and young adults who complete a course of initial training in the company or in training centres</td></tr>
<tr><td>11</td><td>Young people participating in training initiatives designed to prepare them for future employment and for training outside the parental home</td></tr>
<tr><td>12</td><td>Students with learning disabilities and socially disadvantaged</td></tr>
<tr><td>13</td><td>Students with learning disabilities and socially disadvantaged, who have completed compulsory education and do not have a professional qualification in the company</td></tr>
<tr><td>14</td><td>Students with a slow learning rhythm and socially disadvantaged who missed the earlier stages of apprenticeship in the company and/ or those outside the company</td></tr>
</table>

15	Young people needing support through a pre-vocational agreement in accordance with the legal provisions on training. All socio-pedagogical initiatives are demand driven and adjusted between the enterprise and the training provider	
16	Young people seeking apprenticeship but unable to find it until a certain deadline.	
17	Participants must be registered as an applicant for training, vocational guidance or minimum service to be interviewed before the course.	
18	For those who have not found employment, the lack of consistency between training and market requirements of the applicant's personal profile.	
19	Young people already having the required maturity for access apprenticeship or work.	
20	Students may have difficulty getting school graduation certificates and making a successful transition to training	
21	Public priorities	
22	RMI or young people in great need, people receiving social assistance.	
23	Young employed on an employment contract of indefinite duration (FR-76).	
24	Young people who have reached the age of majority and are married and/ or have at least one child	
25	Single parents	
26	Youth aged 16-22 years with low or no qualifications	
27	Young and low-skilled adults	
28	Young people aged 16-25 years with a lower educational level than baccalaureate, and 16 to 25-year-old A+ baccalaureate graduates living in sensitive urban areas (ZUS), benefiting from CIVIS	
29	Young people under 26 without a diploma and social benefits	
30	Young people aged 16-25 who have left early school	
31	Young people aged 16-25 who are experiencing difficulties in finding a job.	
32	Persons aged between 16 and 65 years who have difficulty in entering the labour market	
33	Young people aged 16-25 who face particular problems in terms of their professional and social integration) ** Young people aged up to 25 years with a qualification that does not exceed level IV (BAC). Specific provisions for youth without a diploma (level VI or VBI): "CIVIS reinforced" weekly interviews in the first 3 months and every month thereafter.	
34	Young people aged between 18 and 22 years unemployed/with low qualifications who are experiencing difficulties at school or personal problems of social and professional integration.	
35	Young people aged 18-25 years unemployed or on subsidized contracts (ESC or CEC), or undertaking a training programme, but looking for a job.	
36	Young people aged 26-29 years who are eligible for unemployment benefits	
37	Young people who have left school without any degree.	
38	Young people who cannot find an apprenticeship programme or who previously abandoned their apprenticeship programme	
39	Unregistered/ inactive	
40	Unregistered (disabled)	
41	Immigrants	
42	Ethnic Minorities	

43	Other people who are looking for a job (with disabilities)	
44	Young people looking for a job	
45	Persons seeking employment	unemployment
46	Registered unemployed	
47	Youth who are registered as unemployed	
48	Young people aged between 16 and 30 years who are seeking their first job.	
49	Young people aged between 16 and 30 years old with medium or high education who: are unemployed and who have had no occupation for more than a year; are unemployed and looking for their first job who have had no occupation for more than one year	
50	Young people aged between 16 and 30 years having a certain level of skills through which they gain further qualifications and who have not worked in a given field for more than a year, or are unemployed and looking for their first job, not being occupied for more than one year.	
51	Unemployed people with allowances and following a training recommended by the Pôle Emploi.	
52	Registered unemployed (people with disabilities)	
53	Low-skilled unemployed youth	
54	Long-term unemployed persons	
55	Employed persons	employment
56	Employed persons (persons with disabilities)	
57	Young workers with professional qualifications	
58	Employees at risk	

The specific needs of the beneficiary are to be defined in terms of fulfilment, in order to realise the effective and efficient positive transition towards employment. This takes place by means of the implementation of active measures as a response to an objective situation that generates the demand. Accordingly:

- It is important to define the target group so as to closely consider issues arising from their occupational transitions as well as the costs of activating these measures;

- The target groups are defined by a common need that provides the group with identity and must be compensated through a professional external intervention. This common need in terms of objectives to fulfil is described by some internal characteristics, which differ considerably from other target groups developed and previously described;

- The paradox of target group formation lies in the need of scientific classification and taxonomy described as a rigid standardisation and in that of innovation absorption in pre-existing ones through the identification of a new need;

- Within an institutional framework, the designed active measures must rapidly respond to an objective demand of the individual to be connected to the labour market.

2. The 6 Essential Factors or Constrains Identified through an Overview of Good Practices which Affect the Individual Relations with the Labour Market

In Fig. 4-5 we present the main factors and constraints affecting the individual relation with the labour market that youth have to challenge. The objective is to match the need of the individual to be included and to belong to a specific target group, with a specific active measure. Following the cases of good practices and the typology of the target groups, we identified six essential factors or constraints that are reflected in the exit active measures applied in seven European countries, taking into consideration: age, working capacity, education, work experience, geographic and socio-economic development, and citizenship/minorities. The overall picture including their allocation by type of target group is visible in Figure 4-6.

Fig- 4-5. 6 Essential Factors or Constrains Identified through an Overview of Good Practices which Affect the Individual Relations with the Labour Market.

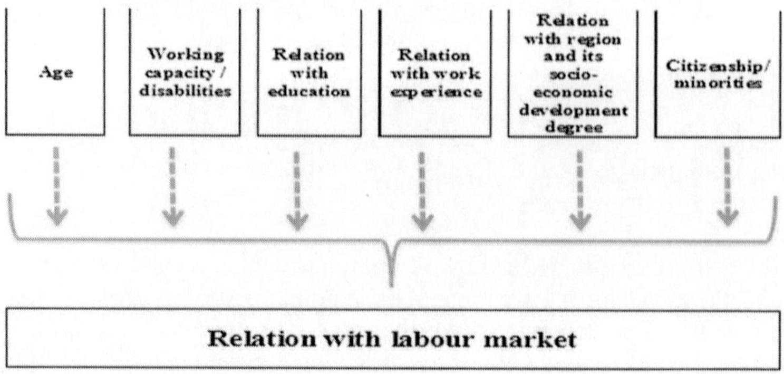

Source: Authors' Own Elaboration.

Fig. 4-6. Main factors and Constraints of Youth Identified in the typology of 48 Target Groups to Increase Youth Employment Active Measures.

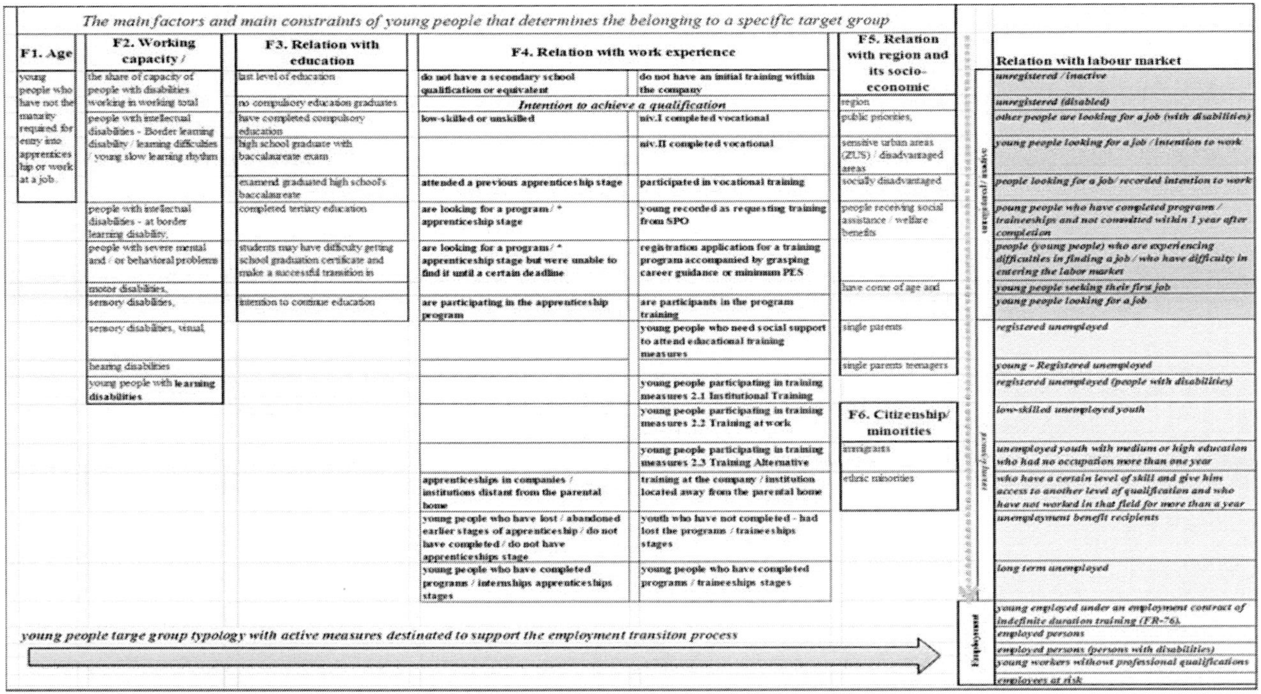

The range of target group typologies could serve as a starting point to develop the procedures for assessing and monitoring the potential and progress of each young person in the process of entering the labour market. The 6 main factors (from F1 to F6) and main constraints could be detailed as follows:

F1. Age

- Young people who do not have the required age for undertaking apprenticeships or work.

F2. Working capacity and disability

- The share of working people with disabilities out of those who are totally capable of work;
- People with intellectual disabilities, border learning disability, learning difficulties, slow learning rhythms.
- People with severe mental or behavioural problems
- Motor disabilities
- Sensory disabilities
- Visual disabilities
- Hearing disabilities
- Young people with learning disabilities

F3. In relation to education

- Low levels of education
- Failure to complete compulsory education
- Completion of compulsory education
- High school graduates with a baccalaureate degree
- Completion of tertiary education
- Students having difficulty obtaining school graduation certificates and moving to training
- Intention to stay on in education

F4. In Relation to Work Experience	
- They do not have a secondary school qualification or equivalent	- They do not have initial training within the company
Intention to achieve a qualification	
- Low-skilled or unskilled	- Level. I completed vocational training
	- Level. II completed vocational training
-They previously attended apprenticeships	- They participated in vocational training
- They are looking for a programme/ * apprenticeships	- Youth found to request training from SPO
- They are looking for a programme/ * apprenticeships but were unable to find them until a certain time	- The application for a training programme was accompanied by grasping career guidance or minimum PES Interviews
- They are participating in the apprenticeship programme	- They are participants in training
	- Young people who need social support to attend educational training measures
	- Young people participating in training programmes 2.1 Institutional Training
	- Young people participating in training initiatives 2.2 On-the-job Training
	- Young people participating in training measures 2. Alternative 3 Training
- Apprenticeships in companies/ institutions distant from the parental home	- Training at the company/ institution located away from the parental home
- Young people quit at the earlier stages of apprenticeships/ have not completed/ do not undertake apprenticeships	- Youth not having completed the programmes/ training
- Young people who have completed programmes/ internships/ apprenticeships	- Young people who have completed programmes/ training

F5. In relation to geographic and socio-economic development

- Region
- Public priorities
- Sensitive urban areas (ZUS)/ disadvantaged areas
- Socially disadvantaged
- People receiving social assistance/ welfare benefits
- They have come of age and are married and/ or have at least one child
- Single parents
- Single teenager parent

F6. Citizenship/ minorities

- Immigrants
- Ethnic minorities.

3. Main Interventions and Types of Action: ALMPs Implemented in Europe in 2010 for Young People Aged 15 to 24 Years old

In 2010, the relationship between active and passive measures could be described taking into account the following aspects (Table 2): the overall costs, the number of beneficiaries aged less than 25 years, the scope of application among youth people and the average cost, measure, year and number of recipients:

- The relationship between the total costs for active and passive measures was 42% in the EU27 and 5.1% in Romania;

- The relationship between the total number of beneficiaries of active measures out of the total number of beneficiaries for passive measures was 62% in the EU27 and 12% in Romania;

- The relationship between recipients of active and passive measures aged less than 25 years old was 113% in the EU27 and 27% in Romania;

- The applicability rate of active measures among young people was 18.6 in the EU27, lower than the 19.3% reported in Romania. As for passive measures, the applicability rate was 10.2% in the EU27, and 8.5% in Romania.

- The relationship between the average cost per measure/beneficiary/year for active and passive measures was 79% in the EU27 and 43% in Romania.

Table 4-8 presents the ALMP Interventions “2 to 7”, concerning:

- Total costs (million Euros)
- Total number of beneficiaries
- Total number of beneficiaries aged less than 25 years old
- The rate of application among young people
- The average value of the cost per measure/beneficiary/year.

a) Total costs (million Euros)

At EU level, the cost concerning ALMP2 (training) was 943 million Euros, that is the largest amount of money devoted to ALMPs, whereas only 316.2 million Euros were set aside for ALMP4 (Employment incentives). In Romania, the financial resources allocated to ALMP4 and ALMP2 were 23 and 2 million Euros, respectively.

b) The total number of beneficiaries

In the EU27, ALMP4 concerned 162,875 individuals, whereas ALMP3 (job rotation and job sharing) involved 30,800 people. In Romania, ALMP4 involved 28,821 individuals, whereas ALMP6 (Direct job creation) reported the lowest number of people involved (7,447).

c) Total number of beneficiaries aged less than 25 years old

In the EU27, ALMP2 concerned 53,380, whereas ALMP7 (Start-up incentives) involved the lowest number of individuals (3,702). In Romania, 4,577 individuals participated in ALMP4, and 1,585 individuals took part in ALMP6.

d) As far as the applicability rate to youth is concerned

In the EU27, 49.5% of youth benefitted from ALMP2, whereas only 6.4% participated in ALMP7. In Romania, ALMP2 and ALMP4 concerned 28% and 15% of young people, respectively.

e) The average cost per measure/beneficiary/year

[The annual average cost by measure for each beneficiary is equal to the total annual cost of the measure divided by the total number of beneficiaries. An attempt was made to calculate the unit cost per person for each measure as a projection base in view of estimating the ALMP budget need].

In 2010, the resources allocated to ALMP5 in the EU27 (in relation to employment and vocational rehabilitation) for these items were €15,364, whereas the unit cost for activating ALMP7 amounted to €6,244.

In Romania, ALMP6 has the highest unit cost (€989) and ALMP2 the lowest unit cost (€431).

Table 4-8. LMP Interventions by Characteristics for EU Countries and Romania in 2010 for all Beneficiaries and Youth.

	measure code	UE countries and Romania	Total expenses [milion Euros]	Total beneficiaries [persons]	Beneficiaries under 25 years old [persons]	Share of young beneficairy in total beneficiaries [%] = [3]/[2]*100	Average cost /measure/ beneficiary/ year [Euro]=[1]/[2]
			1	2	3	4	5
Training	2	Minimum	1	929	204	0,0	64
	2	Mean	942,708	107803	53380	*49,5*	7325
	2	Maximum	7585	774309	473084	61,1	24494
	2	**Romania**	**4**	**9841**	**2756**	**28,0**	**431**
Job rotation and job sharing	3	Minimum	1	199	11	0,0	1140
	3	Mean	41,75	30800	9561	11,9	6869
	3	Maximum	118	103890	25359	24,4	20860
Employment incentives	4	Minimum	1	85	49	0,0	802
	4	Mean	614,083	162875	16416	*10,1*	8622
	4	Maximum	2700	2058840	90565	57,6	59271
	4	**Romania**	**23**	**28821**	**4577**	**15,9**	**802**
Supported employment and rehabilitation	5	Minimum	1	39	26	0,0	1927
	5	Mean	555,059	59835	5523	12,4	15364
	5	Maximum	2811	394488	22055	61,6	78795
Direct job creation	6	Minimum	7	900	96	0,0	216
	6	Mean	449,278	58517	9391	*16,0*	6859
	6	Maximum	4201	292241	67197	23,0	25127
	6	**Romania**	**7**	**7447**	**1585**	**21,3**	**989**
Start-up incentives	7	Minimum	1	103	1	0,0	1401
	7	Mean	316,25	55529	3702	6,4	6244
	7	Maximum	1942	367577	18732	18,1	15686
Out-of-work income maintenance and support	8	Minimum	22	9468	972	0,0	691
	8	Mean	5748,81	618270	75734	*12,2*	7670
	8	Maximum	32580	3468204	423385	28,7	27387
	8	**Romania**	**680**	**390435**	**33074**	**8,5**	**1741**
Early retirement	9	Minimum	65	1372	2	0,0	2667
	9	Mean	690,833	82717	87	0,0	13128
	9	Maximum	2616	312493	172	0,4	47117
Total Active LMP measures (categories 2-7)	*27*	*Minimum*	*2*	*1944*	*0*	*0,0*	*754*
	27	*Mean*	*2545,88*	*408567*	*75993*	*18,6*	*6117*
	27	*Maximum*	*16086*	*2980774*	*654717*	*40,0*	*17166*
	27	***Romania***	***35***	***46109***	***8918***	***19,3***	***754***
Total passives LMP measures, LMP supports (categories 8-9)	*89*	*Minimum*	*22*	*10291*	*0*	*0,0*	*1197*
	89	*Mean*	*6071,96*	*655033*	*67031*	*10,2*	*7769*
	89	*Maximum*	*33147*	*3558560*	*423385*	*28,7*	*29885*
	89	***Romania***	***680***	***390435***	***33074***	***8,5***	***1741***

Source: Authors' Own Elaboration, data from EUROSTAT, Labour market policy statistics Qualitative report by countries.

3.1. Types of LMPs Most Likely to be implemented specifically among Young Persons

In Table 4-9, we present the European countries situation for 2010 relating to the number of beneficiaries of LMP aged less than 25 years old, the share of young beneficiaries under 25 years out of the total beneficiaries, the number of beneficiaries of LMP over 25 years old and for average cost per measure/beneficiary/year by type of LMP measures 2-9 (normalized points). ALMP2 training is the most likely intervention to be implemented for a young person. The ALMP4-employment incentive is the second one, 48pp from the leading one.

Table 4-9. Types of LMP Interventions most likely to be implemented among Youth

	Code LMP 2_7	People under 25	Share of young beneficiary out of total beneficiaries	People over 25 years old	Av. cost
Training	**2**	70	100	6	93
Job rotation and job sharing	**3**	13	63	0	0
Employment incentives	**4**	22	20	24	30
Supported employment and rehabilitation	**5**	7	18	6	100
Direct job creation	**6**	12	32	5	80
Start-up incentives	**7**	5	13	6	55
Out-of-work income maintenance and support	*8*	100	25	100	100
Early retirement	*9*	0	*0*	12	88

Source: Authors' Own Elaboration, data from EUROSTAT, Labour market policy statistics Qualitative report by countries.

3.2. Types of Actions Most Likely to be implemented among Youth

Table 4 presents the most likely types of actions to be implemented among young people according to:

a. ALMP2 types of actions: “Training 2.1. Training at the institutional level”; “2.4. Special support for apprenticeship” and the “2.2. On-the-job training”.
b. ALMP4 types of actions: “Employment incentives” 4.1.1. “Permanent” and “4.1.2. Temporary”.

Table 4-10. Most Likely Types of Actions to be Implemented among Youth.

Type of action	App. rate> 19%	App. rate> 82%	Percentage of total selection; Application rate> 19%	Percentage of total selection; Application rate> 82%
2.1. Training at the institutional level	9	7	19 .1	33.3
2.4. Special support for apprenticeship	6	6	12 .8	28.6
2.2. On-the-job training	9	3	19 .1	14.3
1.1. Management of individual cases	3	2	6 .4	9.5
4.1.1. Permanent	5	1	10 .6	4.8
4.1.2. Temporary	3	1	6.4	4 .8
5.2. Rehabilitation	4	1	8.5	4 .8
2.Formation	3		6.4	
2.3. Alternative training	1		2.1	
5. Employment support and rehabilitation	1		2.1	
5.1. Supported employment	1		2.1	
6. Direct job creation	1		2.1	
8.1.2 Unemployment assistance	1		2.1	
Total	**47**	**21**	**100.0**	**100 .0**

Average unit cost for the 2010/ intervention/ beneficiary/ year was 9,246 (Euro) with a probability of 75%. Source: Authors’ Own Elaboration, data from EUROSTAT, Labour market policy statistics Qualitative report by countries.

4. Conclusions

Romania needs to reform and develop its Active Labour Market Policies through focusing on the following specific issues:

- Increasing investments in ALMPs;
- Improving target group management and the implementation process of ALMPs;
- Diversifying the ALMPs according to the needs of target groups in order to enhance the transition to employment for ALMPs beneficiaries;
- Designing and implementing ALMPs for youth including those inactive and unregistered as unemployed;
- Improving the assessment criteria for ALMPs through a standardised and unique methodology (EUROSTAT&OECD) regardless of funding.

References

European Commission and EUROSTAT, Directorate F: Unit F/2: Labour Market Statistics. 2006. *Labour Market Policy Database Methodology Revision of June 2006*. Brussels: European Commission.

EUROSTAT. 2010. *Labour Market Policy Statistics Qualitative Report, Austria*. Brussels: EUROSTAT.

—. 2010. *Labour Market Policy Statistics Qualitative Report, Denmark*. Brussels: EUROSTAT.

—. 2010. *Labour Market Policy Statistics Qualitative Report, France*. Brussels: EUROSTAT.

—. 2010. *Labour Market Policy Statistics Qualitative Report, Germany*. Brussels: EUROSTAT.

—. 2010. *Labour Market Policy Statistics Qualitative Report, The Netherlands*. Brussels: EUROSTAT.

—. 2010. *Labour Market Policy Statistics Qualitative Report, Portugal*. Brussels: EUROSTAT.

—. 2010. *Labour Market Policy Statistics Qualitative Report, Romania*. Brussels: EUROSTAT.

—. 2010. *Labour Market Policy Statistics Qualitative Report, Spain*. Brussels: EUROSTAT.

COORDINATES FOR NEW ACTIVE LABOUR MARKET POLICIES (ALMPS) FOR YOUTH IN ROMANIA

CRISTINA LINCARU

1. Introduction

This paper analyses young peoples' performances in the Romanian labour market with a view to boosting their employment quality and efficiency. Based on the evaluation of these performances and taking into account some recent EU policies and initiatives, a number of coordinates have been put forward.

The first set of coordinates is a more tangible one and tries to advance some proposals for improving the impact of ALMP on youth employment in Romania, mainly in the short term. Conversely, the second set of coordinates constitutes an attempt to integrate existing ALMPs.

2. Proposed Improvement Measures for the Development of ALMPs among Youth in Romania

Romania should adopt the ILO Standards laid down in the Youth Employment Conventions:

- **Governance Convention on Employment Policy:**

C 142 - The Human Resources Development Convention, 1975 (No. 142), - Convention concerning Vocational Guidance and Vocational Training in the Development of Human Resources (Entry into force: 19 July 1977) Adoption: Geneva, 60th ILC session (23 June 1975) - Status: Up-to-date instrument (Technical Convention), not ratified by Romania.

R 195- Human Resources Development Recommendation, 2004 (No. 195)

- **Conventions concerning Public and Private Employment Services:**

C 181 - Private Employment Agencies Convention, 1997 (No. 181), not ratified by Romania

R188 - Private Employment Agencies Recommendation, 1997
R198 - Employment Relationship Recommendation, 2006 (No. 198)

- **Other important conventions:**

C044 - Conventions: C044 - Unemployment Provision Convention, 1934 (No. 44).

Other suggestions:

1. In the short term, policies concerning youth guarantee employment should be enforced, while supporting youth in the changing labour market through a range of public interventions: services, active measures, passive measures and support measures. Each type of intervention should cover the different dimensions of the labour market for beneficiaries of PES, such as flexibility and security.

2. The characteristics of the unemployed should be redefined, in order to include those with disabilities (following the examples of Austria, Denmark, Portugal, and Germany).

3. The Labour Market Informational System administered by PES should build and maintain a database for active measures in Romania or elsewhere. The creation of an Active Measures Observatory is a useful instrument that could improve coordination, efficiency and effectiveness of all public interventions addressing employment.

4. The EUROSTAT criteria on public interventions in the labour market should be adopted while framing clauses of Law No. 76/2002 concerning the unemployment insurance system and incentives for employment;

5. A method for the identification and characterization of a target group that requires the development of active labour market measures should be adopted. Public interventions in the labour market to increase youth employment are designed for heterogeneous groups by characteristics and scope. In this sense, there is a need to set up criteria to create a target

group methodology to be integrated into the monitoring of labour market active measures to increase effective spending budgets, and so forth.

6. The "Online Journal for those in the Labour Market" should be devised concerning the assessment, diagnosis, control and monitoring of young people's transition from school to work and further developments;

7. Romanian active measures financed by Structural Funds ESF/ ERDF should be reported to international LMP database (EUROSTAT). There is a need to improve the national official statistics regarding ALMPs both in terms of results and budgets. If public expenditure in the labour market is considered, Romania is at the bottom of the pack in terms of the share of expenditure on active measures in Europe (4.8% in 2010).

2.1. Proposals for the Establishment of Active Measures for Young People: Security associated with the Individual rather than the Employment Status

This initiative includes three levels to be carried out simultaneously and considering the past and future status of the beneficiaries of the active measures:

- The flexible component (learning to know and to do);
- The security component (generating income from work);
- The connection to social welfare (links with the community).

Concerning the first point and based on European experience, the following are traditionally provided to young people: institutional training, apprenticeships, on-the-job training (formulations under standardization EUROSTAT / LFS). As for the security level, this should be the base for the complementary flexibility level within ALMPs, together covering both sides of flexicurity: the current income from employment (or replacement income, calculated as a proportion of the gross minimum wage in the economy) and the "learning and doing" needs. Finally, the systems of social protection include safeguards against the main risks (losing jobs and skills, age, illness, and so forth).

2.2. The Estimated Budget Required to Guarantee Normative Levels and to Ensure Positive Transitions, Minimal and Maximal Efforts in Romania in the Short Term

Considering the normative levels and assuming the hypothetical provision of positive transitions, the minimal and maximum effort in Romania in the short term (Table 4-11) were estimated and projected using two algorithms.

Algorithm 1: it calculates the absolute transitions x, y, and z, using real quarterly data for youth (15-24 years) in Romania. Applying examples for the period 2008Q2-2008Q1 with the final time-baseline set at the last quarter Q1 2012.

Algorithm 2: it calculates the simulated transitions x, y, and z, using as a reference the first quarter of 2012, the current quarterly data for youth (15-24 years) in Romania.

The output data were simulated under *ceteris paribus* positive transitions x, z, y for the transition of the 15 to 24 age group, whereas other age groups are ignored. In this sense:

"x" is the difference between the number of people who have left the inactive status and accessed the employment status and the number of persons who have left the employment status and accessed the inactive status = absolute transition from inactive state to employment;

"y" is the difference between the number of people who have left the inactive status and have become unemployed and the number of persons who have left the unemployment status and entered into the inactive status = absolute transition from inactive to unemployment;

"z" is the difference between the number of people who have left the unemployment status and have entered the employment status and the number of persons who have left the employment status and have entered into the unemployment status = absolute transition from unemployment to employment;

Based on simulated positive transitions, the normative values for the Pa active population, Pi inactive population, Ps unemployed population and their corresponding rates were calculated, along with the estimated impact caused by positive transitions relating to simulated performance models of youth employment in Q2 2012 (the 15-24 age group).

Additionally, the effect of this effort in the performance of employment of persons aged 15-64 in employment Q2 2012 was also identified.

Table 4-11. Presumed Normative Levels to ensure Positive Transitions.

	Scenarios I - realist	**Scenarios II - optimist**
	Minimum effort	Maximum effort
simulated unemployment rate 15-24	22	15
x + y + z [thousand persons]	**33,59**	**302,3**
x (absolute transitions from Inactive to Employment) [thousand persons]	6,3	4,2
y (absolute transitions from Inactive to Unemployment) [thousand persons]	7,9	123,8
z (absolute transitions from Unemployment to Employment) [thousand persons]	19,4	174,2
Pa2_15_24 [thousand persons]	800,8	914,7
Po2_15_24 [thousand persons]	624,5	777,4
Ps2_15_24 [thousand persons]	176,2	137,2
Pi2_15_24 [thousand persons]	1935,4	1821,5
ra2_15_24 [%]	29,1	33,4
ro2_15_24 [%]	**22,7**	**28,4**
rs2_15_24 [%]	22,0	15,0
ri2_15_24 [%]	70,4	66,5
ra2-ra1_15_24 [%]	0,4	4,6
ro2-ro1_15_24 [%]	**0,8**	**6,5**
rs2-rs1_15_24 [%]	-1,8	-8,8
ri2_-ri1_15_24 [%]	-0,8	-4,8
ra2-ra1_15_64 [%]	0,1	0,9
ro2-ro1_15_64 [%]	0,2	1,2
rs2-rs1_15_64 [%]	-0,1	-0,6
ri2_-ri1_15_64 [%]	-0,1	-0,9
Pa2-Pa1_15_24 [thousand persons]	**14,2**	**128,1**
Po2-Po1_15_24 [thousand persons]	**25,6**	**178,5**
Ps2-Ps1_15_24 [thousand persons]	**-11,4**	**-50,4**
Pi2-Pi1_15_24 [thousand persons]	**-14,2**	**-128,1**

Source: Authors' Own Elaboration.

In addition to this, we identified two bound scenarios of the required effort spectrum correlated with the possible desired effects (Table 4-12 and Table 4-13).

Table 4-12. Two Bound Scenarios of the Required Effort Spectrum Correlated with the Possible Desired Effect (mentioned hypothesis).

	Estimated additonal budget requsted for youth ALMP's fininc ing *[milion euro]*	The share of estimated budget in total labour market budget *[%]*	executed budget *[milion euro]*	share LMP budget of GDP *[%]*	GDP in 2010 *[milion euro]*
					117109
Labour market services			34,769	0,03	
Active measures on labour market ALMP (categories 2-7)			34,754	0,03	
Financial supports regarding the labour market (categories 8-9)			679,61	0,58	
Labour market budget			714,364	0,61	
Projected budget for active measures on labour market ALMP (categories 2-7)					
Scenarios I. Normative level minimum 33.6 thousand persons, simultaneous positive transitions, projected based on average cost of ALMP's at EU27 in 2010 of 9246 euro/intervention/year/persons.	**311**	**43,5**	**1025,36**	**0,9**	
Scenarios II. Normative level minimum 302.3 thousand persons, simultaneous positive transitions, projected based on average cost of ALMP's at EU27 in 2010 of 9246 euro/intervention/year/persons	**2795**	**391,3**	**3509,36**	**3**	

Source: Authors' Own Elaboration.

The "Minimum effort" scenario (Table 4-11) requires the positive transition of 33.6 thousand youth aged 15 to 24 years to employment (6.3 thousand persons from inactivity to employment, 7.9 thousand people from inactivity to unemployment and 19.4 thousand unemployed people to employment). The impact of these positive transitions is estimated to reduce the youth unemployment rate by 1.8 pp and to increase the employment rate by 0.8 pp. Realising this transition requires an increase of the active population by 14.2 thousand persons, of the employed population of 25.6 thousand people, a decrease of the unemployed population by 11.4 thousand and the decrease of inactive population by 14.2 thousand people.

The estimated impact of these transitions on the employment performances of those aged 15 to 64 years is an increase of the activity rate by 0.1 pp, an increase of the employment rate by 0.2 pp, and the decrease of the unemployment and inactivity rates by 0.1 pp.

Table 4-13. Share of GDP spent on Public Labour Market Policy.

Share of GDP (%)	LMP's expenses as GDP %]	
Ireland	3,95	
Spain	3,9	
Belgium	3,77	
Denmark	3,37	
Netherlands	**2,91**	**Romania in optimist scenarious**
Finland	2,77	
France	2,57	
Austria	2,27	
Germany	2,26	
Portugal	2,08	
Sweden	1,85	
Italy	1,84	
Hungary	1,32	
Latvia	1,25	
Luxembourg	1,24	
Slovenia	1,17	
Estonia	1,09	
Poland	1,04	
Slovakia	0,94	
Greece	0,93	**Romania in realist**
Cyprus	0,88	**scenarious**
Lithuania	0,79	
Czech Republic	0,72	
Romania	0,61	2010 level Romania
Bulgaria	0,58	
Malta	0,5	
United Kingdom	*	

Source: Authors' Own Elaboration.

Based on a minimal effort scenario, the optimist scenario was designed. Scenario II—the normative level is that at least 302.3 thousand people have to realise simultaneous transitions. In considering 2010, in order to implement ALMPs, there is a need to supplement 714.36 million Euros to a budget of 3,059 million Euros, representing 3% of GDP (Table

4-12), in the hypothesis of an average expense of €9,246 per intervention / year / person.

Such an increase of the labour market budget level of the public spending share of GDP would lead to moving up 19 spots at EU level. With a 2.4% rise in GDP, Romania would join the first 7 leading countries, like France, Finland, and The Netherlands (Table 4-13).

One might note that there is no one optimal solution but a wide variety of solutions in between minimum and maximum values which are strongly correlated with objectives and that a dynamic and competitive environment calls for an integrated and systematic approach, highly diversified and finely targeted. Austerity budgets can be effectively exploited through the development and the implementation of sound and innovative active measures.

Labour market reform is a consequence of the operation of the knowledge economy that is characterized by high levels of flexibility and implies the individual-level security on maintenance and growth of an ability to be competitive and able to create added value. The answer could be the harmonization of the individual-level security in the tangible production system associated with industrial relations (focused on job security) and with the intangible production system related to knowledge (focused on employability).

If the pattern of industrial relations was the type: inactive/unemployed/ employed the new knowledge economy pattern is the type specific training/employment simultaneously and/or sequentially.

Through such a new model, unemployment and inactivity do not have the same meaning, as we will explore further.

3. Coordinates for New Active Labour Market Policies (ALMPs) in the Knowledge Economy

In the knowledge economy, some implications exist at the social level allowing us to identify a new socio-economic paradigm manifestation. The hypothesis of this new paradigm considers the intangible value as the main source of growth and that the value creation process is highly differentiated by its creativity. The proper business model is treated as a whole, including the current and potential future configuration of the value creation, through the transformation of knowledge into action and finally into benefit as a consequence of responding to a specific need of the community. Building the individual identity is mostly concerned with following the interaction with one's community. This uniqueness and relative dependence between individuals and their community might give rise to a common identity mark for those actors, followed by some limitations in terms of comparability.

- **Recent Evolutions and Actual Trends pointing to the Knowledge Economy**

After 40 years since the issuing of the "Learning to be" report calling for the need of the entire society to "learn to be", the progress made in terms of implementation can be certainly confirmed:

> Learning to Be (1972) expressed the fear of dehumanization of the world, associated with technical progress and one of its main messages was that education should enable each person: to be able to solve his own problems, make his own decisions and shoulder his own responsibilities. Rather than educating children for a given society, the challenge will be ensuring that everyone always has the personal resources and intellectual tools needed to understand the world and behave as a fair-minded, responsible human being. More than ever before, the essential task of education seems to be to make sure that all people enjoy the freedom of thought, judgment, feeling and imagination to develop their talents and keep control of as much of their lives as they can.[1]

Through scientific progress, the information technology revolution and the shift to the information and knowledge economy, competitiveness has become global (see Table 4-14).

> With the growth in the knowledge-based economy, it is becoming increasingly the case that the intangible assets of the firm and its intellectual capital are the keys to achieving sustainable competitive advantage rather than technology or tangible assets alone. Value creation takes place through innovation, research and development, brand building, relationship and networks—all intangible assets […] Global business is now primarily intangible. Intangibles are the major drivers of growth in any business or economy"[2].

The new global value paradigm creation was reflected in the major restructuring of economies, especially through their specialization in

---

[1] http://www.unesco.org/delors/ltobe.htm (Accessed 12 November 2013).

[2] Mishra, R. K., and S. Jhunjhunwala. 2009. *Valuation of Intangibles.* Research study sponsored by ICAI, the Accounting Research Foundation, Preliminary report, Institute of Public Enterprise.
http://www.icai.org/resource_file/17800valuation_intangibles.pdf (accessed 12 November 2913).

services with intangible products that offer high profit and investment returns in the short term (especially in research and innovation), with associated risks and high (work) income fluctuations. The tendency to product diversification is reflected through the high variability of production demand. The labour market is less and less predictable, while labour flexibility as a response to the need to adapt production to volatile market demand is on the rise. The new model focuses on workers' flexibility and adaptability in order to meet real-time requirements which induce global competitiveness.

> Policy reforms are needed to strengthen innovation and productivity outcomes. […] Reform of labour markets, notably through well-designed employment protection legislation, would help firms to adjust and allow them to draw greater benefits from their investment in innovation and technology.[3]

Consequently, it becomes necessary for individuals to pursue certain educational levels regardless of age, improving skills and qualifications in accordance with labour production and absorption. In the new global economy, processes of education, training and work can take place simultaneously, sequentially and continuously, in the sense that these processes can be paused and resumed by desired objectives and requirements. Individual adaptation to the new economic and social model impacts on fewer children and households. The extension of the educational processes until the age of 30-35 years old and the difficulty of finding and keeping a job discourage to start a family with an effect on birth rates. The risk of being dismissed is associated with unemployment assurance and some social protection instruments (active measures and unemployment benefits) (ESPROSS Manual). The risk of losing the ability/capacity to perform a job is associated with training and education.

Education assurance concerning skills depreciation risks could be considered to be partially covered, or integrated into the unemployment assurance contribution.

> The future of these economies hinges on their ability to turn advances in knowledge into innovations that will generate new businesses and new jobs. "Learning to do" can no longer mean what it did when people were trained to perform a very specific physical task in a manufacturing process.

---

[3] OECD. 2007. Innovation and Growth: Rationale for an Innovation Strategy. Paris: OECD. http://www.oecd.org/science/inno/39374789.pdf (accessed 12 November 2013).

Skills training therefore has to evolve and become more than just a means of imparting the knowledge needed to do a more or less routine job.[4]

Table 4-14. New Paradigms and New Hypotheses Induced by Knowledge Economy Manifestation, Complementary to the Existing Paradigm.

	Existing ALMPs Industrial society (Galilean relativity /invariance and space and time absolute space, universal time, Newtonian Mechanics[5])	**New ALMPs (marginal improvement need) Knowledge society** (Einstein—theory of relativity: space and time should be considered together and in relation to each other[6])
Value	**Tangible**	**Intangible**
Value production system	Serial Value creation chain / Successive mode	Parallel Value creation chain / Simultaneous mode
Time	$\Delta t \rightarrow 0$ Focused on short-term objectives	Long-term objectives
Space	Global (no limit)	Clearly spatial delimited
Education (UNESCO)	Learning to do[7]	Learning to be[8]
Production System	Industrial production system	Knowledge production system; Globalization era
	Industrialization era	Services era
	Quantitative	Qualitative
	Focus to create the solution and then to find the potential users / consumers	Focus on a specific community, identifying and solving an existing problem of the community in a time frame, creating and implementing a solution in partnership with the beneficiary community
Magnifier of value	Accumulation	Sharing
Increasing power	Concentration	Spreading

[4] http://www.unesco.org/delors/ltodo.htm (accessed 12 November 2013).
[5] http://en.wikipedia.org/wiki/Galilean_invariance (accessed 12 November 2013).
[6] http://en.wikipedia.org/wiki/Theory_of_relativity (accessed 12 November 2013).
[7] http://www.unesco.org/delors/ltodo.htm (accessed 12 November 2013).
[8] Faure, E. 1972. *Learning to Be: The World of Education Today and Tomorrow, published,* UNESCO.

Finality	Consumer	Beneficiary
Conservation	Economic value (market value)	Social value (community value)
Production process	Stable for the long term	Variable on the short term
Product	Low diversity	High diversity
Main growth factors	Tangible values (buildings, machinery, production lines, capital, land)	Intangible assets (inventions, innovations, technologies, design, brands, patents)
What to create?	Tangible values	Intangible values
Value creation	Value creation takes place through productivity increase and technology investment.	Value creation takes place through innovation, research and development, brand building, relationship and networks, responding to community specific needs
Competitive advantage specific strategy	Productivity, extensive markets, expanding production through increasing the number of users.	Product variety/diversity increasing fitting to the needs of beneficiaries: "value creation model and profit model fit in with the external market conditions in such a way to be attractive to core target groups and other company stakeholders, thus resulting in a competitive advantage"[9]
Risk / profit distribution	Owners of productive factors (tangible values) take the risk and profit	Owners of the productive factors (intangible values) take the risk and profit
The right business model	Controlling the environment	Responding to the environment
	It is an important internal perspective—the value chain creation is realized inside the company.	Looking at the business model as a whole—both at its current structure and orientation and at the yet unused and hidden potential.

[9] http://www.iioe.eu/fileadmin/files/projects/Sustainable_Value_Creation.pdf (accessed 20 December 2013).

	Making the product available in the right market at the right time (product creates the market) Managers view the market and technology from the inside.	"considering the current and potential future value added offering for stakeholders, viewed from the perspective of each of the target groups involved; considering the current and potential future configuration of the value creation model of added value, that consists of business processes, organizations, business infrastructure, business partner relations, core competencies, and corporate culture; and also considering the current and potential profit model defining revenue sources and cost structure".[10]
The Management system		
Structures and relations	Specialization (Fayol, 1916)	Cooperation
	Labour/ Work division (A. Smith)	Decision division / Communication
	Hierarchy-Professionalization of the management functions at the individual level (see the ISCO standardisation)	Network: (variable) degree of integration of the management skills in view to perform management functions, role, skills, the hierarchy is flattened at the individual level (see *Annex 2)*
	Many to one (syndicates, etc.)—the higher is the representation base the more powerful is the structure	One to many (network membership)
Relationship with society	The individual must be it into social norms /system—pre existent and rigid "given society"	The individual creates their own society in a responsible and conscious—dynamic process (local autonomy, empowerment, participation)
Activity orientation	Task orientation [classical school of management theory, Taylor and Scientific Management]	People orientation [behavioural school of management] Hawthorne's argument was that human relations and the social needs of workers are crucial aspects of business management[11]
Main questions	Management questions. How and When productivity needs increasing	Leadership questions. What and Why diversity needs increasing

10 http://www.iioe.eu/fileadmin/files/projects/Sustainable_Value_Creation.pdf (accessed 20 December 2013).

11 http://www.cliffsnotes.com/study_guide/Behavioral-Management-Theory.topicArticleId-8944,articleId-8852.html (accessed 20 December 2013).

<table>
<tr><td>Focusing</td><td>Objectives</td><td>Needs</td></tr>
<tr><td></td><td>Terms / deadlines</td><td>Results /impact</td></tr>
<tr><td>Priority</td><td>Short term</td><td>Long term</td></tr>
<tr><td>Executioner / beneficiary</td><td>Individual is performing tasks/actions for the organization benefit</td><td>Community (partnership created with participation of regions, state, business, research, civil society) created in view to perform tasks / action for the individual benefit—here ALMPS are applied</td></tr>
<tr><td rowspan="14">Main vector
Differences between leader & manager[12]
Management thoughts: Industrial revolution, scientific management, management theory, Era of behavioural Science</td><td>Manager</td><td>Leader</td></tr>
<tr><td>To administer</td><td>To innovate</td></tr>
<tr><td>He is a copy</td><td>He is the original</td></tr>
<tr><td>To maintain</td><td>To develop</td></tr>
<tr><td>He focuses on systems and structures</td><td>He focuses on people</td></tr>
<tr><td>He relies on control</td><td>He inspires the truth</td></tr>
<tr><td>He has a short-range view</td><td>He has a long-range perspective</td></tr>
<tr><td>He asks how and when</td><td>He asks what and why</td></tr>
<tr><td>He has an eye on the bottom line</td><td>He has an eye on horizon</td></tr>
<tr><td>He initiates</td><td>He originates</td></tr>
<tr><td>He accepts the status quo</td><td>He challenges it</td></tr>
<tr><td>He does things right</td><td>He does the right thing</td></tr>
<tr><td></td><td>Manager: Skills / abilities to translate knowledge into action</td></tr>
<tr><td></td><td>Entrepreneur: Skills / abilities to translate knowledge (output) into profit (knowledge impact assessment)</td></tr>
<tr><td colspan="3">Business model generation</td></tr>
<tr><td rowspan="2"></td><td>Fayol's 14 principles of management [1]</td><td>Knowledge society functioning mirrored possible principles</td></tr>
<tr><td>Specialization of labour. Specializing Esprit de corps. He encourages continuous improvement in skills and the development of improvements in methods.</td><td>Communication in view to work in ad hoc created groups in view to solve a problem using multidisciplinary and multidisciplinary approaches. Cooperation and connectivity skills improve the efficiency of the group work results. Individual affiliation to professional network. The ability of the group to transform intangible into tangible value.</td></tr>
</table>

[12] Sanjay Kumar Jha. *General Management Theory and Practice*, Kathmandu Academy of Tourism & Hospitality Management (KATHM). http://www.slideshare.net/sanjayjha/unit-igeneral-management-theory-and-practicebtts (accessed 20 December 2013).

	Authority. The right to give orders and the power to demand obedience.	Participation, individual negotiation, risk assuming
	Discipline. No slacking, bending of rules.	Flexibility. Individual responsibility, collaboration protocols
	Unity of command. Each employee has one and only one boss.	Multi-poles of commands / multi-action plans. Each member of the community has multiple relations both master and slave type, for a short time, in the context of problem solving.
	Unity of direction. A single mind generates a single plan and all play their part in that plan.	Unity of receiving –solutions packages for the beneficiaries from a specific community.
	Subordination of Individual Interests. When at work, only work things should be pursued or thought about.	Subordination of collective interests. When at work, the integration of any vulnerable individual should be pursued or thought about regardless of one's background (education, work capacity, minority group belonging, ageing problems, etc.). Life and work balance.
	Remuneration. Employees receive fair payment for services, not what the company can get away with. Paid jobs are those jobs where the incumbents hold explicit (written or oral) or implicit employment contracts which give them a basic remuneration which is not directly dependent upon the revenue of the unit for which they work (this unit can be a corporation, a non-profit institution, a government unit or a household) [13]	Work income is in concordance with the risk and profit company/ network profile (box office type quotation, international benchmarking by specific characteristics—researchers, international services for profile providers ex IDEAS, Research Gate, RePEC) Self-employment jobs are those jobs where remuneration is directly dependent upon the (potential) profits derived from the goods and services produced (where one's consumption is considered to be part of the profits).[14]

[13] http://laborsta.ilo.org/applv8/data/icsee.html (accessed 20 November 2013).
[14] http://laborsta.ilo.org/applv8/data/icsee.html (accessed 20 November 2013).

	Centralization. Consolidation of management functions. Decisions are made from the top.	Decentralisation. Increasing autonomy and individual decision. Concordance risks benefit at the individual level.
	Scalar Chain (line of authority). Formal chain of command running from the top to the bottom of the organization.	Network flat relationships. Multidimensional directions of command like the human brain and neural network
	Order. All materials and personnel have a prescribed place, and they must remain there.	Short-term, high fidelity and sensitivity response in view to solve a specific problem of a specific community. Flexibility and adaptability. The allocation of personnel and materials is provisionally generated in concordance with the common function / task that is identified and agreed to be performed.
	Equity. Equality of treatment (but not necessarily identical treatment)	Inequity. Risk and profit return profile (IPE model, blockbuster model[15], stars box office model)
	Personnel tenure. Limited turnover of personnel. Lifetime employment for good workers.	High turnover of personnel. Temporary employment for the highly qualified - they are too expensive to be full-time employed.
	Initiative. Thinking out a plan and do what it takes to make it happen.	Community is the beneficiary/ integrator of the long-term plan and employs forces (actors, organisations, networks) in view to fulfil its identity
	Esprit de corps. Harmony, cohesion among personnel.	Community spirit. Harmony, cohesion among the host/partnership community
	Source: http://www.analytictech.com/ mb021/fayol.htm	Source: Formulated by authors
	Among the 14 most important elements are specialization, unity of command, scalar chain, and, coordination by managers (an amalgam of authority and unity of direction).	

[15] Sundelin, A. 2008. *What is a Blockbuster Business Model?* http://tbmdb.blogspot.ro/2008/12/blockbuster-business-model.html (accessed 20 November 2013).

Labour market role challenges to face	To allocate labour force offer according to labour demand needs (in the context of specialisation). The process of job creation and job destruction is slow and concerns specific intra-sectoral allocations.	To creates chains of demand and offer (in the context of cooperation)—new jobs creation. "The challenge is to ensure that the adjustment process involved in matching available workers with new job openings works as smoothly as possible" (OECD 25 July 2005) The process of job creation and job destruction is rapid and concerns specific inter-sectoral allocations.
Labour market good functioning means	To respond to a stable demand where value creation takes place through productivity increasing, technology investment.	To support the creation of new demand and to respond rapidly to variable demand where value creation takes place through innovation, research and development, brand building, relationship and networks
Priority	"To do" then "to be" The executioner & product dichotomy	"to be" then "to do" (first property rights ownership, then production) The individual identity is built relatively to a community
Action	Action is standardised/ clearly decrypted by a procedure (the "slave" level executing is functional isolated by the "master" level.)	Action is intelligent / reactive /adaptive and responding to the beneficiary needs, therefore it is difficult to be rigid.
Implementing process	The (technological) process of implementation is rigid. The chain of command / execution sequences is distributed spatially and hierarchically.	The (methodological) process of implementation is flexible. The chain of command / execution sequences is distributed spatially through a network.
Main role of PES (Public Employment Services) on the labour market	Allocation of labour force offer according to demand. PES realise the matching of the worker (according to his characteristics, qualification, skills, experience) with a job (attribution, responsibilities, tasks), according to hierarchical positions.	Transparency increasing "a solution providing market" where communities close representation pays leaders to find solutions and management contracts for managers so as to implement the community objectives.

Work income	Constant / predictable	Variable/ unpredictable
Duty performing requests	Predictable	Difficult / with limited predictability
Main relationship	Many to one Subordination/ including members in a structure/hierarchy	Self knowledge and relationship with other people/One to many, members (node) in a network
Evaluation	Certified skills / employer evaluation	Personal competence[16] /self evaluation
Solution	Outside / Hierarchical received	Internal process resulted / research/Investigating Individuals in the community context/ Horizontal
	Dependency: Responsibility outside the Execution	Independency: Responsibility of Execution
Risk assured by social protection system	Unemployment benefits for losing a job	Unemployment benefits for losing the mandate risk: Losing capacity to find and offer a solution in a flexible manner to the beneficiary // losing contact with the community/ losing the representation mandate.

Source: Authors' Own Elaboration.

Table 4-14 summarizes some management principles based on an interdisciplinary perspective along with knowledge management relatedness (Fig. 4-15), considering the neoclassical definition of economy "space".

Below we widen this definition to integrate some approaches proposed by the spatial economy, the evolutionary economy and the Bio-economy School. The need for such integration to offer a holistic approach was recently formulated (1965) through the "entropy and bioeconomics, linking environment, institutions and production"[17] system of Georgescu

[16] This includes a range of skills and talents, thus combining certified skills acquired through technical and vocational training, social behaviour, personal initiative and a willingness to take risks, http://www.unesco.org/delors/ltodo.htm (accessed 20 November 2013).

[17] Gowdy, J., and S., Mesner. 1998. "The Evolution of Georgescu-Roegen's Bioeconomics," *Review of Social Economy*, Rensselaer Polytechnic Institute, 56, No. 2, Association of social Economics.

Roegen.[18] Roegen put forward a comprehensive theory of economy and society under biophysical constraints.[19]

According to this perspective, the economic process is purely entropic and the economic race is explained through the pursuing of low entropy.

A continuator of the Bio-economic School initiated by Roegen was Bran[20] and his 2003 *Economic Value* (awarded by the Romanian Academy). Bran considers that by combining the values of life, the transformations taking place in different systems are linked in succession (production, consumption, production, etc.) rather than in intermediate forms (product or service) of economic potential.

In order to stimulate positive transitions to employment, there is a need to localize the area of action and intervention and to ensure the implementation of this process. We know now that the challenge is global and is amplified by some tension. We also know that there are many systems that act concurrently following their internal laws, yet we are unable to see the relationship between those systems. This is the real challenge, namely to unify all systems in an organic manner, considering that they are functioning even though their coordination is not clear. In considering these theories as a starting point, we further propose our suggestion to explain the socio-economic system based on perennial transforming chain reaction functions.

- **An Organic and Holistic Model for Individual and Community System Integration: "The Intangible Feeds the Tangible and the Tangible feeds the Intangible"**

This model will be figured assuming as an axiomatic dichotomy that the new and the old are relatively dependent on each another and have a dichotomist relationship so that their existence is reciprocally conditioned (Fig. 4-7).

---

[18] Georgescu-Roegen, N. 1999. *The Entropy Law and the Economic Process, Bioeconomics and Sustainability*; Beard, T. R., and G. A. Lozada. 1999. *Economics*, *Entropy and the Environment*. US: Edward Elgar. [The total energy is said to be conserved over time, Georgescu Roegen-Economics, *Entropy and the Environment* (1999)].

[19] Acad. Aurel IANCU, Georgescu-Roegen, N. Întemeietor De Şcoală Economică, discurs de recepţie la Academia Română, 9.

[20] Bran, P. "Mecanismul monetar", "Finanţele întreprinderii", "Gestiunea financiară a întreprinderii", "Relaţii monetare şi financiare internaţionale", "Managementul prin valoare"—alte lucrări ale Prof. Univ. dr. Paul Bran.

Fig. 4-7. The Organic and Holistic Model for Individuals and Communities System Integration, where "the Intangible Feeds the Tangible and the Tangible Feeds the Intangible".

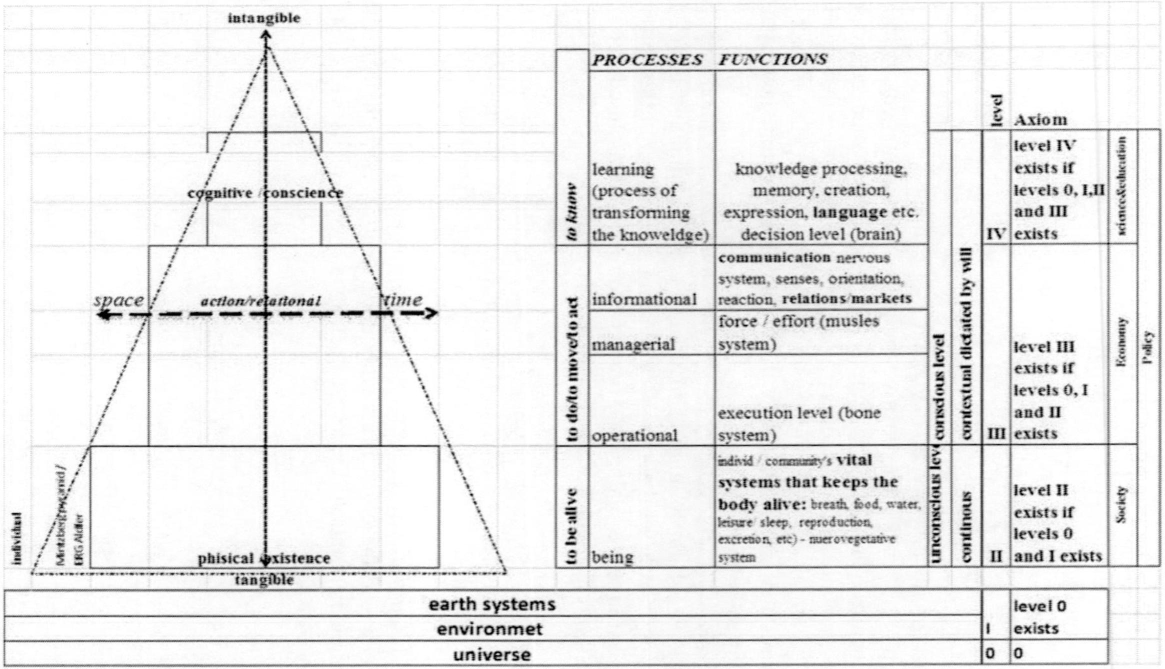

Source: Authors' Own Elaboration.

The dichotomist relationship is not a linear one but consists of a continuously transforming chain reaction from the intangible to the tangible and vice versa. This process reflects the probabilistic reciprocal dependency of both functions. Its existence is sustained by 2 different functions, input/inspiration and output/expiration, within a system which includes two vital functions, which are as complementary as different.

Evidently, the same function is realized by the socio-economic component: tangible production feeds individuals to ensure their living functions, allowing them to produce the intangible products requested by tangible production.

The input is internalized, processed, absorbed and has the role of maintaining the vital functions of the organism, to allow the manifestation in space and time through relationship and action, and to perform cognitive conscience processes that enhance the output response in both intangible and tangible forms.

The holistic approach is offered by the dichotomous relationship of two vital functions, which are complementary but incomparable, reflecting an altered relation. Following this logic, the possible tensions become essential links in the chain of life:

- The local feeds the global and vice versa;
- The universe feeds the individual and vice versa;
- Tradition feeds modernity and vice versa;
- The long term feeds the short term and vice versa;
- Competition feeds cooperation and vice versa;
- The distribution of knowledge feeds the reception of knowledge and vice versa;
- The spiritual feeds the material and vice versa (see Annex1);
- The male/female relationship is then an altered relation and the masculine and feminine components are not comparable (their functions are different).

This is the chain of life, which is continuously subject to the hypothesis that the intangible feeds the tangible and vice versa (Figure 2).

Back to Figure 1, the focus turns on visible levels of dependency (conditional probabilities) as axiomatically induced by the living organism law:

- **The universe is the "0 level"** and provides the space for the special existence of the Earth and the Sun. The Earth represents the life environment support and the Sun is the main flow energy and light source which is essential for our existence;

Fig. 4-8. The Intangible Feeds the Tangible and the Tangible Feeds the Intangible.

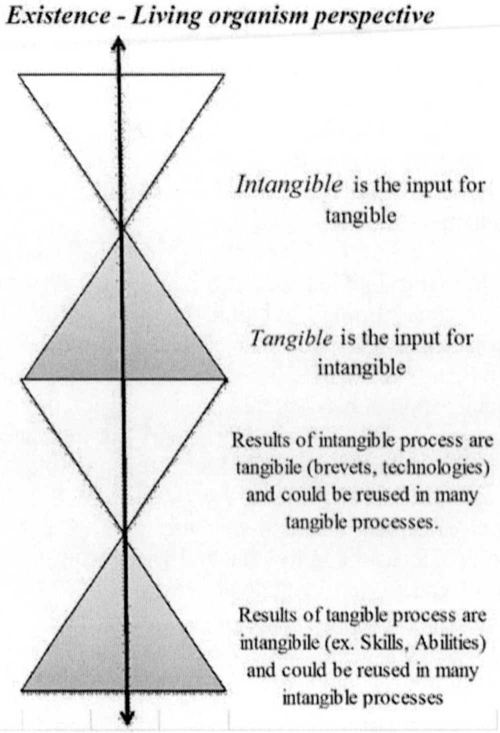

Source Authors' Own Elaboration.

- Level I (the Earth Systems) deals with nature – climate (temperature, precipitation, extreme events and the sea level rise), ecosystems, water resources, and atmosphere[1] – supports and provides the environment for the Human Systems and its development. The Human and Earth Systems are dependent on one another in terms of co-evolution. The impact of the Earth System over the human species survival probability is crucial from the

[1] IPCC (Intergovernmental Panel on Climate Change). 2007. *Climate Change 2007: Synthesis Report.* IPCC. It is the leading body for the assessment of climate change, established by the United Nations Environment Programme (UNEP) and World Meteorological Organization (WMO) to provide the world with a clear picture of the state of climate science and environmental change and its potential socio-economic consequences.

perspective of climate change and the entropic negative impact (pollution, greenhouse gases, aerosols, emissions) with high risks over the human health, food security, and so forth. The reaction chain of the Human System to feed and not destroy the Earth System reflects the dependency of existence of level 1 on the existence of level 0, is outside level 1 and is not under the control of the organism, but could be changed through it.

- Level II (the vital system that keeps the organism alive) includes and reflects the individual level or the community/society level. Level II (existence) is conditioned by the existence of the two foregoing levels (level 0 and level I). At this level, the human organism has the neuro-vegetative system that realises the continuous function of keeping the organism alive: breathing, eating, drinking, sleeping, and reproducing. This system is realized unconsciously and the organism sends input in cases of shocks (diseases, injuries, risks). The organic system is aware of this mechanisms only in emergency situations but is not able to control the internal process of vital functions while happening;
- Level III consists of the organic system interaction with the exterior of the organism. Interaction refers to the external process of transforming the intangible into tangible and the tangible into intangible through controlled and conscious actions and relationships of development in space and time. This system includes the operational, managerial and informational processes (hence the market). The operational process is realized by the execution level (the bone system in the living organism), the managerial process is the coordination and commanding level of the effort to transform the intangible into action (which is the equivalent of the muscles system in the human body) and the informational processes ensuring the functions of communication, orientation, reaction, change/transactions (transactions results are replacing the tangible/merchandise with intangible/money). At this level there are the markets, the inclusive labour market and the economic activity. The existence of level III is conditioned by the existence of all the three previous levels (level 0, I and II).
- Level IV is the cognitive level, which deals with the learning process as the main knowledge processing. This includes: memory, creation, expression, and language. This is a highly conscious level and refers to research and education activities. The cognitive processes interfere with level II in a conscious manner and with

level III in an unconscious manner. The existence of level IV is conditioned by the existence of the previous levels.

In Table 4-14 we present the intangible production system (modelled on the industrial society) in a dichotomy relationship with the tangible production system (knowledge production system). In Fig. 4-9, we modelled the occupational pyramid in the case of tangible production (labour division system) and intangible service production (decision division system).

Fig. 4-9. Occupational Pyramid for Tangible Production and Intangible Service Production.

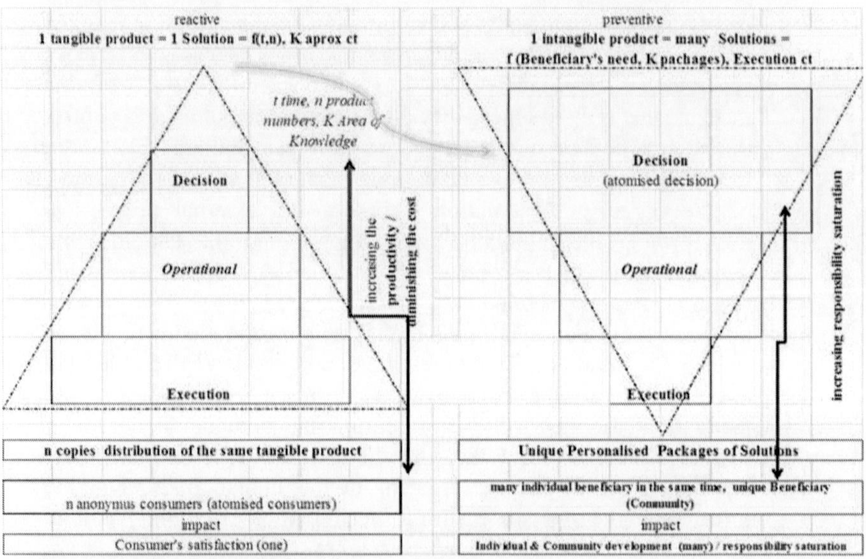

Source: Authors' Own Elaboration.

In the case of tangible products manufacturing, the system is serial and implies the division of labour. Knowledge-based solutions are almost invariant in time; strategies are competitive and focused to diminish the costs and time and increasing production, and implicitly, productivity.

Decision-making is professionalized and the operational level is set to organize production and execution processes. The mass of employment is located at the execution level, followed by the operational level and the decisional one.

In the case of intangible products manufacturing, the system is parallel and simultaneous and implies sharing decisions and communication. The knowledge solutions change in time, strategies are cooperative and focused to saturate the community responsibilities, the uniqueness and quality of intangible product are essential, centered implicitly on increasing the impact on community in regard to the problems to be solved. The mass of employment is located at the decision level, followed by the operational level and the lowest employment level is realised at the execution level.

Assuming that the intangible feeds the tangible and vice versa, then those two production systems are the units of the living organism as it was presented in Fig. 4-7. The transversal level (the continuous level) is simply to exist and to be alive and concurrently there are intangible and tangible sequences of the chain of life. The continuous level is the result of discontinuous/dichotomous reactions and those reactions could be processed only by the organism internalization. It is no longer a simple and two-tier hierarchy within a "master/servant" relationship, but a threefold one including the organism, intangible and tangible processes.

In this sense, we provide the historical evolution of the value production systems (Fig. 4-10). Starting from the Mintzberg's pyramid (and Aldfer's ERG) we combined the management levels with the tangible and intangible evolutionary scale (in space and time) of those social production systems. Accordingly:

- The labour intensive social system (the society effort was towards assuring the mass for the physical work) develops into:
- The operational social system (the society effort was to formalize the explicit into tacit knowledge see Fig. 4-10), which in turn, develops into:
- Decision-making social system (the society effort will be focused to create decision-making processes, cognitive/conscience social processes, knowledge intensive processes).

From a holistic perspective, if the entire functioning system is considered (Fig. 4-11a), the horizontality of the intangible production and the verticality of the tangible production become evident. In terms of impact, the axes are rotated by 180 degrees, so the intangible impact is vertical (community development regardless of the characteristics), and the tangible one is horizontal (individuals with the same characteristics).

Fig. 4-9. Occupational Pyramid for Tangible Production and Intangible Service Production.

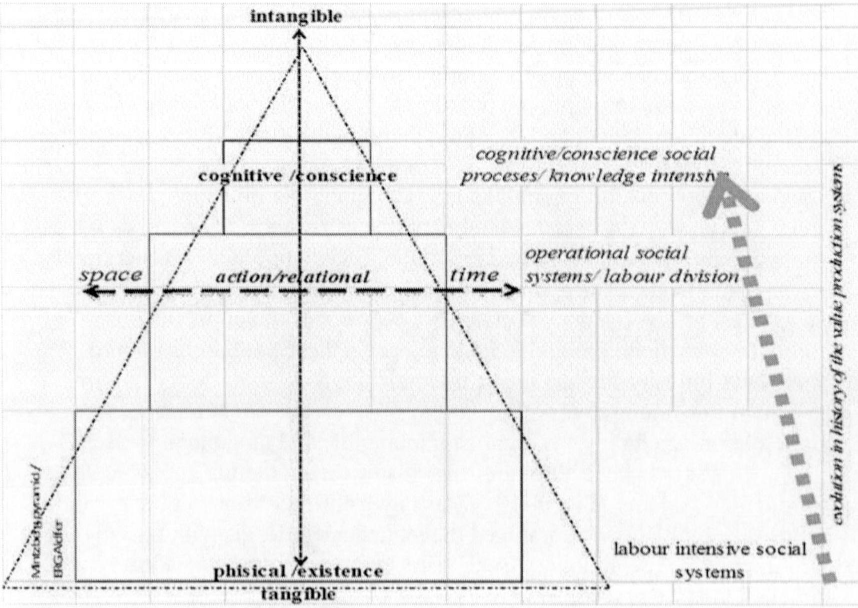

Source: Authors' Own Elaboration.

Fig. 4-11a. Knowledge Typology Map.

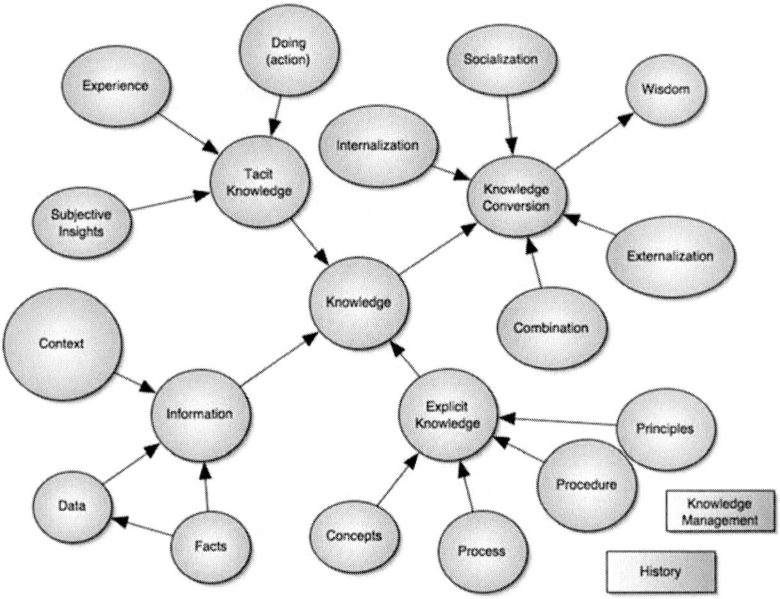

Source: http://www.nwlink.com/~donclark/knowledge/knowledge_typology.html (accessed 20 November 2013).

Fig. 4-11b. Model of the Generation of a New Business System.

Generation of a New Bussiness System						
structures		*individuals*	Institutions		Agents (market)	
Knowledge domain	*Value space*	*irationale*	rationale			
Vector		***Leader***		**Researcher**	**Manager**	**Operator**
Action	Transforms	***Irational knowledge into New rational knowledge***		***New Rationale knowledge into Explicit knowledge***	***Explicit knowledge into action***	***Explicit knowledge into tacit knowledge and produce tangibile value***
	Communicate	***Information***				
Receptor of the process result		**Beneficiary**				**Consumer**
Space of the resulted value		intangibile				tangible
Reaction /effect	impact on tangibile dimension **community development**					impact in intangibile dimension **individual satisfaction**
structures	leaders and community					demand and offer
chaneel of transaction	policy decision process					market

Source: Authors' Own Elaboration.

Both the intangible and tangible production systems are coordinated and linked together by information and communication. This is the new challenge to accomplish the integration system of the production chains and the receptors of the results. Communication at this moment is an impossible mission. How to manage and develop a new language for a new business system where people from disjunctive knowledge areas are brought together? This new Business System is a functional one and starts from intangible production. Leaders transform irrational knowledge into new rational knowledge, researchers transform new rational knowledge into explicit knowledge, managers transform explicit knowledge into action and all of them produce intangible value. Operators transform explicit knowledge into tacit knowledge and produce tangible value. The production process includes both tangible and intangible sequences and is built on a specific organism (the individual, the community, etc.).

Under the paradigm that the intangible component is the major driver of growth, the greatest challenge faced by labour market actors concerns the implementation of the new security model in conditions of value creation through innovation, research and development, brand building, relationship and networks as a response to the specific needs of the community. For this purpose, the labour market actors have to consider and address both demand and supply as a whole. To originate the chains of demand and supply (in the context of cooperation), revisiting the new leadership role of PES and devising ALPMs could be a solution. ALMPs reflect the subordination of collective interests to a living organism that could be an individual, a group and a community. When at work, the integration of any vulnerable individual should be pursued or pondered, regardless of one's background and potential. The community delegates PES to perform tasks or action for the individual benefit through the implementation of ALMPs.

As a synthesis of this analysis, Fig. 6 presents the pathway to employment for youth under 25 years old from a behavioural and management perspective, and the steps to implement the education results (Delors), to perform the role of manager (Mintzberg) of one's own life and to develop ALMPs, PALMs and SLMPs (active and passive measures and services developed by PES). Considering essential the interaction between the individual and the community as a "one-to-many" relationship type, then the problem of being out of work is an issue for the community in terms of the main beneficiary of the work results and the full sustainable development of youth.

In the knowledge society and economy, the labour market is the space for transforming the intangible assets into tangible ones in a controlled manner, using and exploiting knowledge. Admitting this as an axiom, then the occupational behaviour that is focused on transforming knowledge into action and action into profit concerns the manager. The radical change for the labour market is that this is no longer a labour market, yet a solution providing market. This market reflects the relationship within the industrial production between the employee and the employer, and the subordination relationship space where the majority of participants are workers. They provide their labour force in exchange of remuneration.[2] To succeed means to develop especially "technical" skills according to the specialization level and the hierarchy position in the workplace.

The new "labour market" is the "solutions providing market", the actors are the "managers", and the employment contract is the "management contract" that provides participation to profit and risk. In the knowledge society and economy each individual acts rationally and needs to:

- Have the know-how to create knowledge but also to transform the intangible into the tangible in technical terms. This level is the equivalent of the low level of management and needs especially technical skills (emotional intelligence & coaching for performance).
- Living together, building the relationship in order to transfer knowledge, building long-term relationships with a beneficiary community and with networks of members organized by problem-solving needs, focused to provide solutions to the analysis to identify common problems; this level is the equivalent of middle management (problem solving, team building, talent development, performance management) —relationship level— knowledge which translates into action;- Being the master of one's own life in order to exploit knowledge and realise income from this activity; this level is the equivalent of the top management level/conceptual level and needs especially technical skills: executive coaching, change management, leadership, delegation and empowerment.

Learning and doing are continuous and sequential in each of the 4 dimensions. We have everything we need, but first of all we need to understand who we are and what we need.

---

[2] Raboaca, G. 2003. "Piata muncii si dezvoltarea durabila," *Tribuna Economica*.

Fig. 4-12. The Pathway to Employment for Youth under 25 Years from the Behaviour/Management Perspective.

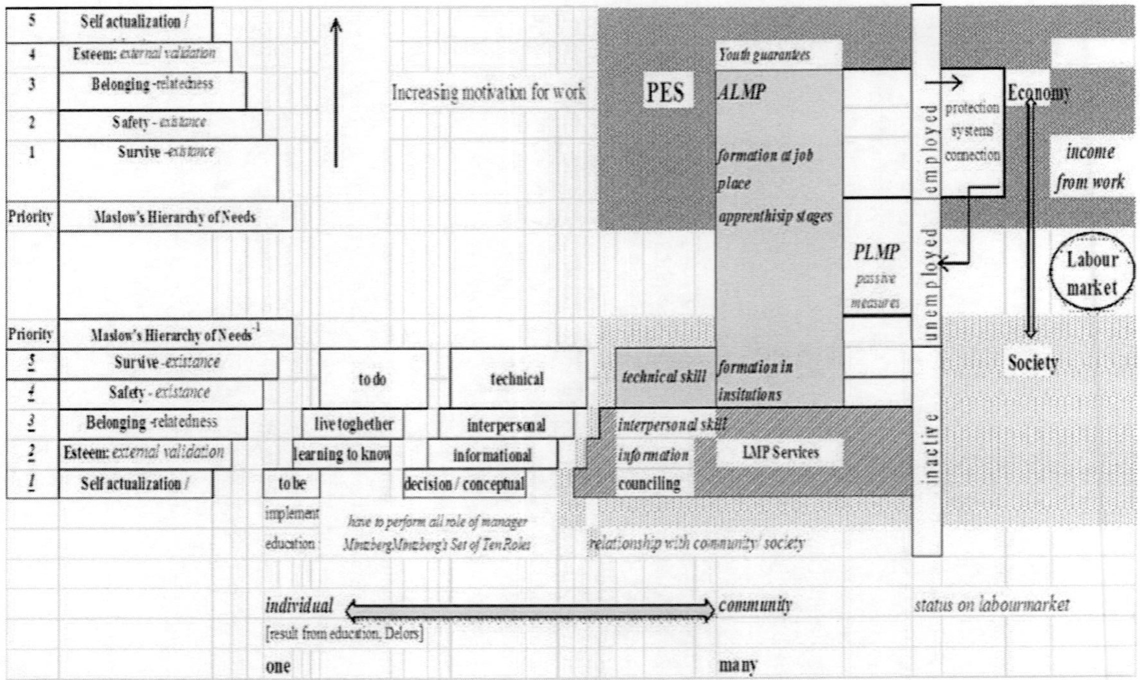

Source: Author's own elaboration.

4. Conclusions

In the four pillars of the education context the validation of the learning process is the capacity to transform the intangible assets into tangible assets and to produce a consequence following the realized action.

Education is the space where forging intangible assets at the individual level, regardless of the age, whereas the labour market is the space of transforming the intangible assets into tangible ones in a controlled manner. The transformation process is not clearly defined in time and is dependent on the knowledge to be exploited requested by a specific need of a community. Are we able *to be, to know, to live together* and *to do,* overcoming the tension between the global and the local, the universal and the individual, tradition and modernity, the long term and the short term, the need for competition and the need for cooperation, the extraordinary expansion of knowledge and the capacity to assimilate it, and the tension between the spiritual and the material? From a labour market perspective, these tensions are not insurmountable and the difficulty of the transition from education to work process is further evidence of that. The foregoing organic holistic model can help in this exercise.

References

Delors J., and F. Mayo. 1996. "Education: The Necessary Utopia," UNESCO Headquarters, Paris in April 1996 at the presentation of the report to UNESCO of the International Commission on Education for the Twenty-first Century, Learning: the treasure within. http://www.unesco.org/delors/utopia.htm.

Faure, E., F. Herrera, A.-R. Kaddoura, H. Lopes, H. V. Petrovsky, H. Rahnema, and C.F:, Ward. 1972. *Learning to Be, The World of Education Today and Tomorrow.* UNESCO.

Georgescu-Roegen, N. 1999. "The Entropy Law and the Economic Process, Bioeconomics and Sustainability," in *Economics, Entropy and the Environment*, eds. Beard, T. R., and G.A. Lozada, (U.S.: Edward Elgar).

Gowdy, J., and S., Mesner. 1998. "The Evolution of Georgescu-Roegen's Bioeconomics," *Review of Social Economy*, Rensselaer Polytechnic Institute 56 No. 2.

Iancu, A. 2009. "Nicholas Georgescu-Roegen—Întemeietor De Şcoală Economică," discurs de recepţie la Academia Română, 9.

IPCC (Intergovernmental Panel on Climate Change). 2007. *Climate Change 2007: Synthesis Report*. IPCC.

Mishra R. K., and S. Jhunjhunwala. 2009. *Valuation of Intangibles.* Study sponsored by ICAI, Accounting research foundation, Preliminary report, Institute of Public Enterprise. http://www.icai.org/resource_file/17800valuation_intangibles.pdf

OECD. 2007. *Innovation and Growth: Rationale for an Innovation Strategy*. Paris: OECD, http://www.oecd.org/science/inno/39374789.pdf.

Raboaca, G. 2003. "Piata muncii si dezvoltarea durabila," *Tribuna Economica*.

Sanjay Kr Jha. 2010. *General Management Theory and Practice*. Kathmandu Academy of Tourism & Hospitality Management (KATHM).

Sundelin, A. 2008. *What is a Blockbuster Business Model*? http://tbmdb.blogspot.ro/2008/12/blockbuster-business-model.html.

Annex 1: Tensions to be overcome[1]

"To this end, we have to confront, the better to overcome them, the main tensions that, although they are not new, will be central to the problems of the twenty-first century, namely:

The tension between the global and the local: people need gradually to become world citizens without losing their roots and while continuing to play an active part in the life of their nation and their local community.

The tension between the universal and the individual: culture is steadily being globalized, but as yet only partially. We cannot ignore the promises of globalization nor its risks, not the least of which is the risk of forgetting the unique character of individual human beings; it is for them to **choose their own future and achieve their full potential** within the carefully tended wealth of their traditions and their own cultures which, unless we are careful, can be endangered by contemporary developments.

The tension between tradition and modernity, which is part of the same problem: how is it possible to adapt to change without turning one's back on the past, how can autonomy be acquired along with the free development of others and how can scientific progress be assimilated? This is the spirit in which the challenges of the new information technologies must be met.

The tension between long-term and short-term considerations: this has always existed but today it is sustained by the predominance of the ephemeral and the instantaneous, in a world where an over-abundance of transient information and emotions continually keeps the spotlight on immediate problems. Public opinion cries out for quick answers and ready solutions, whereas many problems call for a patient, concerted, negotiated strategy of reform. This is precisely the case where education policies are concerned.

The tension between, on the one hand, the need for competition, and on the other hand, the concern for equality of opportunity: this is a classic issue, which has been facing both economic and social policy-makers and educational policy-makers since the beginning of the century.

Solutions have sometimes been proposed but they have never stood the test of time. Today, the Commission ventures to claim that the pressures of competition have caused many of those in positions of

[1] Jacques Delors, Mr Federico Mayo, Education: The Necessary Utopia, at UNESCO Headquarters, Paris in April 1996 at the presentation of the report to UNESCO of the International Commission on Education for the Twenty-first Century, Learning: the treasure within. http://www.unesco.org/delors/utopia.html.

authority to lose sight of their mission, which is to give each human being the means to take full advantage of every opportunity. This has led us, within the terms of reference of the report, to rethink and update the concept of lifelong education so as to reconcile three forces: competition, which provides incentives; co-operation, which gives strength; and solidarity, which unites.

The tension between the extraordinary expansion of knowledge and human beings' capacity to assimilate it: the Commission was unable to resist the temptation to add some new subjects for study, such as self-knowledge, ways to ensure physical and psychological well-being or ways to provide an improved understanding of the natural environment, preserving it better. Since there is already increasing pressure on curricula, any clear-sighted reform strategy must involve making choices, providing always that the essential features of a basic education that teaches pupils how to improve their lives through knowledge, through experiment and through the development of their own personal cultures are preserved.

Lastly - another perennial factor - **the tension between the spiritual and the material:** often without realizing it, the world has a longing, often unexpressed, for an ideal and for values that we shall term 'moral'. It is thus the education's noble task to encourage each and every one, acting in accordance with their traditions and convictions and paying full respect to pluralism, to lift their minds and spirits to the plane of the universal and, in some measure, to transcend themselves. It is no exaggeration on the Commission's part to say that the survival of humanity depends thereon".

Table 4-15 Mintzberg's Set of Ten Roles Performed by Managers.[2]

Category	Role	Activity
Informational	Monitor	To seek and to receive information; to scan periodicals and reports; to maintain personal contact with stakeholders.
	Disseminator	To forward information to organization members via memos, reports, and phone calls.
	Spokesperson	To transmit information to outsiders via reports, memos, and speeches.
Interpersonal	Figurehead	To perform ceremonial and symbolic duties, such as greeting visitors and signing legal documents.
	Leader	To direct and to motivate subordinates; to counsel and to communicate with subordinates.
	Liaison	To maintain information links both inside and outside organization via mail, phone calls, and meetings.
Decisional	Entrepreneur	To initiate improvement projects; to identify new ideas and to delegate idea responsibility to others.
	Disturbance handler	To take corrective action during disputes or crises; to resolve conflicts among subordinates; to adapt to environments.
	Resource allocator	To decide who gets resources; to prepare budgets; to set schedules and to determine priorities.
	Negotiator	To represent department during negotiations of union contracts, sales, purchases, and budgets.

Skills / abilities to translate knowledge into action[3]:

- **Technical skills**— specialisation, e.g. to perform a particular task (accountants, engineers, market researchers, and computer sciences);
- **Human skills** (the ability to work well in cooperation with others. Human skills emerge in the workplace as a spirit of trust, enthusiasm, and genuine involvement in interpersonal relationships);

---

2 http://www.cliffsnotes.com/study_guide/Functions-of-Managers.topicArticleId-8944,articleId-8848.html.

3 http://www.cliffsnotes.com/study_guide/Functions-of-Managers.topicArticleId-8944,articleId-8848.html.

- **Conceptual skills** (the ability to think analytically. Analytical skills enable managers to break down problems into smaller parts, to see the relations among the parts, and to recognize the implications of anyone's problems on others. As managers assume ever-higher responsibilities in organizations, they must deal with more ambiguous problems that have long-term consequences).

The skills and personal characteristics that the **American Assembly of Collegiate Schools of Business (AACSB)** is urging business schools to help their students develop are:

- **Leadership**—the ability to influence others to perform tasks;
- **Self-objectivity**—the ability to evaluate yourself realistically;
- **Analytic thinking**—the ability to interpret and explain patterns of information;
- **Behavioural flexibility**—the ability to modify personal behaviour to react objectively rather than to accomplish organizational goals subjectively;
- **Oral communication**—the ability to express ideas in words;
- **Written communication**—the ability to clearly express ideas in writing;
- **Personal impact**—the ability to create a good impression and instil confidence;
- **Resistance to stress**—the ability to perform under stressful conditions;
- **Tolerance for uncertainty**—the ability to perform in ambiguous situations.

The Management level (combined with generic skills)

- Low level: (emotional intelligence & coaching for performance); technical level: knowledge creation level.
- Middle management (problem solving, team building, talent development, performance management); relationship level: knowledge-to-action translation.
- Top management: (executive coaching, change management, leadership, delegation and empowerment); conceptual level: system of business generation in view to gain knowledge that translates into profit.

CONTRIBUTORS

Draga Atanasiu, Mathematician, Senior Researcher at the INCSMPS, Romania.

Beatrice Monica Chiriac, Researcher at the INCSMPS, Romania.

Ghenadie Ciobanu, Senior Researcher at the INCSMPS, Associate Professor at the Academy of Economic Studies of Bucharest, the Academy of Economic Studies from the Republic of Moldova.

Vasilica Ciucă, Ph.D. in Economics, Senior Researcher, General Manager at the INCSMPS, Bucharest, Romania, Associate Professor at ALMA Mater Sibiu Romania and at Valahia University, Romania.

Codruta Ilinca Drăgoiu, Senior Researcher at the INCSMPS, Romania.

Cristina Lincaru, Ph.D. in Economics, Senior Researcher at the INCSMPS, Romania.

Eliza-Olivia Lungu, Senior Researcher at the INCSMPS, Romania.

Maer-Matei Monica Mihaela, Ph.D., Researcher at the INCSMPS, Romania.

Eva Militaru, Ph.D. in Economics, Senior Researcher at the INCSMPS, Romania.

Cristina Mocanu, Ph.D. Candidate at the University of Bucharest, Senior Researcher at the INCSMPS, Romania.

Speranţa Pirciog, Ph.D. in Economics, Senior Researcher and Scientific Manager at the INCSMPS, Romania.

Gabriela Predoşanu, Ph.D. in Economics, Senior Researcher at the INCSMPS, Romania.

Ana-Maria Zamfir, Head of the Education and Labour Market Department, Researcher at the INCSMPS, Romania.

INDEX